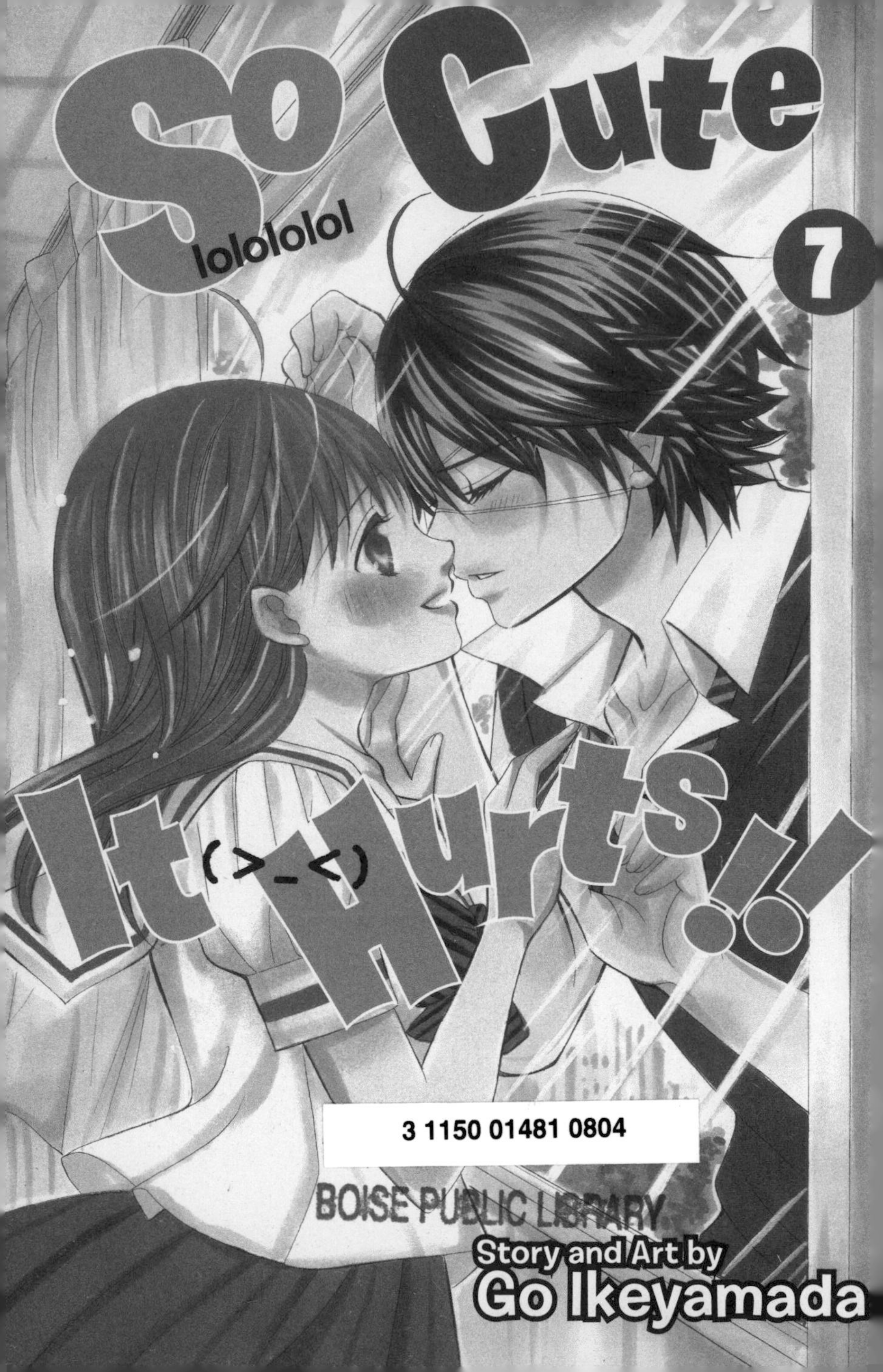
So Cute
lololololol
7
It (>_<) Hurts!!
Story and Art by
Go Ikeyamada

CHARACTERS

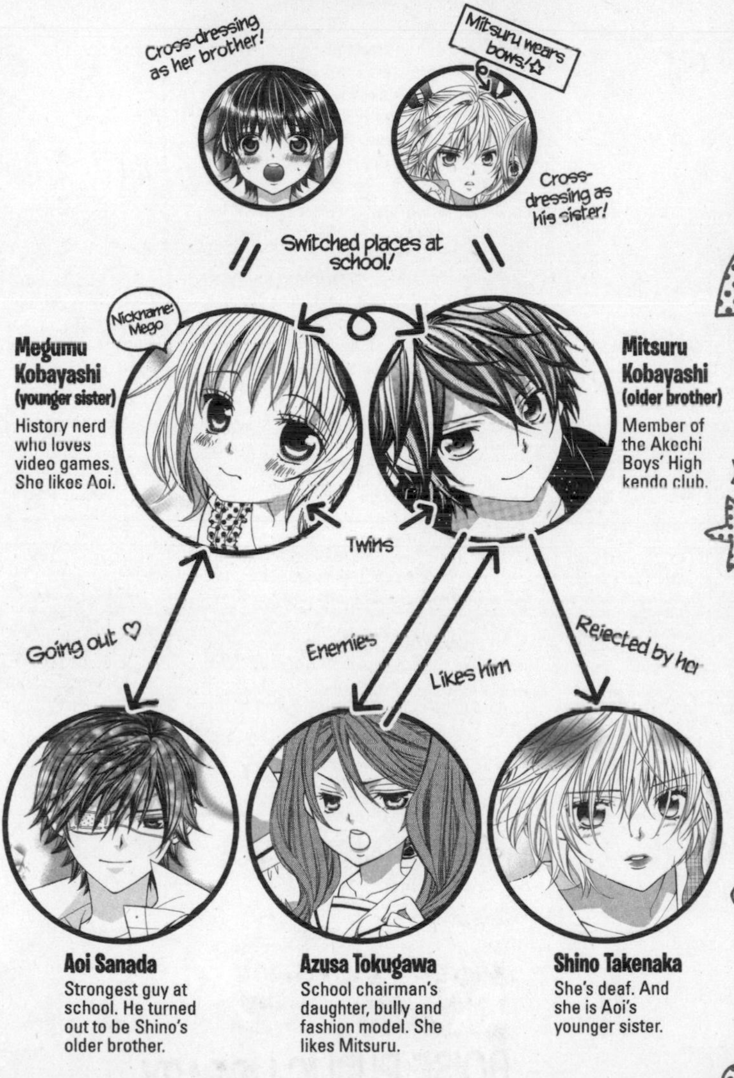

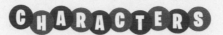

Cross-dressing as her brother!
Mitsuru wears bows!☆
Cross-dressing as his sister!
Switched places at school!
Nickname: Mego
Megumu Kobayashi (younger sister)
History nerd who loves video games. She likes Aoi.
Mitsuru Kobayashi (older brother)
Member of the Akechi Boys' High kendo club.
Twins
Going out ♡
Enemies
Likes him
Rejected by her
Aoi Sanada
Strongest guy at school. He turned out to be Shino's older brother.
Azusa Tokugawa
School chairman's daughter, bully and fashion model. She likes Mitsuru.
Shino Takenaka
She's deaf. And she is Aoi's younger sister.

STORY

★ Mitsuru and Megumu are twins. One day they switch places and go to each other's school for a week! That's when Megumu falls in love with Aoi and Mitsuru falls in love with Shino. Azusa and Aoi both discover the twins' ruse but keep quiet for reasons of their own. When the week is over, Megumu declares her love for Aoi, and they start dating. They need to stay two feet apart because of Aoi's extreme discomfort around women, but they plan to work on it. Mitsuru is rejected by Shino, but Azusa starts to have feelings for him.

★ Megumu is trying to improve her drawing by sketching in the park, when she meets a boy who reminds her of Aoi. But when he sees her drawing of Aoi, he flips out! Megumu runs away but wonders why he seemed so angry about Aoi.

★ Meanwhile, Mitsuru rescues Azusa from an attack and swaps places with Megumu again so he can be Azusa's bodyguard. Then the boy Megumu met in the park shows up at Akechi High as a transfer student. Aoi is disturbed to find out the new student's name is Chiharu Uesugi, but why...?!

CONTENTS

So Cute It Hurts!! (>_<)

Chapter 31

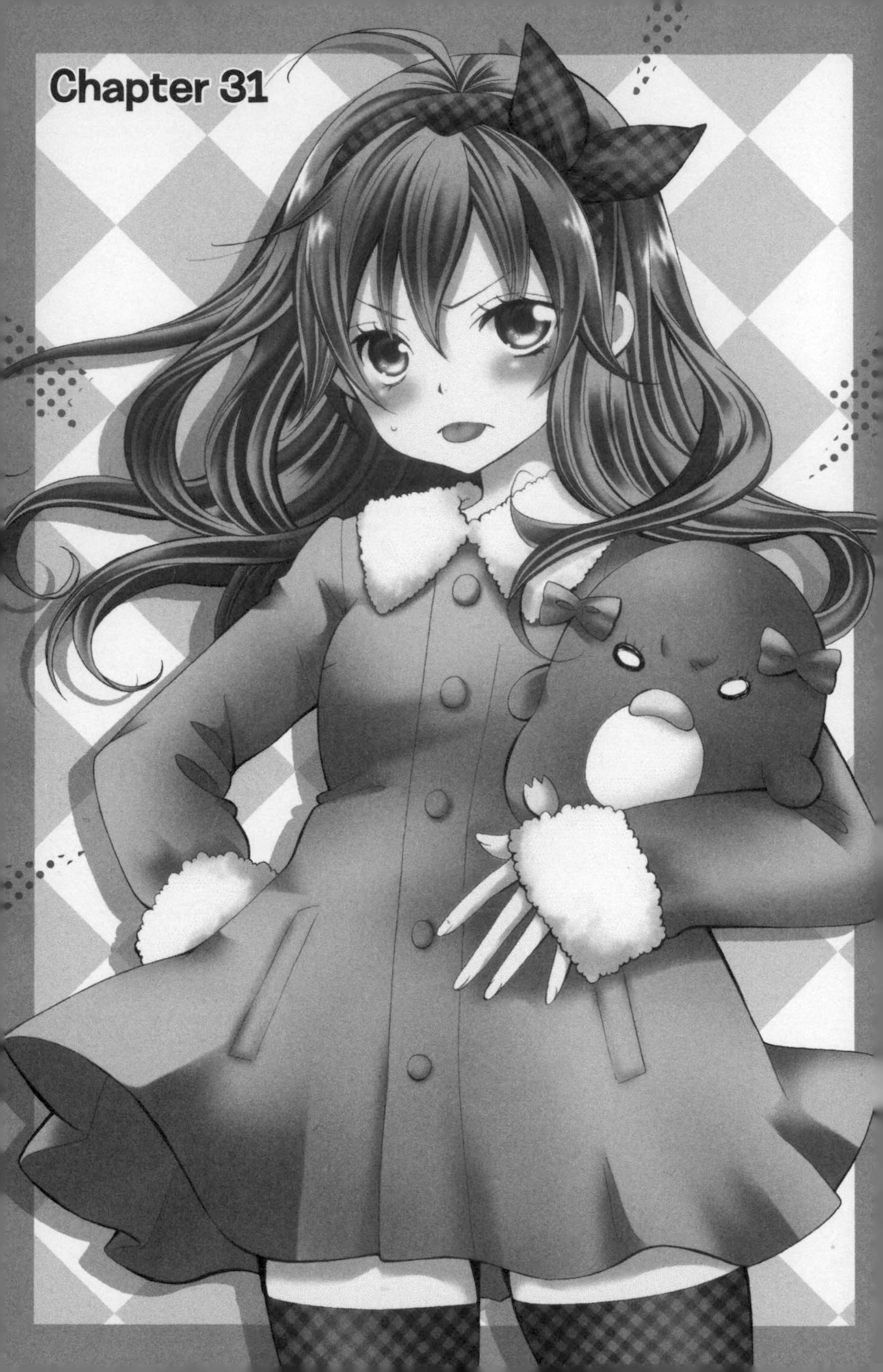

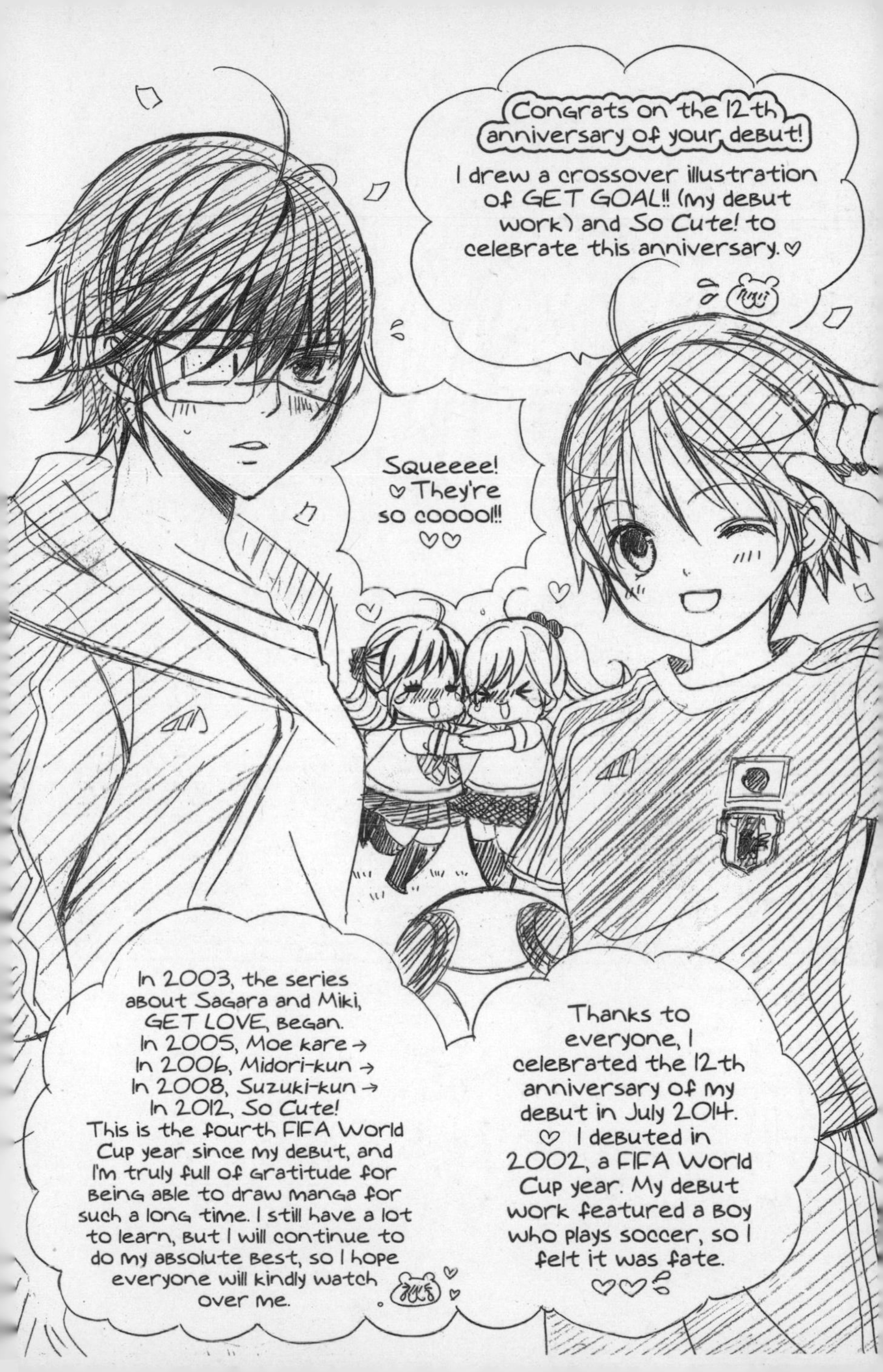
Congrats on the 12th anniversary of your debut!
I drew a crossover illustration of GET GOAL!! (my debut work) and So Cute! to celebrate this anniversary. ♡
Squeeee! ♡ They're so cooool!! ♡♡
Thanks to everyone, I celebrated the 12th anniversary of my debut in July 2014. ♡ I debuted in 2002, a FIFA World Cup year. My debut work featured a boy who plays soccer, so I felt it was fate. ♡♡
In 2003, the series about Sagara and Miki, GET LOVE, began. In 2005, Moe kare → In 2006, Midori-kun → In 2008, Suzuki-kun → In 2012, So Cute! This is the fourth FIFA World Cup year since my debut, and I'm truly full of gratitude for being able to draw manga for such a long time. I still have a lot to learn, but I will continue to do my absolute best, so I hope everyone will kindly watch over me.

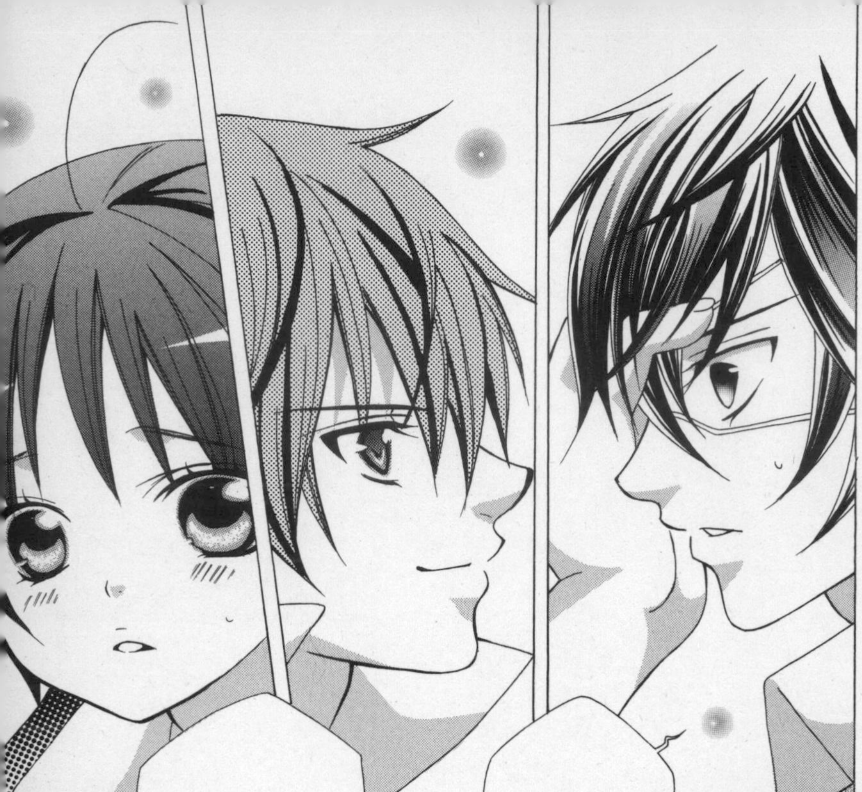
CHIHARU...
...UESUGI?

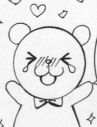

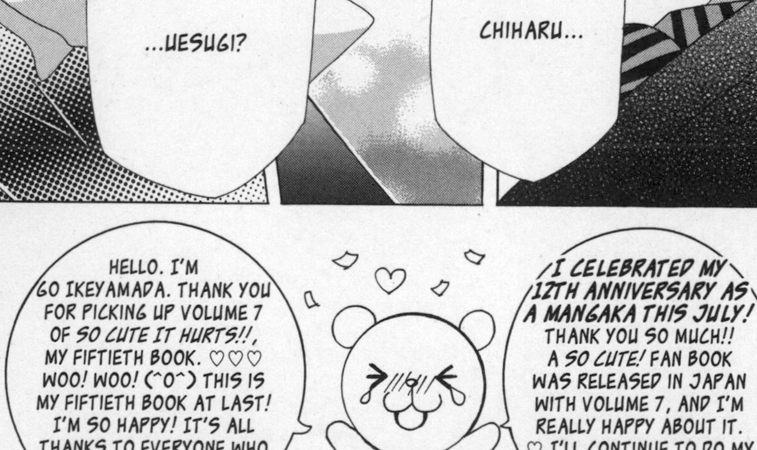
HELLO. I'M GO IKEYAMADA. THANK YOU FOR PICKING UP VOLUME 7 OF *SO CUTE IT HURTS!!*, MY FIFTIETH BOOK. ♡♡♡ WOO! WOO! (^O^) THIS IS MY FIFTIETH BOOK AT LAST! I'M SO HAPPY! IT'S ALL THANKS TO EVERYONE WHO HAS LOVINGLY CHEERED ME ON!
I CELEBRATED MY 12TH ANNIVERSARY AS A MANGAKA THIS JULY! THANK YOU SO MUCH!! A *SO CUTE!* FAN BOOK WAS RELEASED IN JAPAN WITH VOLUME 7, AND I'M REALLY HAPPY ABOUT IT. ♡ I'LL CONTINUE TO DO MY ABSOLUTE BEST, SO KEEP READING!! (ToT)

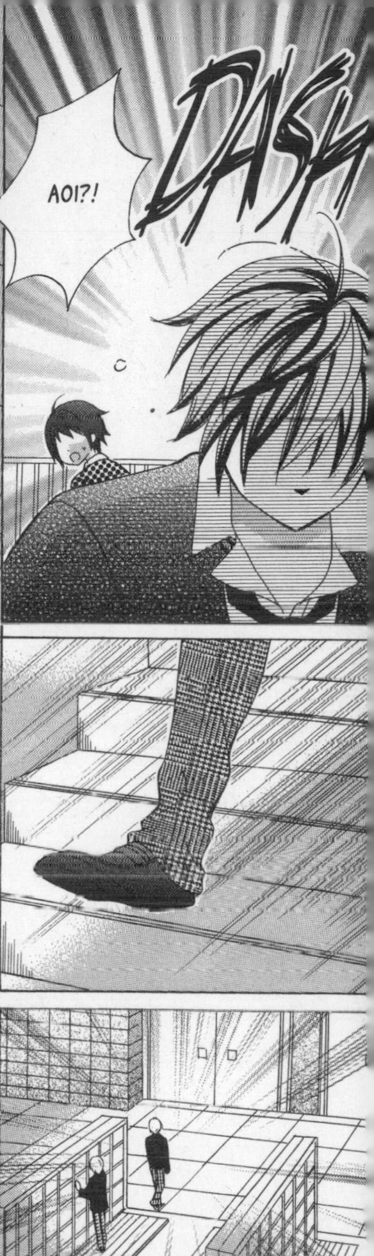
DASH
AOI?!

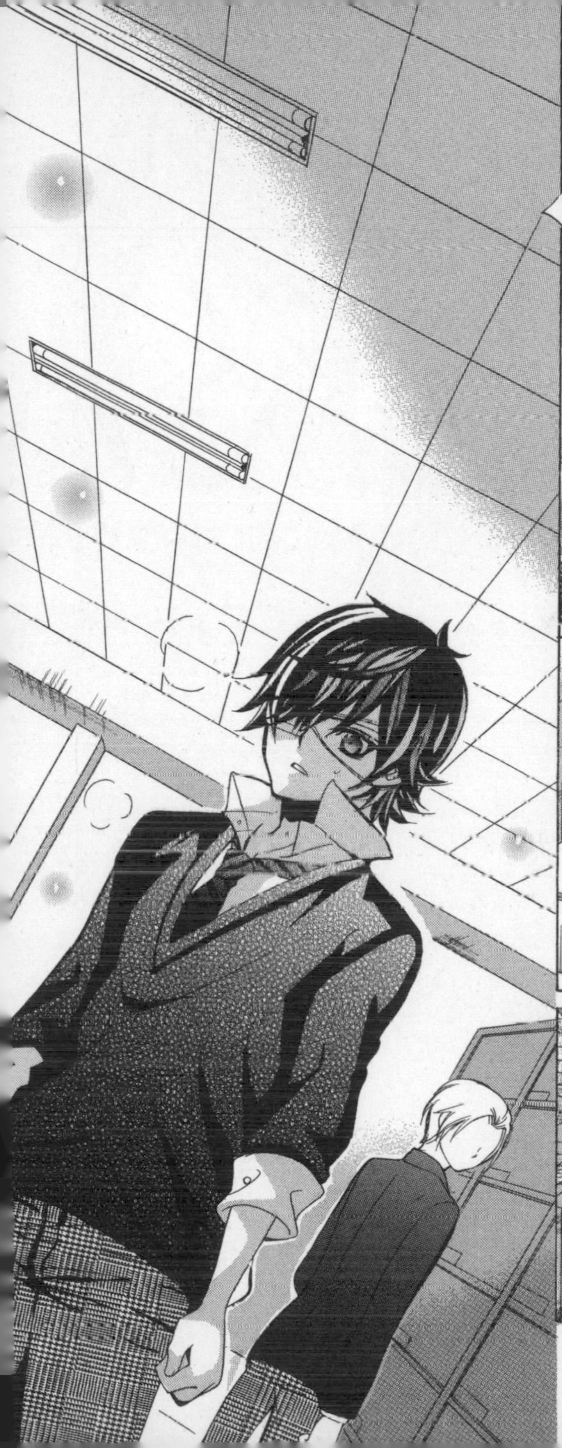

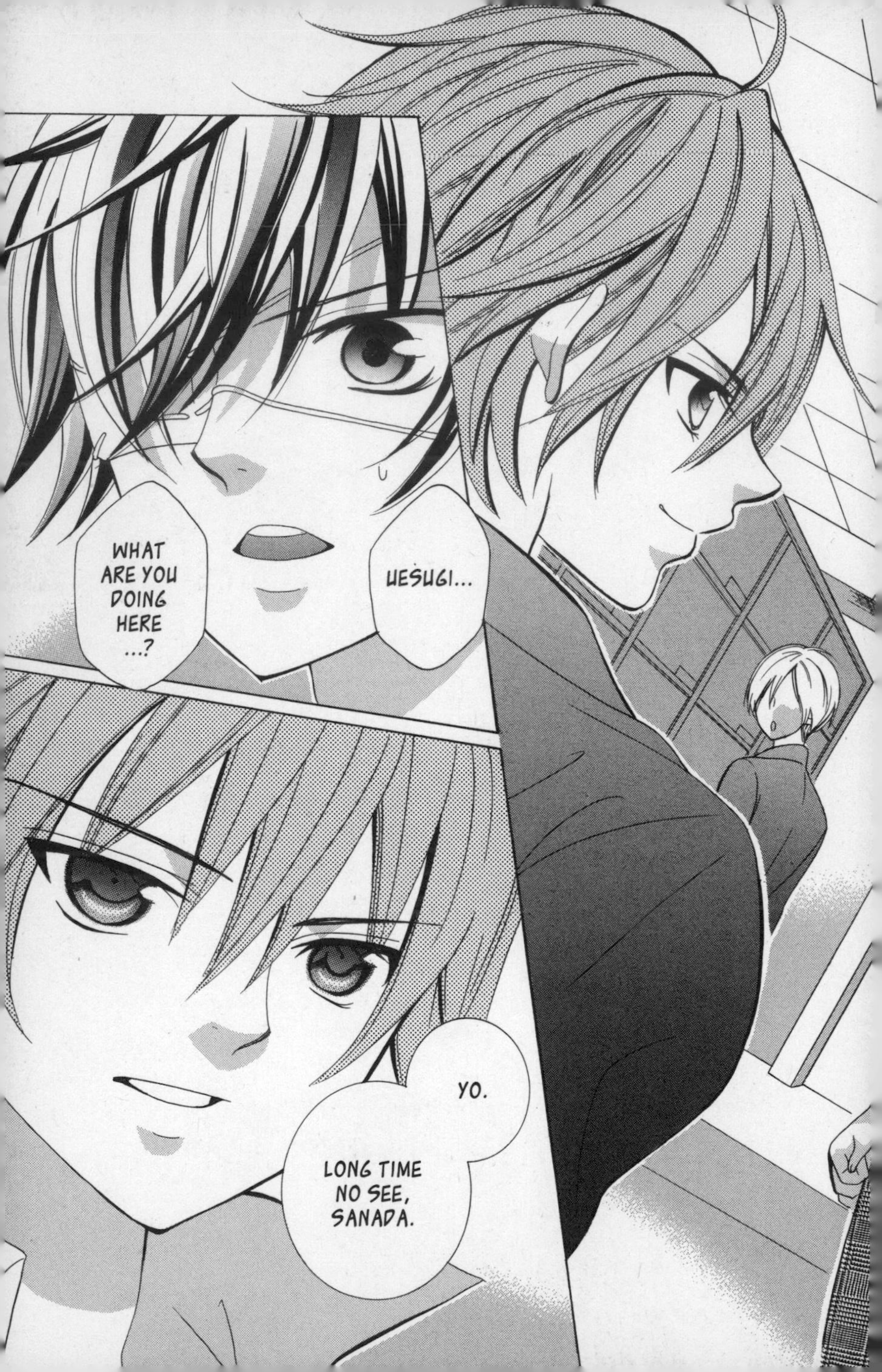
UESUGI...
WHAT ARE YOU DOING HERE ...?
YO.
LONG TIME NO SEE, SANADA.

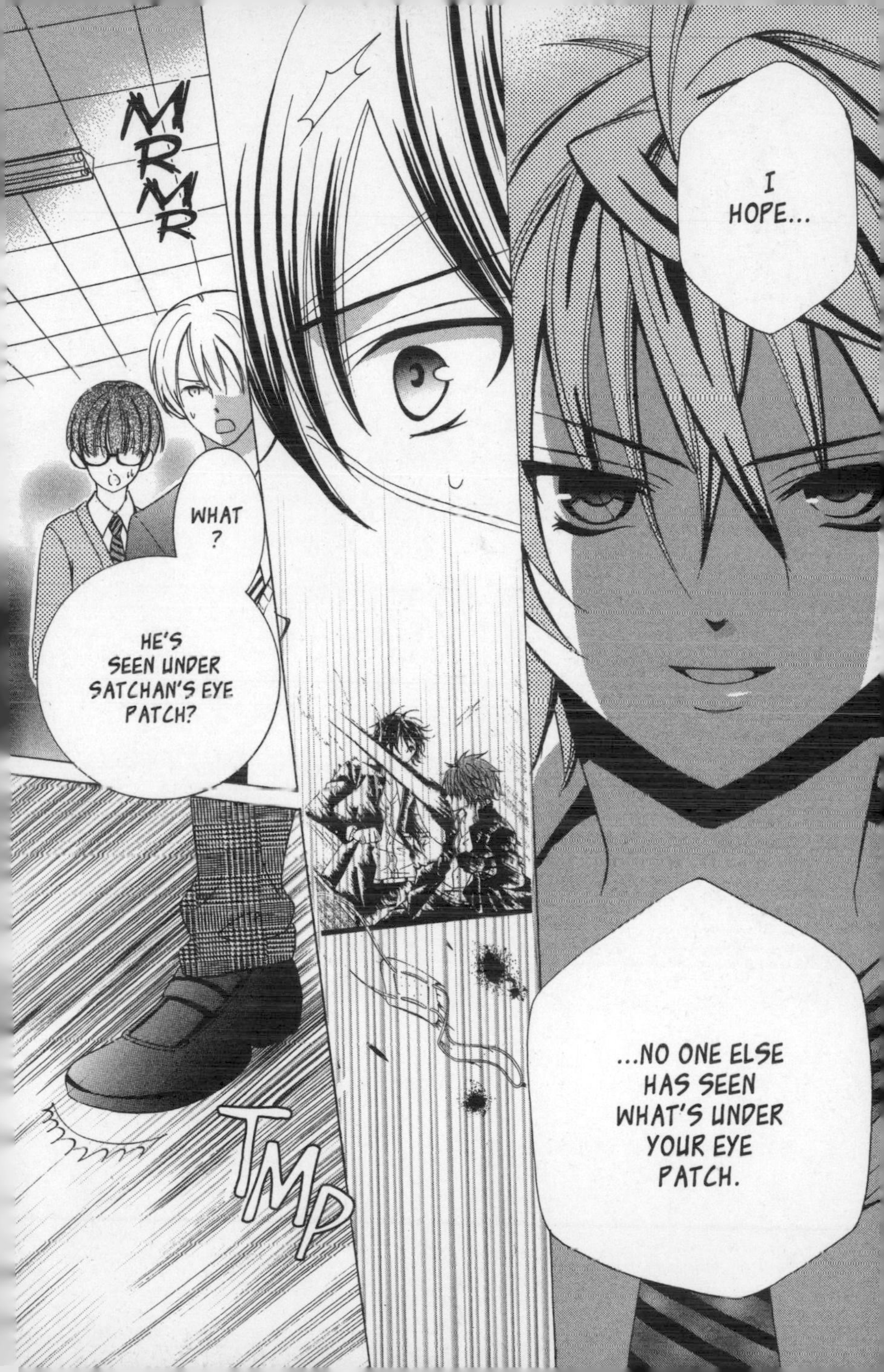
I HOPE...
...NO ONE ELSE HAS SEEN WHAT'S UNDER YOUR EYE PATCH.
MRMR
WHAT?
HE'S SEEN UNDER SATCHAN'S EYE PATCH?
TMP

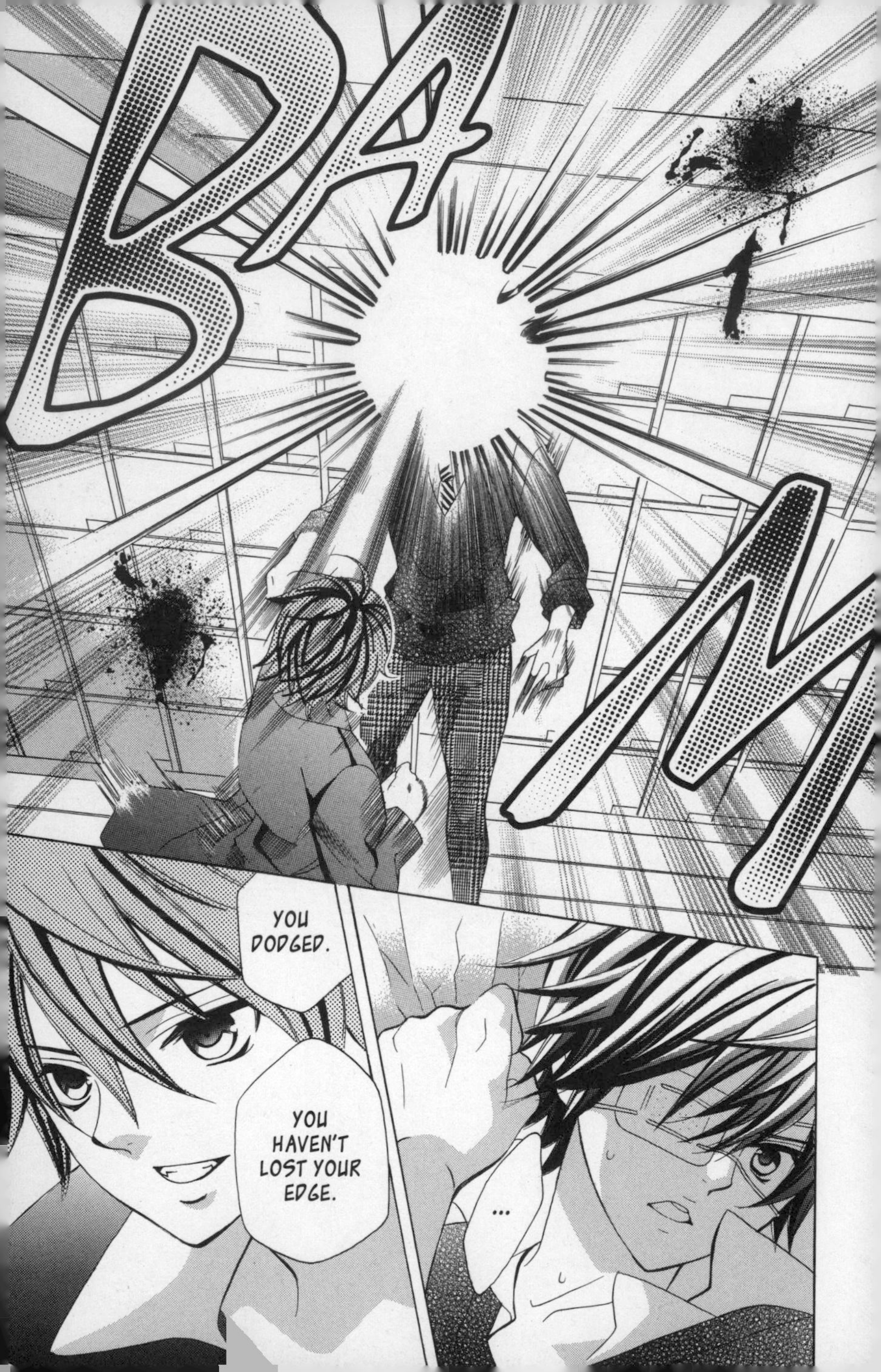
BAM
YOU DODGED.
...
YOU HAVEN'T LOST YOUR EDGE.

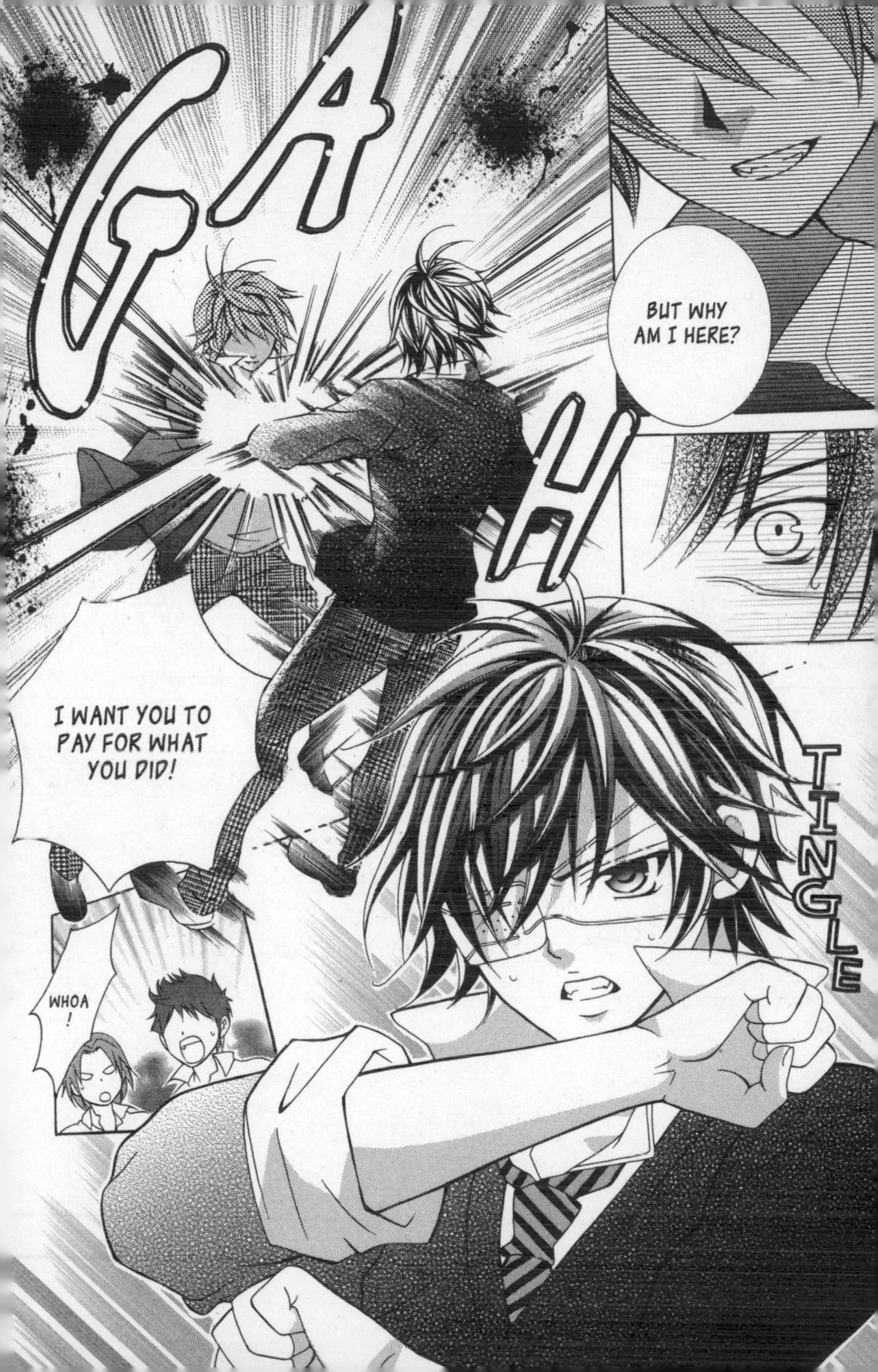
BUT WHY AM I HERE?
GAAH
I WANT YOU TO PAY FOR WHAT YOU DID!
TINGLE
WHOA!

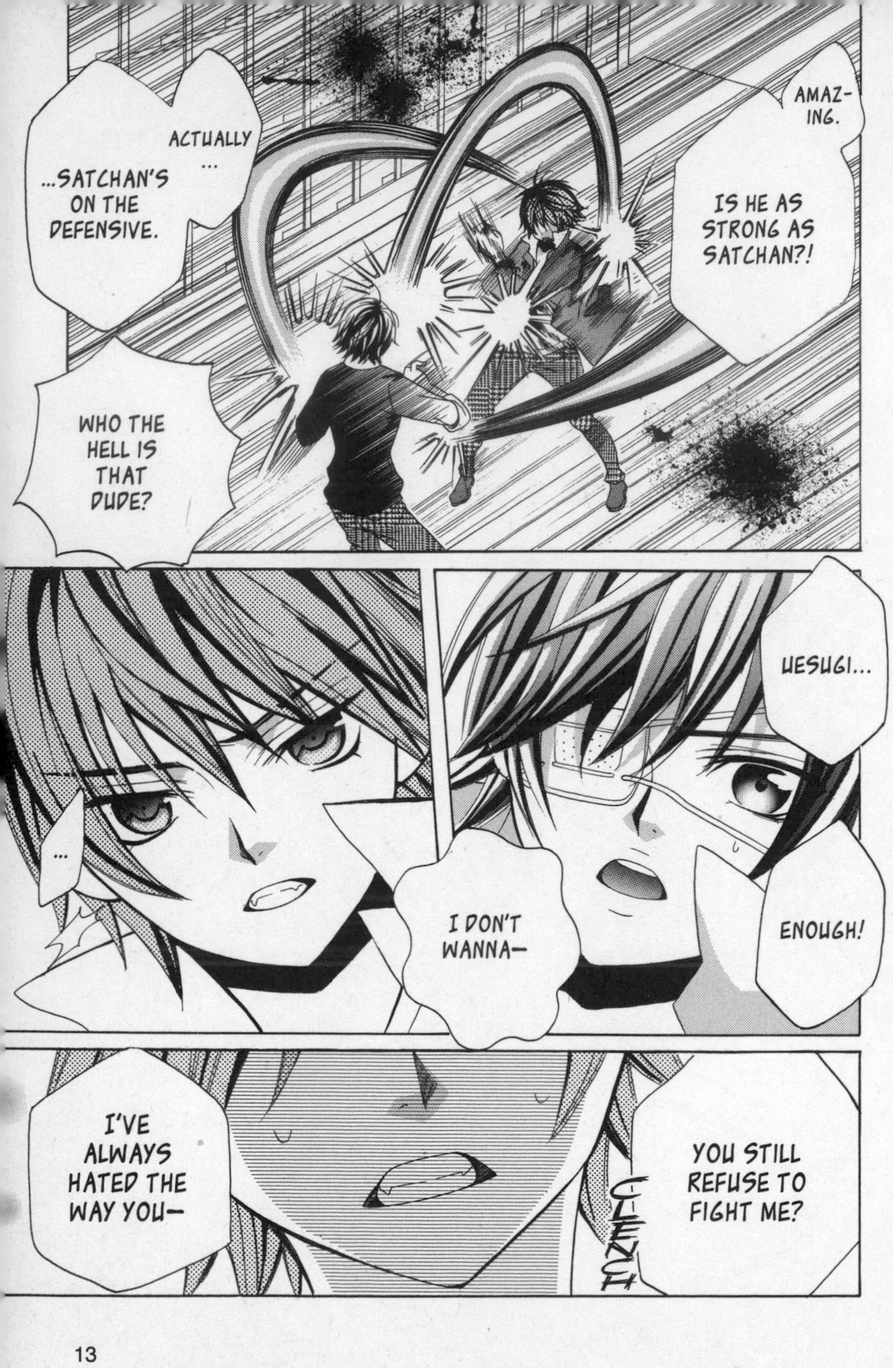
AMAZ-ING.
IS HE AS STRONG AS SATCHAN?!
ACTUALLY ...
...SATCHAN'S ON THE DEFENSIVE.
WHO THE HELL IS THAT DUDE?
UESUGI...
ENOUGH!
I DON'T WANNA—
...
YOU STILL REFUSE TO FIGHT ME?
CLENCH
I'VE ALWAYS HATED THE WAY YOU—

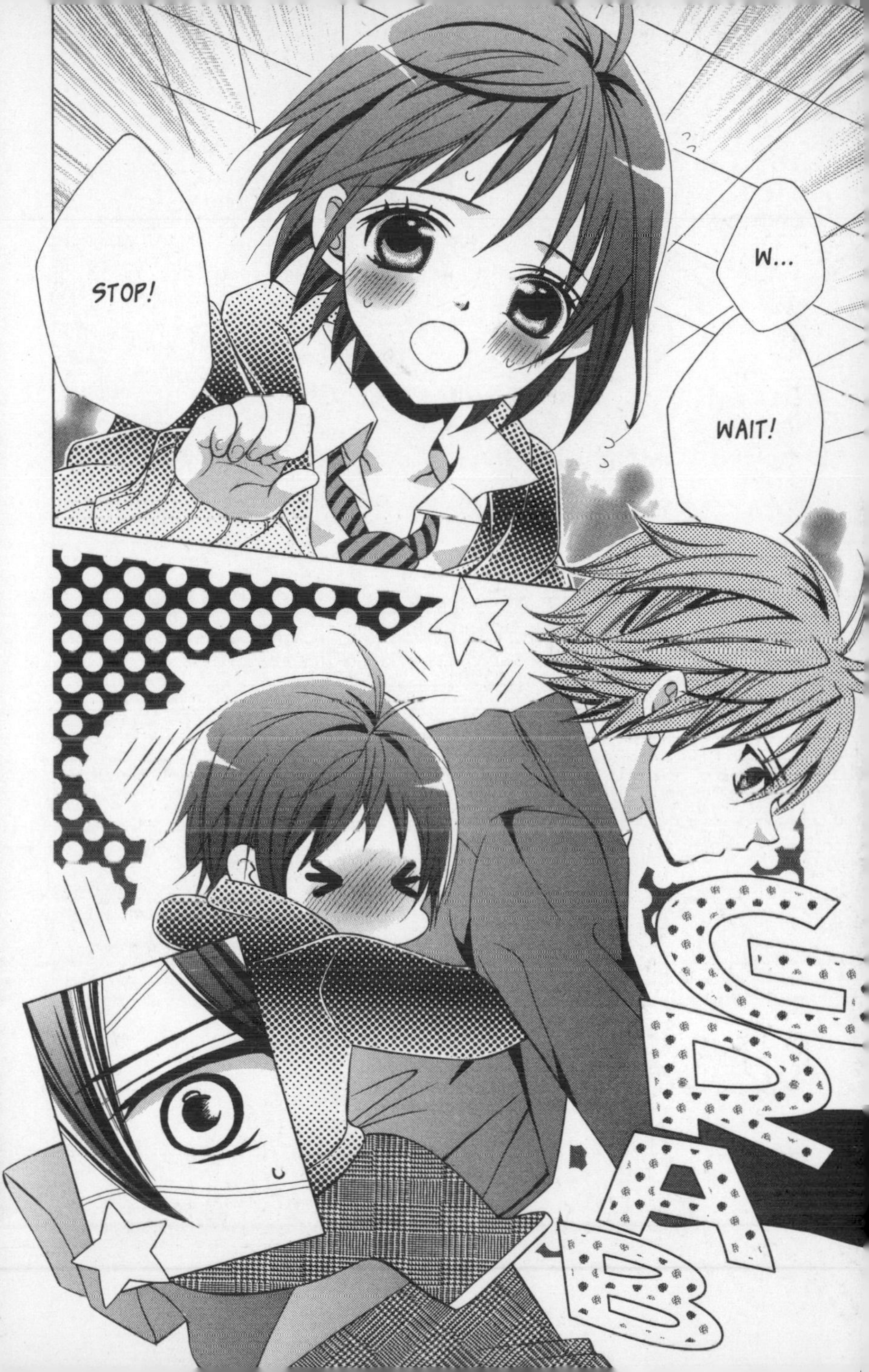
W...
WAIT!
STOP!
GRAB

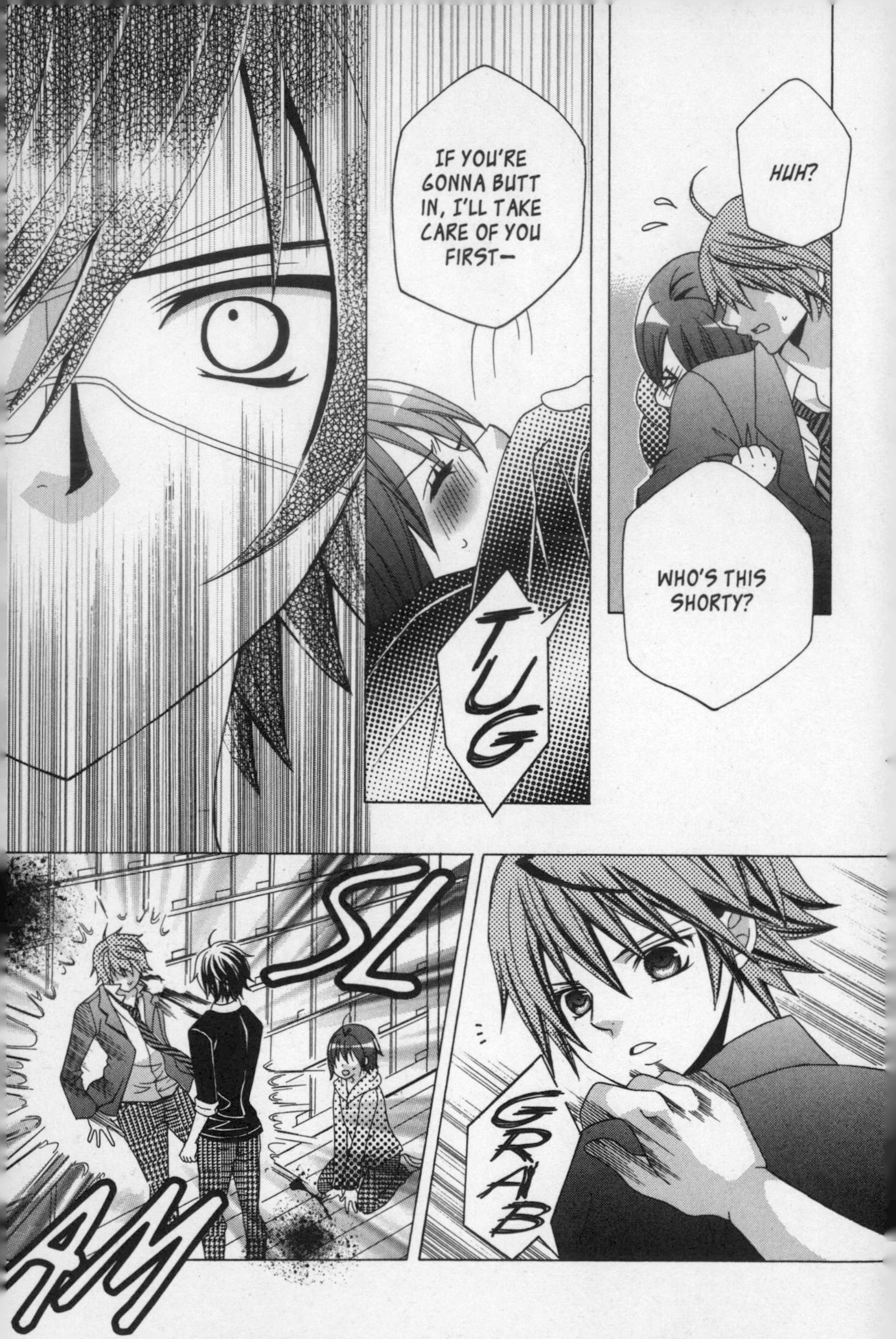
HUH?
WHO'S THIS SHORTY?
IF YOU'RE GONNA BUTT IN, I'LL TAKE CARE OF YOU FIRST—
TUG
GRAB
SL
AM

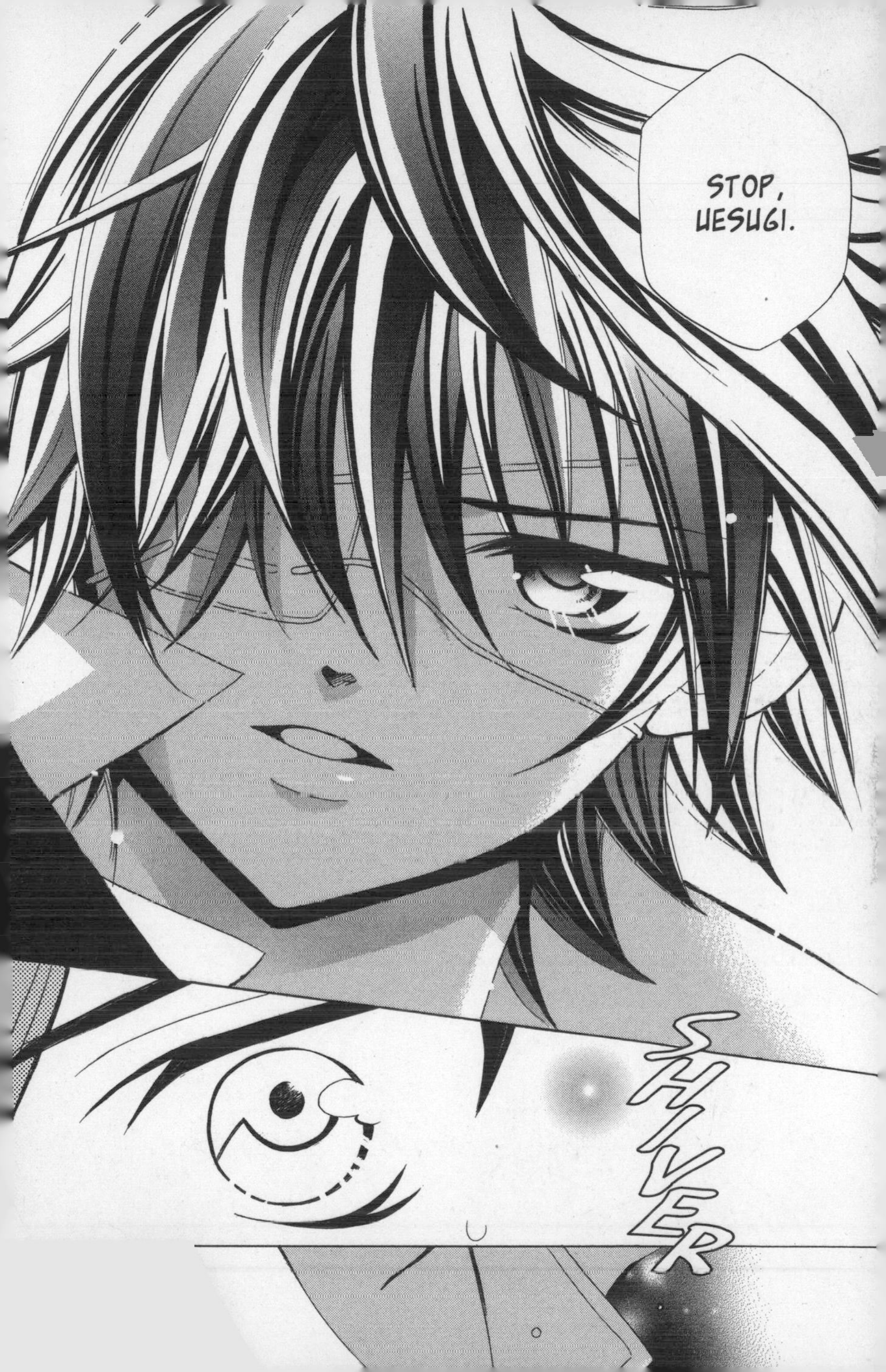
STOP, UESUGI.
SHIVER

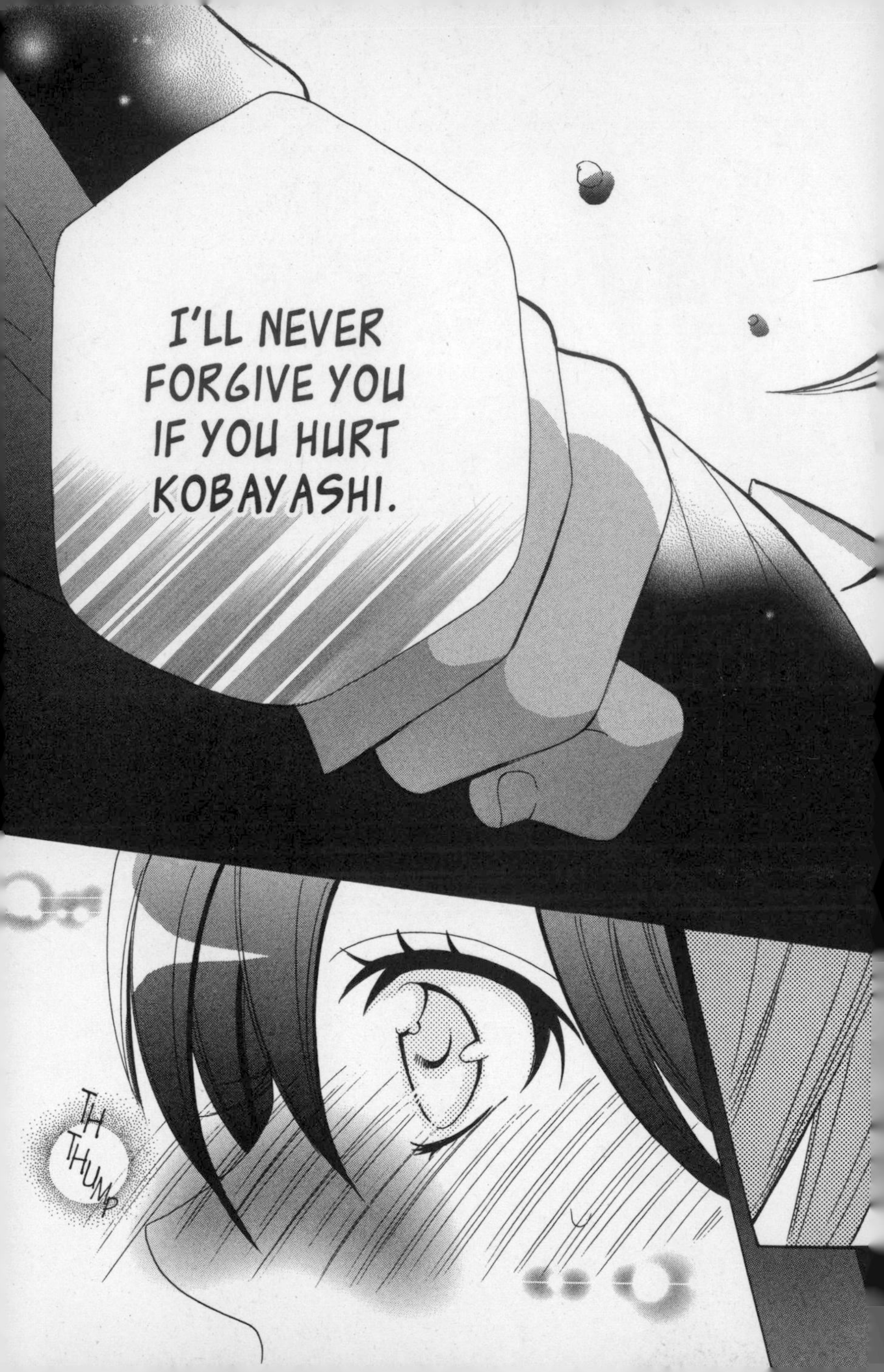
I'LL NEVER FORGIVE YOU IF YOU HURT KOBAYASHI.
TH THUMP

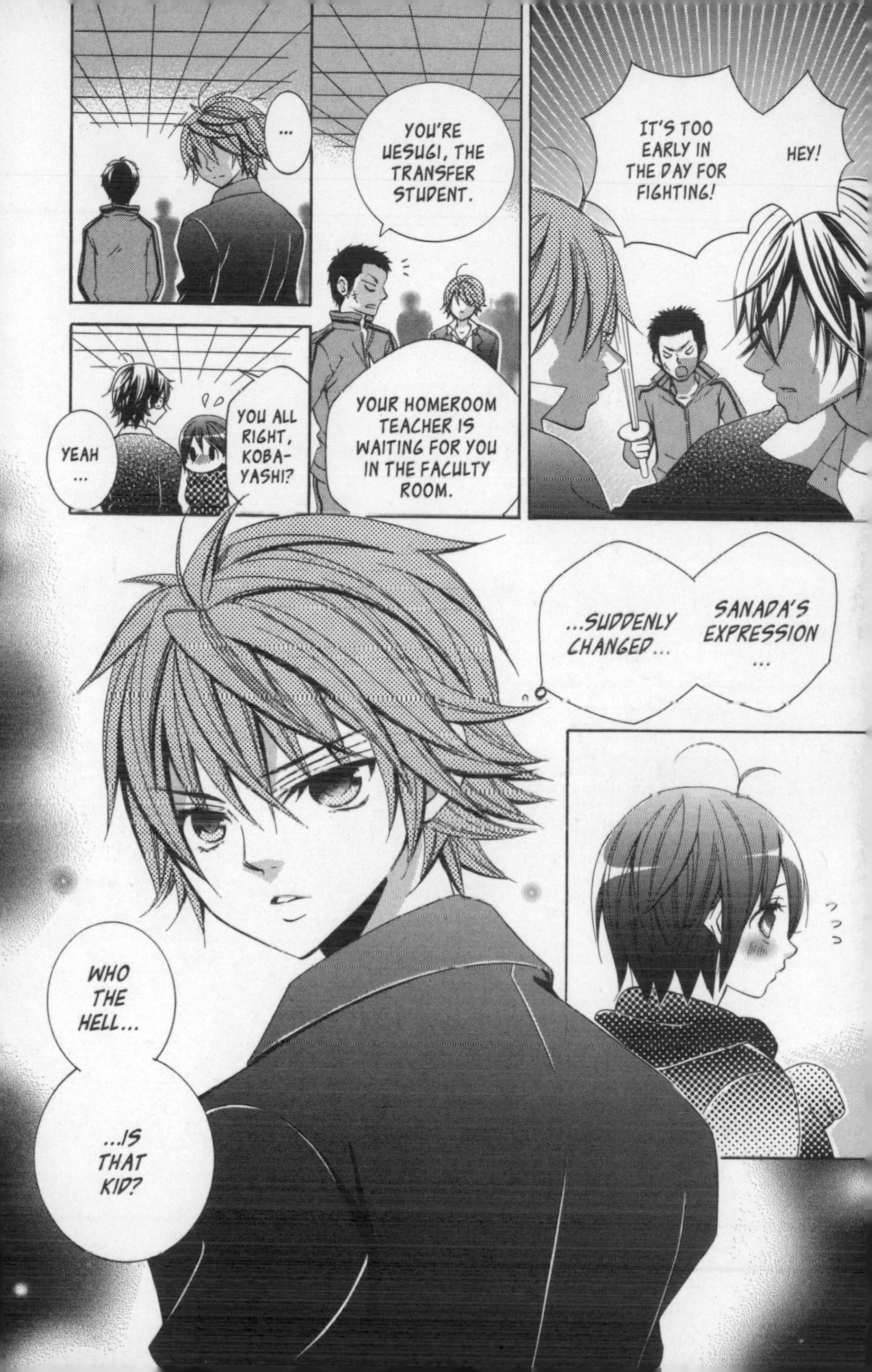
HEY!
IT'S TOO EARLY IN THE DAY FOR FIGHTING!
YOU'RE UESUGI, THE TRANSFER STUDENT.
YOUR HOMEROOM TEACHER IS WAITING FOR YOU IN THE FACULTY ROOM.
...
YOU ALL RIGHT, KOBAYASHI?
YEAH ...
SANADA'S EXPRESSION ...
...SUDDENLY CHANGED...
WHO THE HELL...
...IS THAT KID?

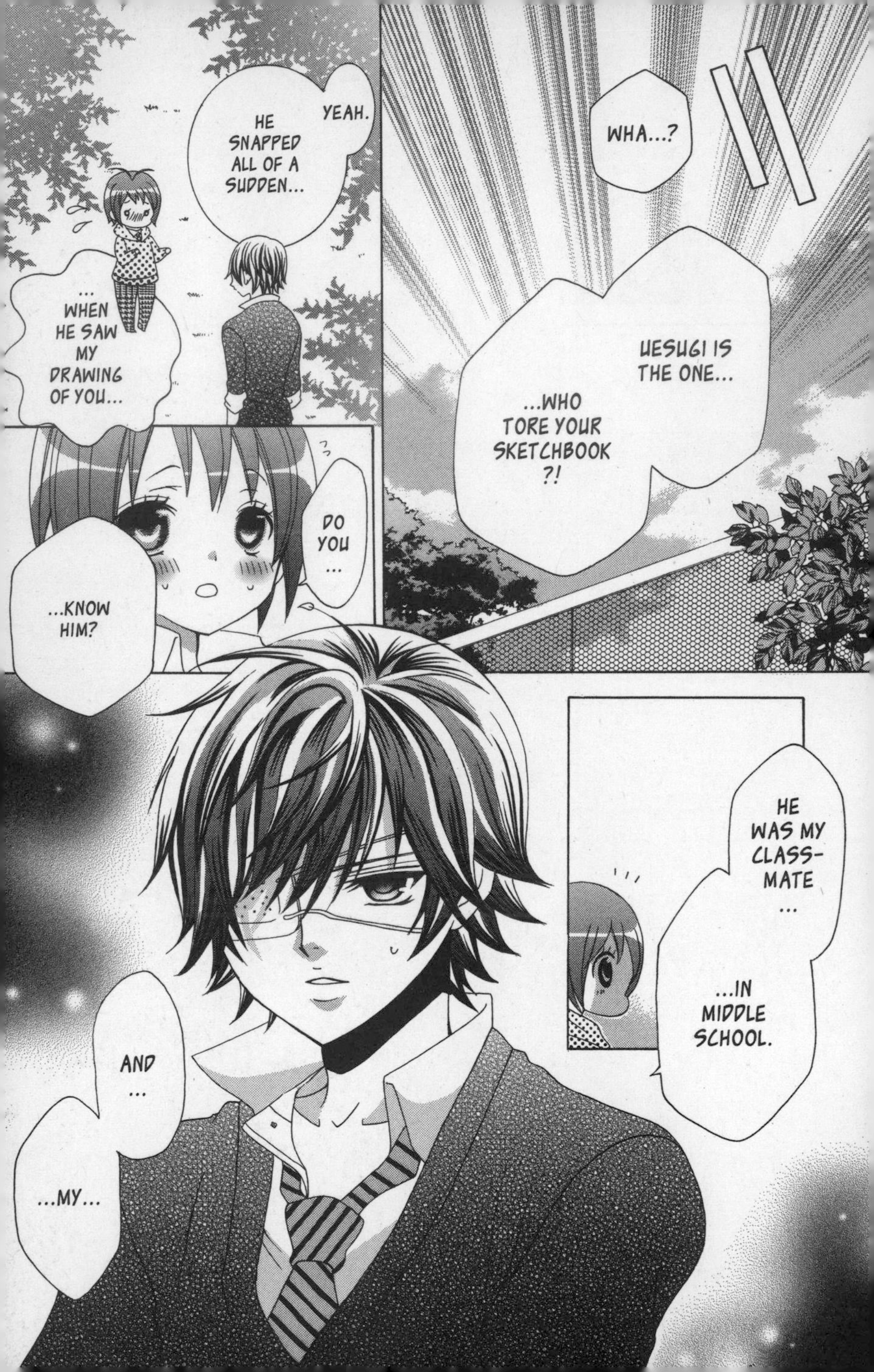
WHA...?
UESUGI IS THE ONE...
...WHO TORE YOUR SKETCHBOOK?!
YEAH.
HE SNAPPED ALL OF A SUDDEN...
...WHEN HE SAW MY DRAWING OF YOU...
DO YOU...
...KNOW HIM?
HE WAS MY CLASSMATE...
...IN MIDDLE SCHOOL.
AND...
...MY...

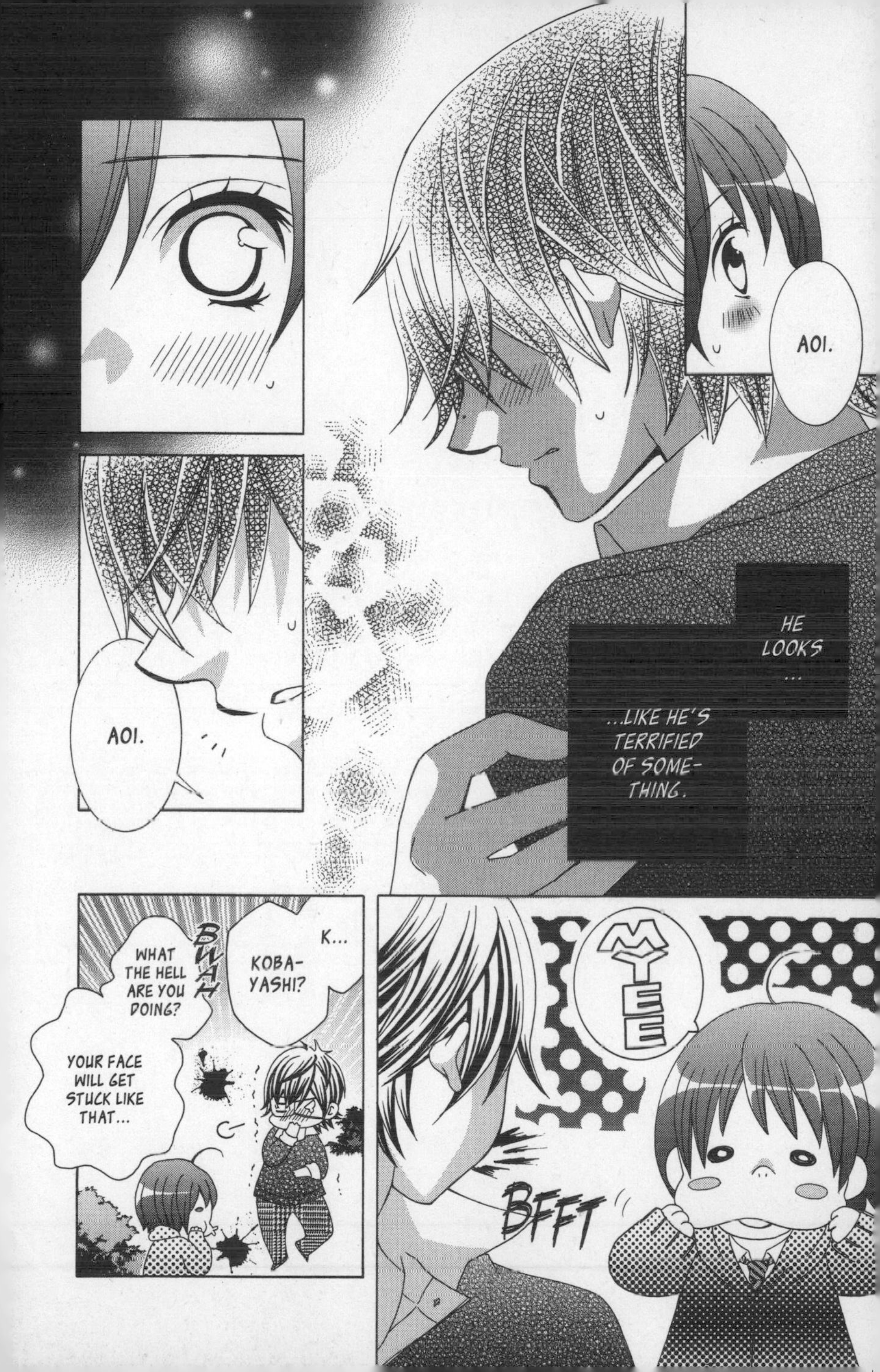
AOI.
HE LOOKS ...
...LIKE HE'S TERRIFIED OF SOME-THING.
AOI.
MYEE
BFFT
K...
KOBA-YASHI?
BWAH
WHAT THE HELL ARE YOU DOING?
YOUR FACE WILL GET STUCK LIKE THAT...

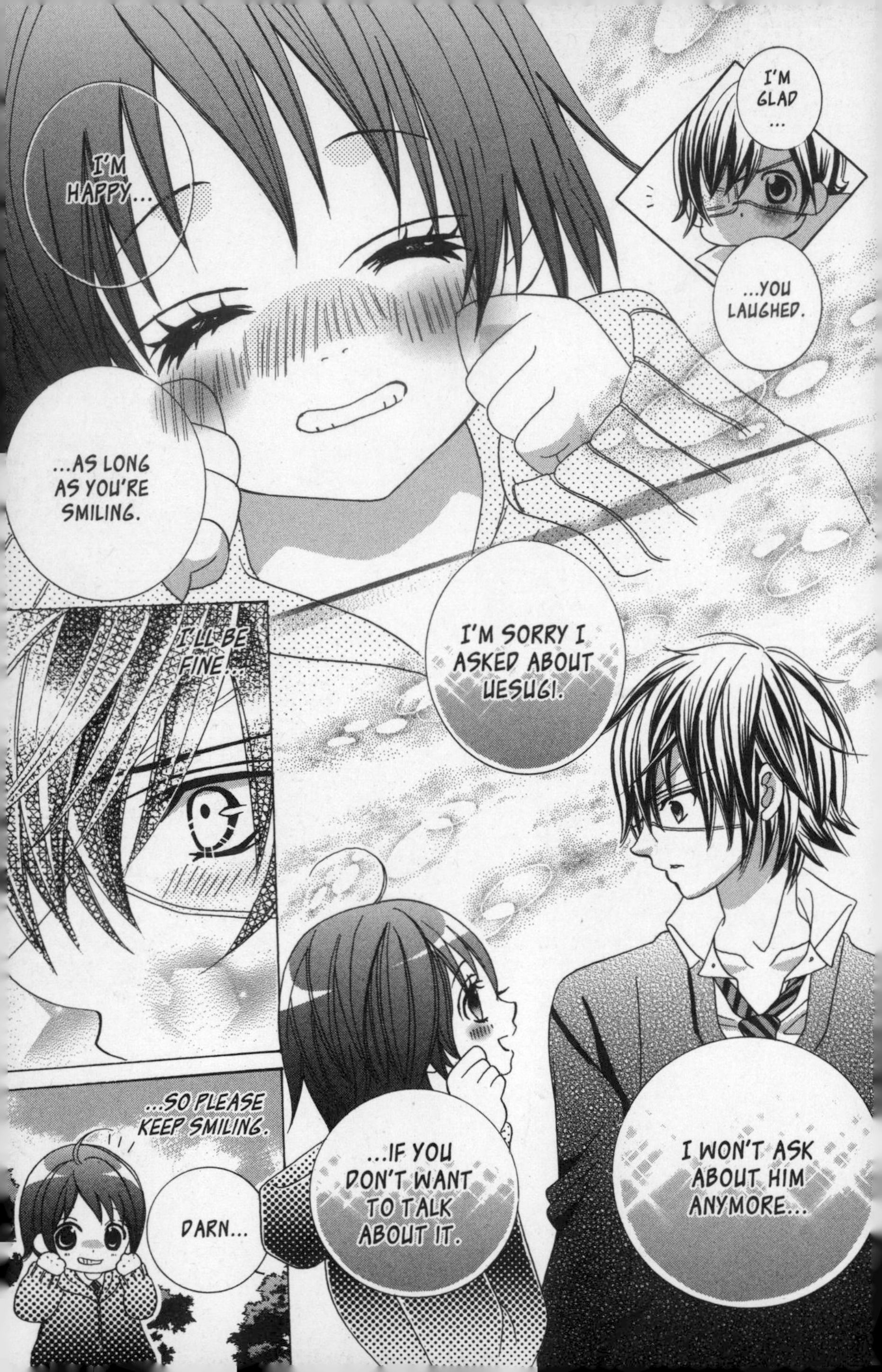
I'M GLAD...
...YOU LAUGHED.
I'M HAPPY...
...AS LONG AS YOU'RE SMILING.
I'M SORRY I ASKED ABOUT UESUGI.
I'LL BE FINE...
I WON'T ASK ABOUT HIM ANYMORE...
...IF YOU DON'T WANT TO TALK ABOUT IT.
...SO PLEASE KEEP SMILING.
DARN...

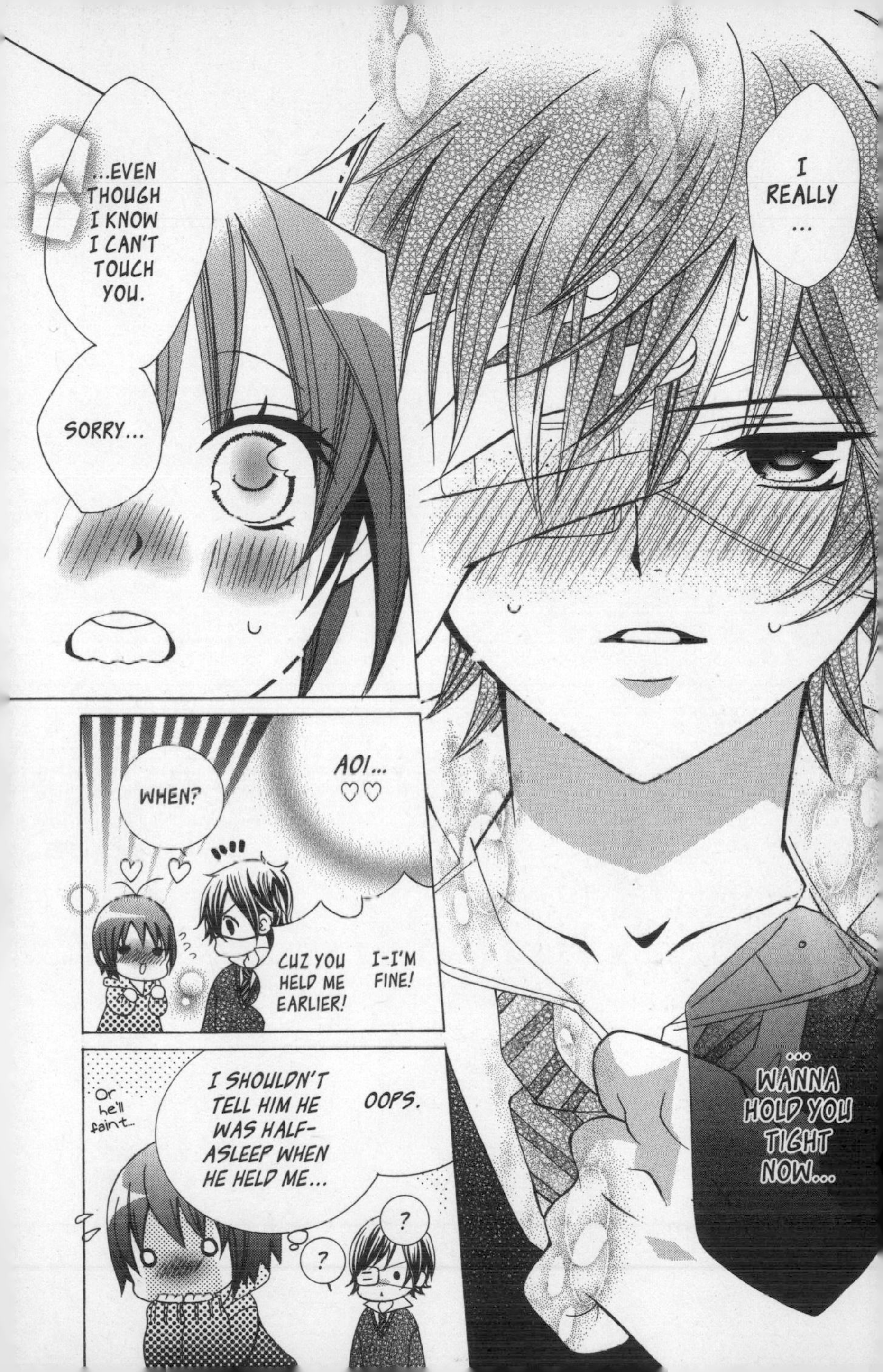
I REALLY...
...WANNA HOLD YOU TIGHT NOW...
...EVEN THOUGH I KNOW I CAN'T TOUCH YOU.
SORRY...
AOI... ♡♡
WHEN?
I-I'M FINE!
CUZ YOU HELD ME EARLIER!
OOPS.
I SHOULDN'T TELL HIM HE WAS HALF-ASLEEP WHEN HE HELD ME...
Or he'll faint...
?
?

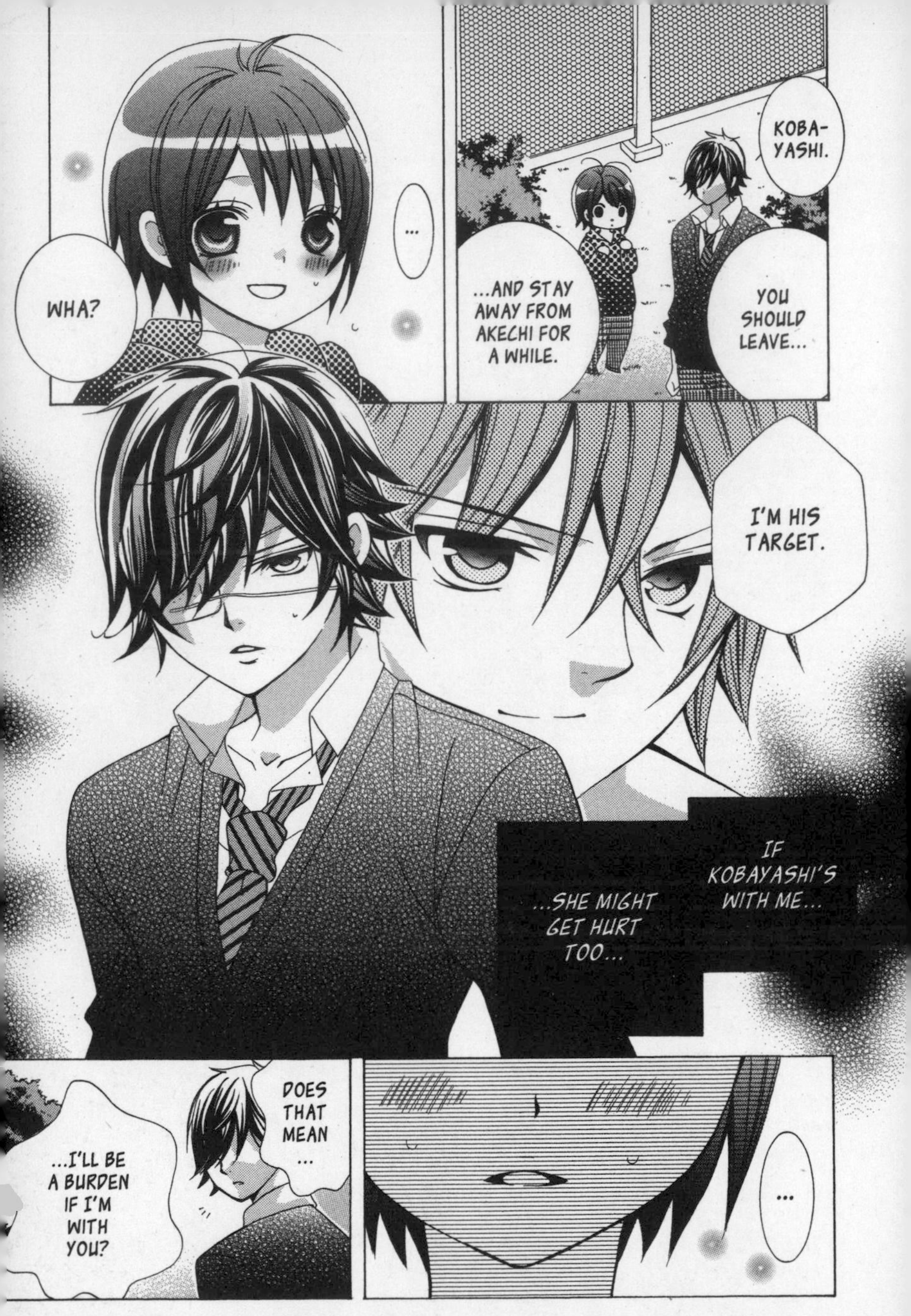
KOBA-YASHI.
YOU SHOULD LEAVE...
...AND STAY AWAY FROM AKECHI FOR A WHILE.
...
WHA?
I'M HIS TARGET.
IF KOBAYASHI'S WITH ME...
...SHE MIGHT GET HURT TOO...
...
DOES THAT MEAN ...
...I'LL BE A BURDEN IF I'M WITH YOU?

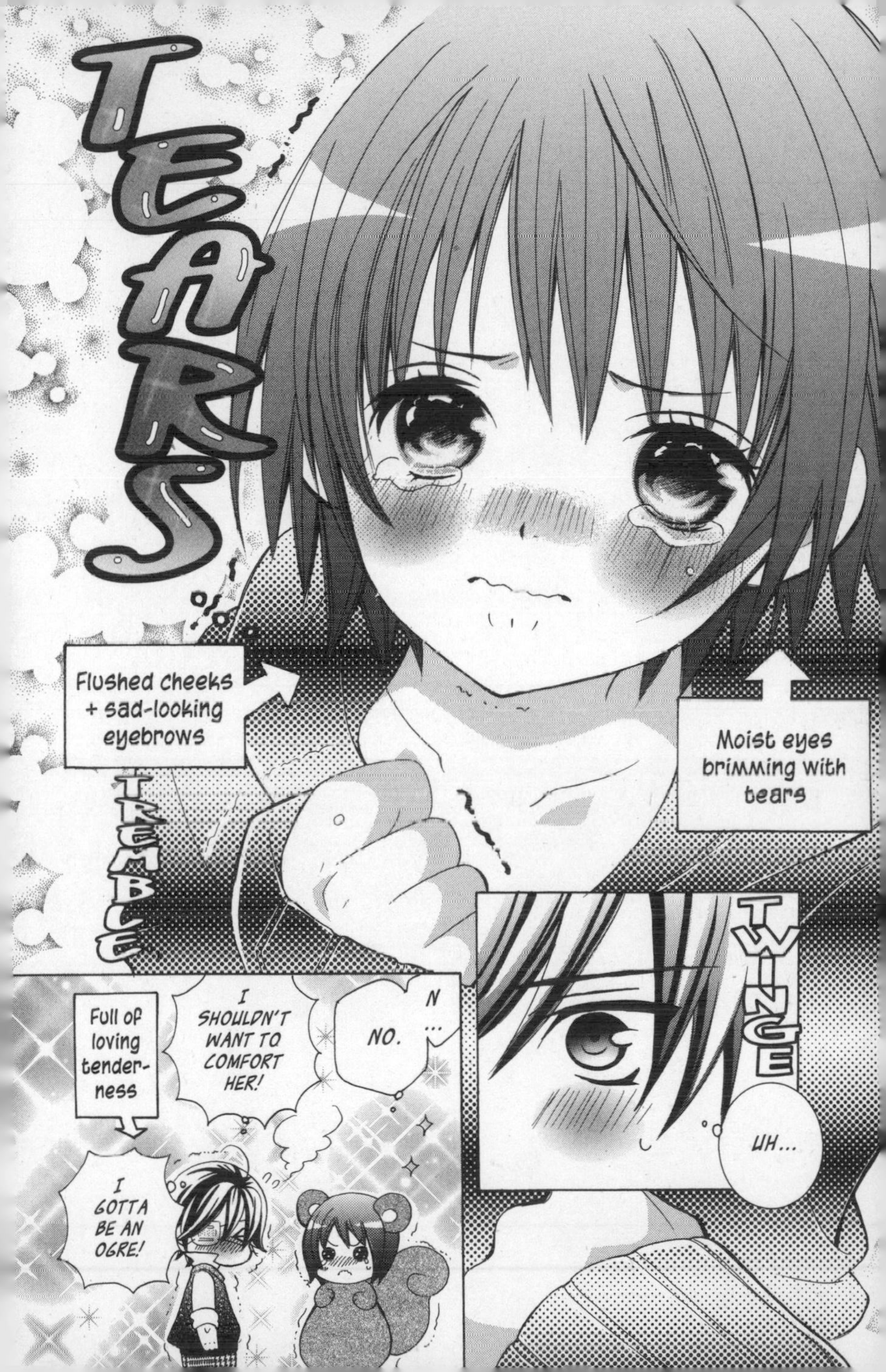
TEARS
Moist eyes brimming with tears
Flushed cheeks + sad-looking eyebrows
TREMBLE
TWINGE
UH...
N...
NO.
I SHOULDN'T WANT TO COMFORT HER!
Full of loving tender-ness
I GOTTA BE AN OGRE!

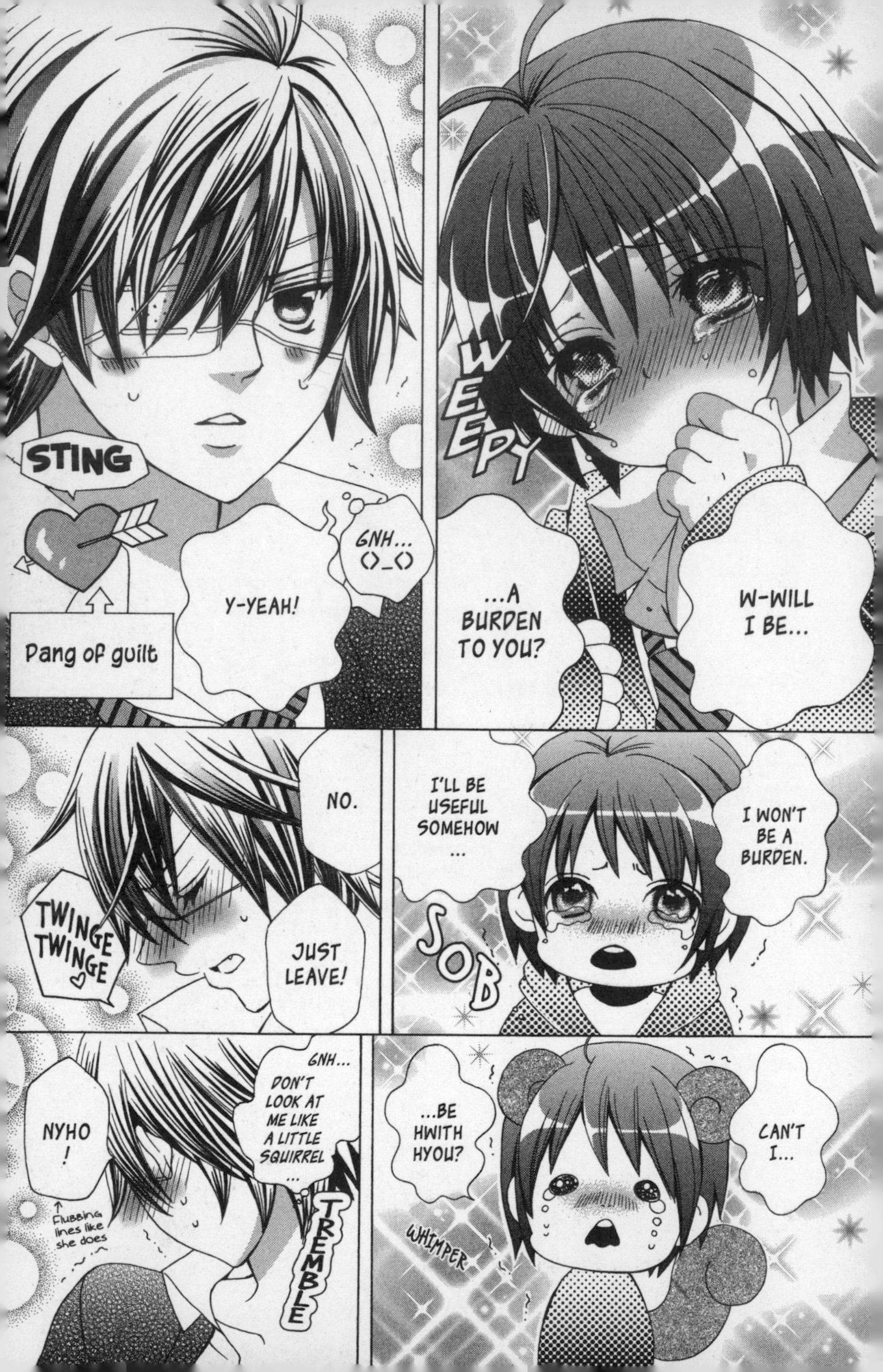
W-WILL I BE...
...A BURDEN TO YOU?
WEEPY
GNH... ()_()
Y-YEAH!
STING
Pang of guilt
I WON'T BE A BURDEN.
I'LL BE USEFUL SOMEHOW ...
SOB
NO.
JUST LEAVE!
TWINGE TWINGE ♡
CAN'T I...
...BE HWITH HYOU?
WHIMPER
GNH... DON'T LOOK AT ME LIKE A LITTLE SQUIRREL ...
TREMBLE
NYHO !
Flubbing lines like she does

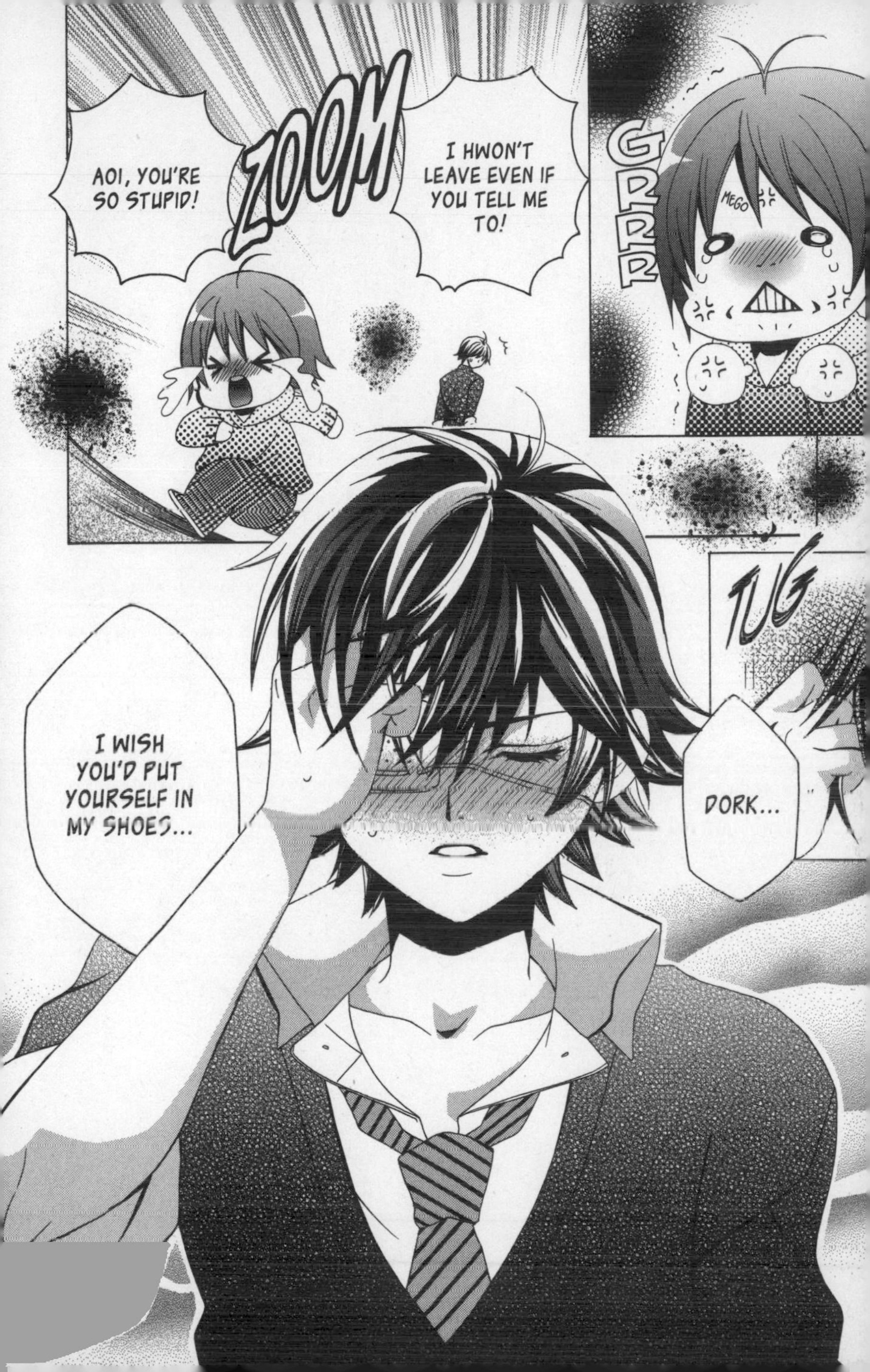
GRRR
MEGO
I HWON'T LEAVE EVEN IF YOU TELL ME TO!
ZOOM
AOI, YOU'RE SO STUPID!
TUG
DORK...
I WISH YOU'D PUT YOURSELF IN MY SHOES...

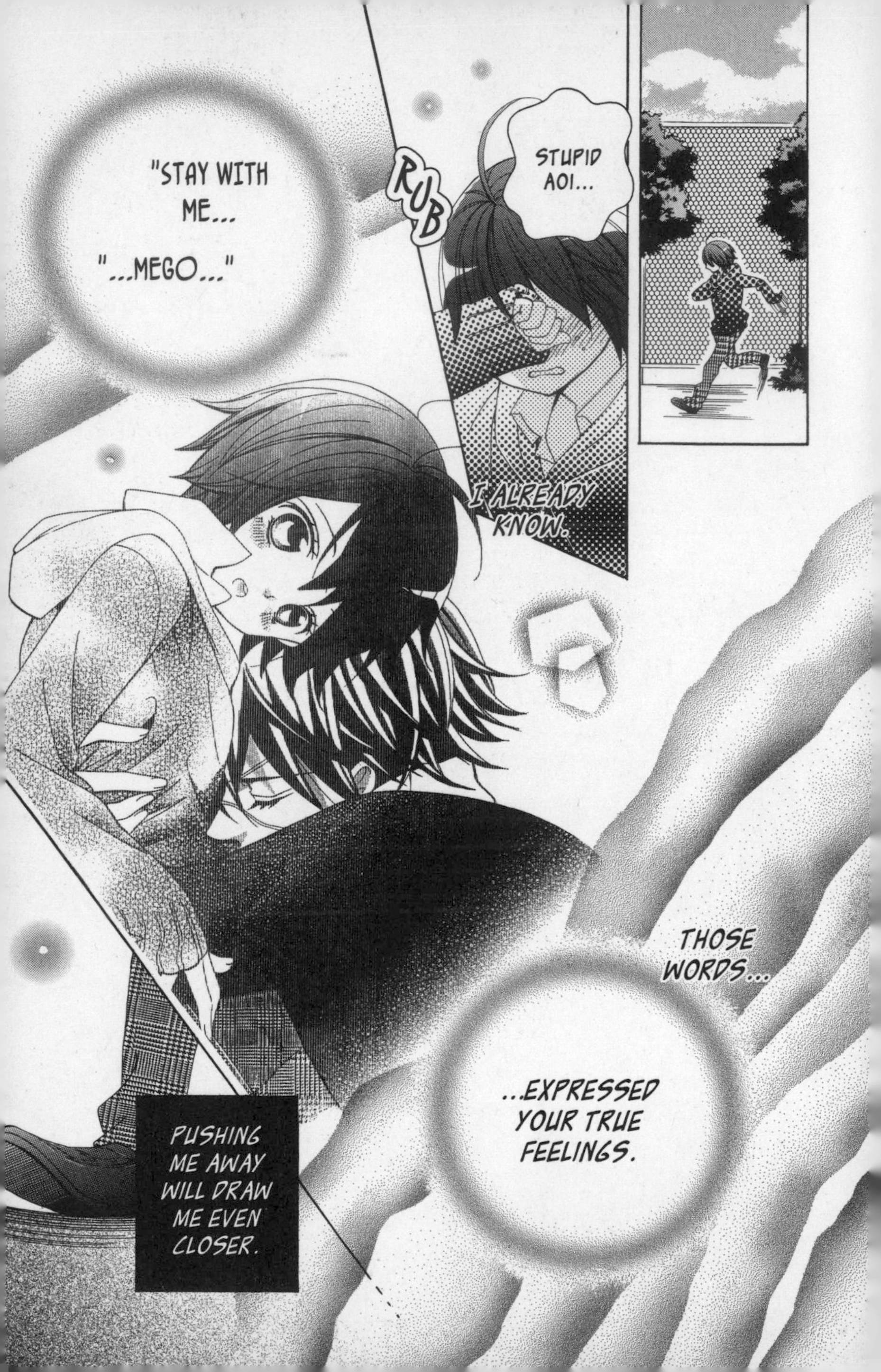
RUB
STUPID AOI...
I ALREADY KNOW.
"STAY WITH ME...
"...MEGO..."
THOSE WORDS...
...EXPRESSED YOUR TRUE FEELINGS.
PUSHING ME AWAY WILL DRAW ME EVEN CLOSER.

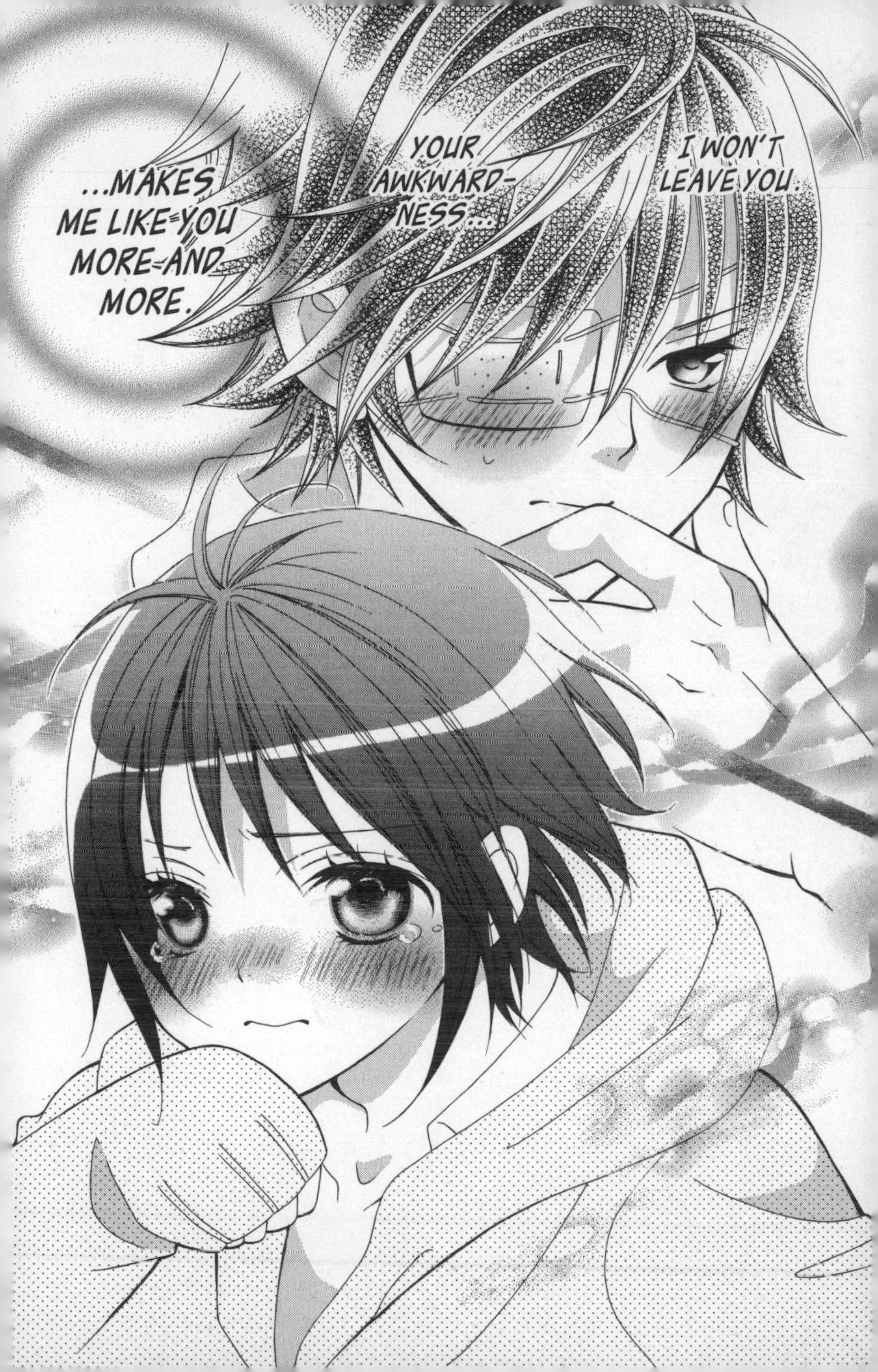
I WON'T LEAVE YOU.
YOUR AWKWARD-NESS...
...MAKES ME LIKE YOU MORE AND MORE.

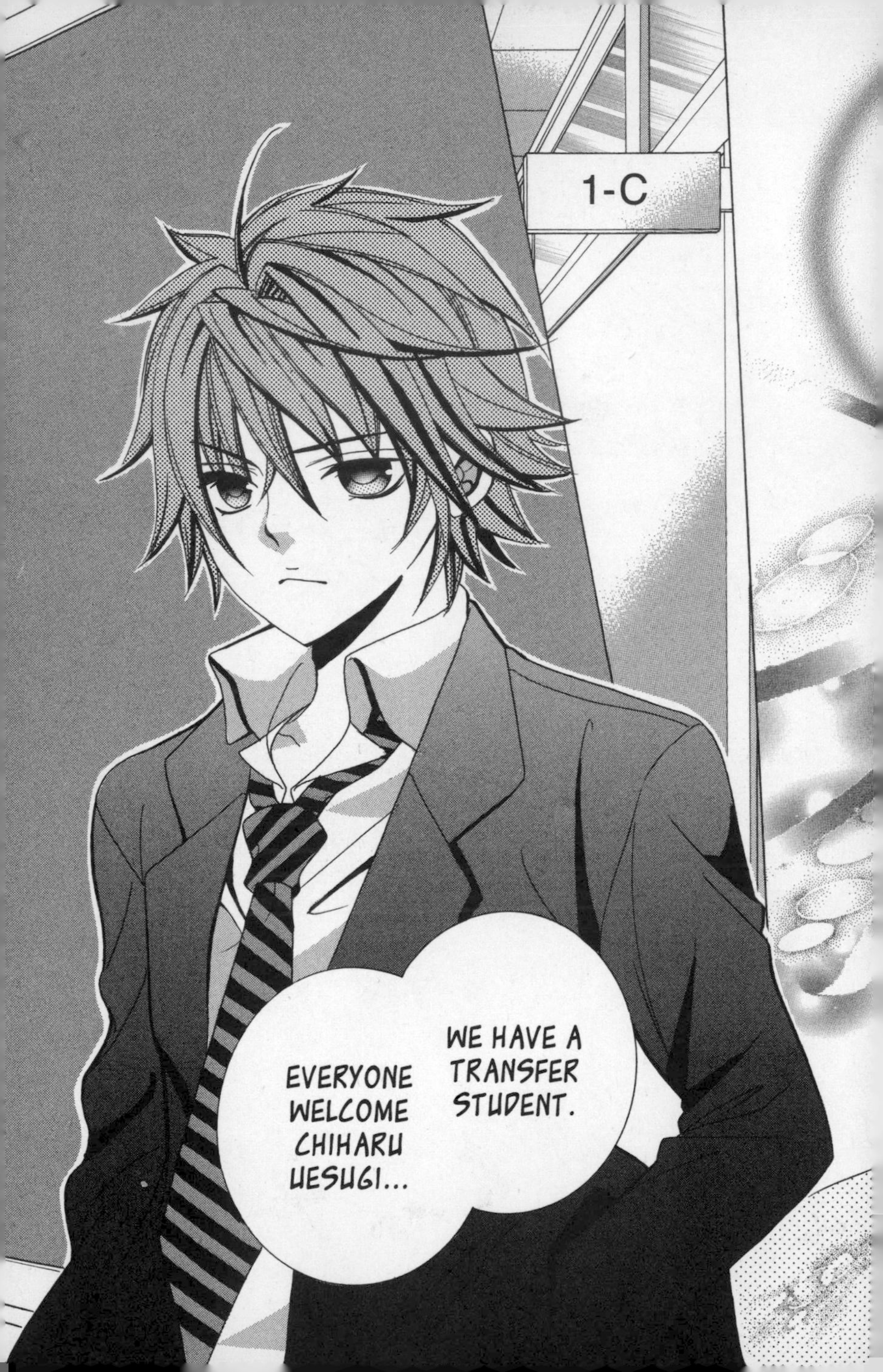
1-C
WE HAVE A TRANSFER STUDENT.
EVERYONE WELCOME CHIHARU UESUGI...

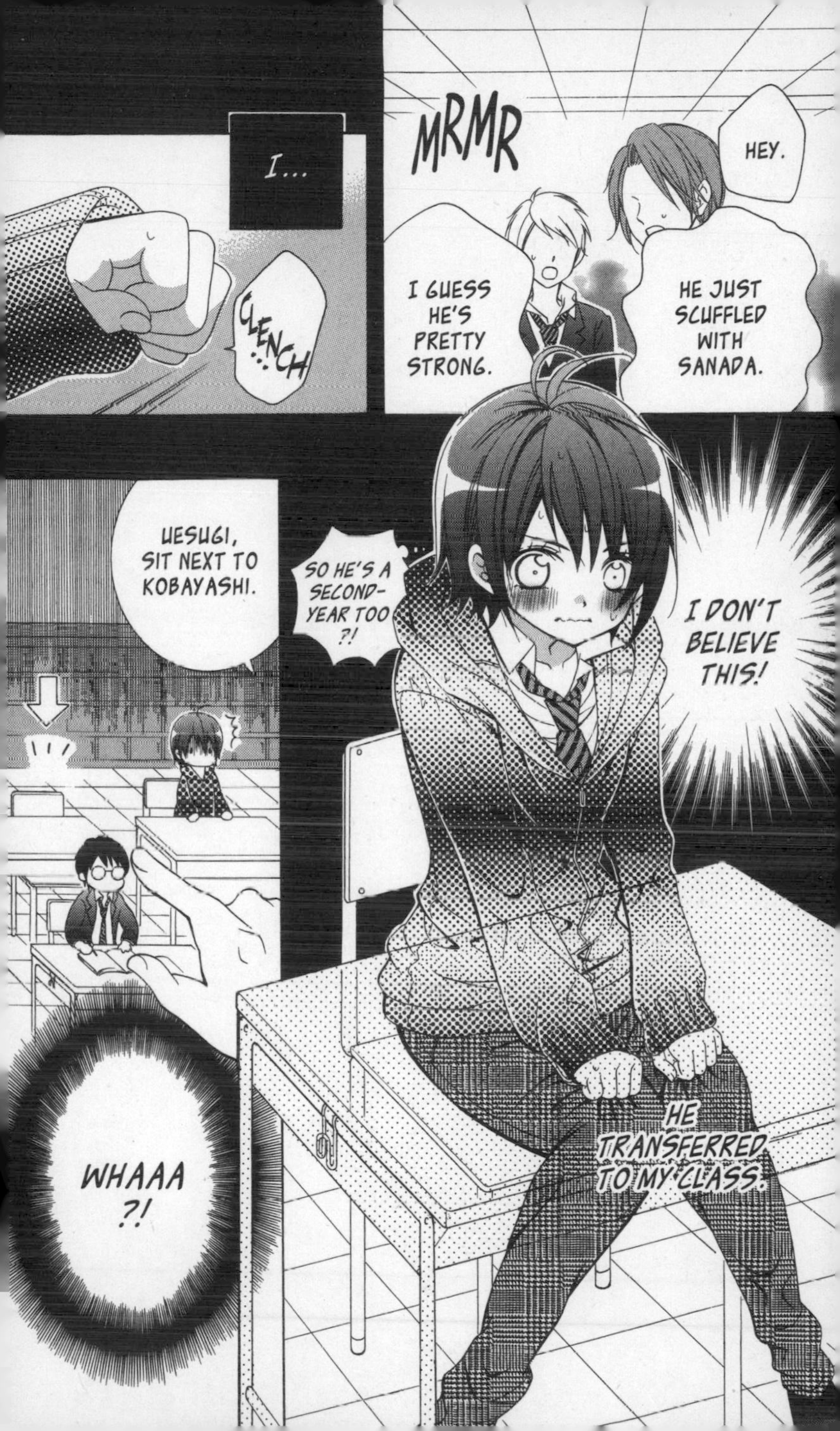
MRMR
HEY.
HE JUST SCUFFLED WITH SANADA.
I GUESS HE'S PRETTY STRONG.
I...
CLENCH...
I DON'T BELIEVE THIS!
SO HE'S A SECOND-YEAR TOO?!
HE TRANSFERRED TO MY CLASS.
UESUGI, SIT NEXT TO KOBAYASHI.
WHAAA?!

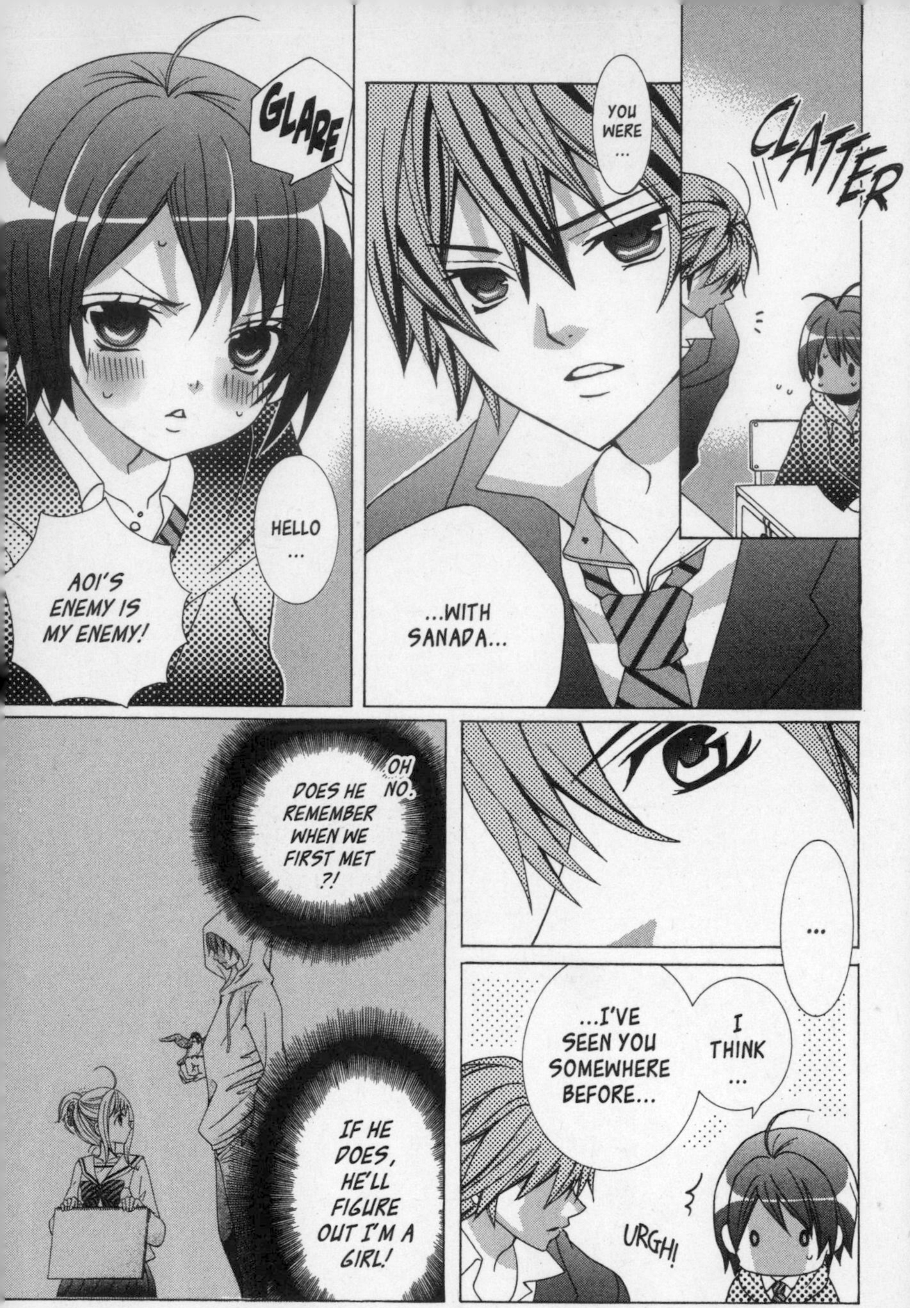
CLATTER
YOU WERE ...
...WITH SANADA...
GLARE
HELLO ...
AOI'S ENEMY IS MY ENEMY!
...
I THINK ...
...I'VE SEEN YOU SOMEWHERE BEFORE...
URGH!
OH NO.
DOES HE REMEMBER WHEN WE FIRST MET ?!
IF HE DOES, HE'LL FIGURE OUT I'M A GIRL!

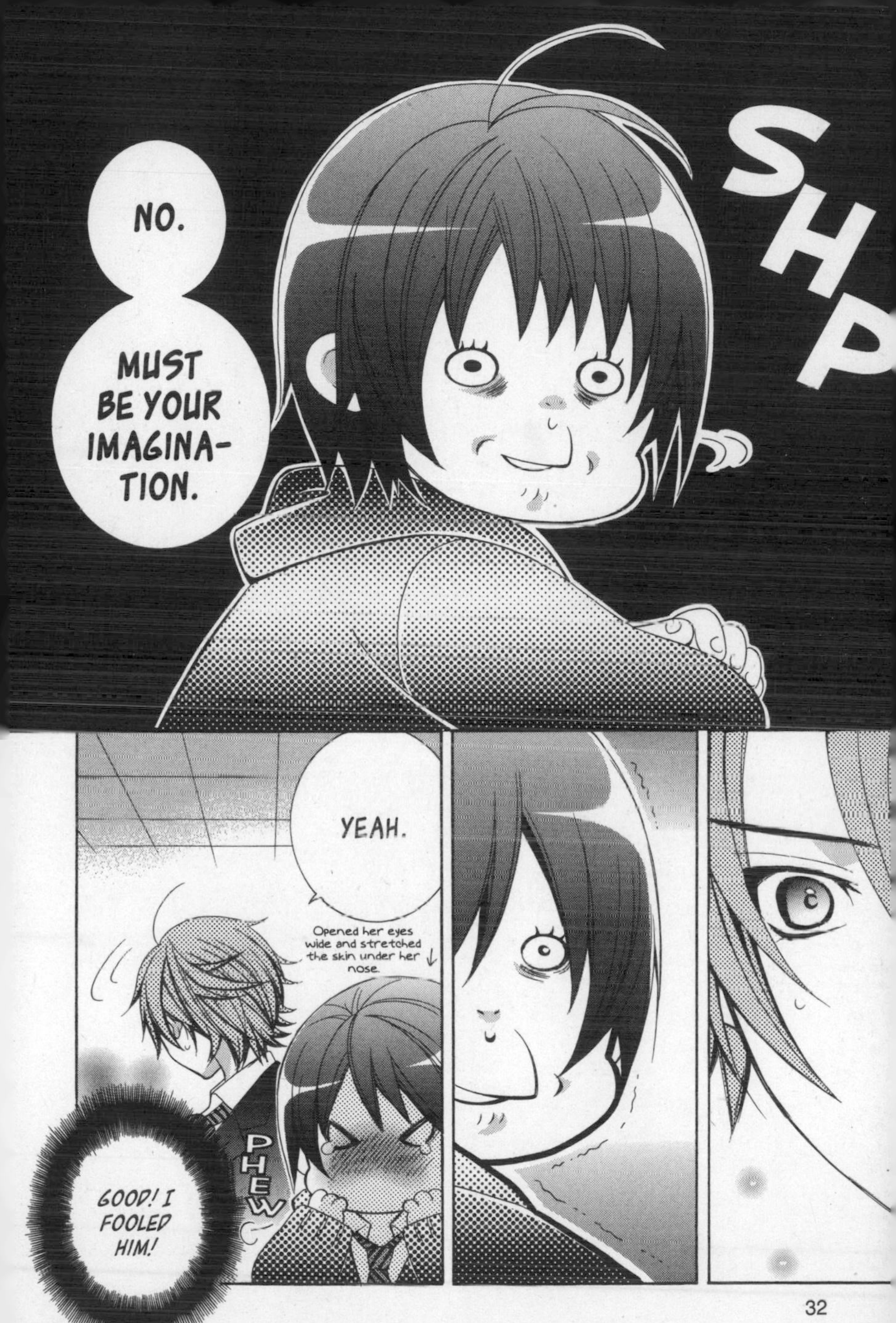
SHP
NO.
MUST BE YOUR IMAGINA-TION.
YEAH.
Opened her eyes wide and stretched the skin under her nose.
PHEW
GOOD! I FOOLED HIM!

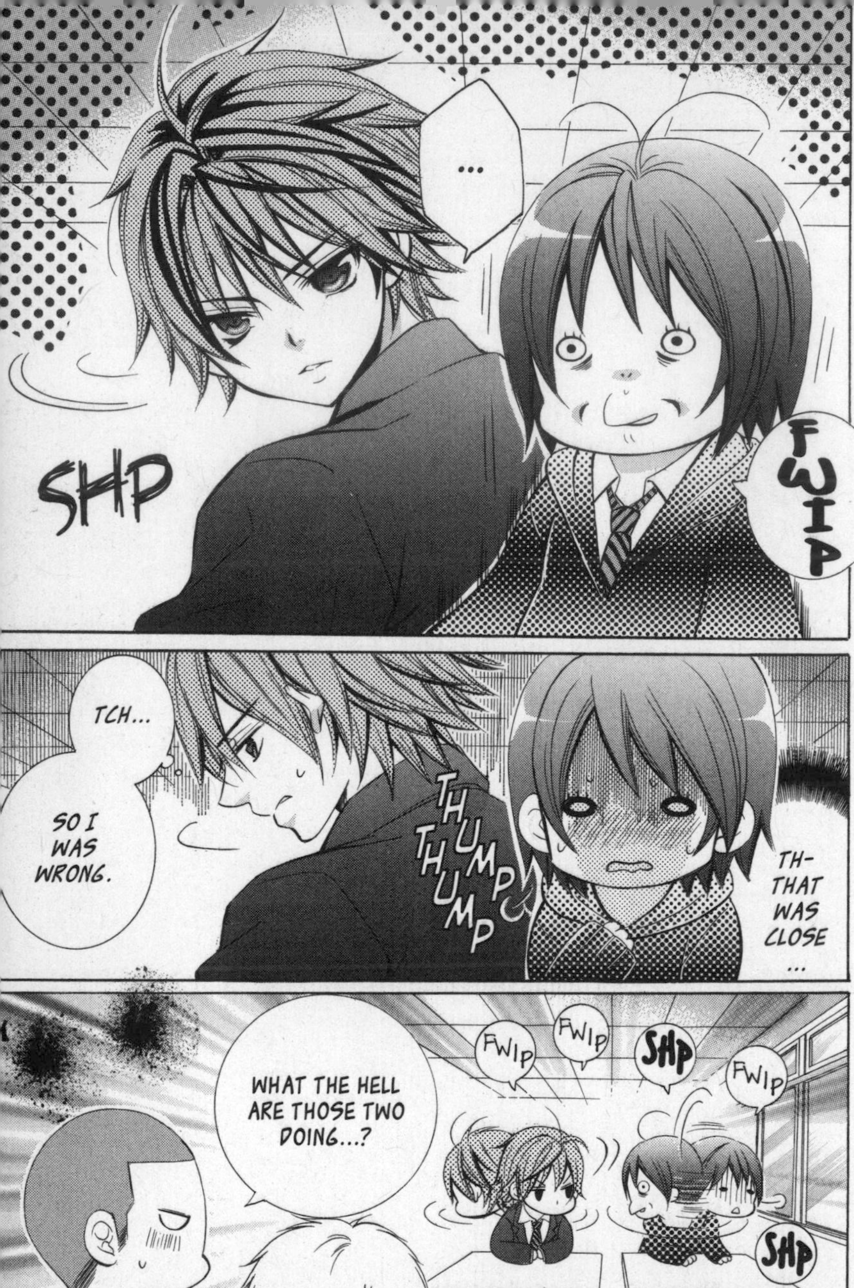
FWIP
...
SHP
TH- THAT WAS CLOSE ...
THUMP THUMP
TCH...
SO I WAS WRONG.
FWIP
SHP
FWIP
FWIP
WHAT THE HELL ARE THOSE TWO DOING...?
SHP

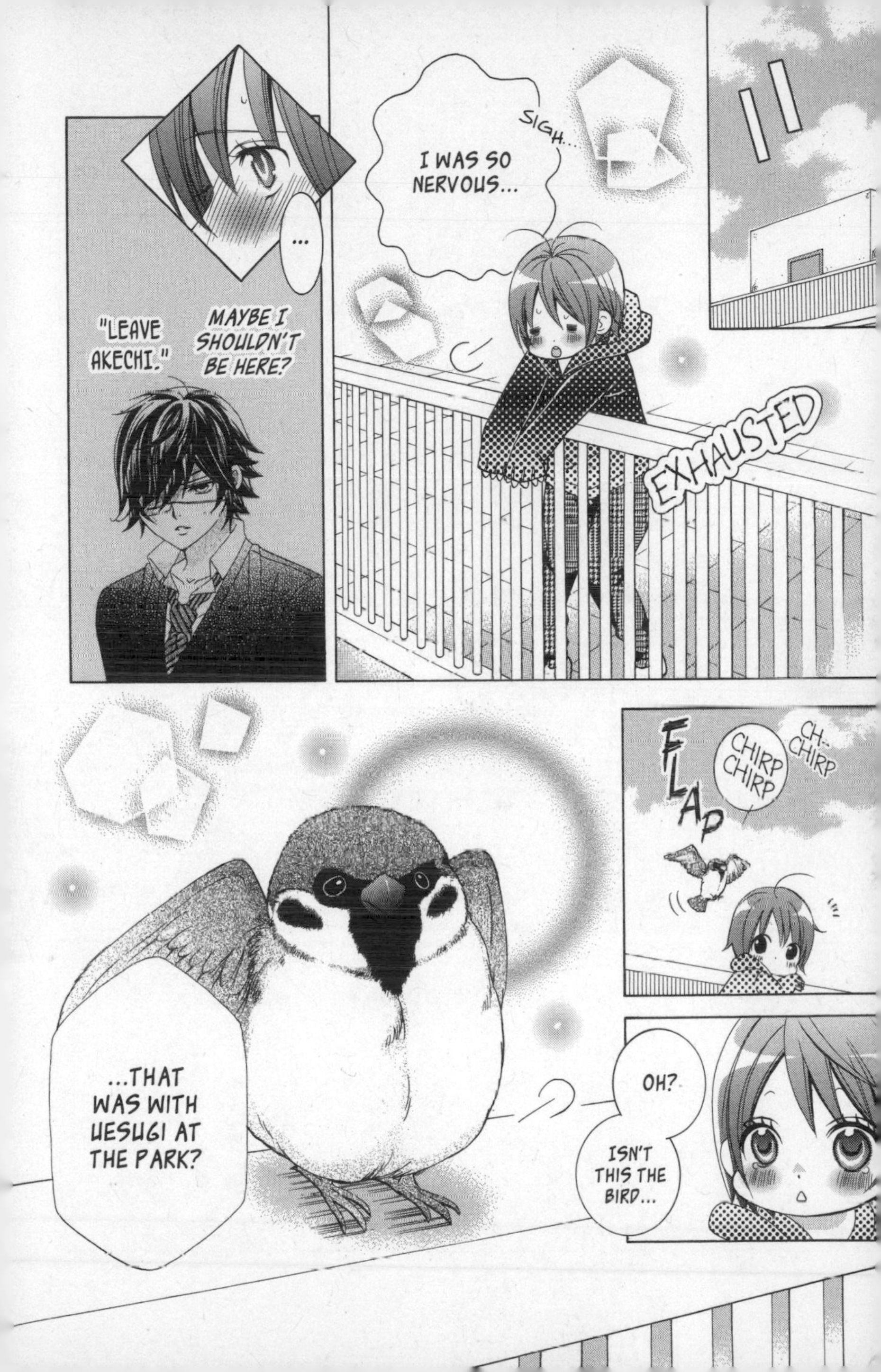
SIGH...
I WAS SO NERVOUS...
EXHAUSTED
...
MAYBE I SHOULDN'T BE HERE?
"LEAVE AKECHI."
CH-CHIRP
CHIRP CHIRP
FLAP
OH?
ISN'T THIS THE BIRD...
...THAT WAS WITH UESUGI AT THE PARK?

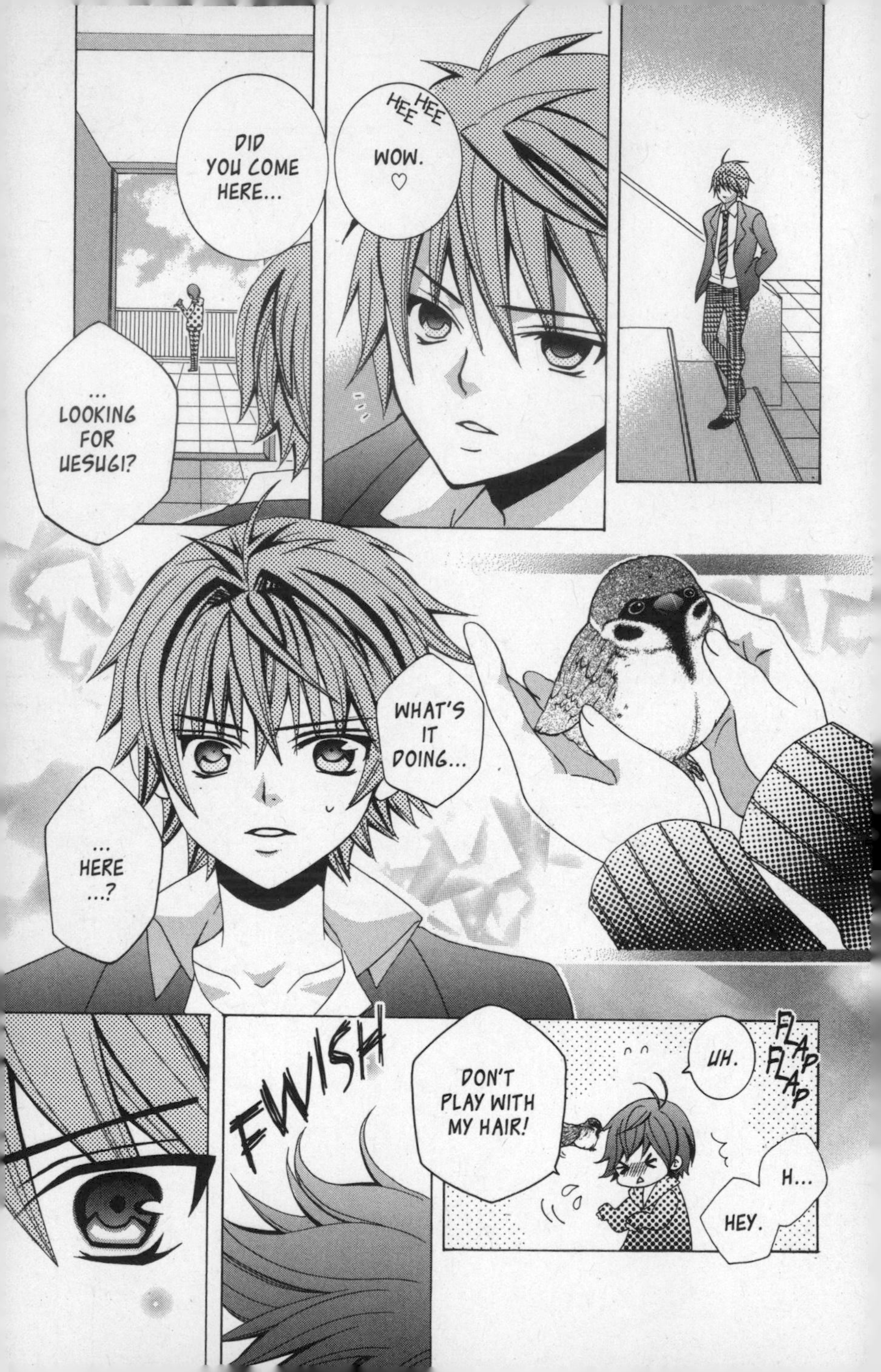
HEE HEE
WOW. ♡
DID YOU COME HERE...
...LOOKING FOR UESUGI?
WHAT'S IT DOING...
...HERE...?
FLAP FLAP
UH.
H... HEY.
DON'T PLAY WITH MY HAIR!
FWISH

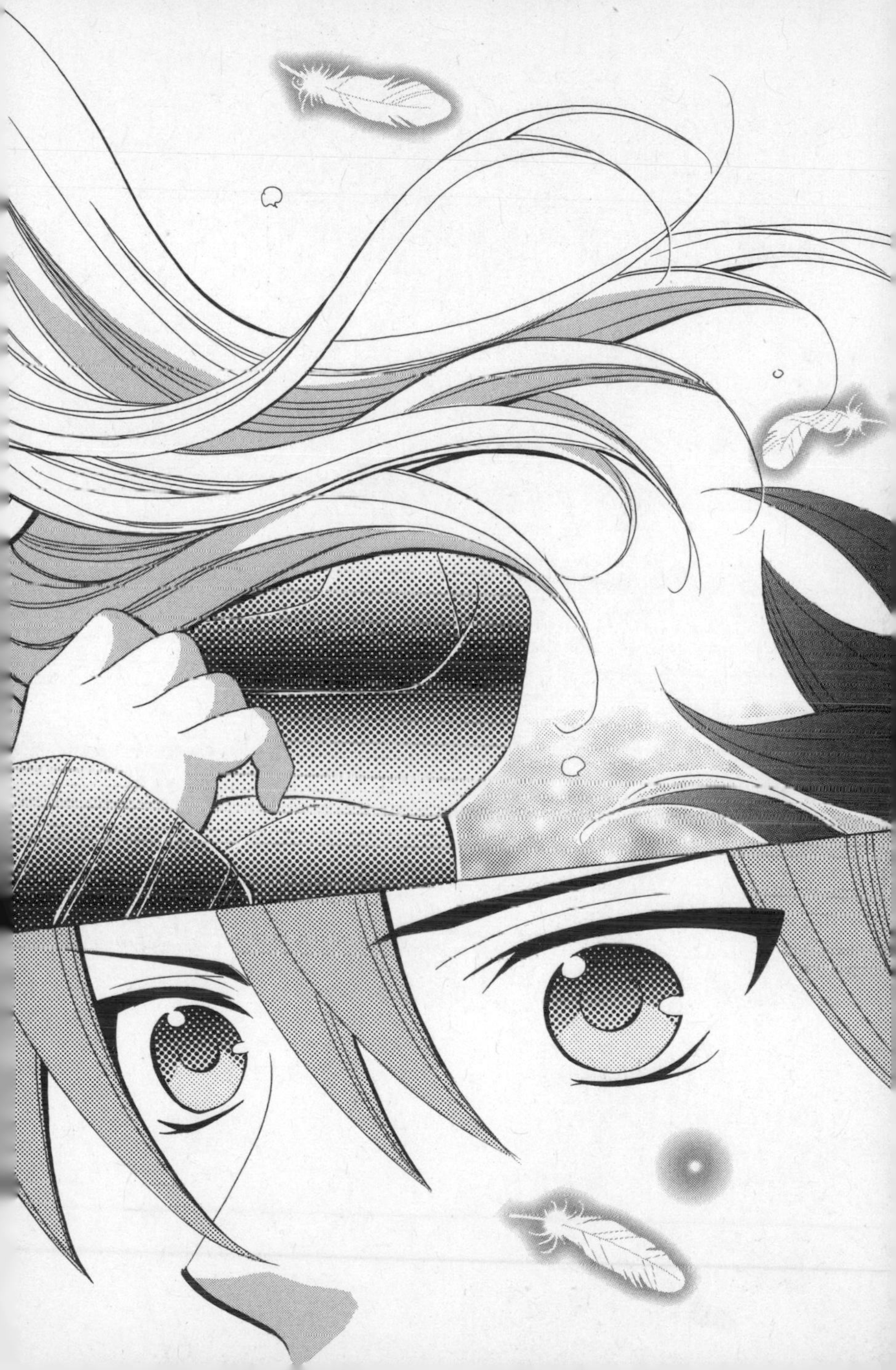

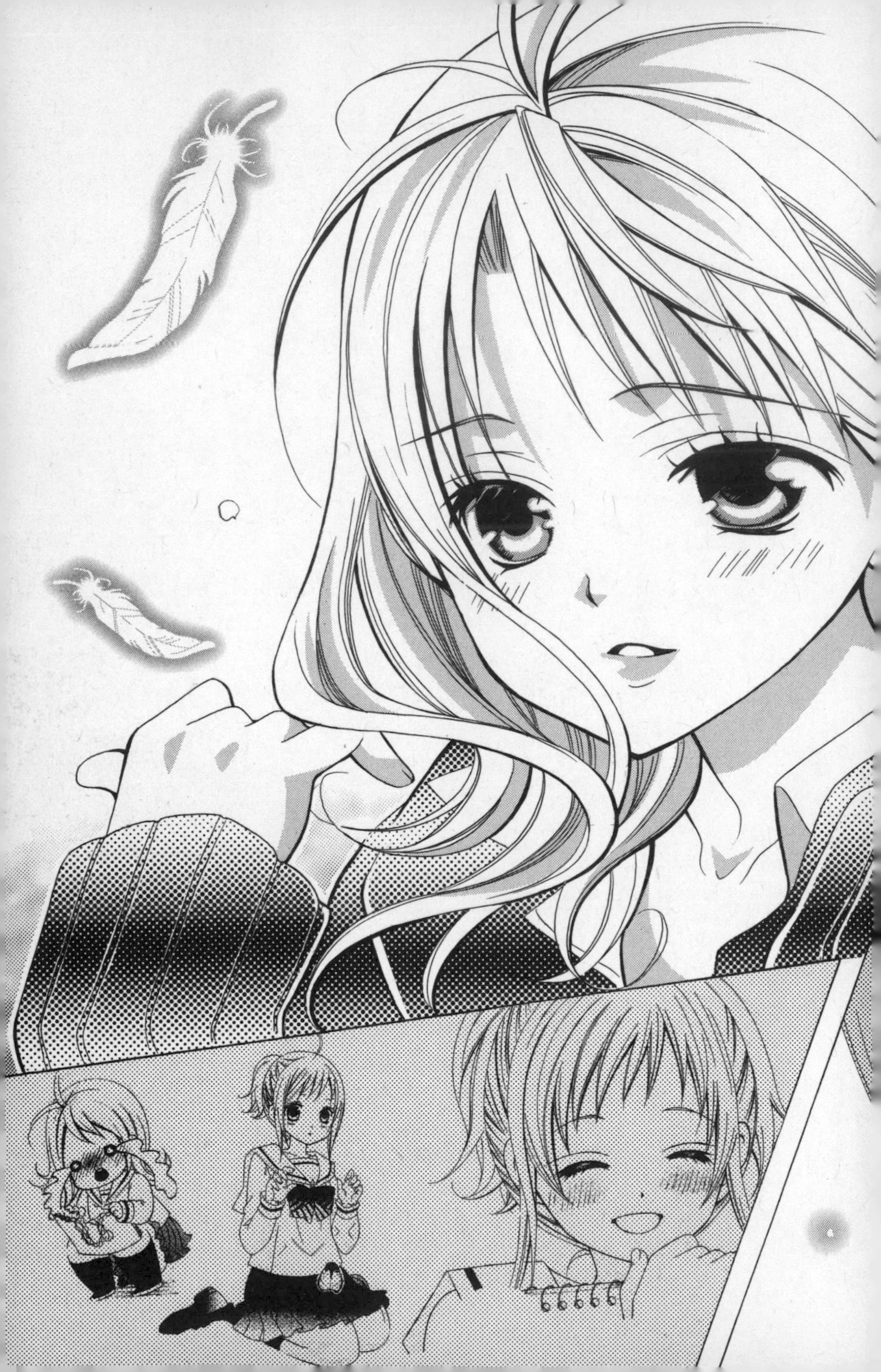

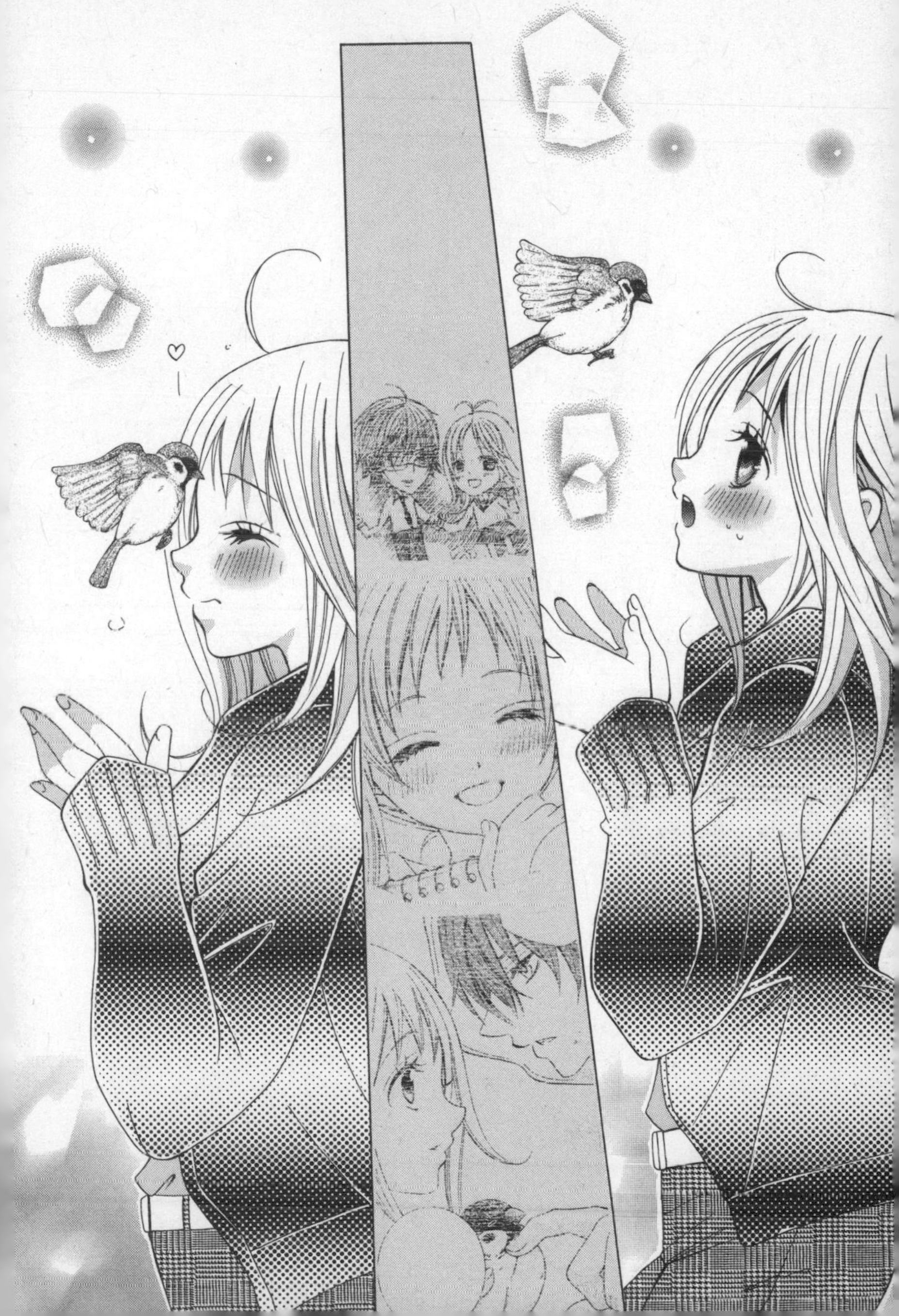

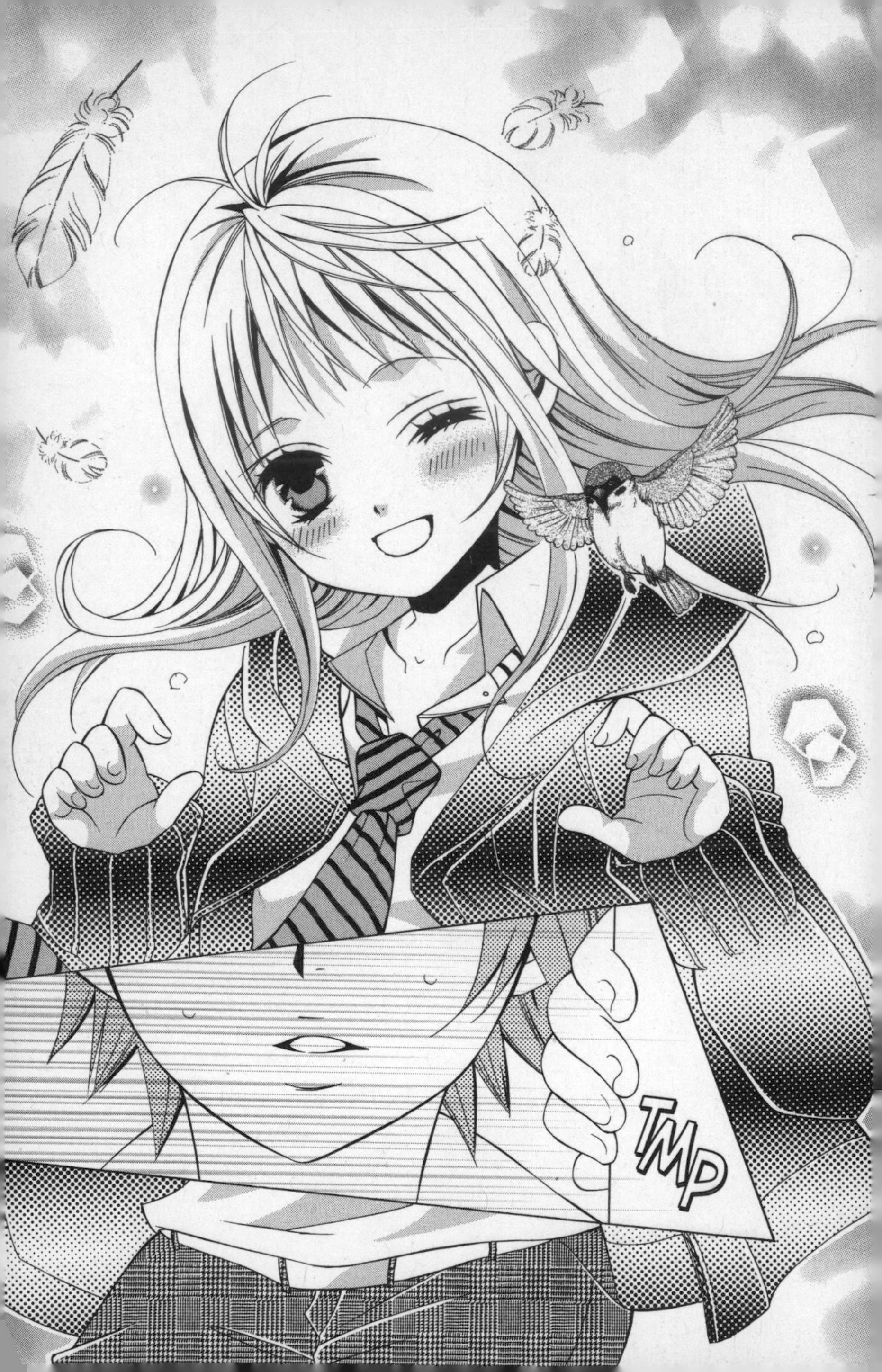
TMP

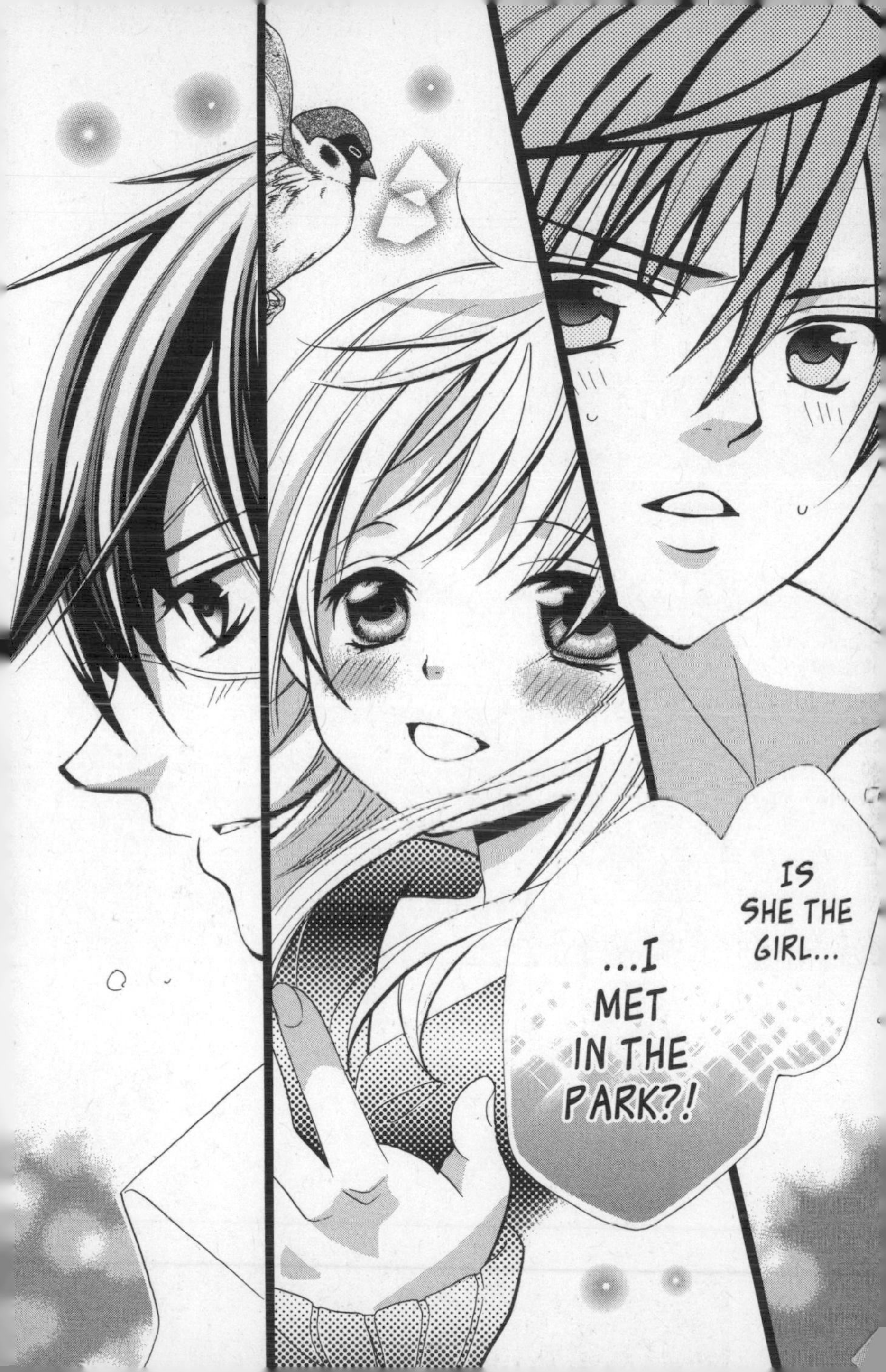
IS SHE THE GIRL...
...I MET IN THE PARK?!

Chapter 32

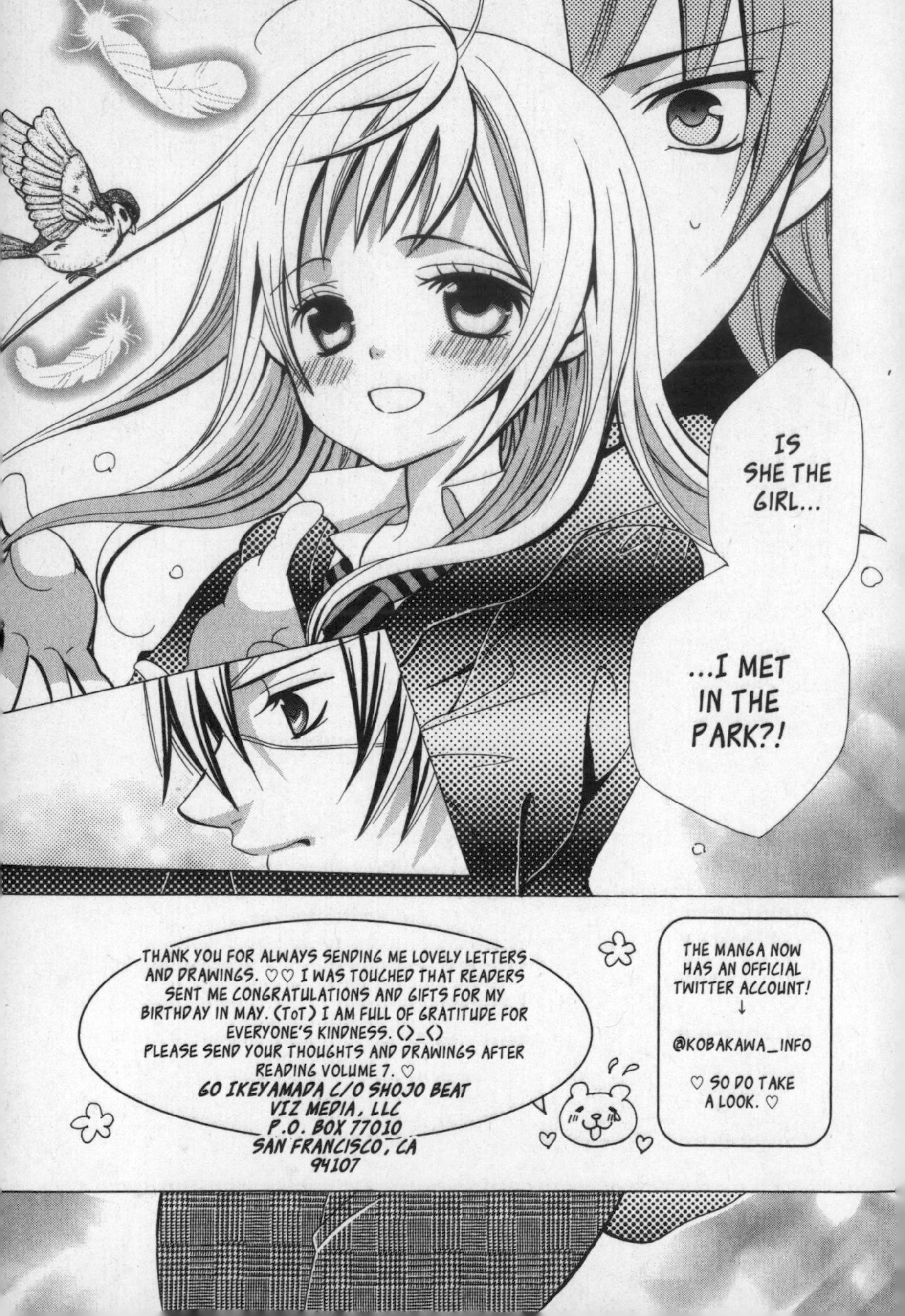
IS SHE THE GIRL...
...I MET IN THE PARK?!
THE MANGA NOW HAS AN OFFICIAL TWITTER ACCOUNT! ↓ @KOBAKAWA_INFO ♡ SO DO TAKE A LOOK. ♡
THANK YOU FOR ALWAYS SENDING ME LOVELY LETTERS AND DRAWINGS. ♡♡ I WAS TOUCHED THAT READERS SENT ME CONGRATULATIONS AND GIFTS FOR MY BIRTHDAY IN MAY. (ToT) I AM FULL OF GRATITUDE FOR EVERYONE'S KINDNESS. (>_<) PLEASE SEND YOUR THOUGHTS AND DRAWINGS AFTER READING VOLUME 7. ♡
GO IKEYAMADA C/O SHOJO BEAT
VIZ MEDIA, LLC
P.O. BOX 77010
SAN FRANCISCO, CA
94107

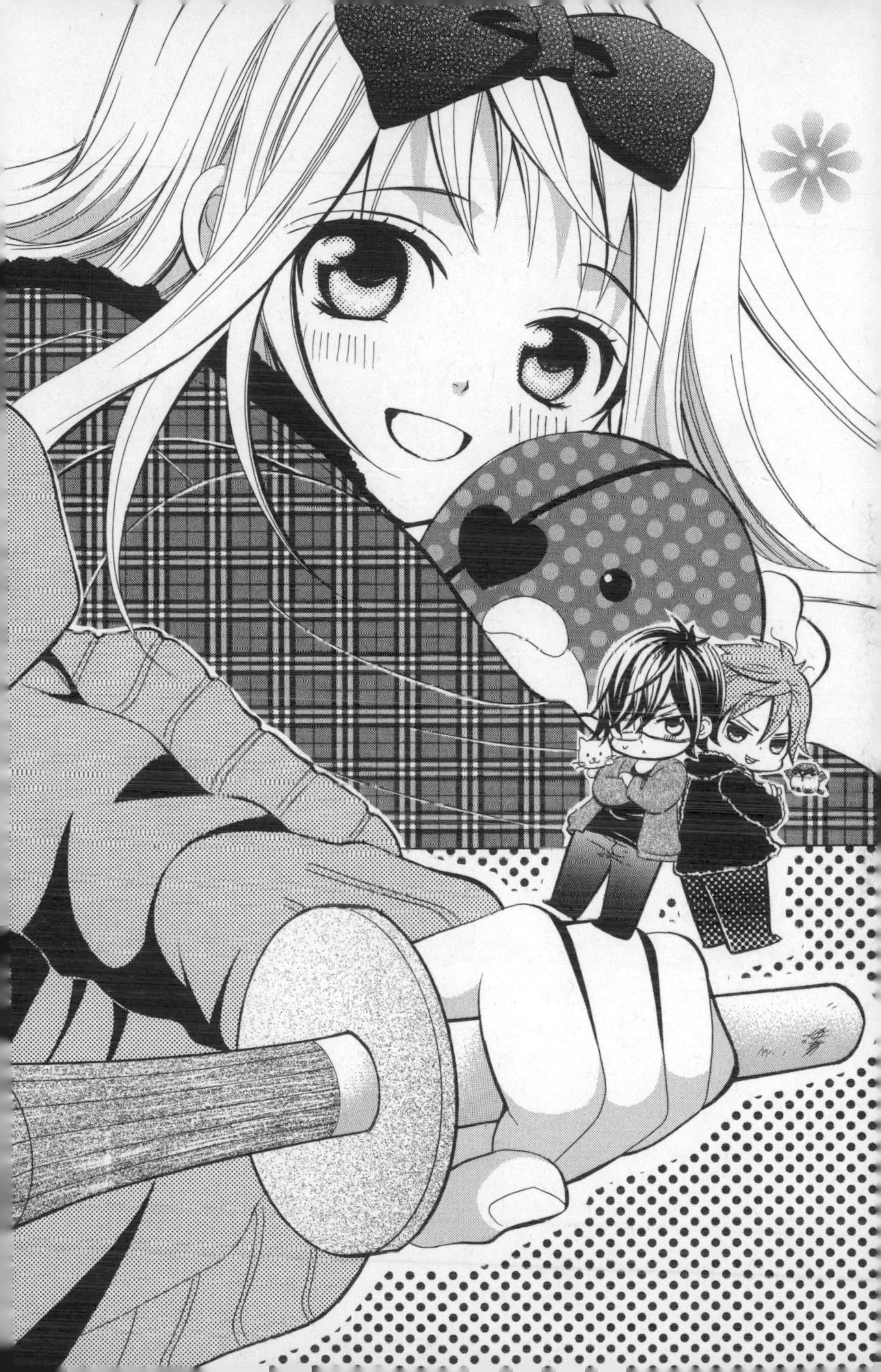

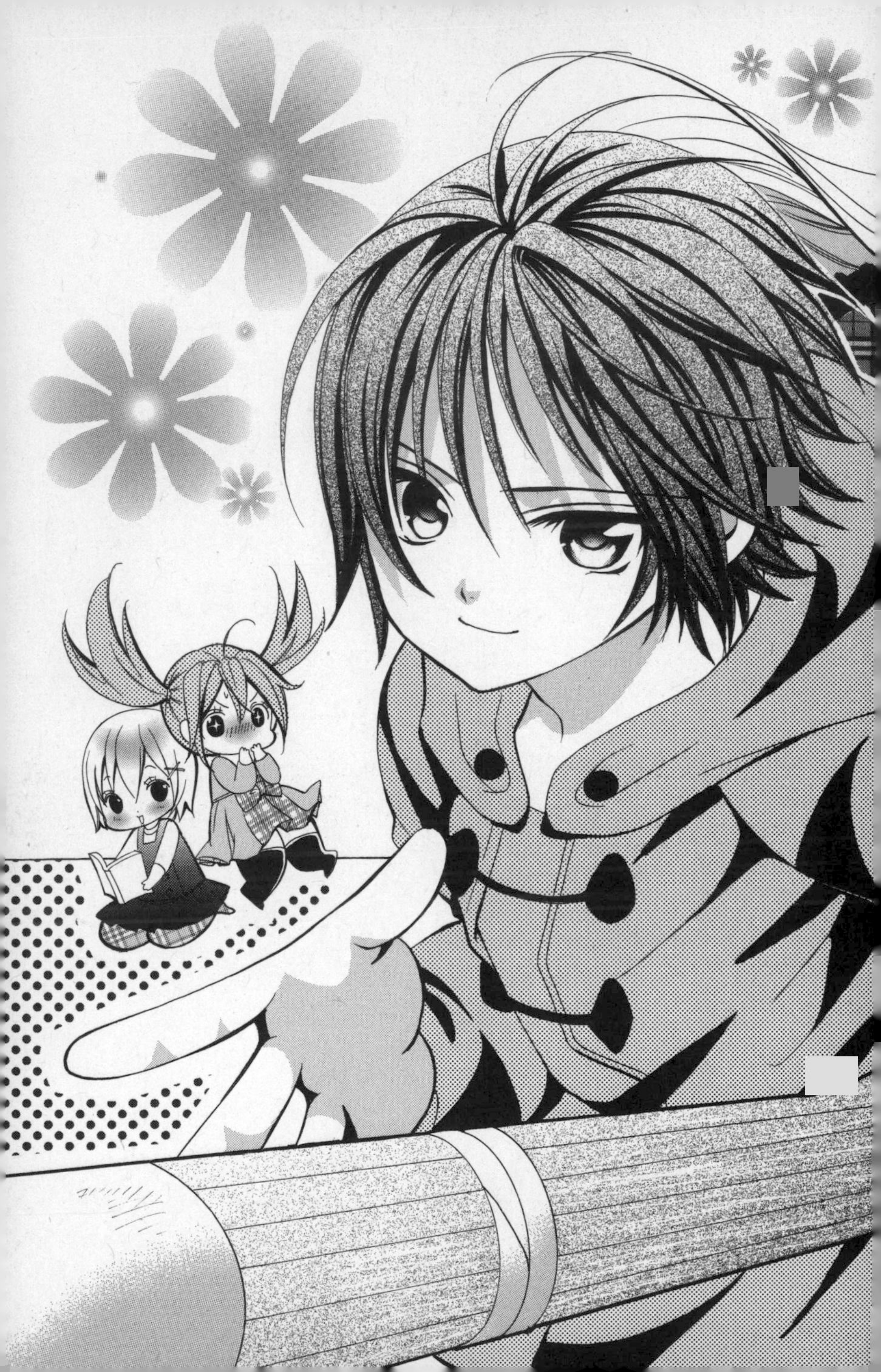

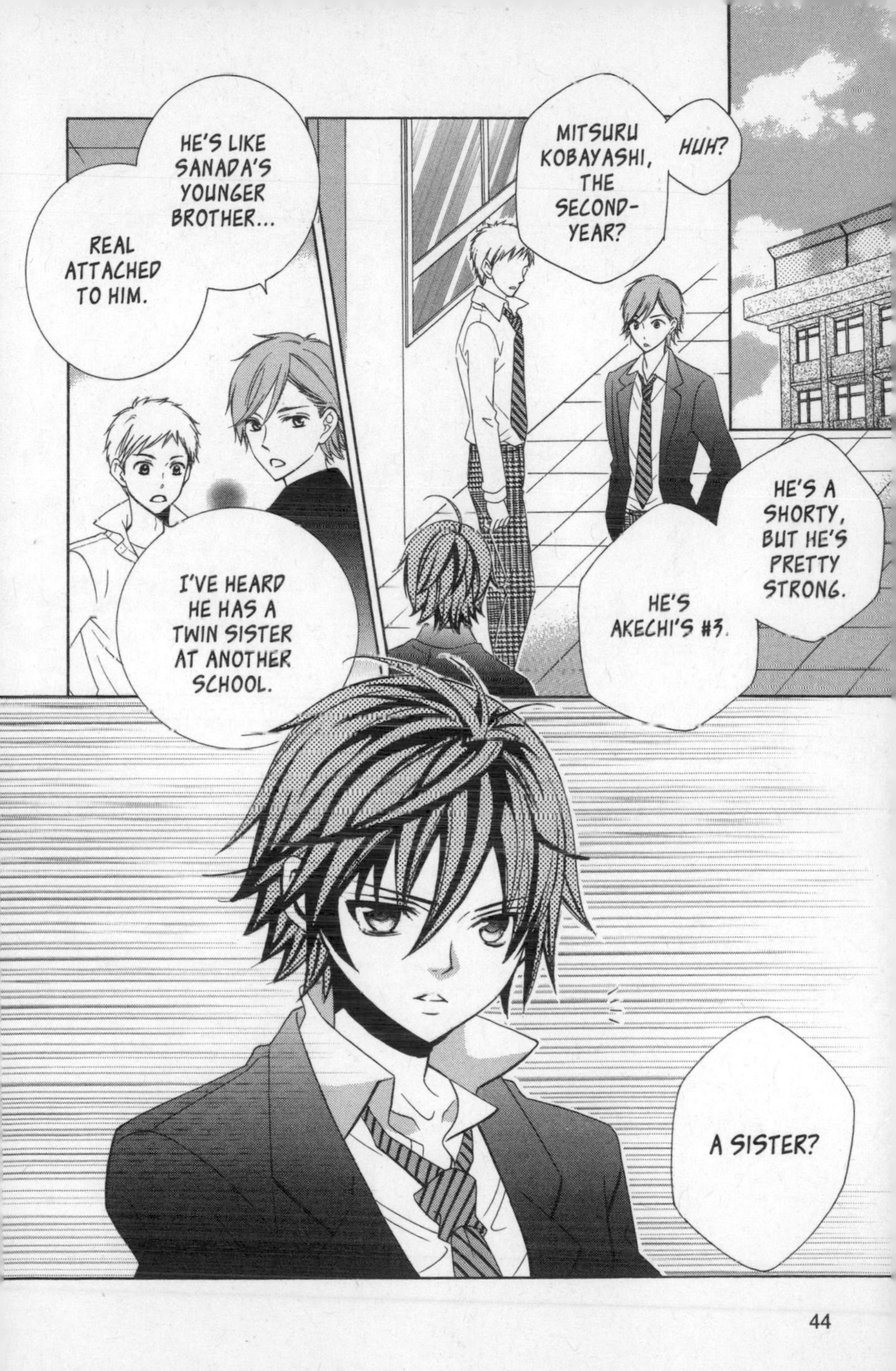
HUH?
MITSURU KOBAYASHI, THE SECOND-YEAR?
HE'S A SHORTY, BUT HE'S PRETTY STRONG.
HE'S AKECHI'S #3.
HE'S LIKE SANADA'S YOUNGER BROTHER...
REAL ATTACHED TO HIM.
I'VE HEARD HE HAS A TWIN SISTER AT ANOTHER SCHOOL.
A SISTER?

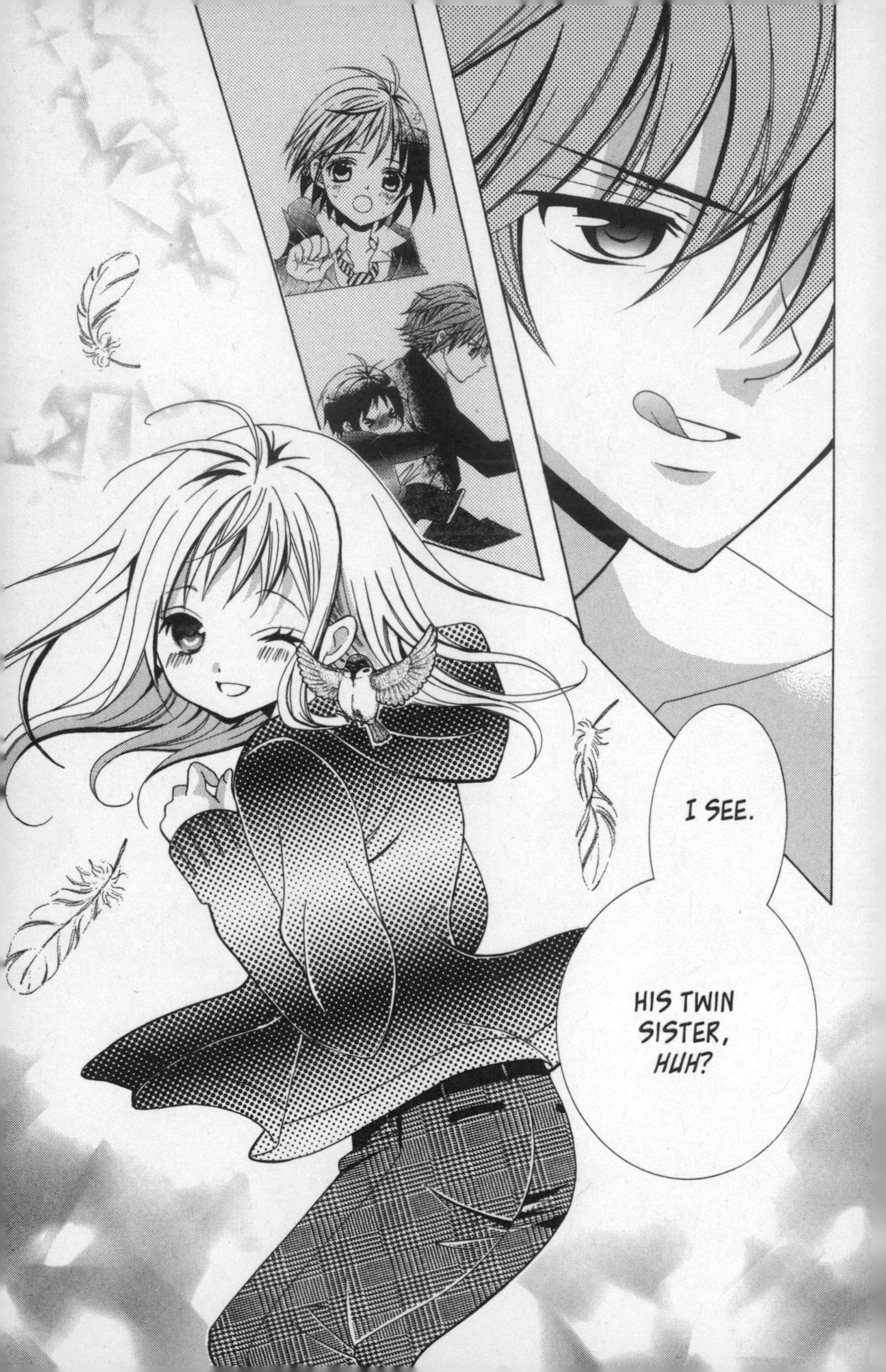
I SEE.
HIS TWIN SISTER, HUH?

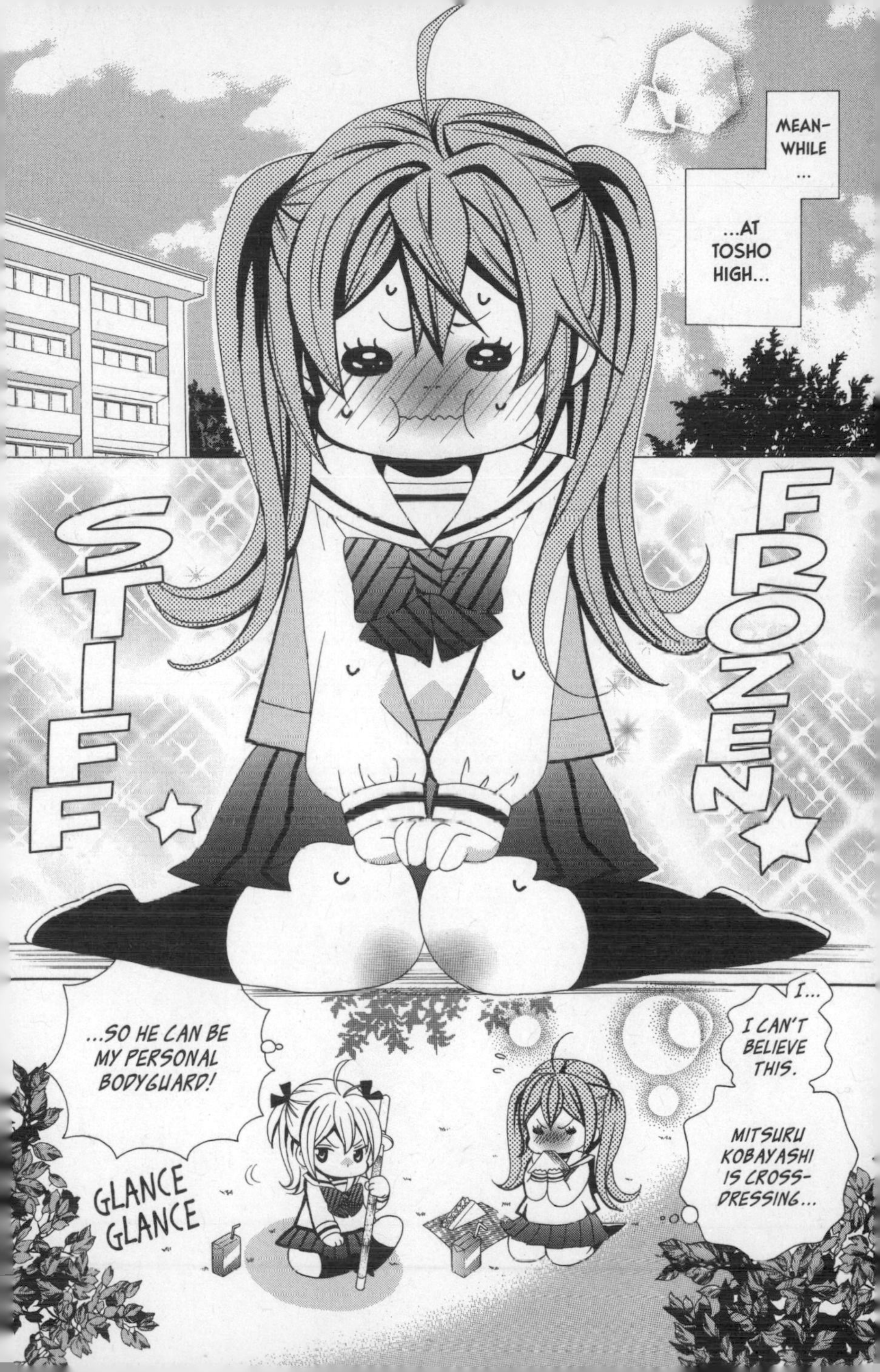
MEAN-WHILE...
...AT TOSHO HIGH...
FROZEN
STIFF
I... I CAN'T BELIEVE THIS.
MITSURU KOBAYASHI IS CROSS-DRESSING...
...SO HE CAN BE MY PERSONAL BODYGUARD!
GLANCE GLANCE

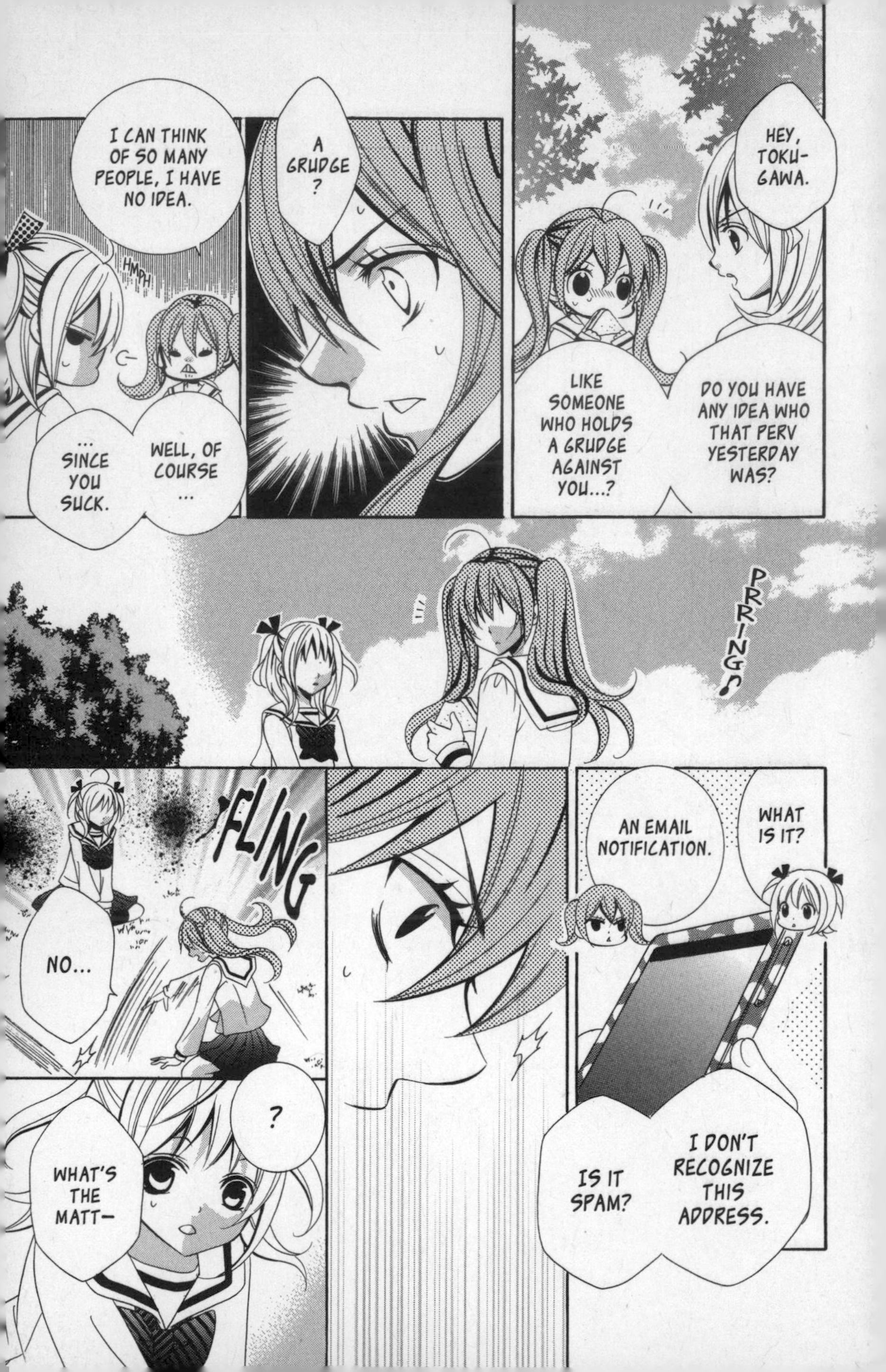

HEY, TOKU-GAWA.
DO YOU HAVE ANY IDEA WHO THAT PERV YESTERDAY WAS?
LIKE SOMEONE WHO HOLDS A GRUDGE AGAINST YOU...?
A GRUDGE?
I CAN THINK OF SO MANY PEOPLE, I HAVE NO IDEA.
HMPH
WELL, OF COURSE...
...SINCE YOU SUCK.
PRRRING♪
WHAT IS IT?
AN EMAIL NOTIFICATION.
I DON'T RECOGNIZE THIS ADDRESS.
IS IT SPAM?
FLING
NO...
?
WHAT'S THE MATT—

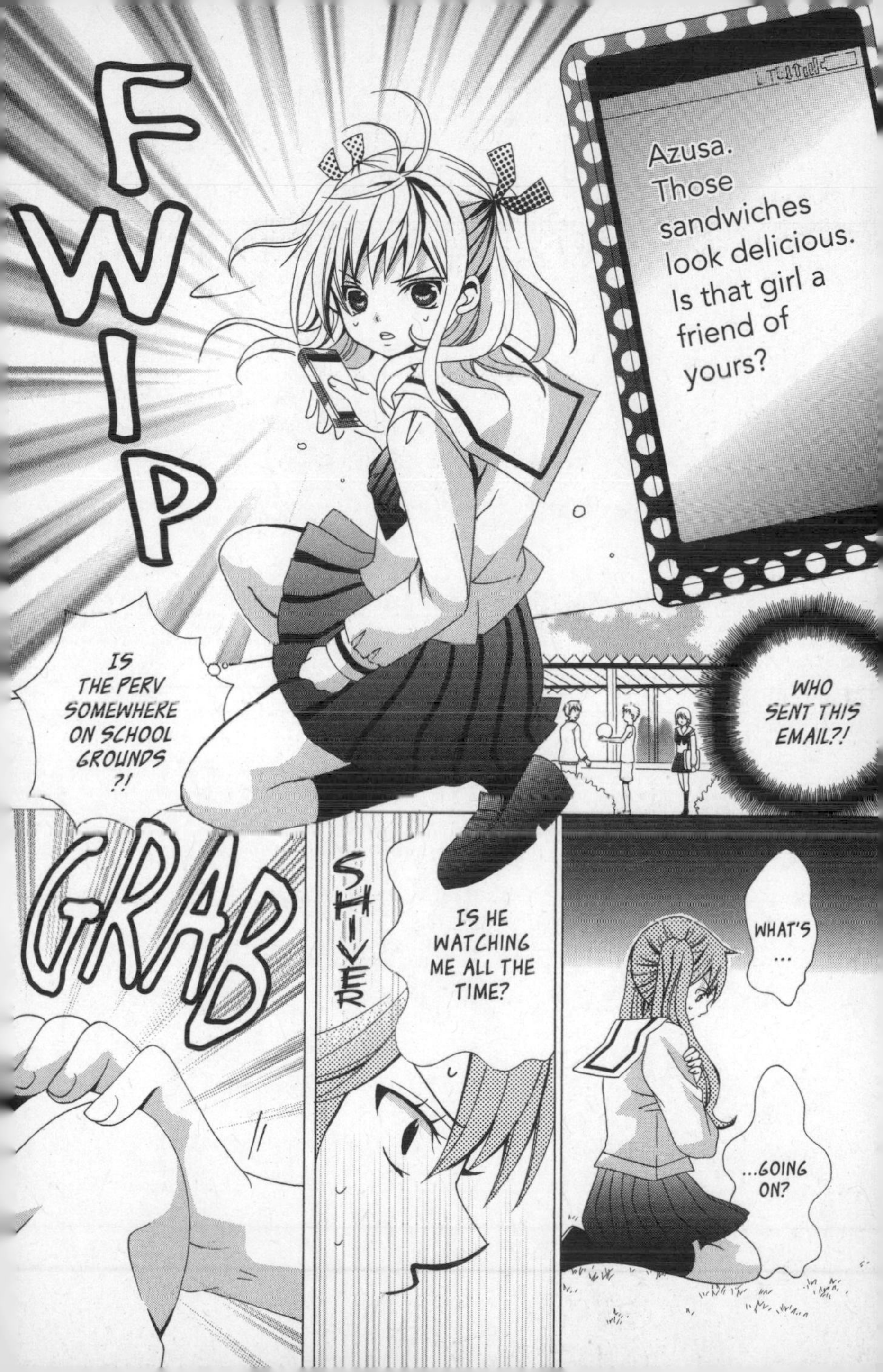
Azusa. Those sandwiches look delicious. Is that girl a friend of yours?
FWIP
WHO SENT THIS EMAIL?!
IS THE PERV SOMEWHERE ON SCHOOL GROUNDS ?!
WHAT'S ...
...GOING ON?
SHIVER
IS HE WATCHING ME ALL THE TIME?
GRAB

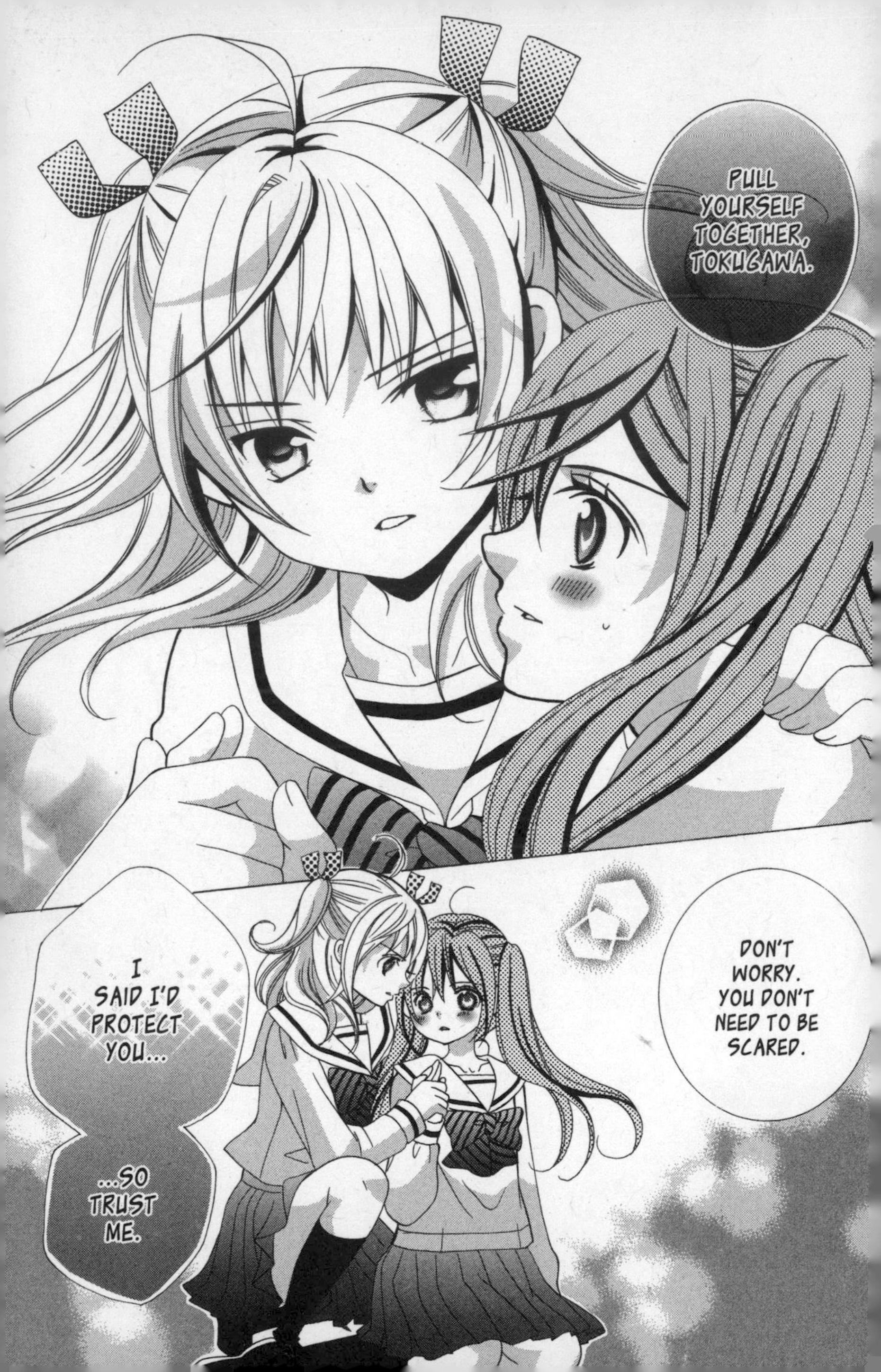
PULL YOURSELF TOGETHER, TOKUGAWA.
DON'T WORRY. YOU DON'T NEED TO BE SCARED.
I SAID I'D PROTECT YOU...
...SO TRUST ME.

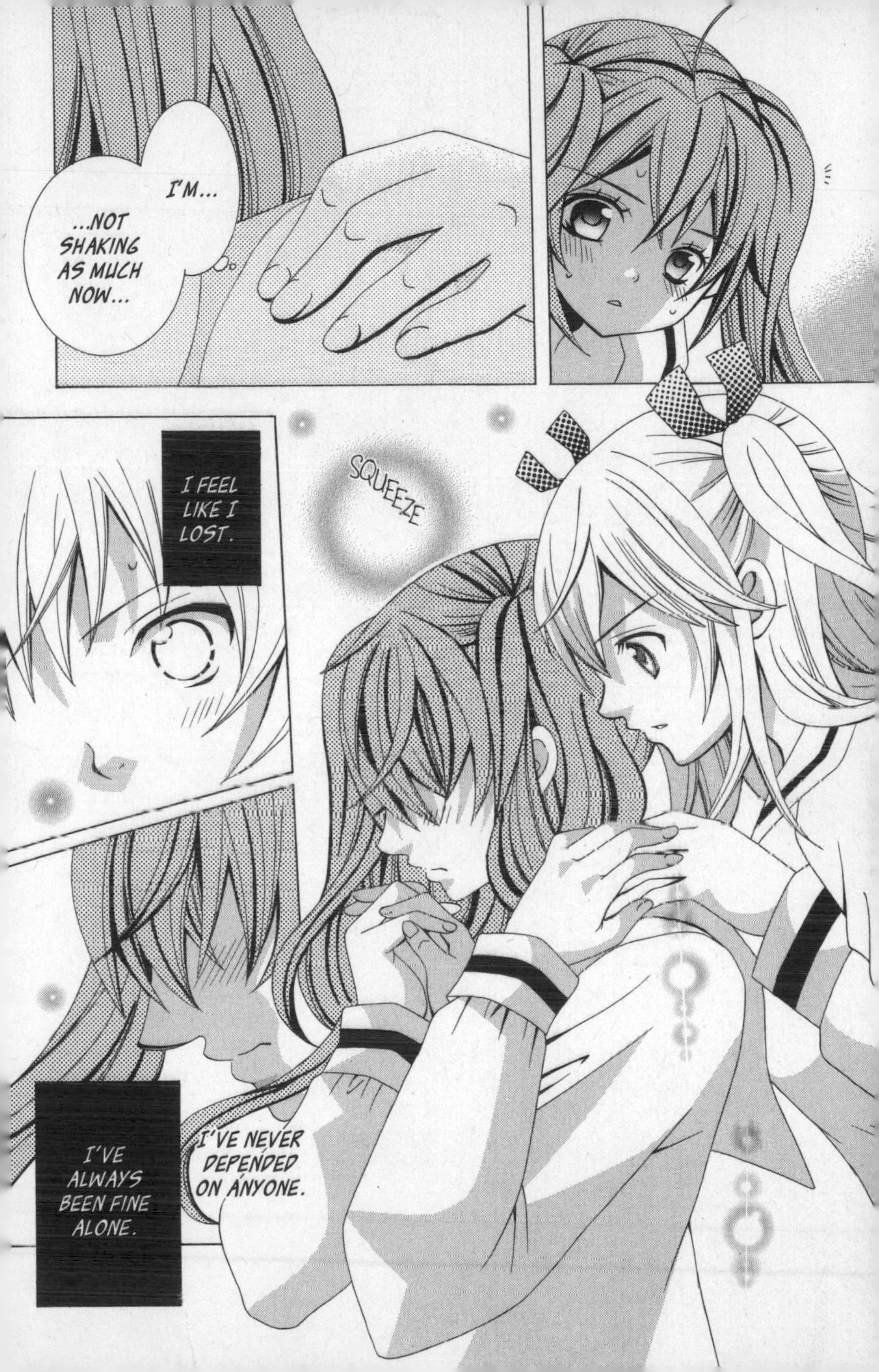
I'M...
...NOT SHAKING AS MUCH NOW...
SQUEEZE
I FEEL LIKE I LOST.
I'VE ALWAYS BEEN FINE ALONE.
I'VE NEVER DEPENDED ON ANYONE.

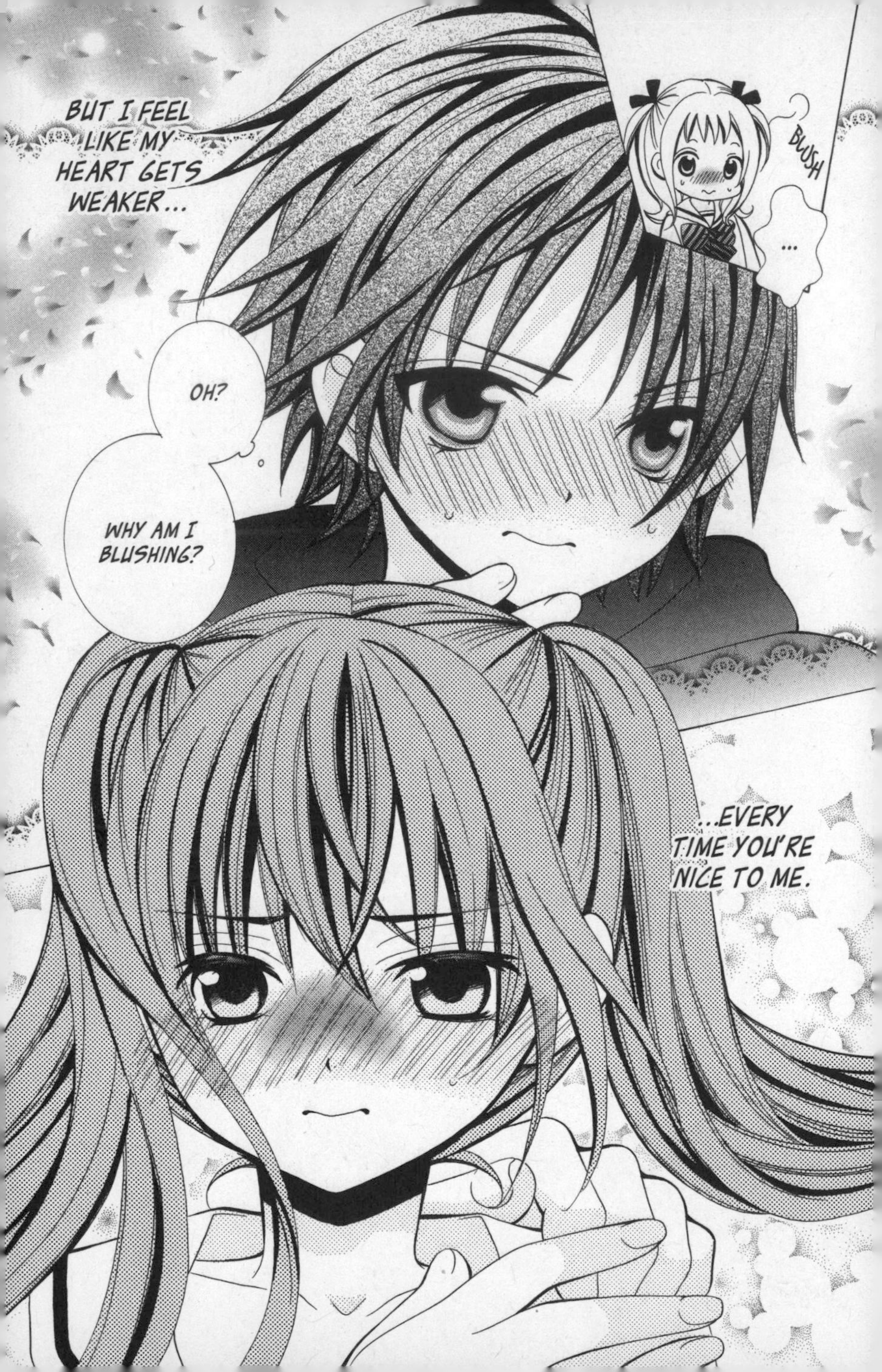
BLUSH
...
BUT I FEEL LIKE MY HEART GETS WEAKER...
OH?
WHY AM I BLUSHING?
...EVERY TIME YOU'RE NICE TO ME.

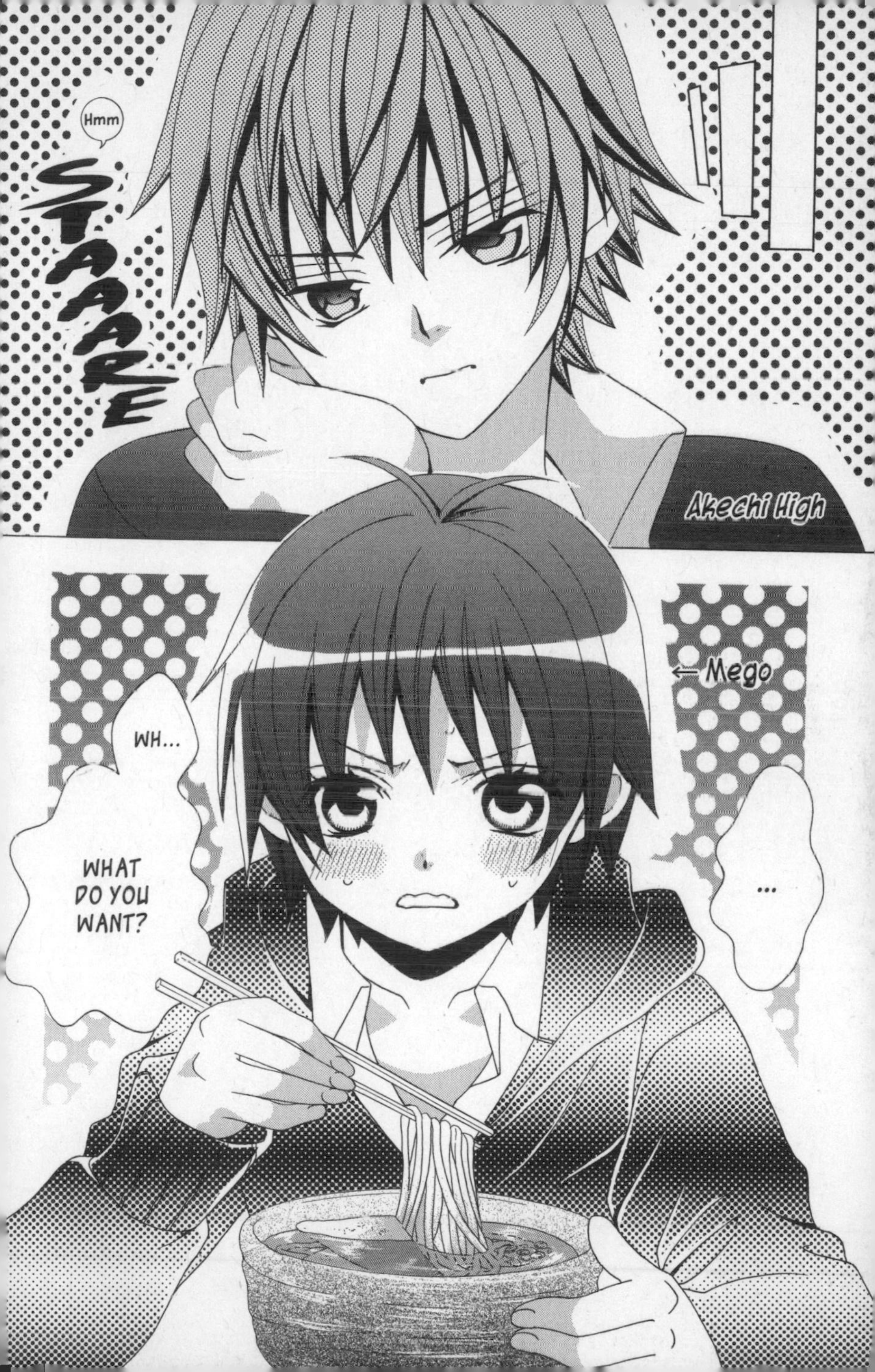
Akechi High
Hmm
STAAARE
← Mego
...
WH...
WHAT DO YOU WANT?

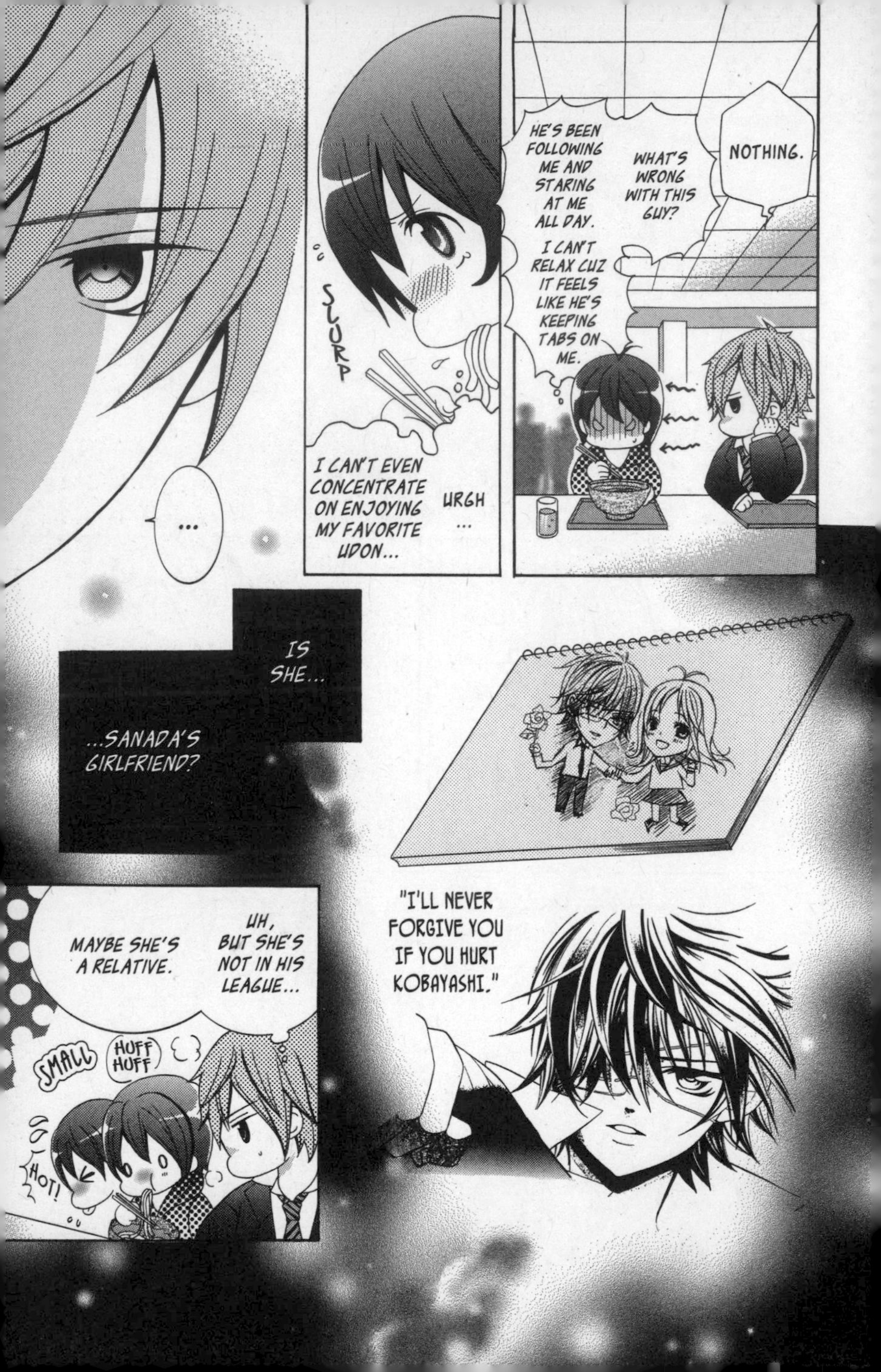
NOTHING.
WHAT'S WRONG WITH THIS GUY?
HE'S BEEN FOLLOWING ME AND STARING AT ME ALL DAY.
I CAN'T RELAX CUZ IT FEELS LIKE HE'S KEEPING TABS ON ME.
SLURP
URGH ...
I CAN'T EVEN CONCENTRATE ON ENJOYING MY FAVORITE UDON...
...
IS SHE...
...SANADA'S GIRLFRIEND?
"I'LL NEVER FORGIVE YOU IF YOU HURT KOBAYASHI."
UH, BUT SHE'S NOT IN HIS LEAGUE...
MAYBE SHE'S A RELATIVE.
HUFF HUFF
SMALL
HOT!

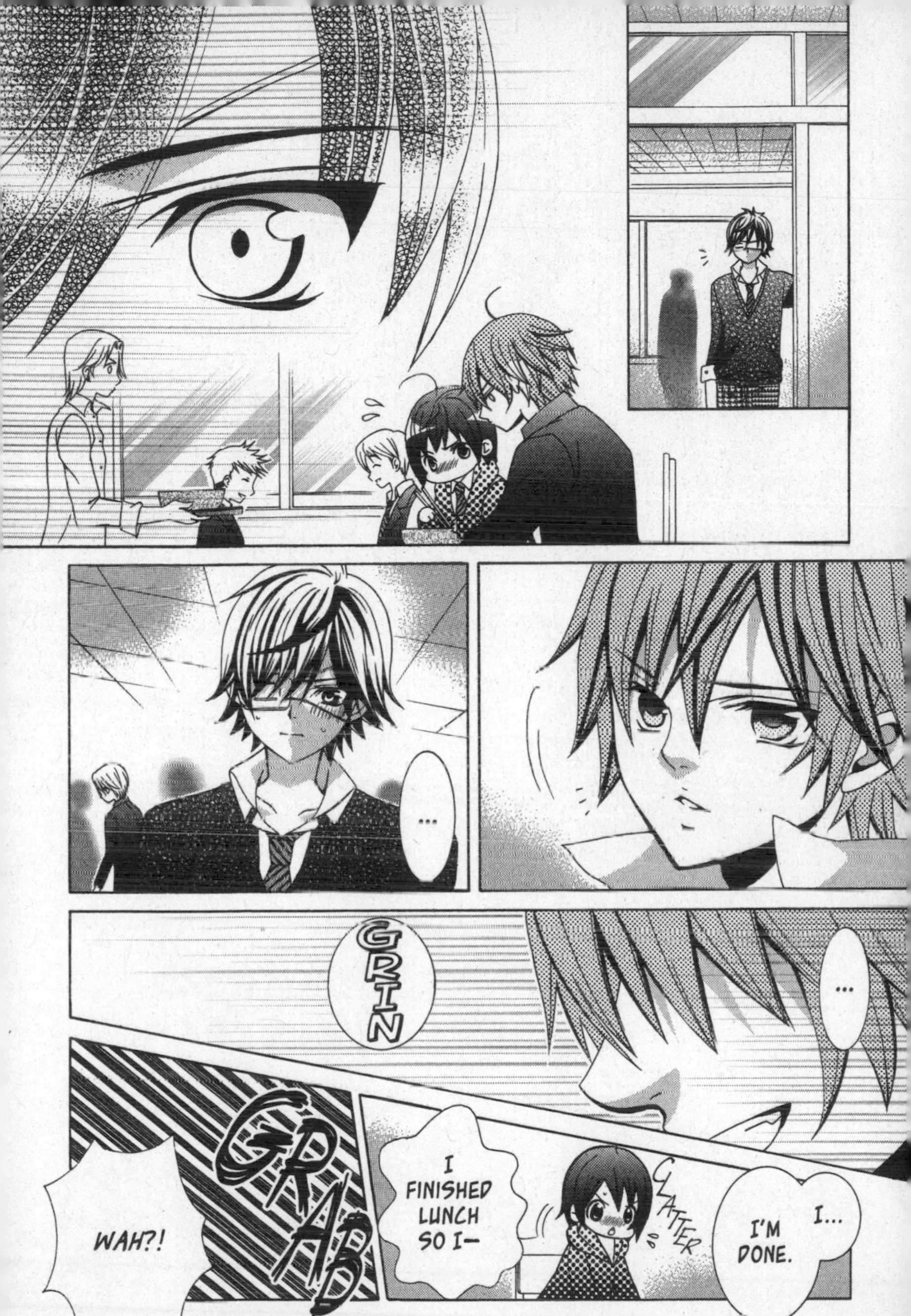
...
...
GRIN
I... I'M DONE.
CLATTER
I FINISHED LUNCH SO I—
GRAB
WAH?!

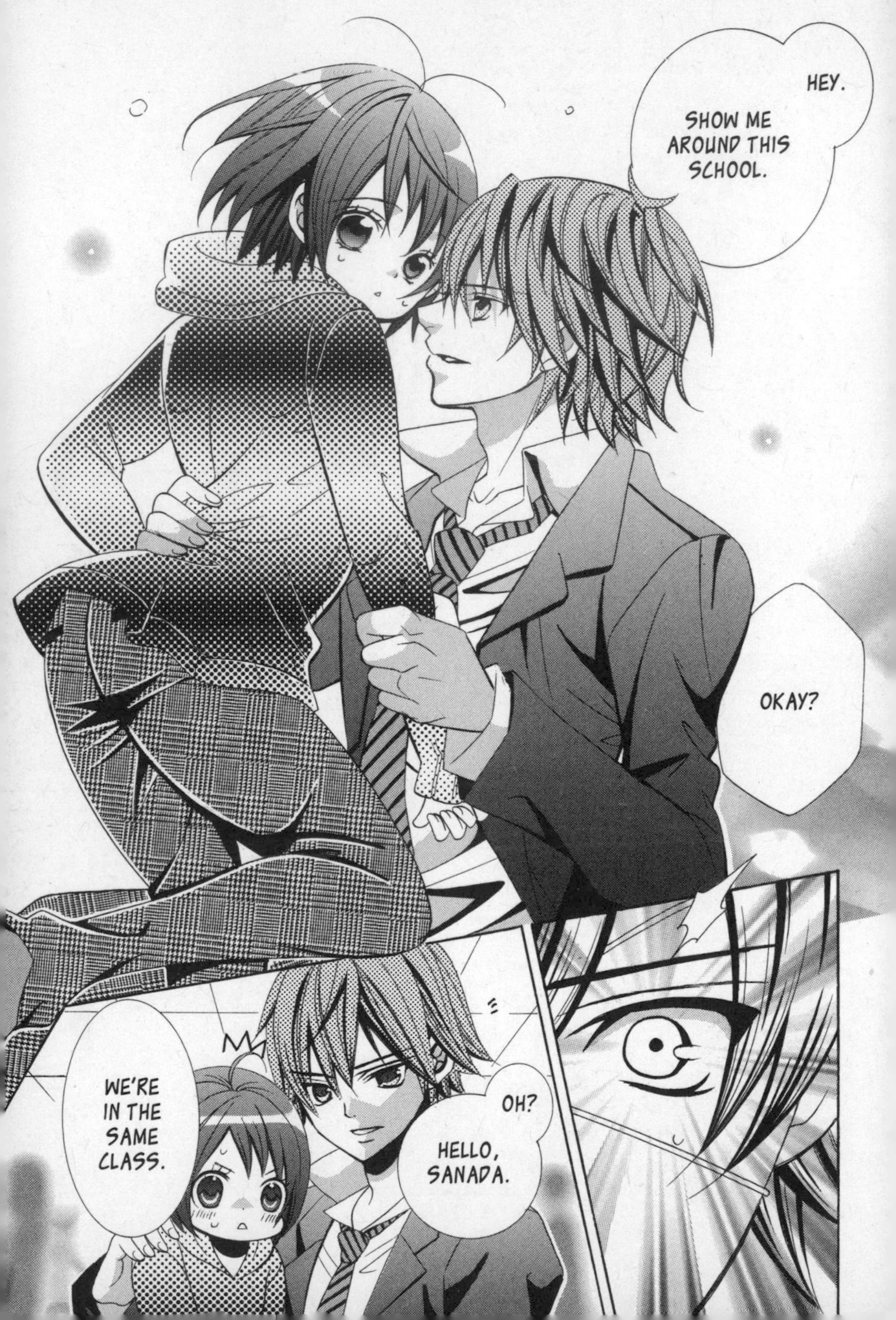
HEY.
SHOW ME AROUND THIS SCHOOL.
OKAY?
OH?
HELLO, SANADA.
WE'RE IN THE SAME CLASS.

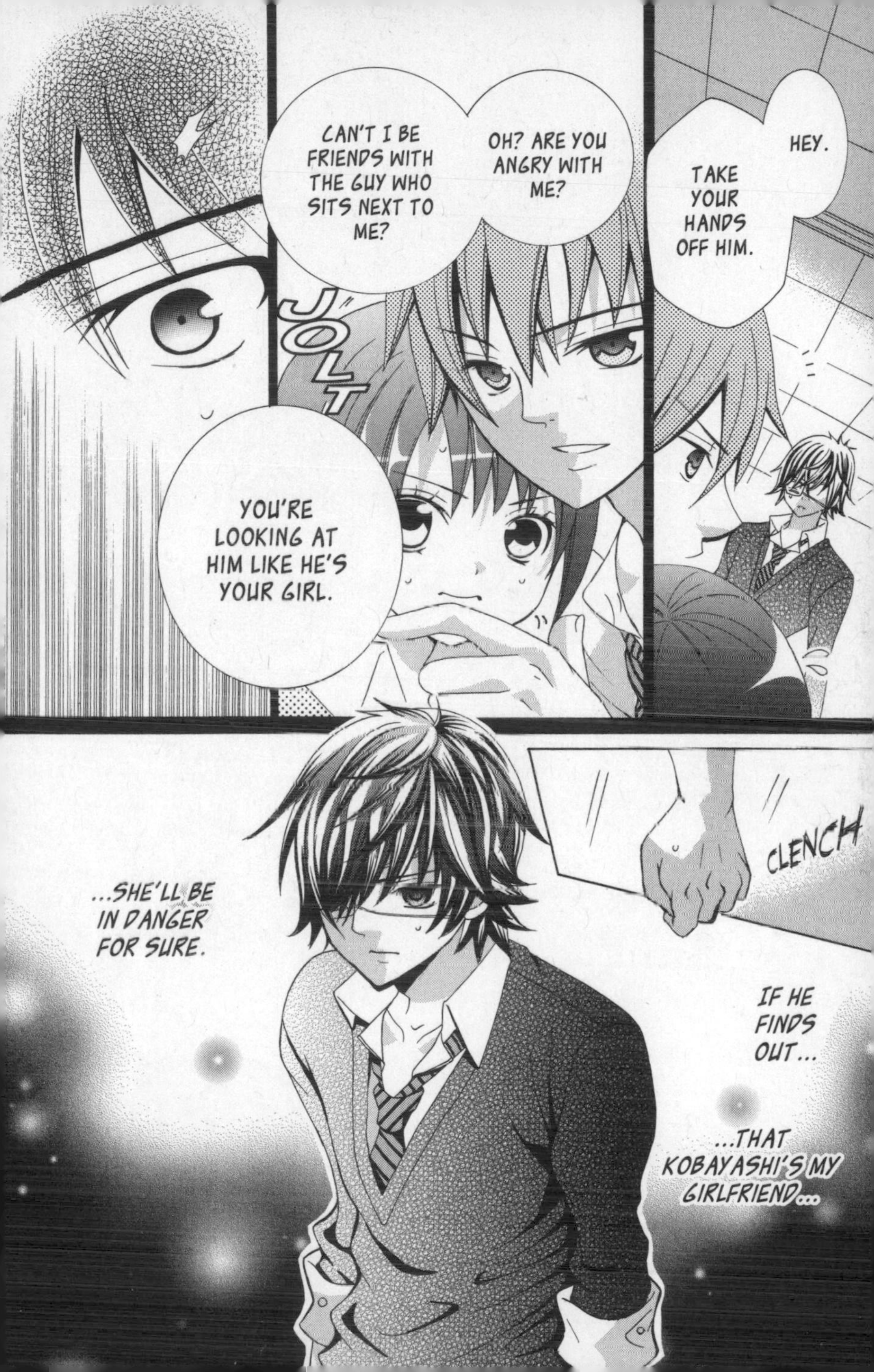
HEY.
TAKE YOUR HANDS OFF HIM.
OH? ARE YOU ANGRY WITH ME?
CAN'T I BE FRIENDS WITH THE GUY WHO SITS NEXT TO ME?
JOLT
YOU'RE LOOKING AT HIM LIKE HE'S YOUR GIRL.
CLENCH
IF HE FINDS OUT...
...THAT KOBAYASHI'S MY GIRLFRIEND...
...SHE'LL BE IN DANGER FOR SURE.

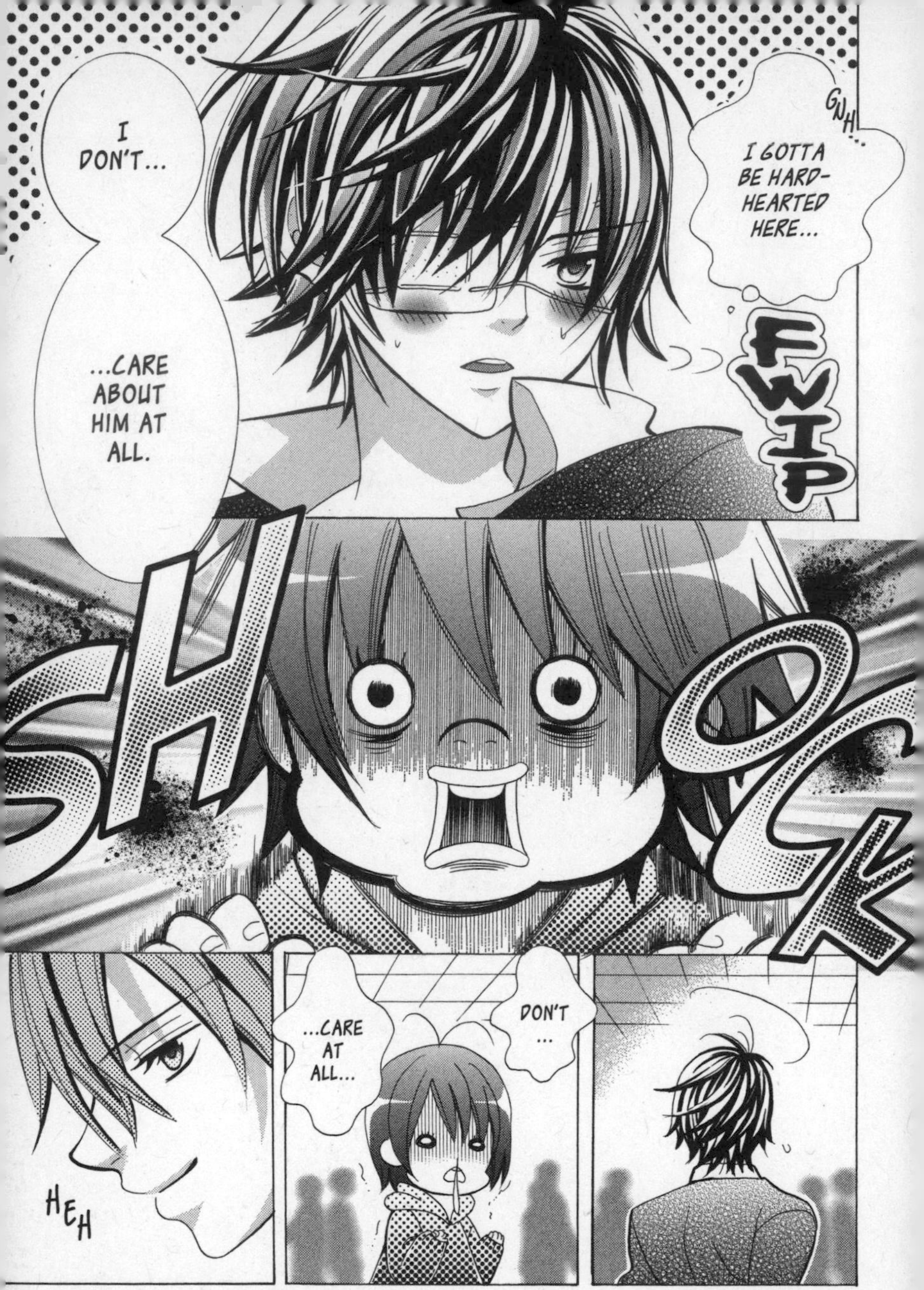
GNH...
I GOTTA BE HARD-HEARTED HERE...
FWIP
I DON'T...
...CARE ABOUT HIM AT ALL.
SHOCK
DON'T ...
...CARE AT ALL...
HEH

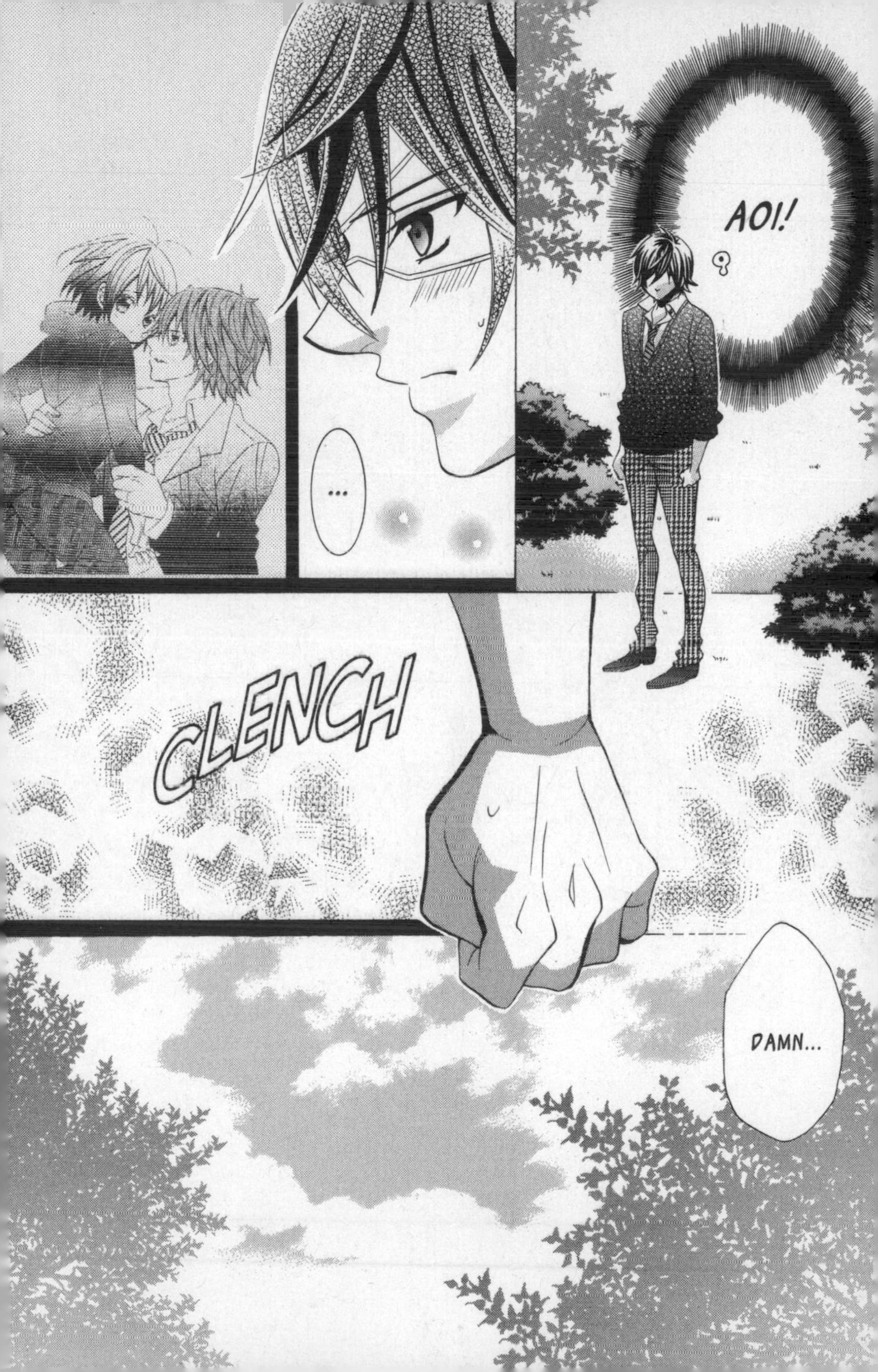
AOI!
?
...
CLENCH
DAMN...

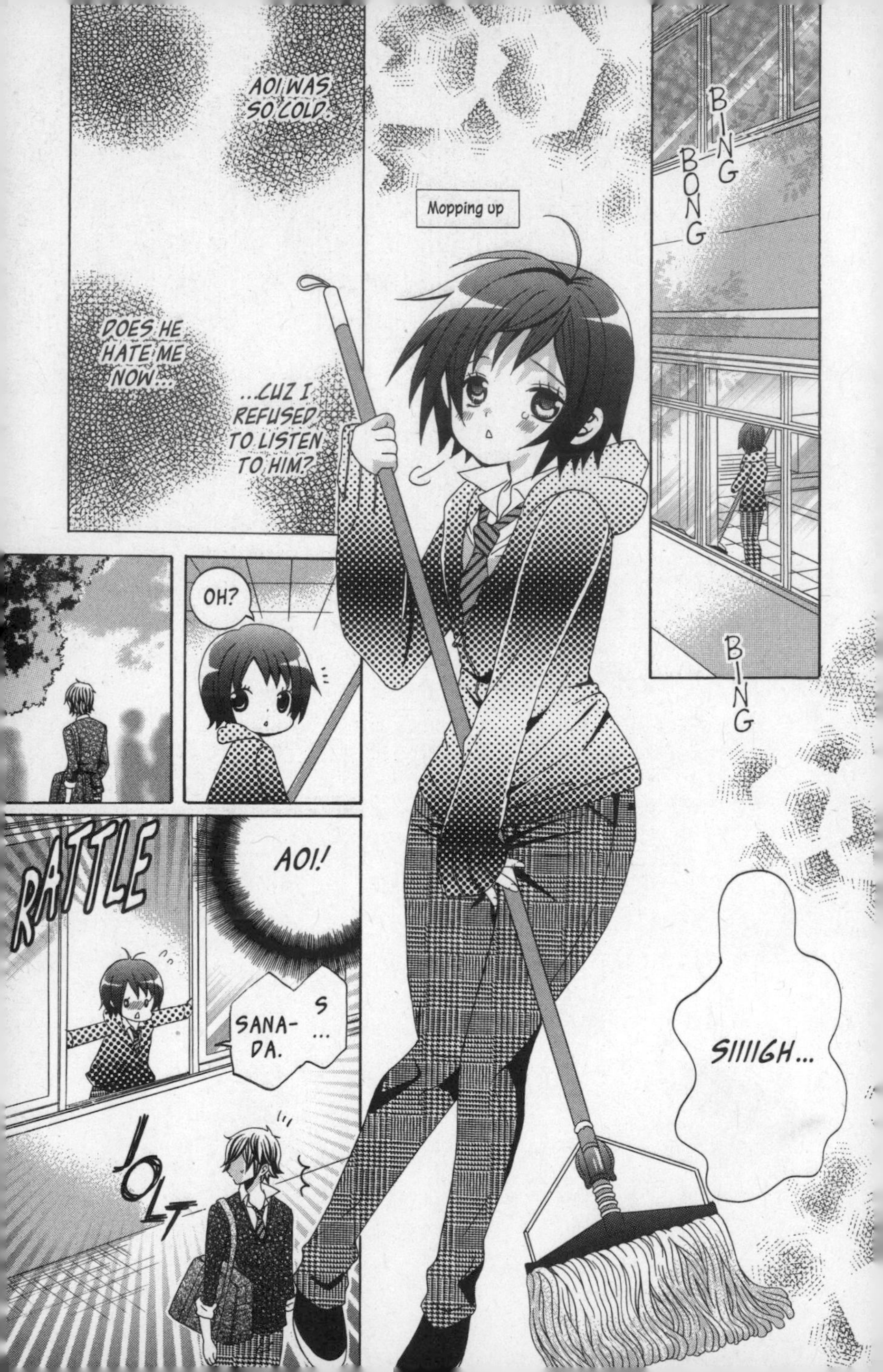
BING BONG
BING BING
Mopping up
SIIIIGH...
AOI WAS SO COLD.
DOES HE HATE ME NOW...
...CUZ I REFUSED TO LISTEN TO HIM?
OH?
RATTLE
AOI!
SANA-DA.
S...
JOLT

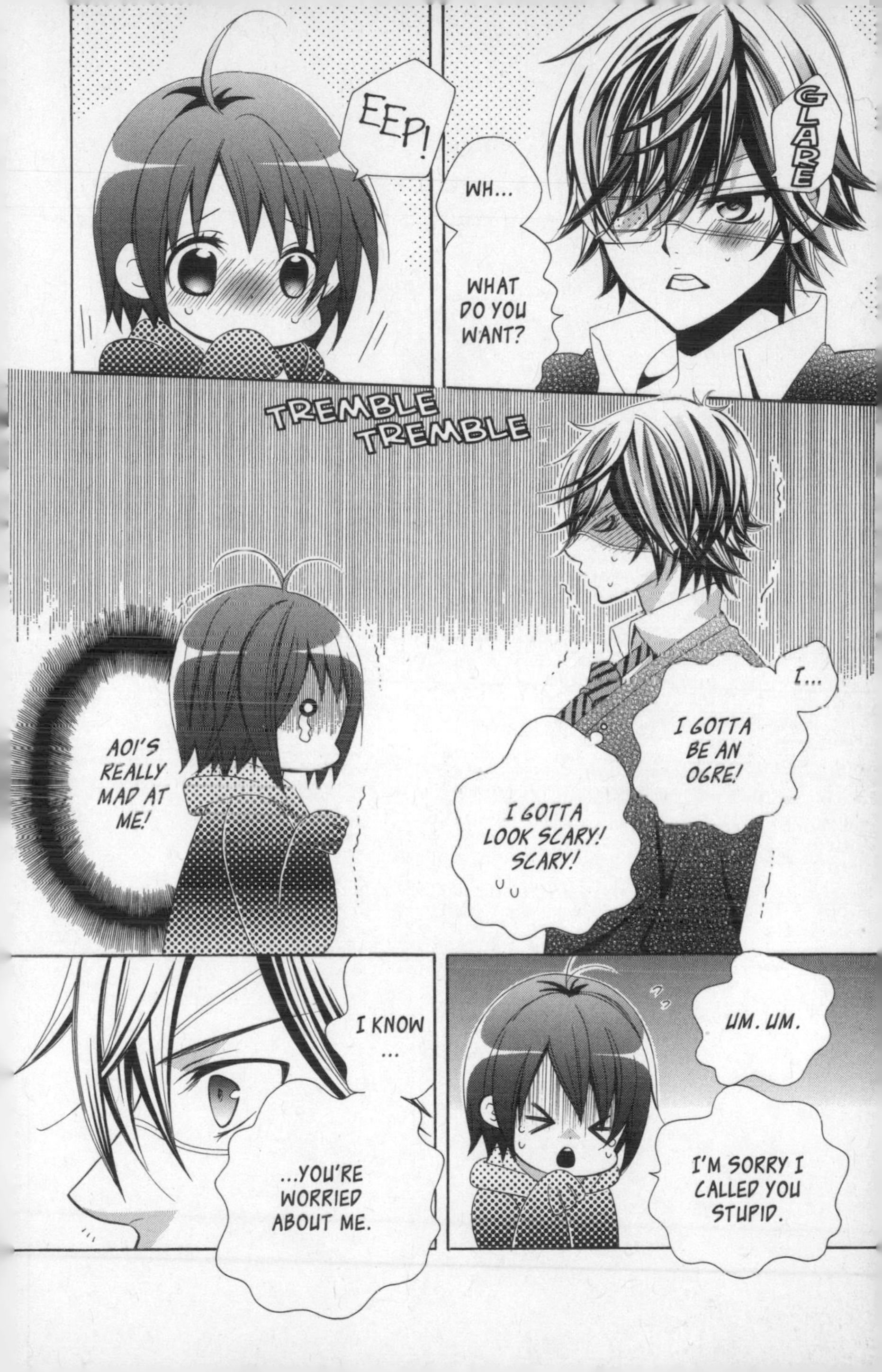
GLARE
WH...
WHAT DO YOU WANT?
EEP!
TREMBLE TREMBLE
I...
I GOTTA BE AN OGRE!
I GOTTA LOOK SCARY! SCARY!
AOI'S REALLY MAD AT ME!
UM. UM.
I'M SORRY I CALLED YOU STUPID.
I KNOW ...
...YOU'RE WORRIED ABOUT ME.

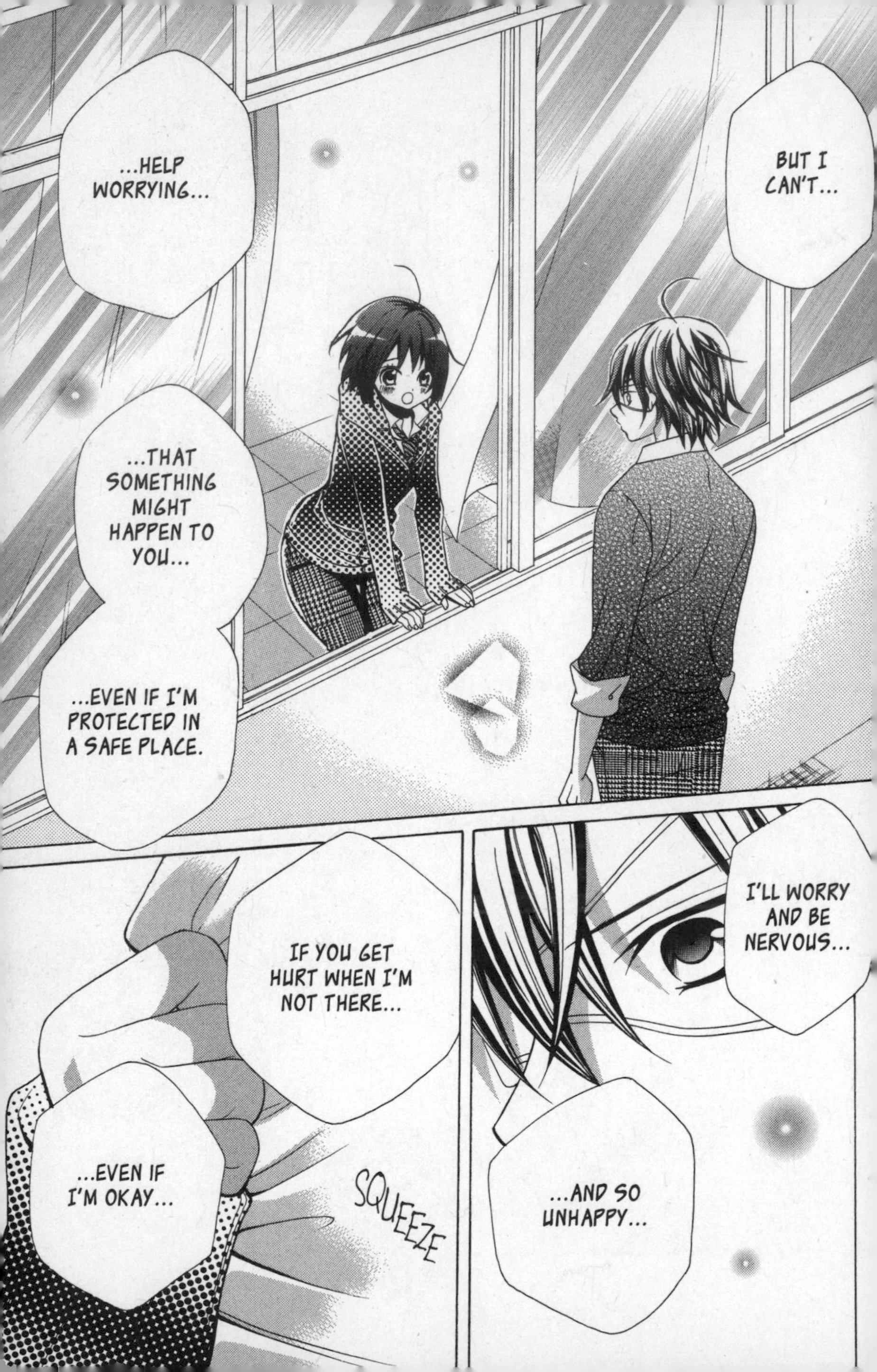
BUT I CAN'T...
...HELP WORRYING...
...THAT SOMETHING MIGHT HAPPEN TO YOU...
...EVEN IF I'M PROTECTED IN A SAFE PLACE.
I'LL WORRY AND BE NERVOUS...
...AND SO UNHAPPY...
IF YOU GET HURT WHEN I'M NOT THERE...
...EVEN IF I'M OKAY...
SQUEEZE

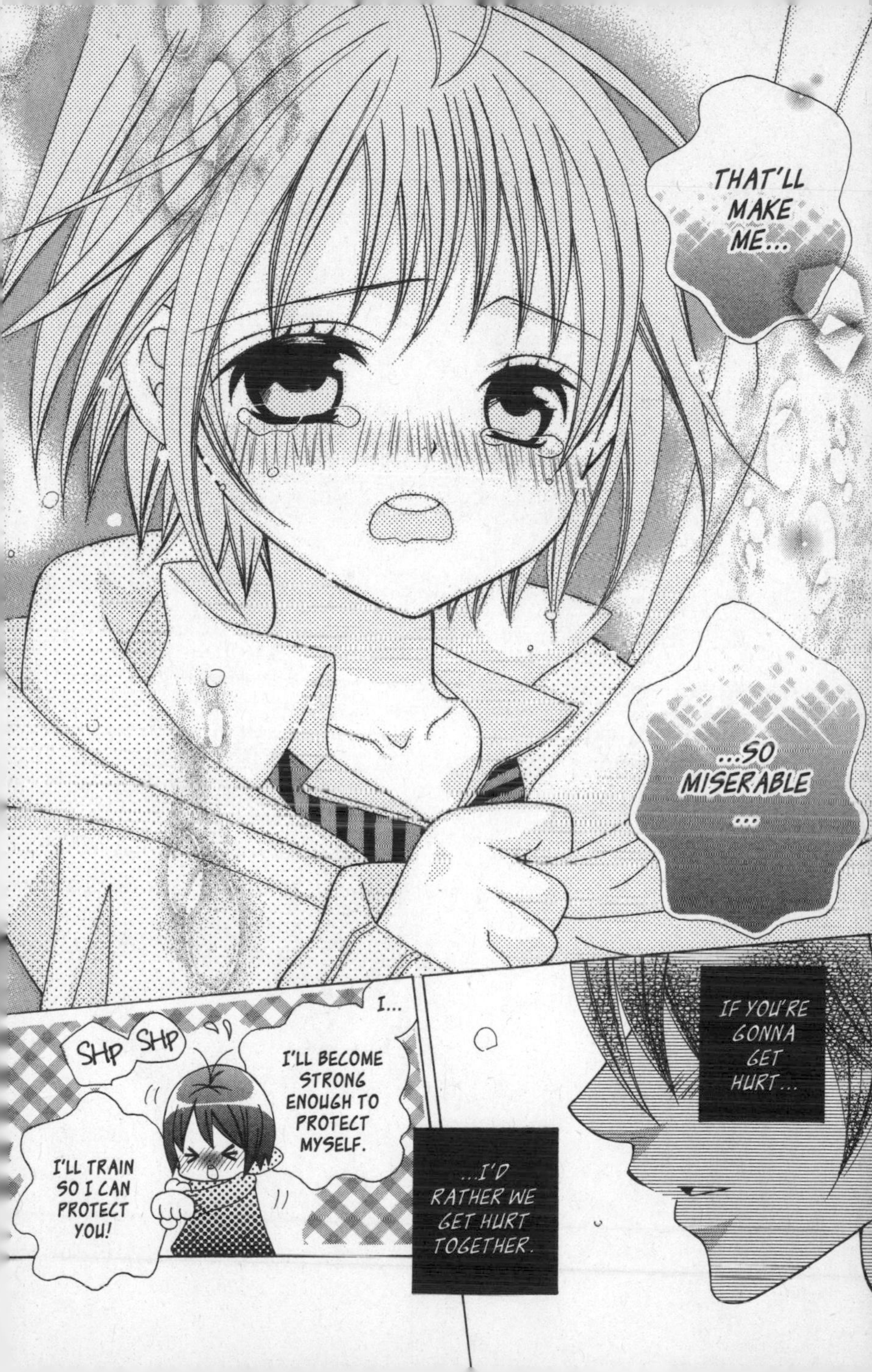
THAT'LL MAKE ME...
...SO MISERABLE ...
IF YOU'RE GONNA GET HURT...
...I'D RATHER WE GET HURT TOGETHER.
I...
I'LL BECOME STRONG ENOUGH TO PROTECT MYSELF.
SHP SHP
I'LL TRAIN SO I CAN PROTECT YOU!

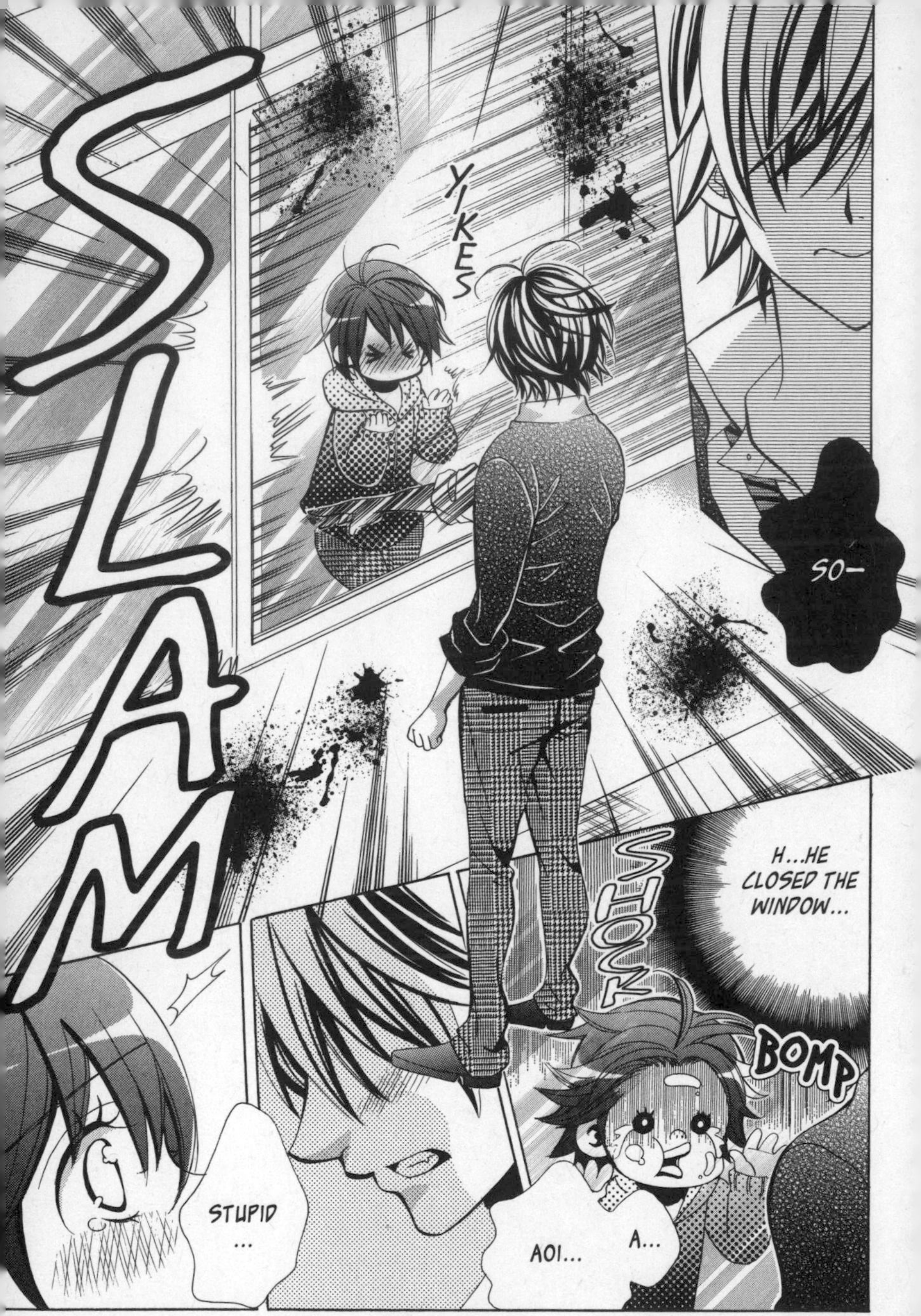
SO–
YIKES
SLAM
H...HE CLOSED THE WINDOW...
SHOOK
BOMP
A...
AOI...
STUPID ...

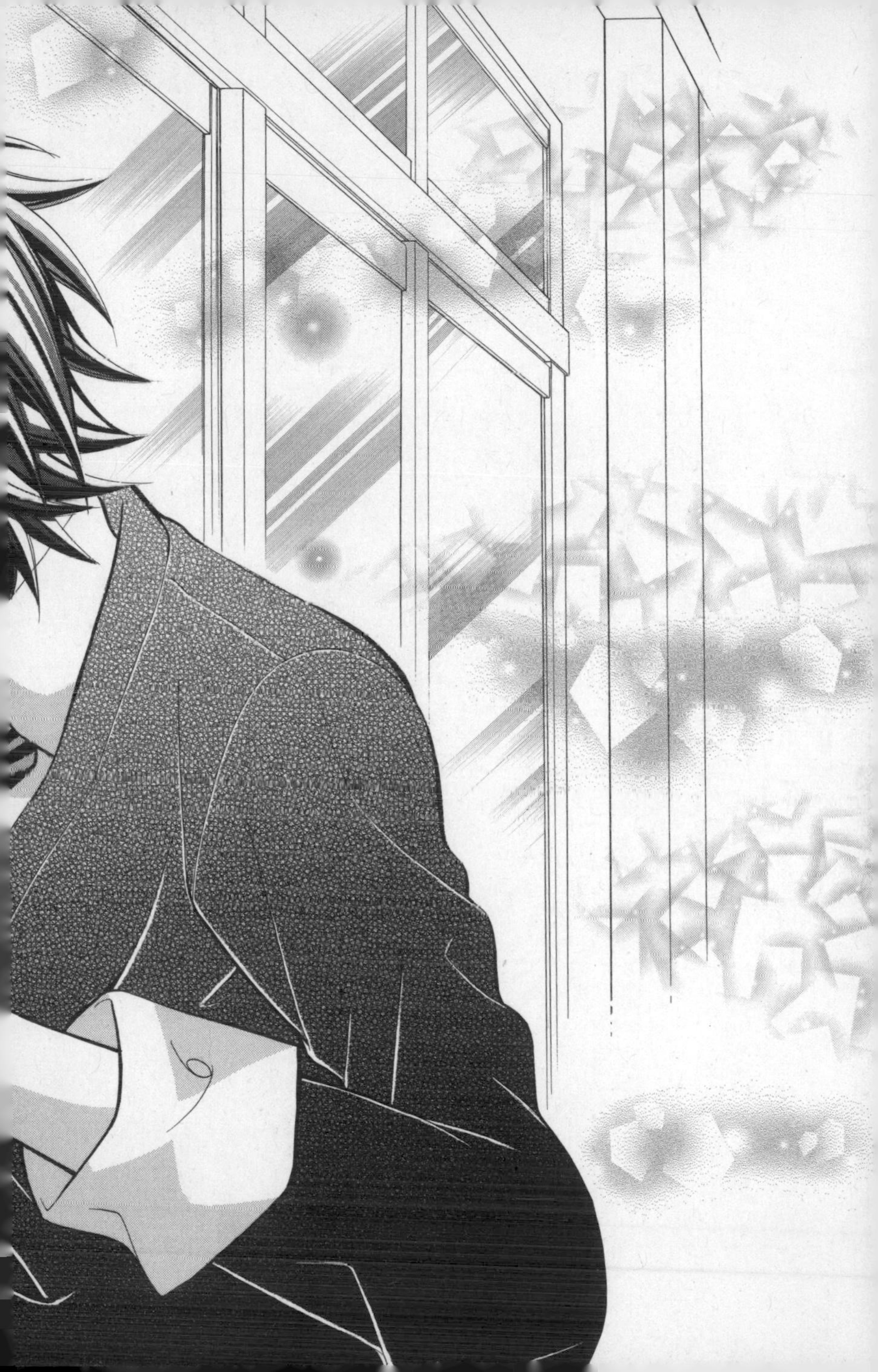

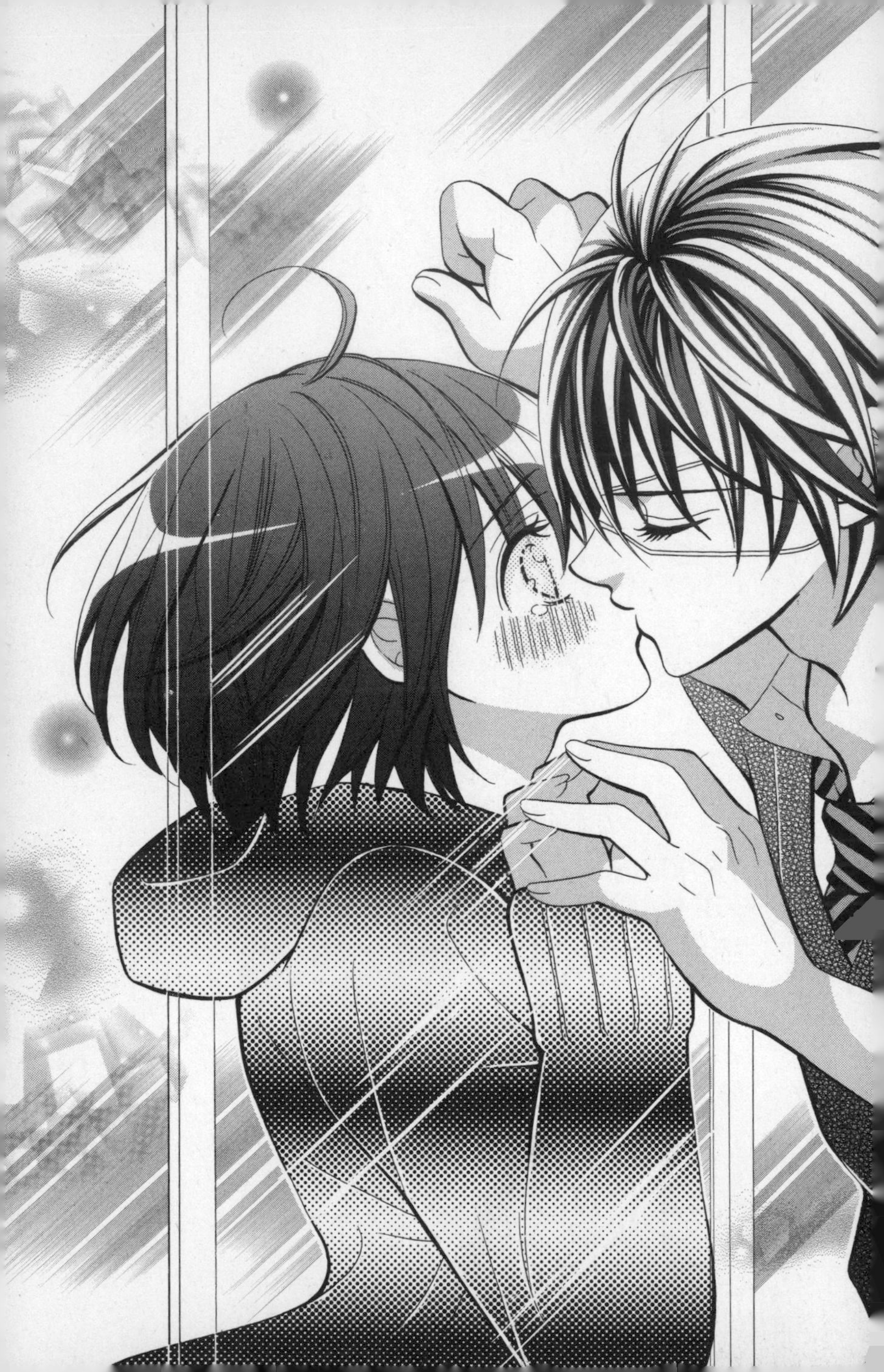

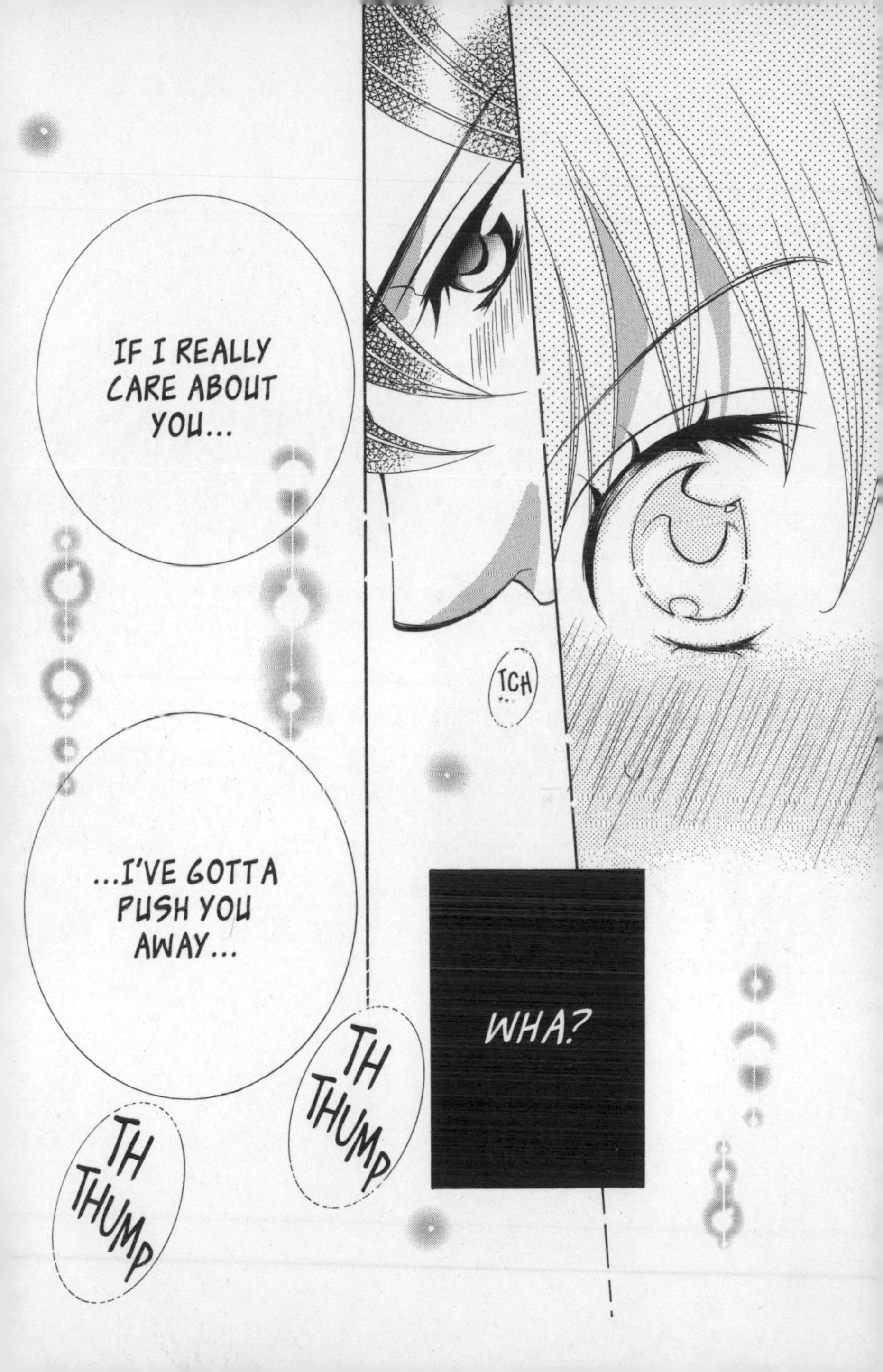
WHA?
TCH...
IF I REALLY CARE ABOUT YOU...
...I'VE GOTTA PUSH YOU AWAY...
TH THUMP
TH THUMP

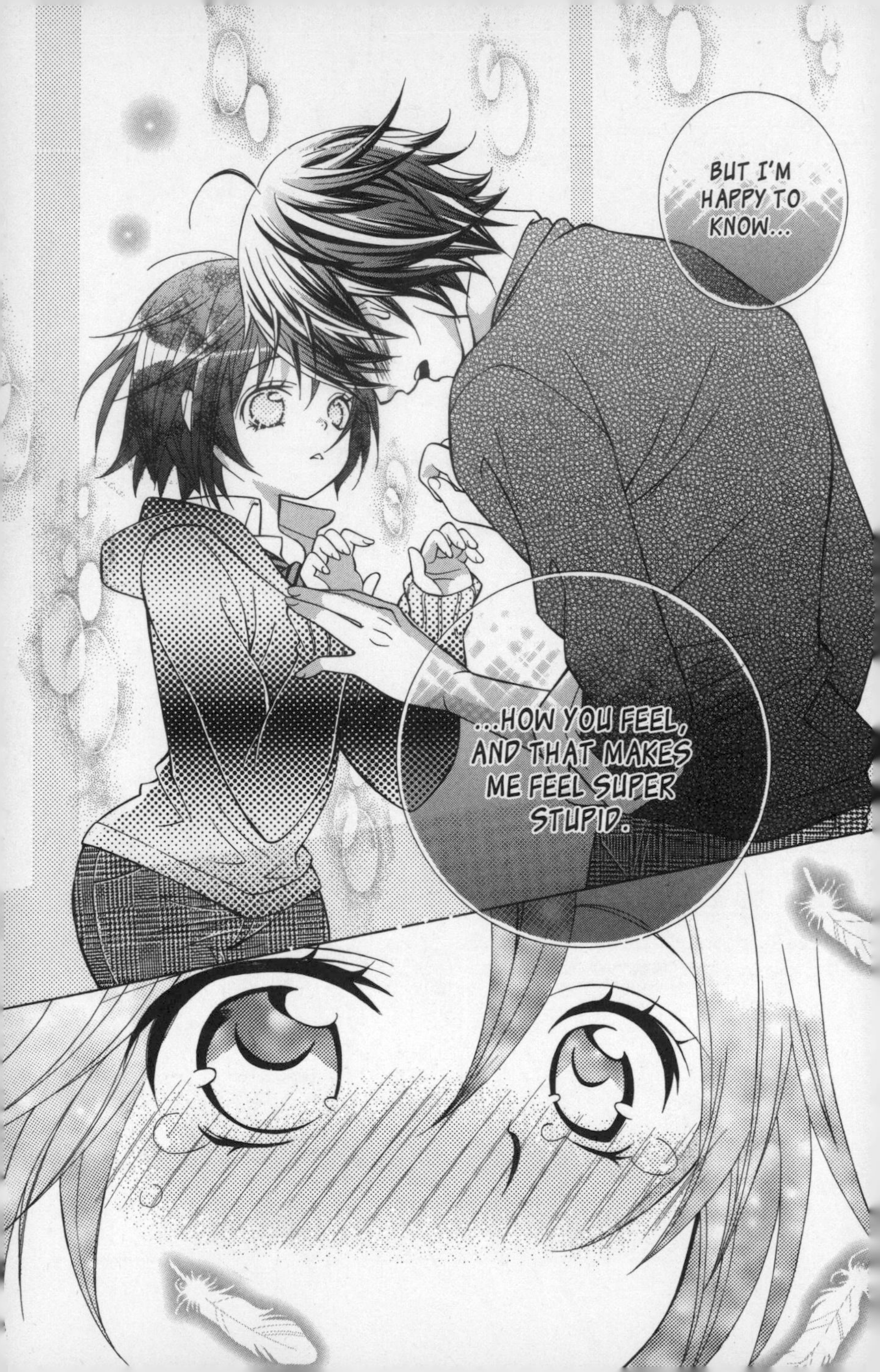
BUT I'M HAPPY TO KNOW...
...HOW YOU FEEL, AND THAT MAKES ME FEEL SUPER STUPID.

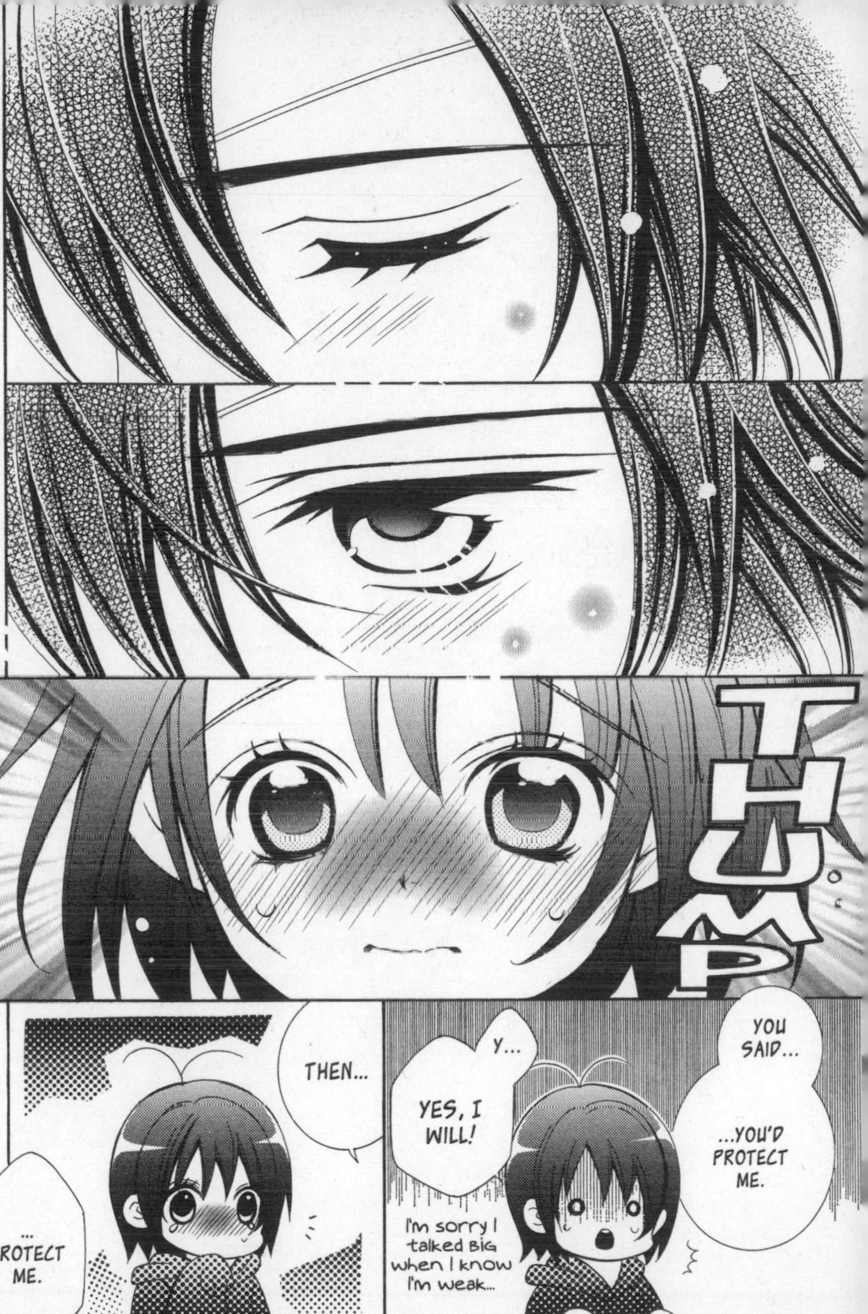
THUMP
YOU SAID...
...YOU'D PROTECT ME.
Y...
YES, I WILL!
I'm sorry I talked BIG when I know I'm weak...
THEN...
... PROTECT ME.

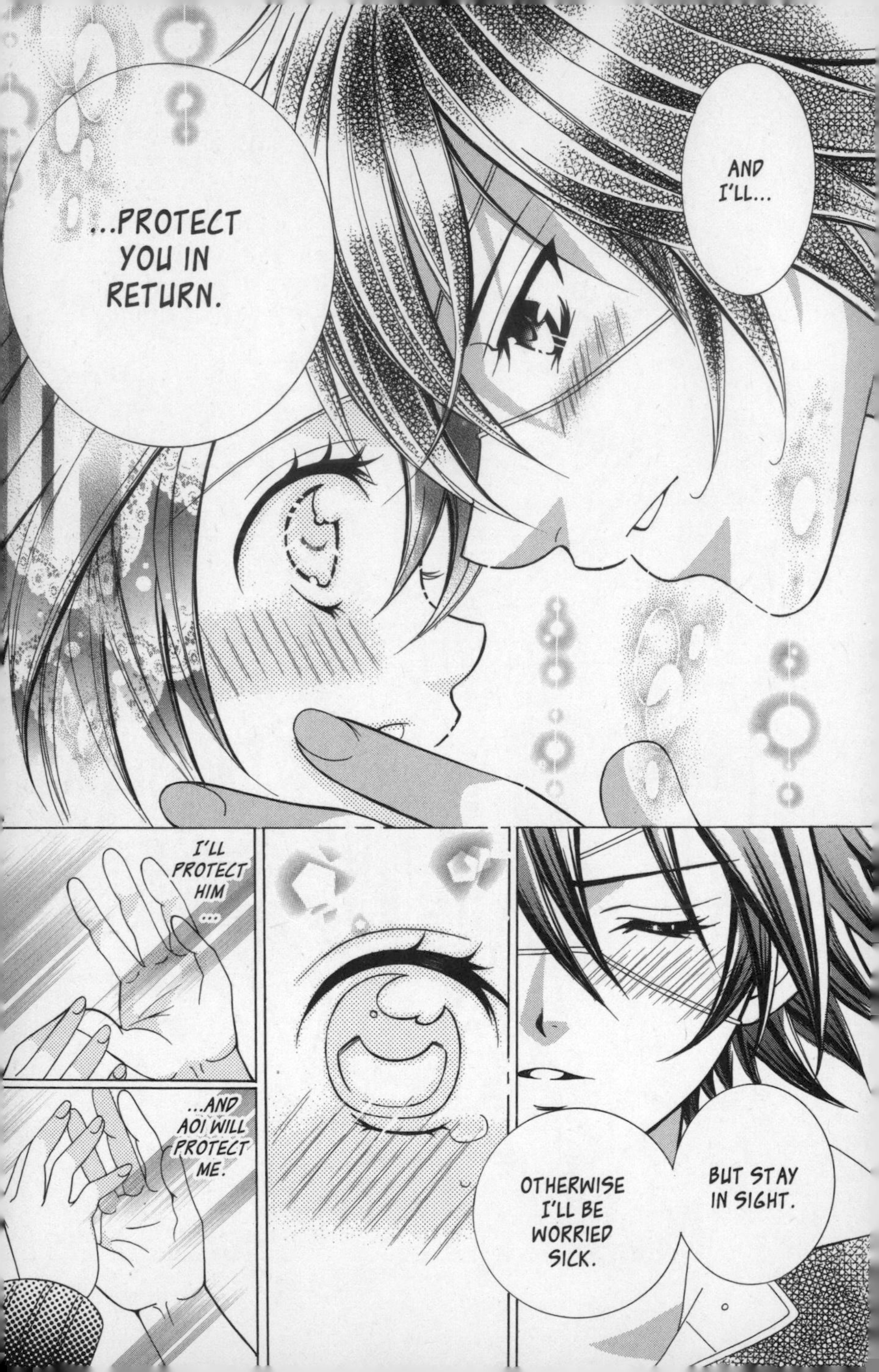

AND I'LL...
...PROTECT YOU IN RETURN.
BUT STAY IN SIGHT.
OTHERWISE I'LL BE WORRIED SICK.
I'LL PROTECT HIM...
...AND AOI WILL PROTECT ME.

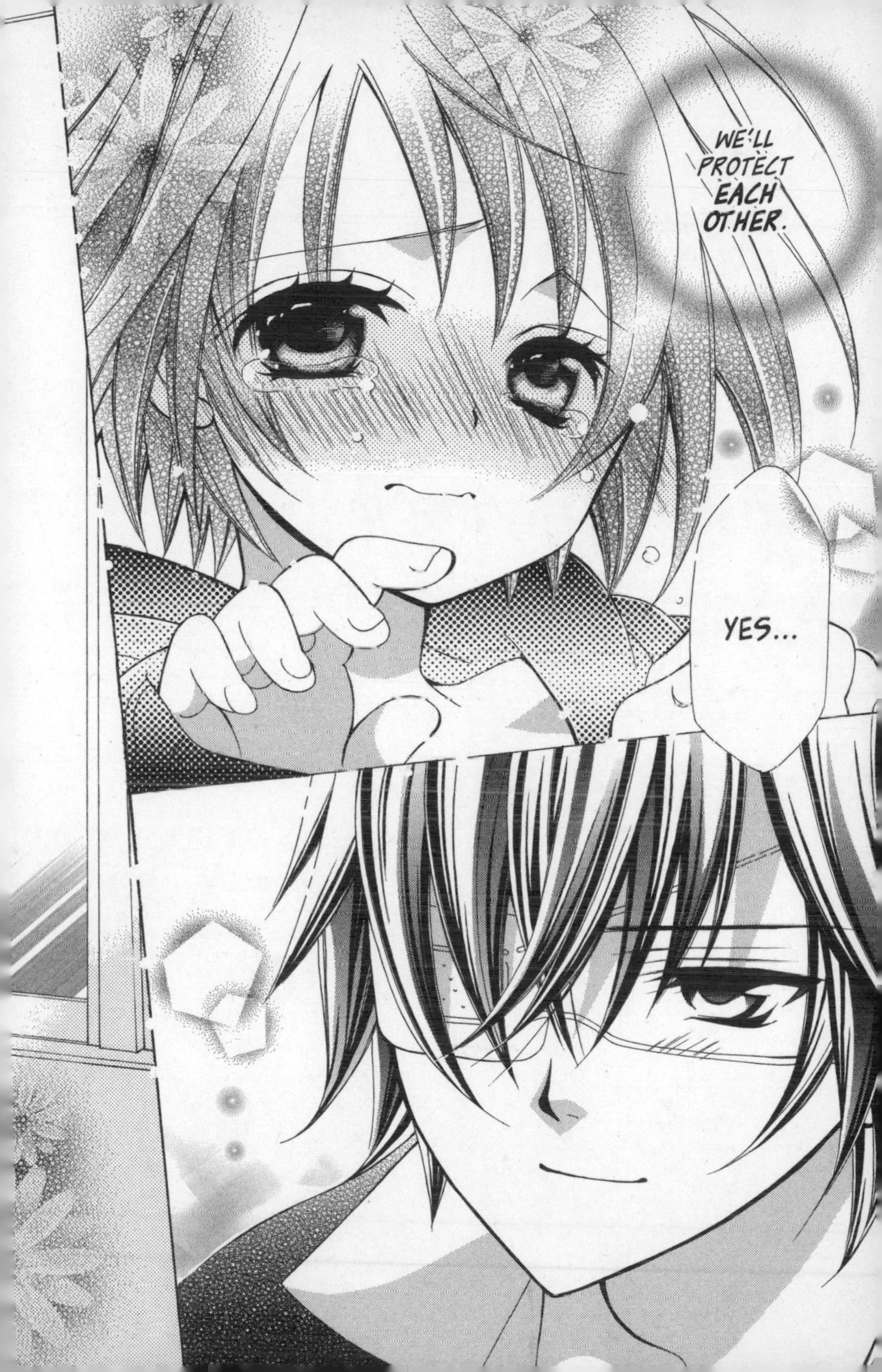
WE'LL PROTECT EACH OTHER.
YES...

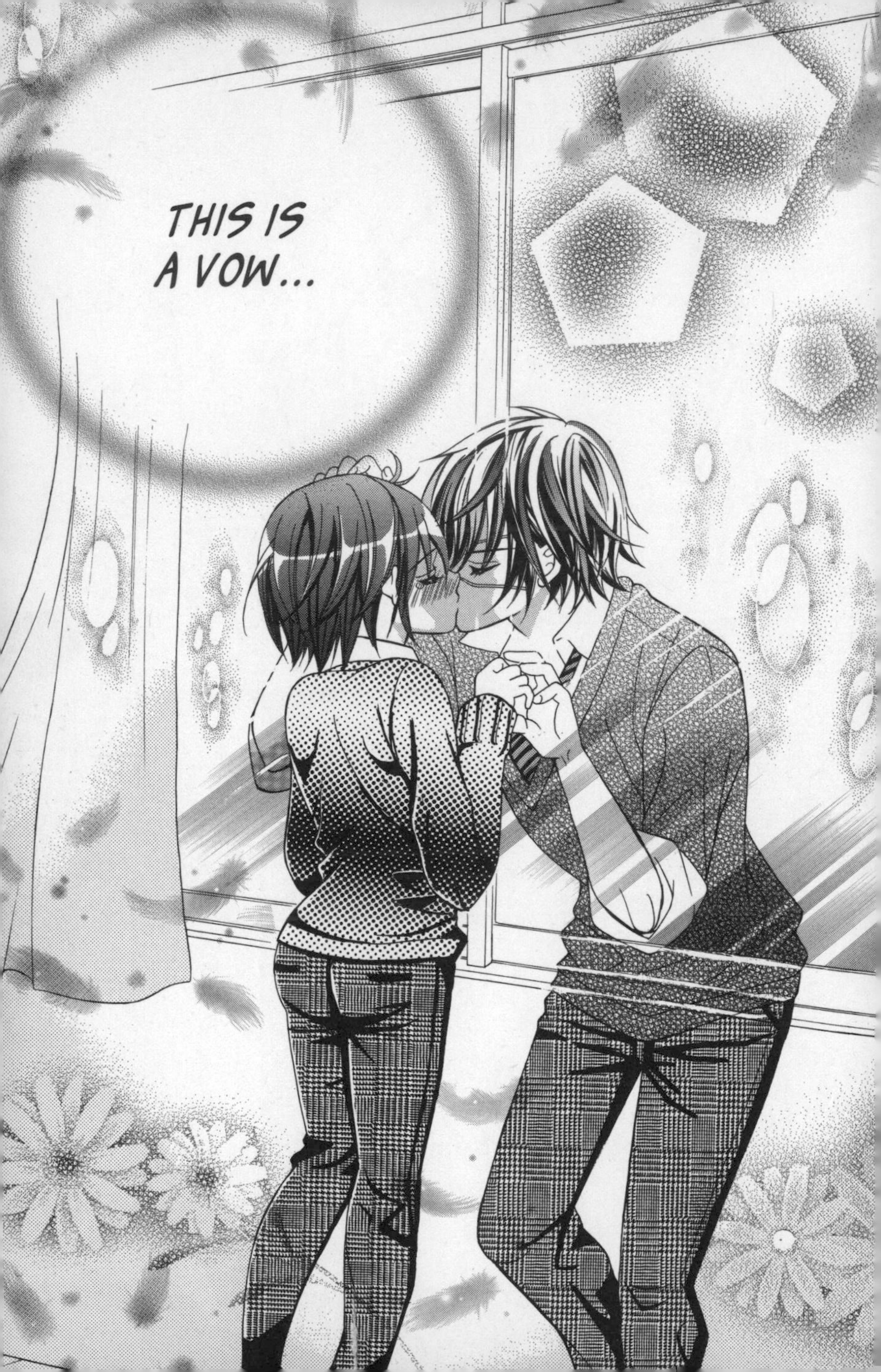
THIS IS A VOW...

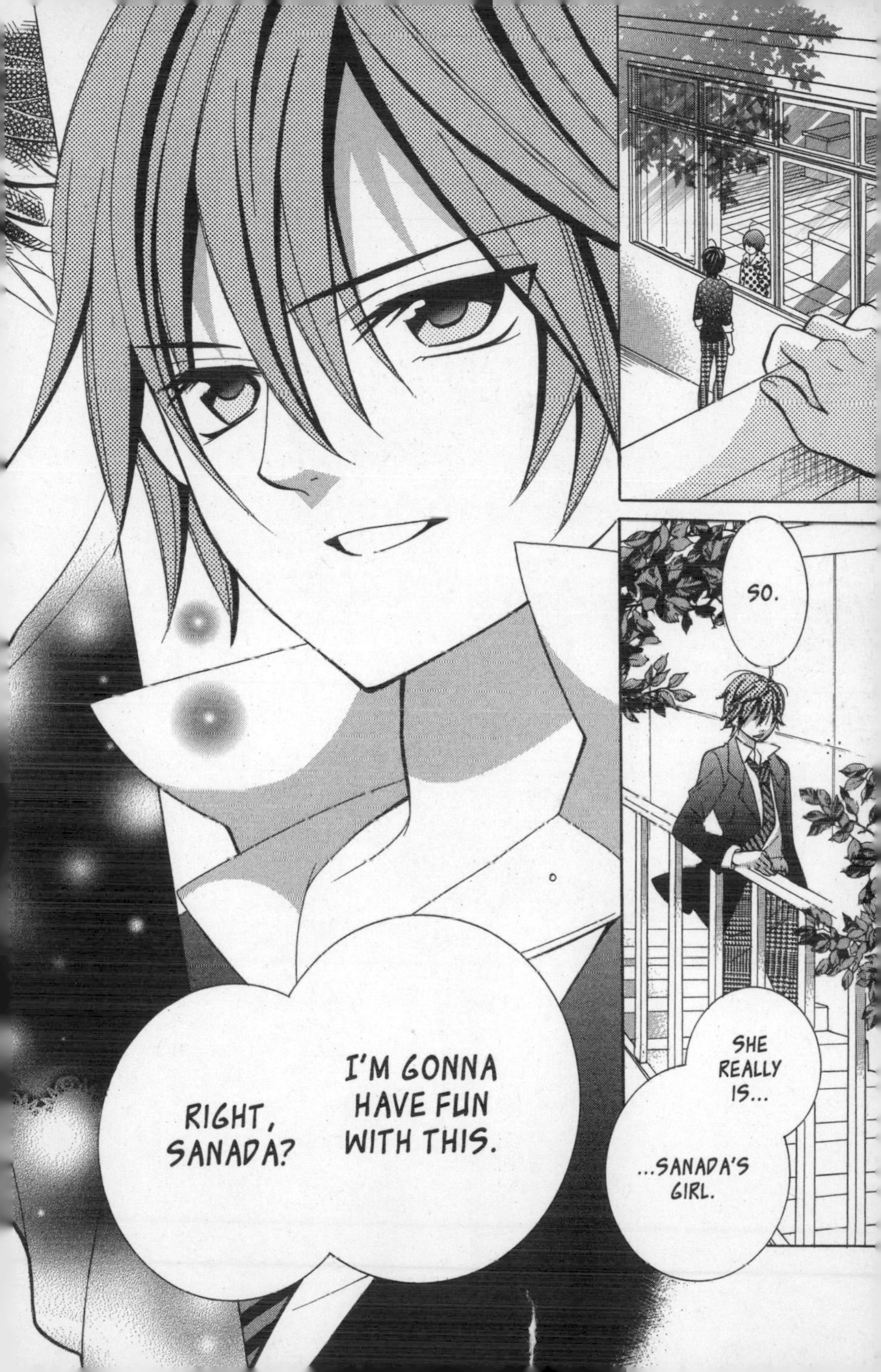
SO.
SHE REALLY IS...
...SANADA'S GIRL.
I'M GONNA HAVE FUN WITH THIS.
RIGHT, SANADA?

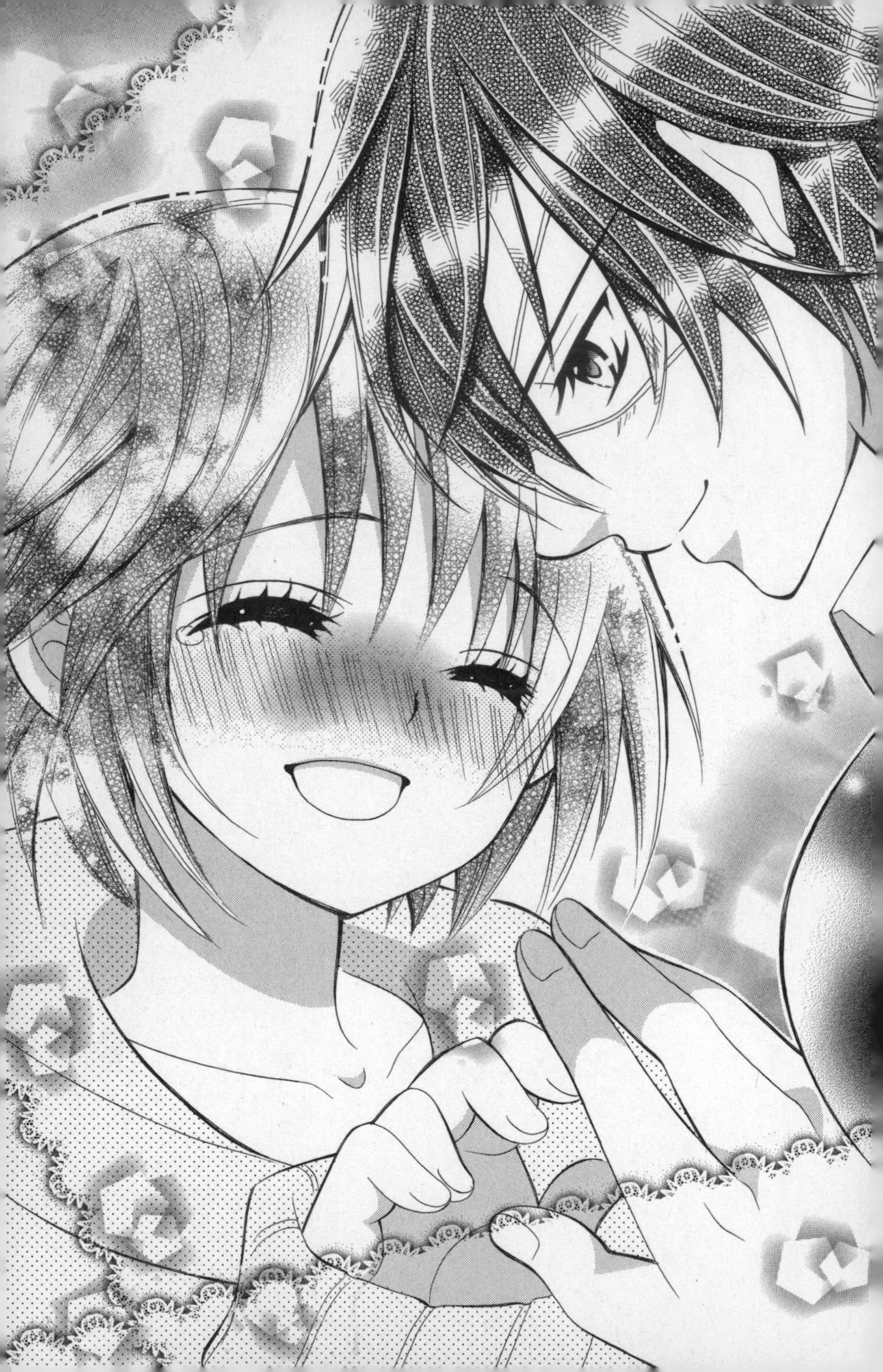

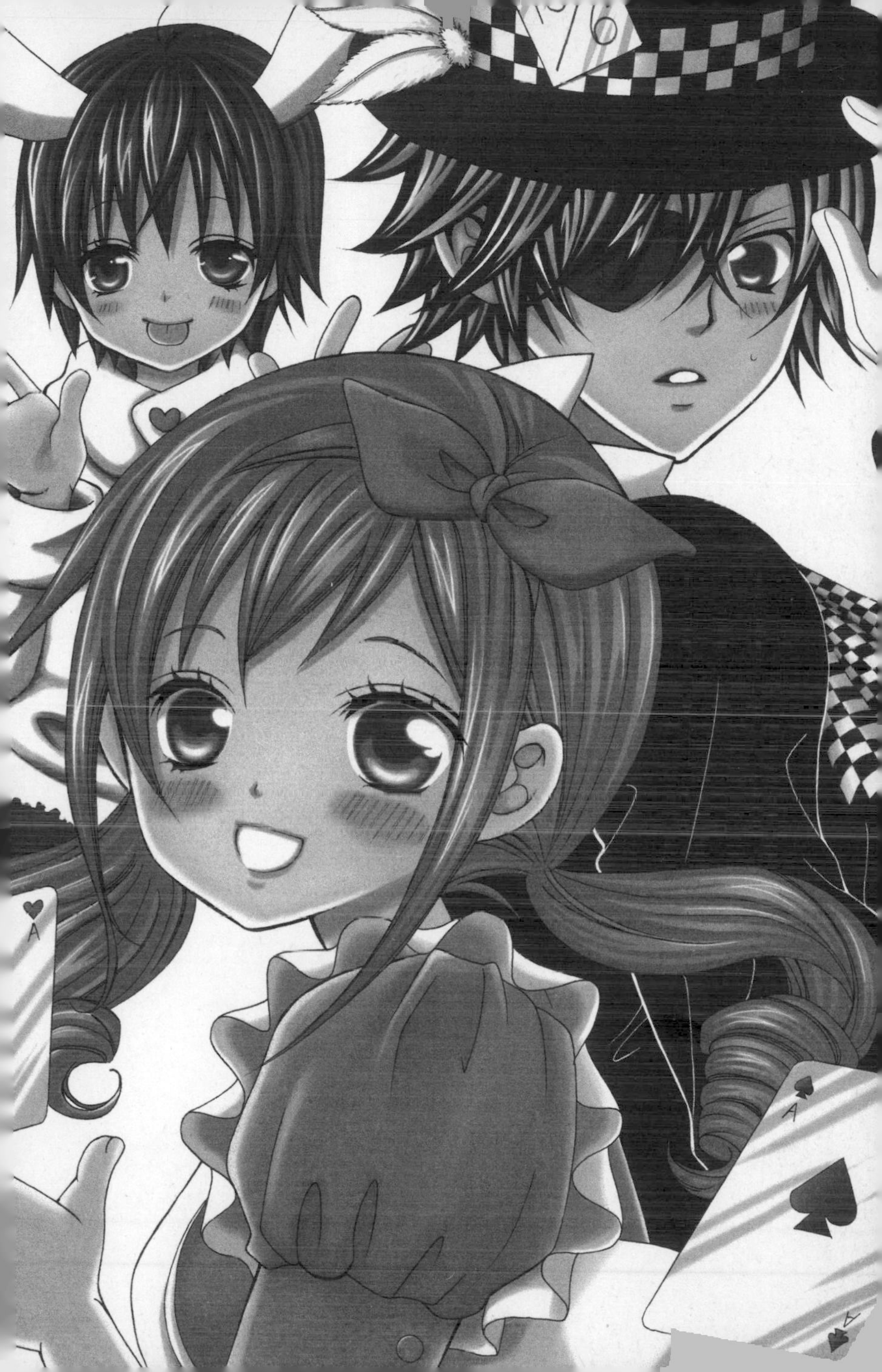

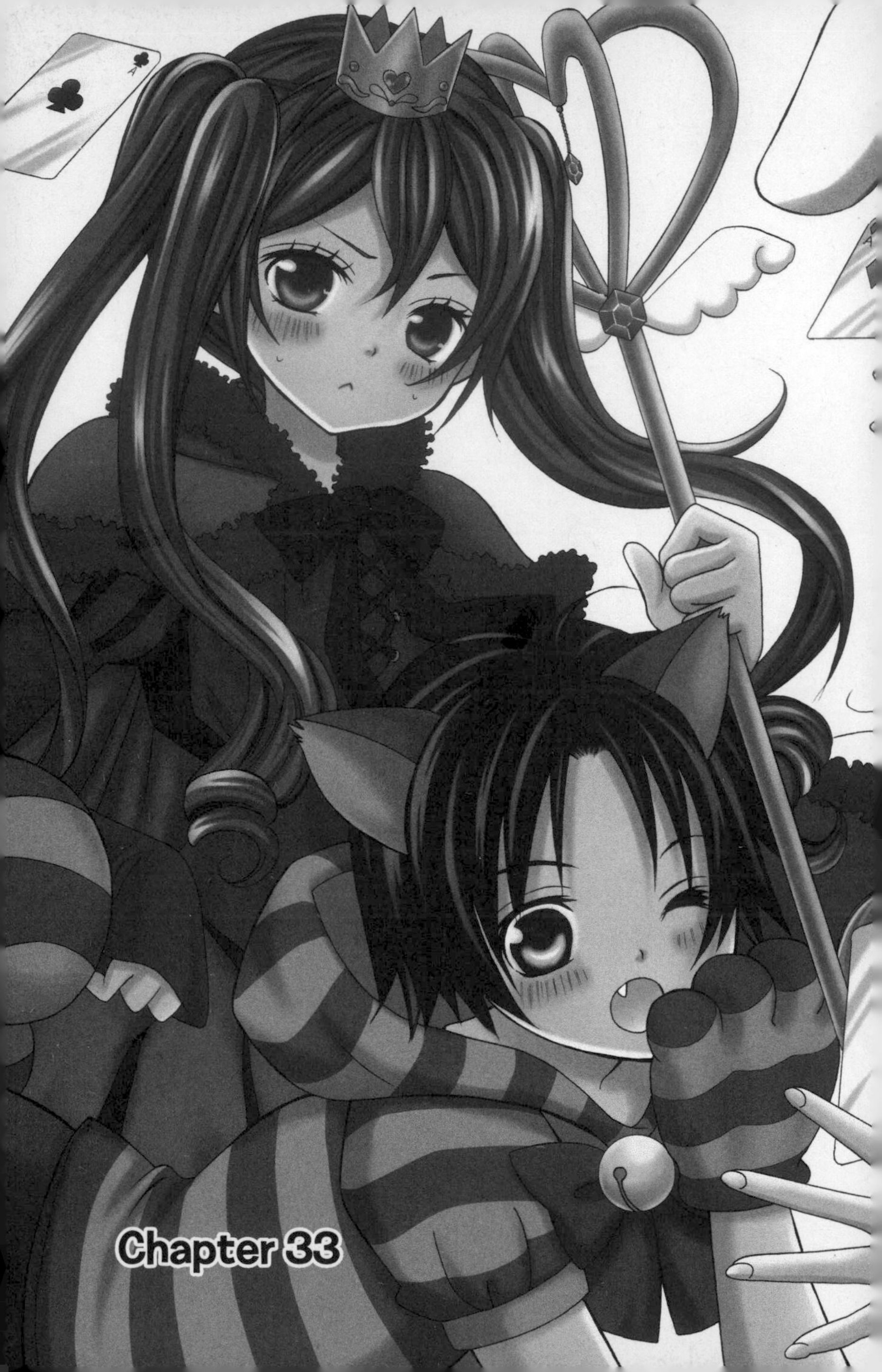
Chapter 33

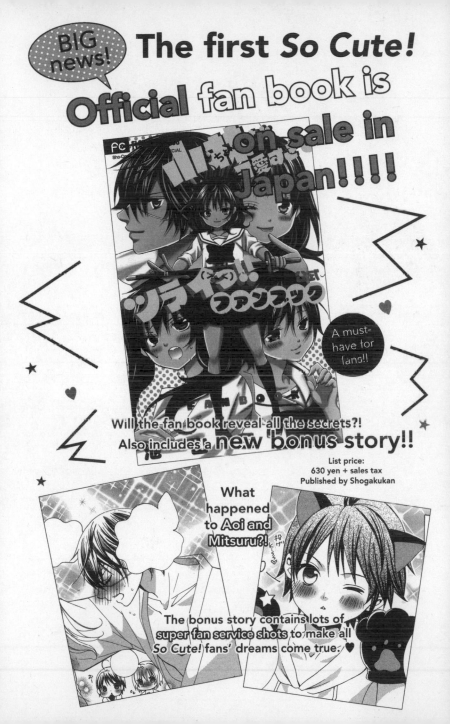

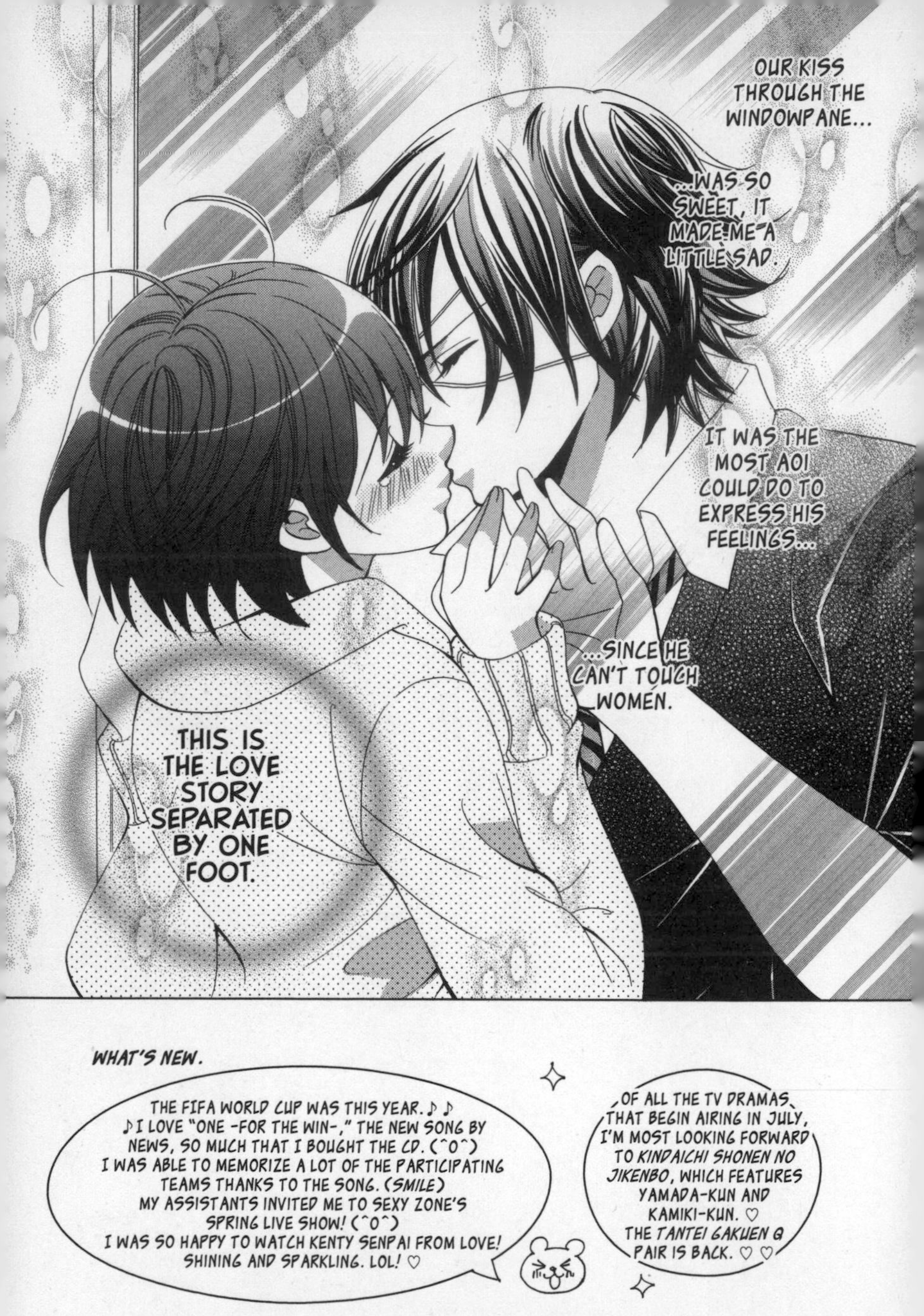
OUR KISS THROUGH THE WINDOWPANE...
...WAS SO SWEET, IT MADE ME A LITTLE SAD.
IT WAS THE MOST AOI COULD DO TO EXPRESS HIS FEELINGS...
...SINCE HE CAN'T TOUCH WOMEN.
THIS IS THE LOVE STORY SEPARATED BY ONE FOOT.

WHAT'S NEW.

THE FIFA WORLD CUP WAS THIS YEAR. ♪ ♪
♪ I LOVE "ONE -FOR THE WIN-," THE NEW SONG BY NEWS, SO MUCH THAT I BOUGHT THE CD. (^O^)
I WAS ABLE TO MEMORIZE A LOT OF THE PARTICIPATING TEAMS THANKS TO THE SONG. (*SMILE*)
MY ASSISTANTS INVITED ME TO SEXY ZONE'S SPRING LIVE SHOW! (^O^)
I WAS SO HAPPY TO WATCH KENTY SENPAI FROM LOVE! SHINING AND SPARKLING. LOL! ♡

OF ALL THE TV DRAMAS THAT BEGIN AIRING IN JULY, I'M MOST LOOKING FORWARD TO *KINDAICHI SHONEN NO JIKENBO*, WHICH FEATURES YAMADA-KUN AND KAMIKI-KUN. ♡
THE *TANTEI GAKUEN Q* PAIR IS BACK. ♡ ♡

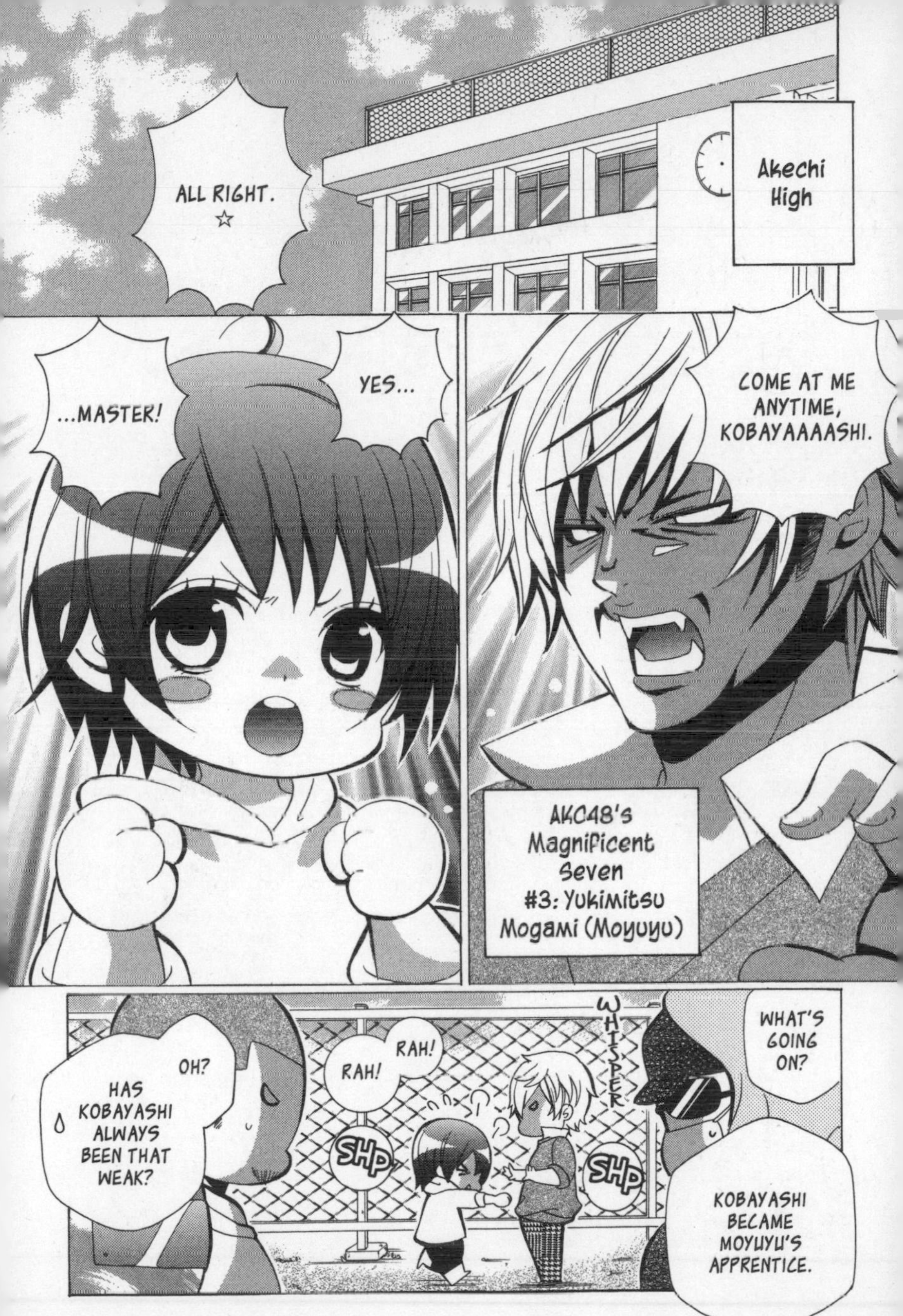
Akechi High
ALL RIGHT. ☆
COME AT ME ANYTIME, KOBAYAAAASHI.
AKC48's Magnificent Seven #3: Yukimitsu Mogami (Moyuyu)
YES...
...MASTER!
WHAT'S GOING ON?
WHISPER
KOBAYASHI BECAME MOYUYU'S APPRENTICE.
SHP
RAH!
RAH!
SHP
OH?
HAS KOBAYASHI ALWAYS BEEN THAT WEAK?

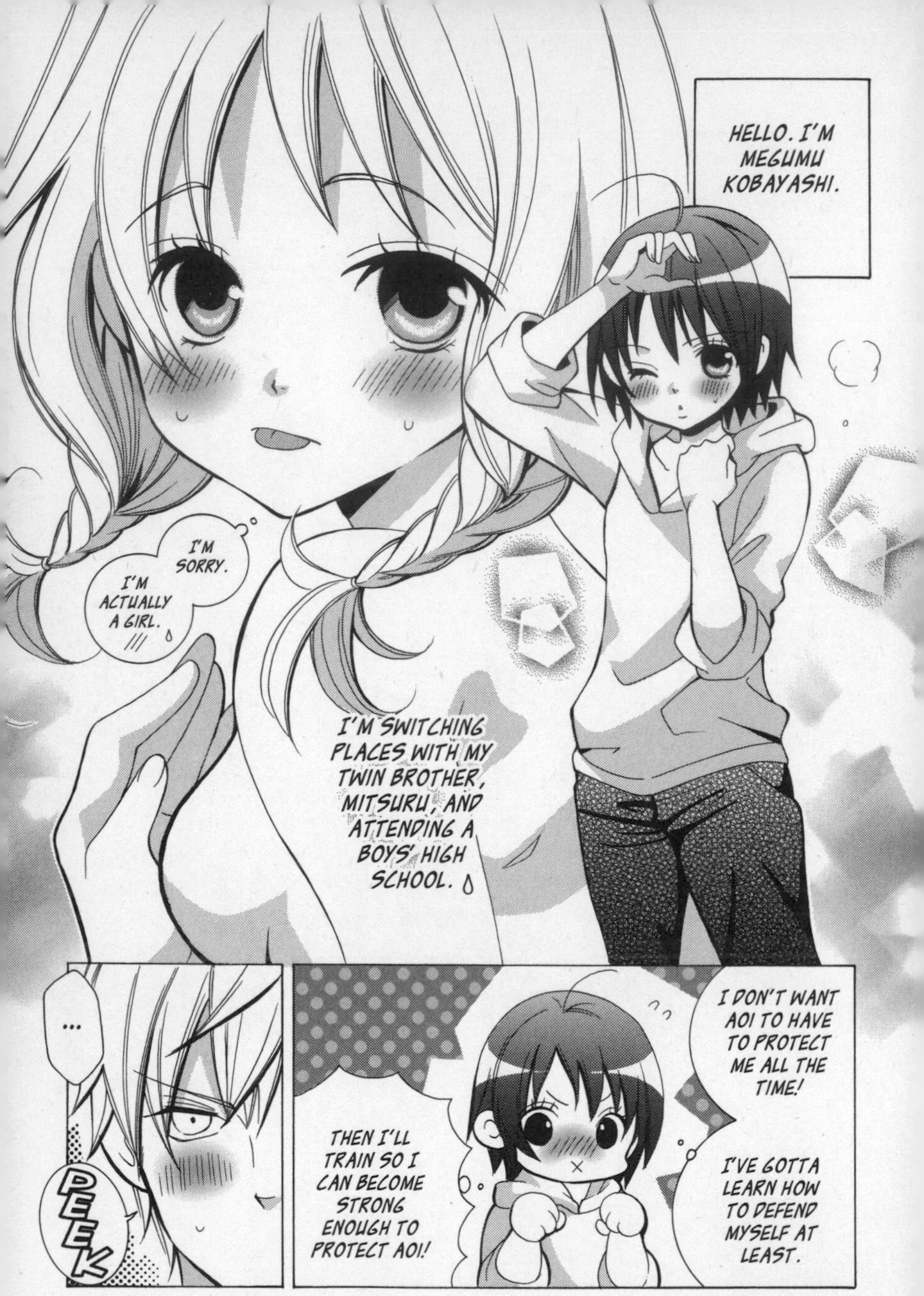
HELLO. I'M MEGUMU KOBAYASHI.
I'M SORRY. I'M ACTUALLY A GIRL. ///
I'M SWITCHING PLACES WITH MY TWIN BROTHER, MITSURU, AND ATTENDING A BOYS' HIGH SCHOOL.
I DON'T WANT AOI TO HAVE TO PROTECT ME ALL THE TIME!
I'VE GOTTA LEARN HOW TO DEFEND MYSELF AT LEAST.
THEN I'LL TRAIN SO I CAN BECOME STRONG ENOUGH TO PROTECT AOI!
...
PEEK

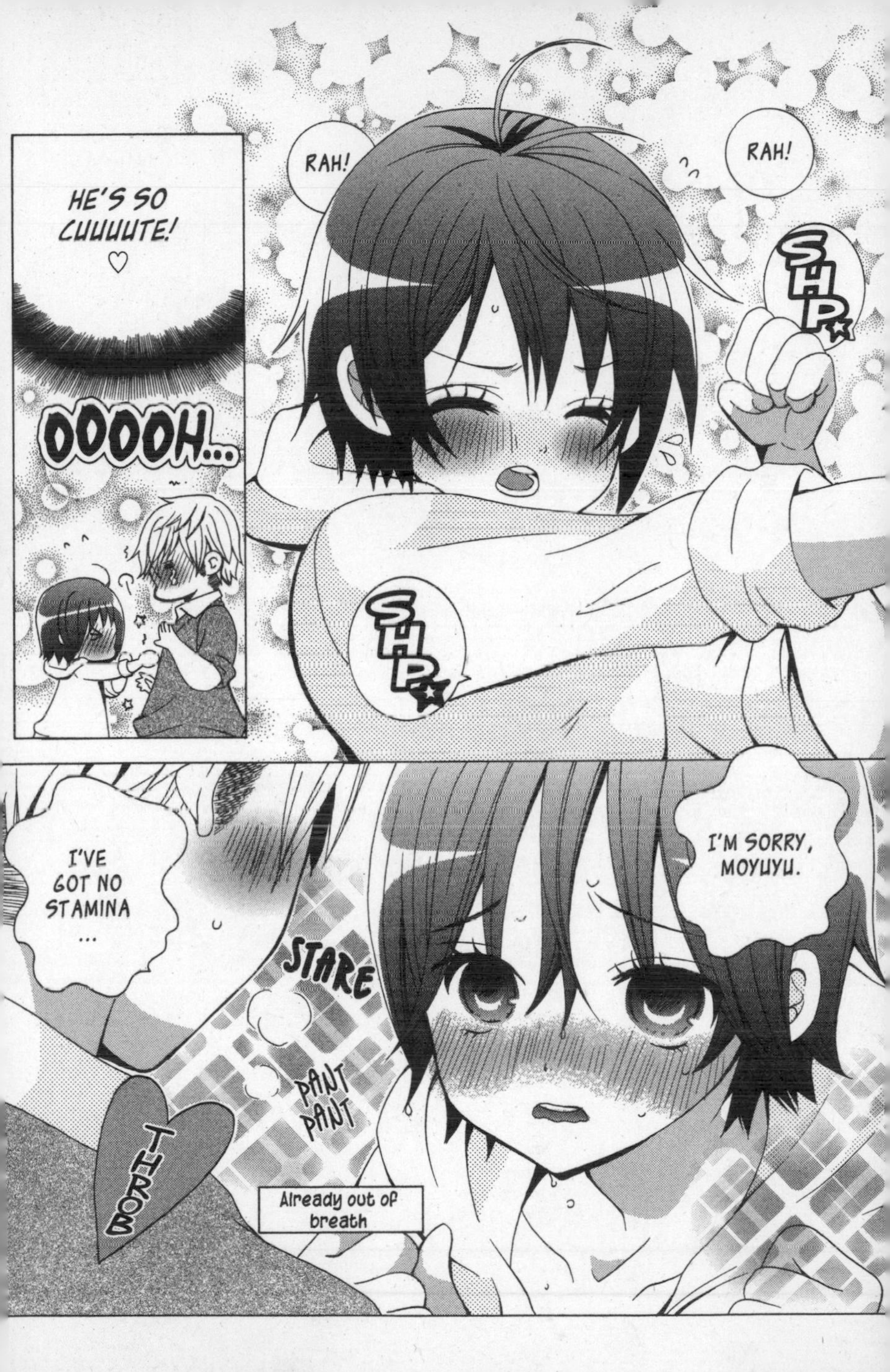
RAH!
RAH!
SHP☆
SHP☆
HE'S SO CUUUUTE! ♡
OOOOH...
I'M SORRY, MOYUYU.
STARE
PANT PANT
I'VE GOT NO STAMINA ...
THROB
Already out of breath

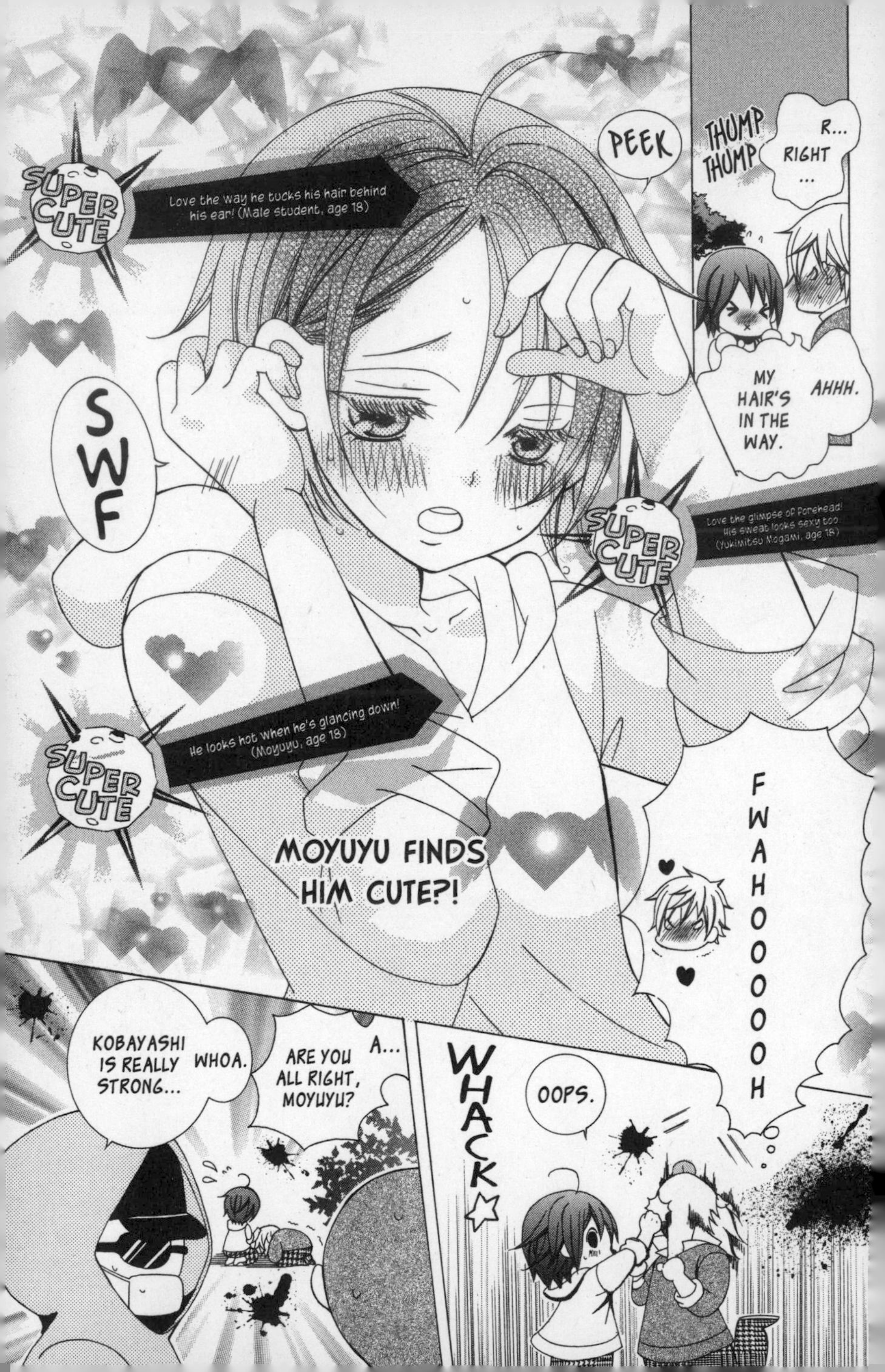
THUMP THUMP
R... RIGHT ...
AHHH.
MY HAIR'S IN THE WAY.
PEEK
SUPER CUTE
Love the way he tucks his hair behind his ear! (Male student, age 18)
SWF
SUPER CUTE
Love the glimpse of forehead! His sweat looks sexy too. (Yukimitsu Mogami, age 18)
SUPER CUTE
He looks hot when he's glancing down! (Moyuyu, age 18)
MOYUYU FINDS HIM CUTE?!
FWAHOOOOOOH
WHACK
OOPS.
A...
ARE YOU ALL RIGHT, MOYUYU?
WHOA.
KOBAYASHI IS REALLY STRONG...

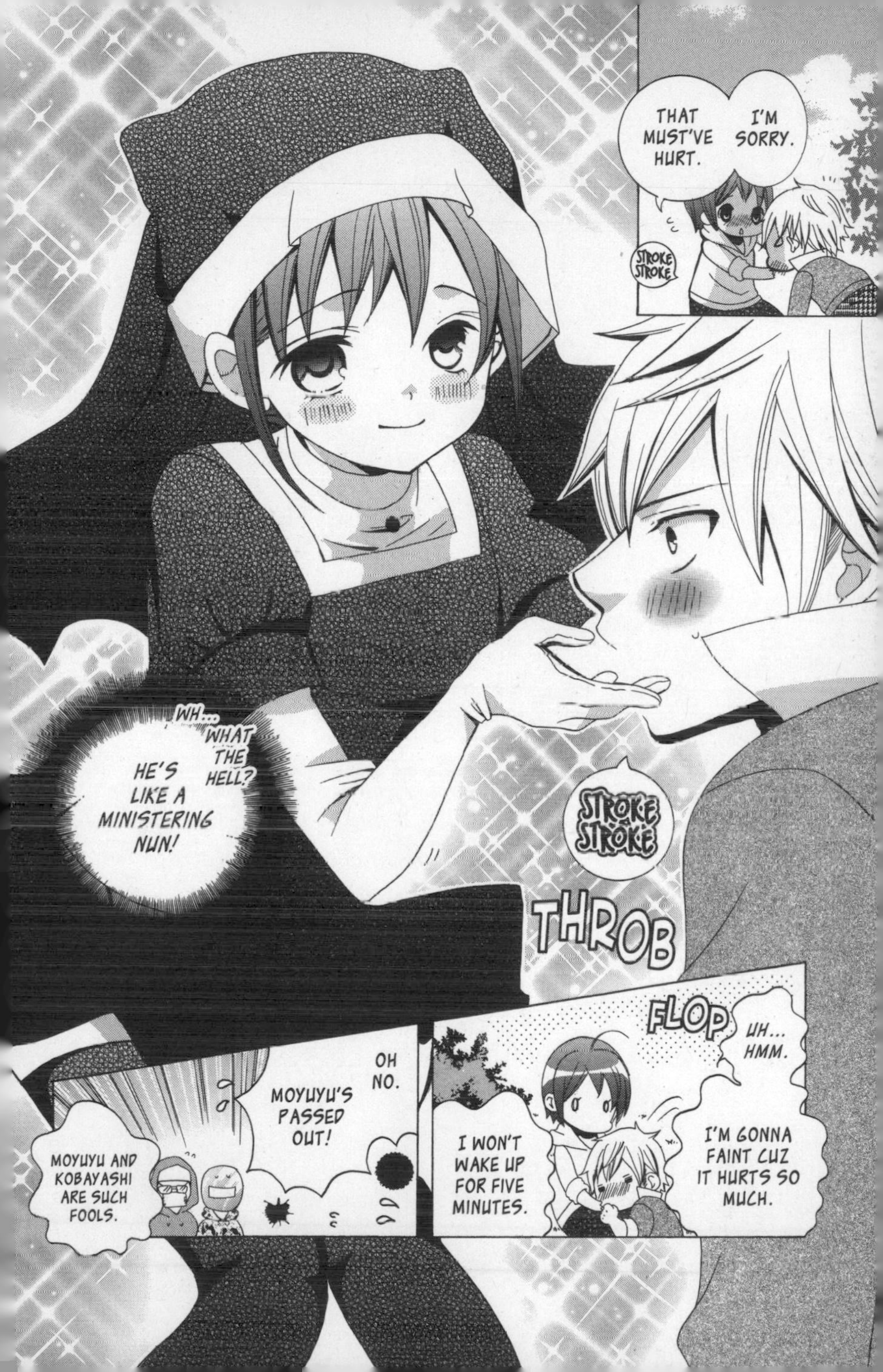
I'M SORRY.
THAT MUST'VE HURT.
STROKE STROKE
STROKE STROKE
THROB
WH... WHAT THE HELL?
HE'S LIKE A MINISTERING NUN!
FLOP
UH... HMM.
I'M GONNA FAINT CUZ IT HURTS SO MUCH.
I WON'T WAKE UP FOR FIVE MINUTES.
OH NO.
MOYUYU'S PASSED OUT!
MOYUYU AND KOBAYASHI ARE SUCH FOOLS.

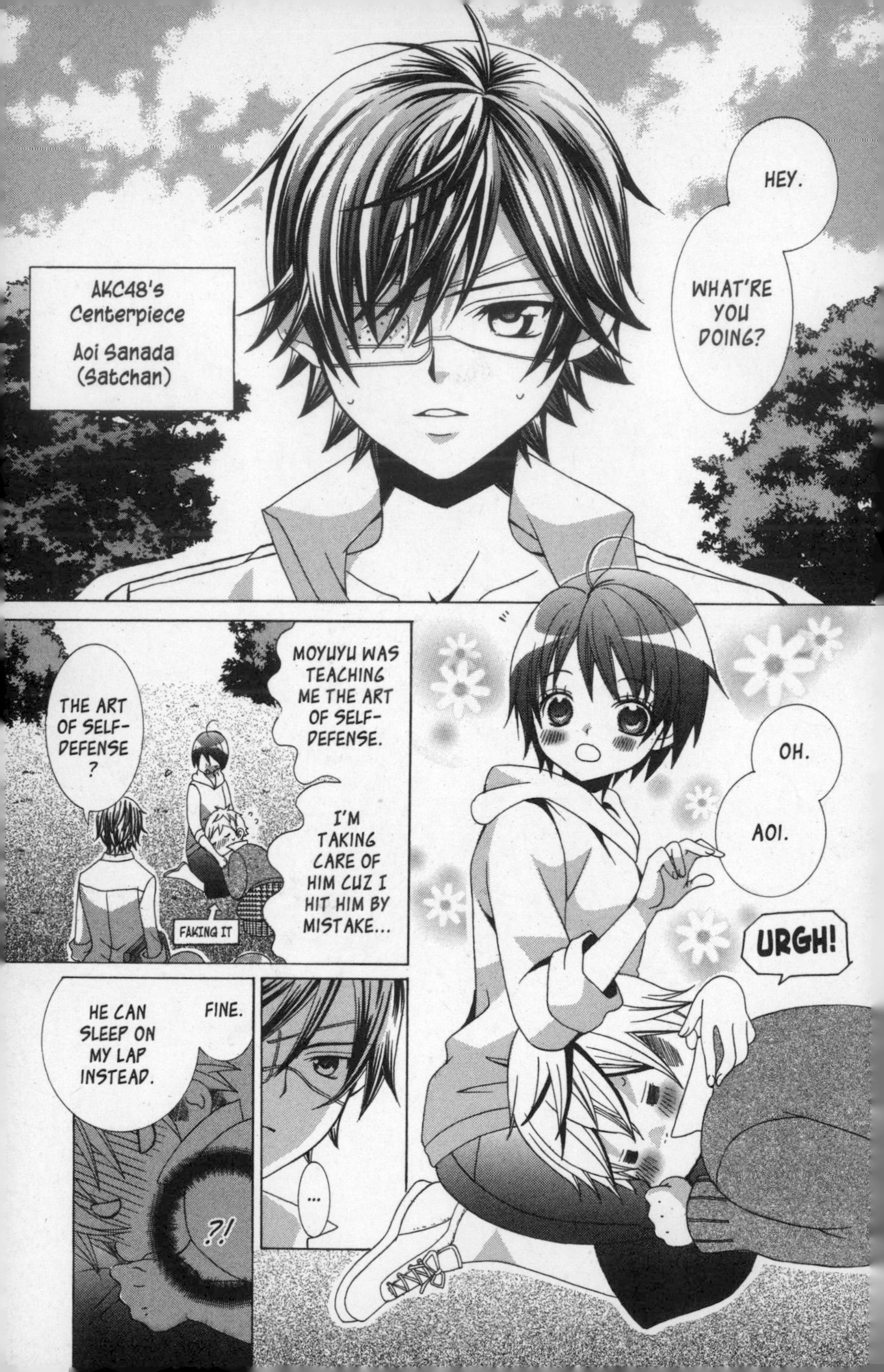
HEY.
WHAT'RE YOU DOING?
AKC48's Centerpiece
Aoi Sanada (Satchan)
OH.
AOI.
URGH!
MOYUYU WAS TEACHING ME THE ART OF SELF-DEFENSE.
I'M TAKING CARE OF HIM CUZ I HIT HIM BY MISTAKE...
THE ART OF SELF-DEFENSE?
FAKING IT
...
FINE.
HE CAN SLEEP ON MY LAP INSTEAD.
?!

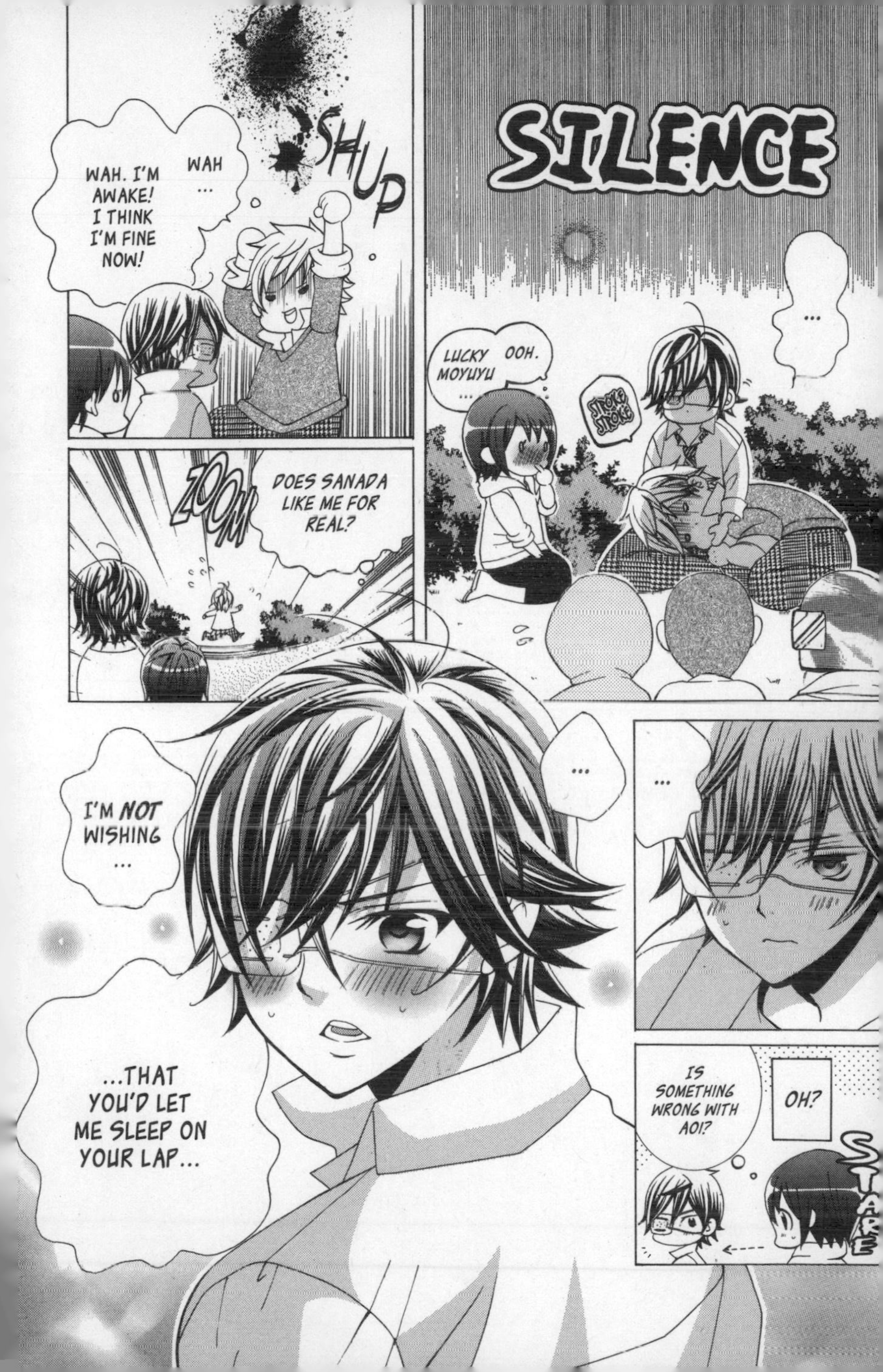
SILENCE
...
OOH. LUCKY MOYUYU ...
STROKE STROKE
SHUP
WAH ...
WAH. I'M AWAKE! I THINK I'M FINE NOW!
ZOOM
DOES SANADA LIKE ME FOR REAL?
...
OH?
IS SOMETHING WRONG WITH AOI?
STARE
...
I'M *NOT* WISHING ...
...THAT YOU'D LET ME SLEEP ON YOUR LAP...

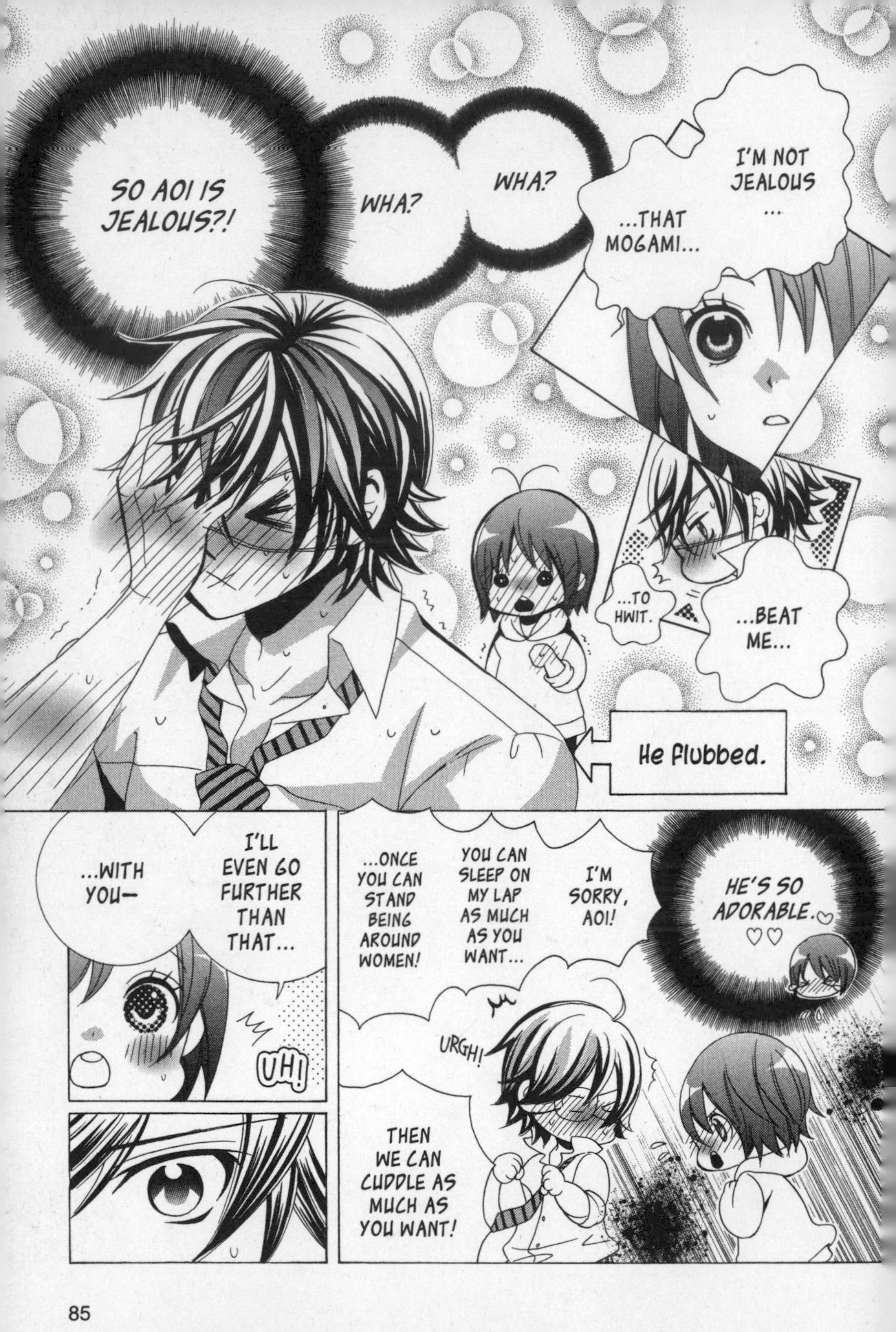
I'M NOT JEALOUS...
...THAT MOGAMI...
...BEAT ME...
...TO HWIT.
He flubbed.
WHA?
WHA?
SO AOI IS JEALOUS?!
HE'S SO ADORABLE. ♡ ♡♡
I'M SORRY, AOI!
YOU CAN SLEEP ON MY LAP AS MUCH AS YOU WANT...
...ONCE YOU CAN STAND BEING AROUND WOMEN!
URGH!
THEN WE CAN CUDDLE AS MUCH AS YOU WANT!
I'LL EVEN GO FURTHER THAN THAT...
...WITH YOU—
UH!

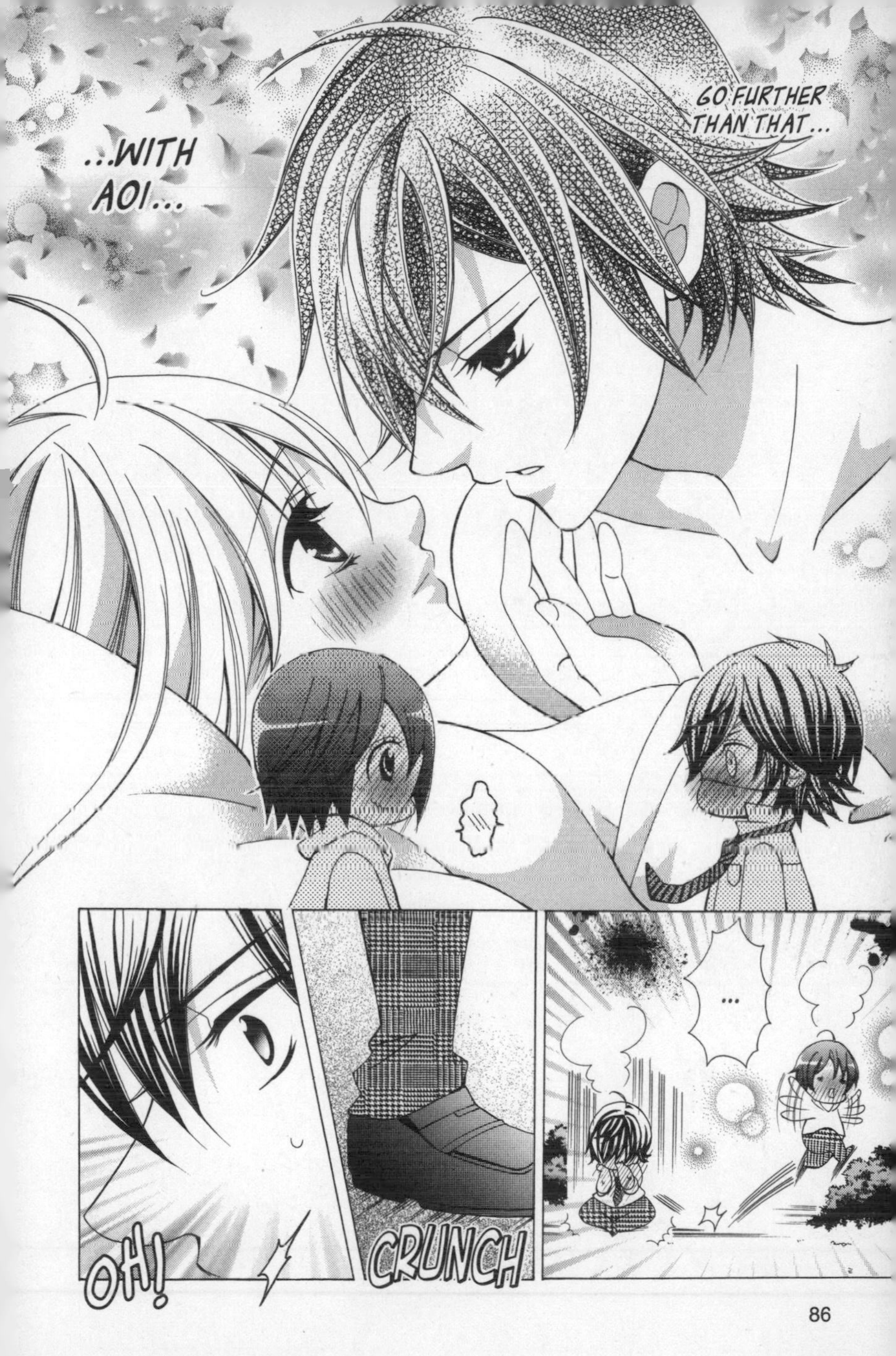
GO FURTHER THAN THAT...
...WITH AOI...
...
CRUNCH
OH!

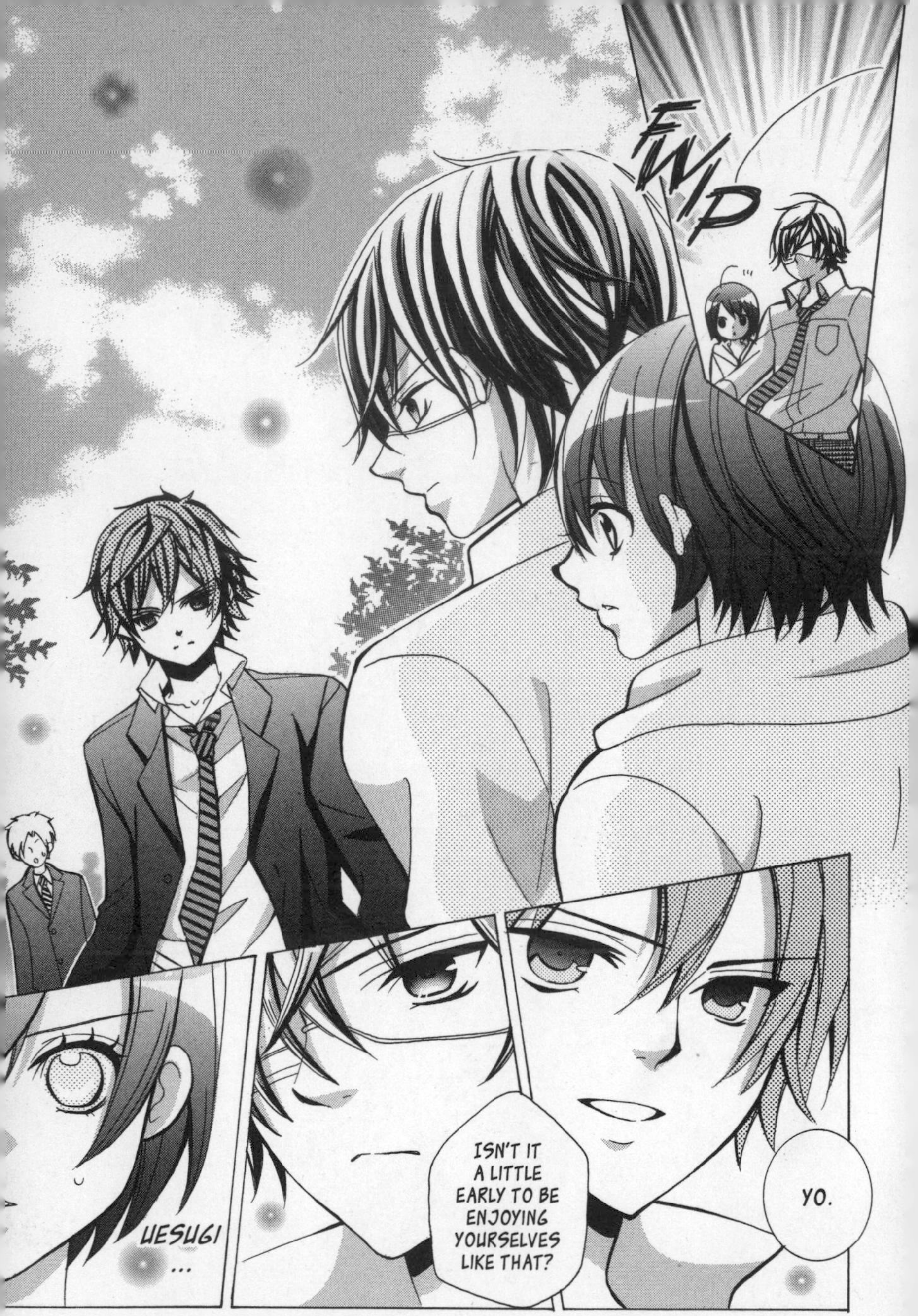
FWIP
YO.
ISN'T IT A LITTLE EARLY TO BE ENJOYING YOURSELVES LIKE THAT?
UESUGI ...

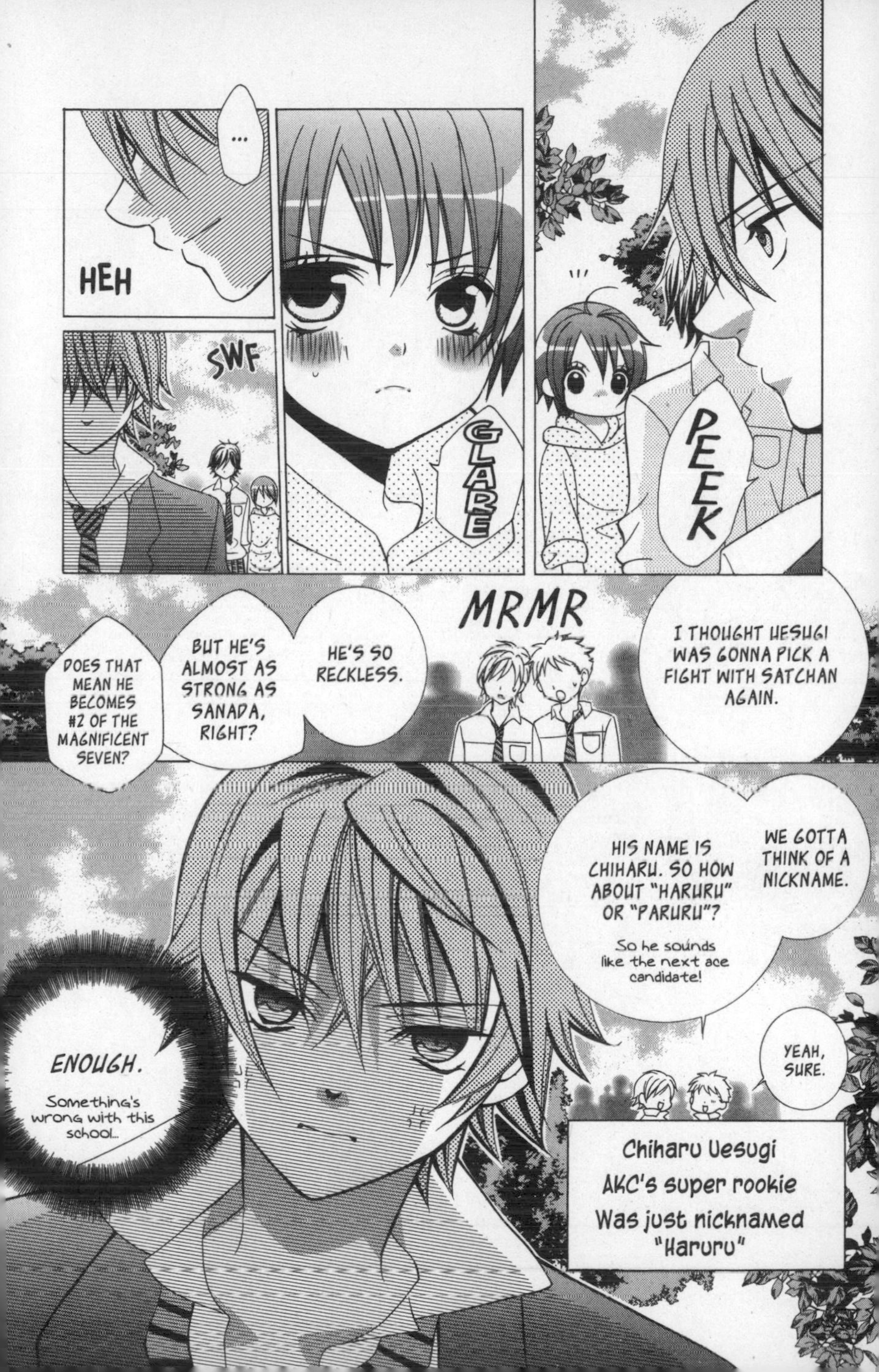
!!
PEEK
GLARE
...
HEH
SWF
I THOUGHT UESUGI WAS GONNA PICK A FIGHT WITH SATCHAN AGAIN.
MRMR
HE'S SO RECKLESS.
BUT HE'S ALMOST AS STRONG AS SANADA, RIGHT?
DOES THAT MEAN HE BECOMES #2 OF THE MAGNIFICENT SEVEN?
WE GOTTA THINK OF A NICKNAME.
HIS NAME IS CHIHARU. SO HOW ABOUT "HARURU" OR "PARURU"?
So he sounds like the next ace candidate!
YEAH, SURE.
Chiharu Uesugi AKC's super rookie Was just nicknamed "Haruru"
ENOUGH.
Something's wrong with this school...

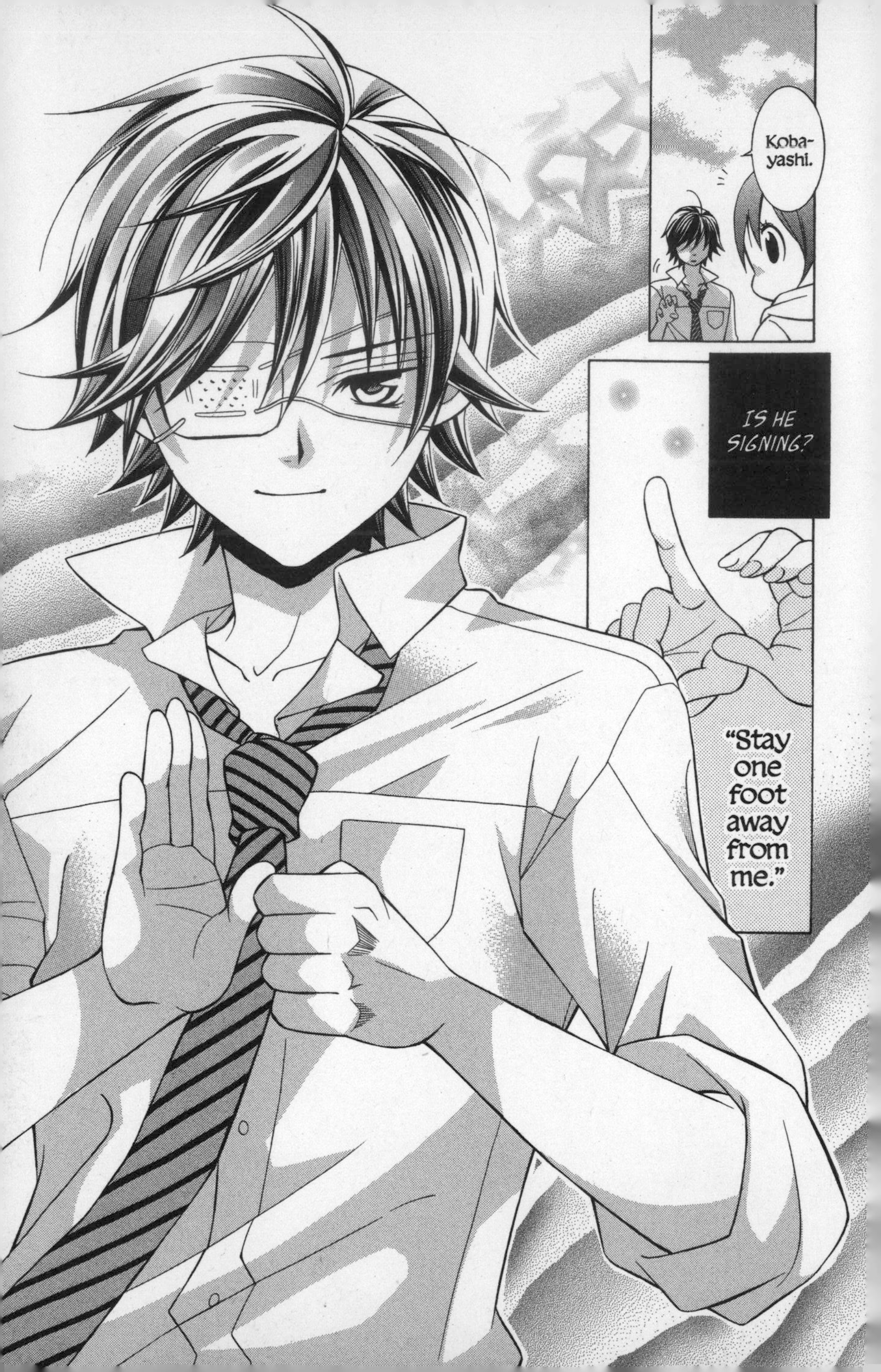
Koba-yashi.
IS HE SIGNING?
"Stay one foot away from me."

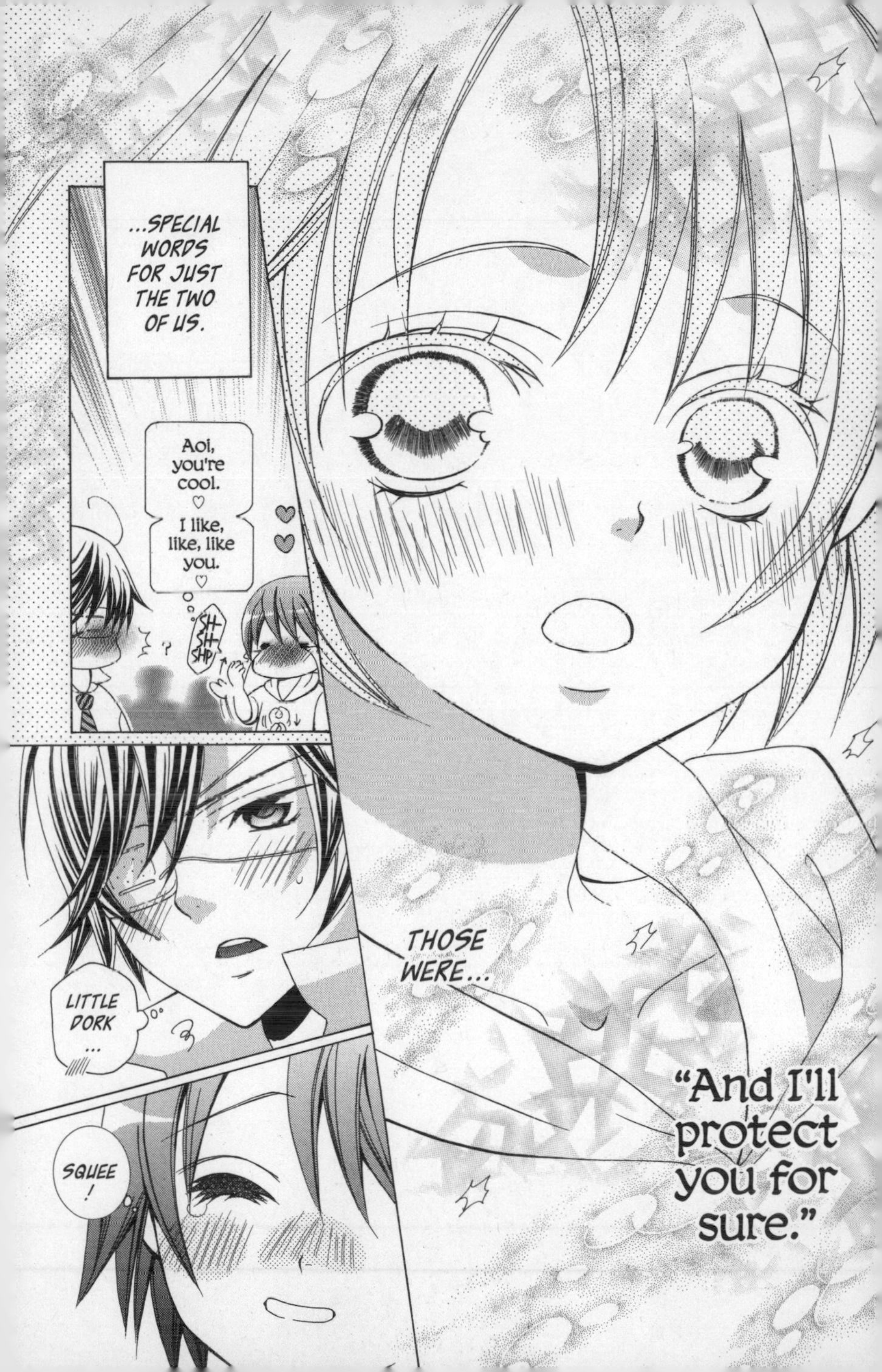
THOSE WERE...
"And I'll protect you for sure."
...SPECIAL WORDS FOR JUST THE TWO OF US.
Aoi, you're cool. ♡ I like, like, like you. ♡
SH SH SHP
LITTLE DORK ...
SQUEE!

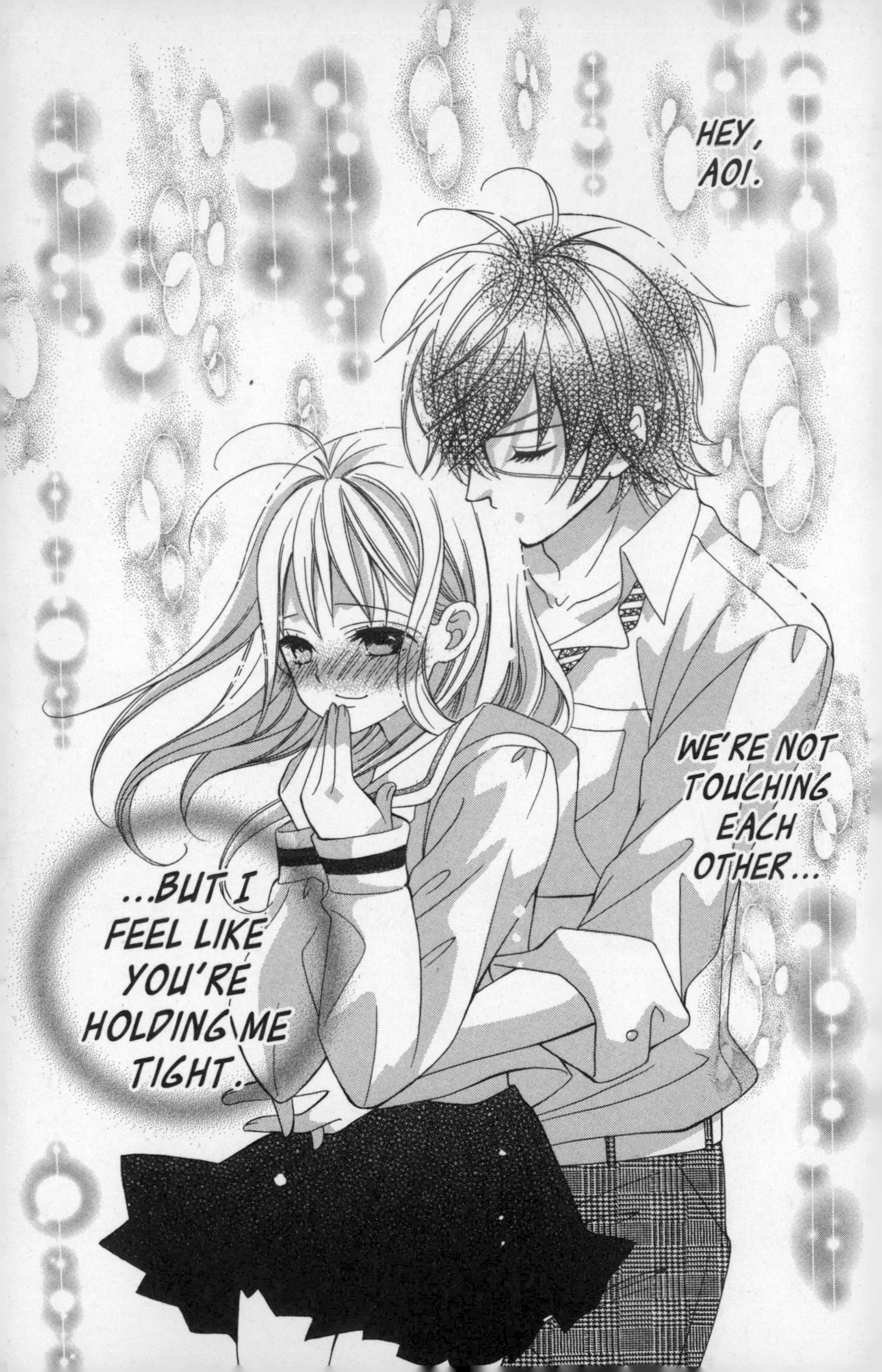
HEY, AOI.
WE'RE NOT TOUCHING EACH OTHER...
...BUT I FEEL LIKE YOU'RE HOLDING ME TIGHT.

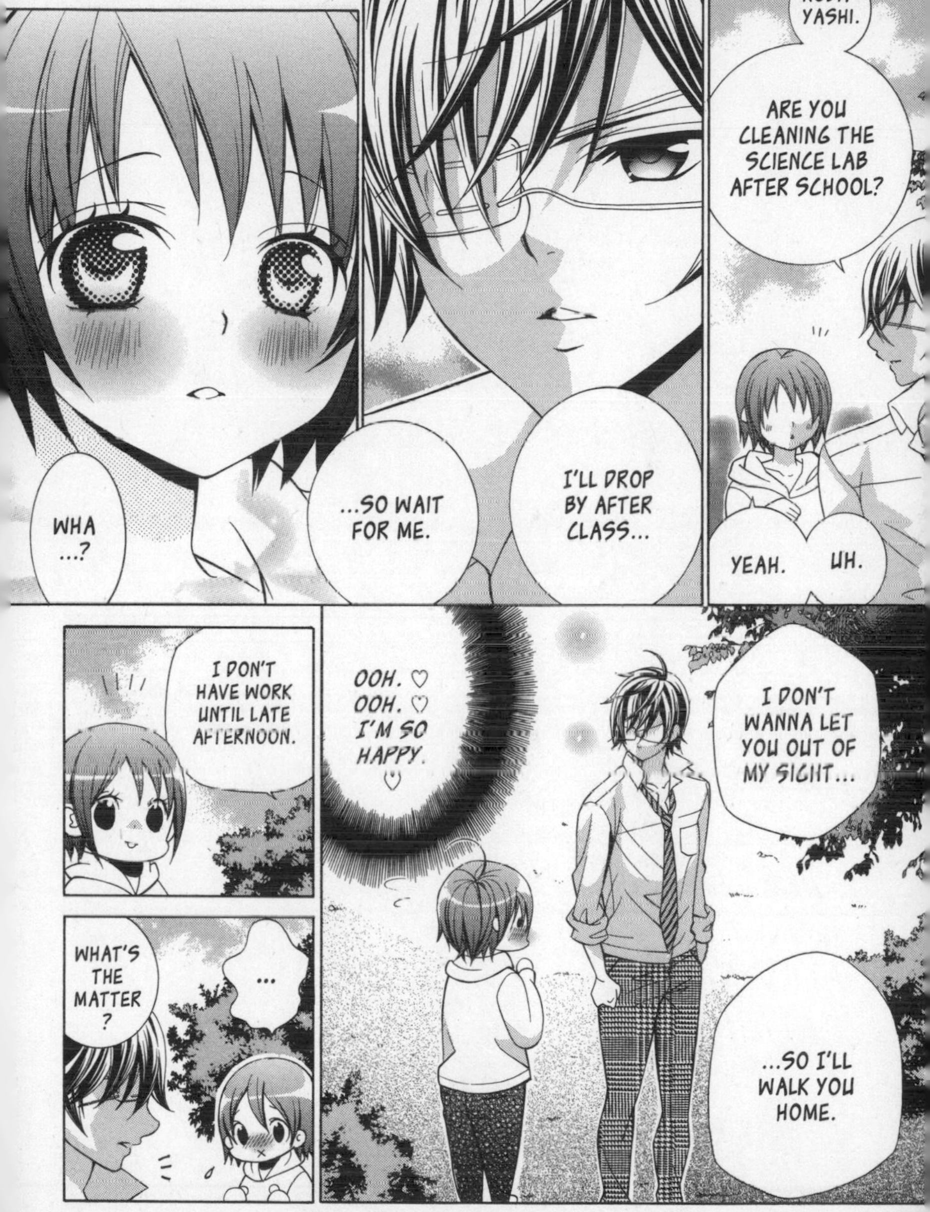
KOBA-YASHI.
ARE YOU CLEANING THE SCIENCE LAB AFTER SCHOOL?
UH.
YEAH.
I'LL DROP BY AFTER CLASS...
...SO WAIT FOR ME.
WHA ...?
I DON'T WANNA LET YOU OUT OF MY SIGHT...
...SO I'LL WALK YOU HOME.
OOH. ♡ OOH. ♡ I'M SO HAPPY.
I DON'T HAVE WORK UNTIL LATE AFTERNOON.
...
WHAT'S THE MATTER ?

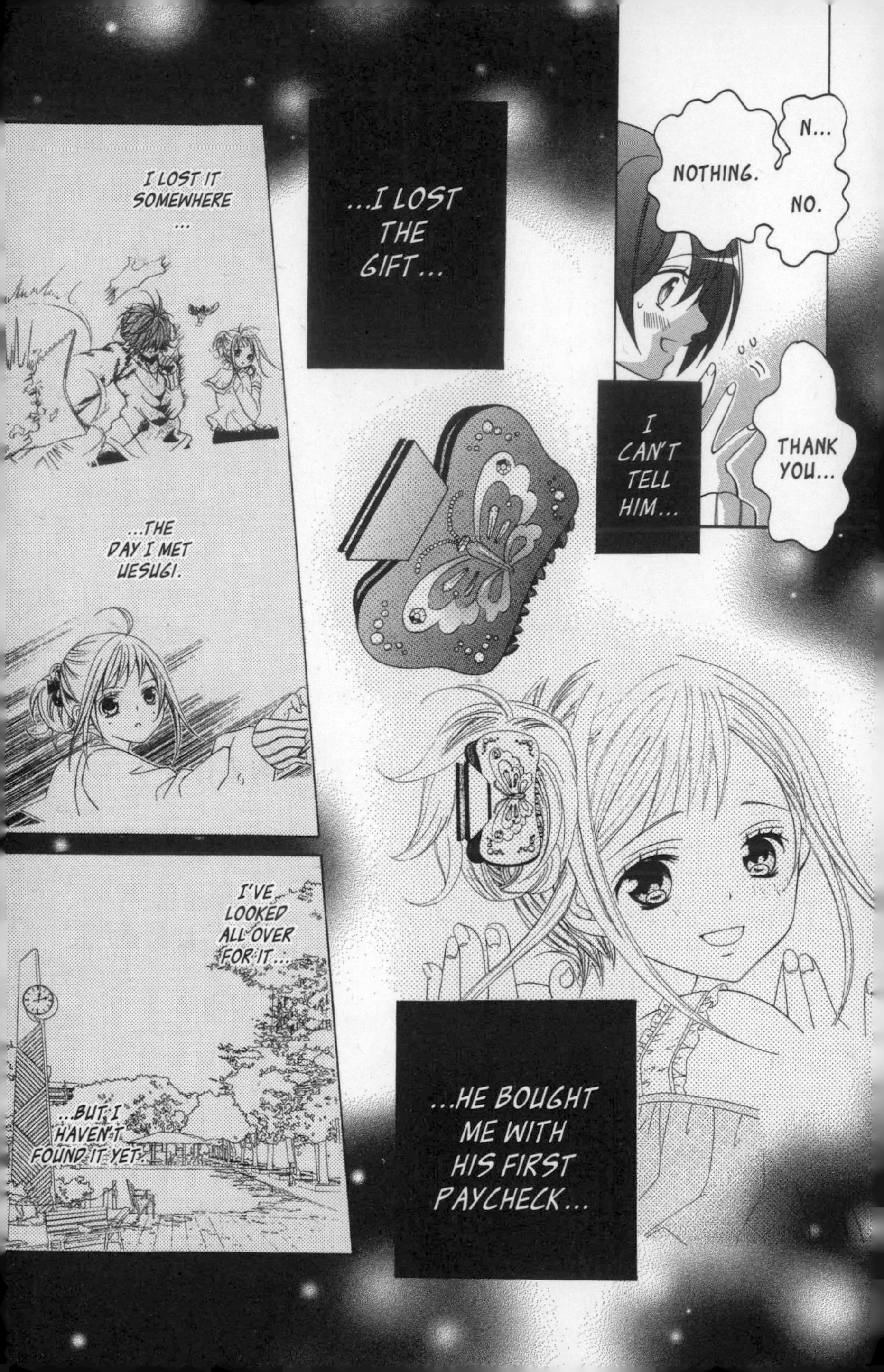
N...
NO.
NOTHING.
THANK YOU...
I CAN'T TELL HIM...
...I LOST THE GIFT...
I LOST IT SOMEWHERE ...
...THE DAY I MET UESUGI.
...HE BOUGHT ME WITH HIS FIRST PAYCHECK...
I'VE LOOKED ALL OVER FOR IT...
...BUT I HAVEN'T FOUND IT YET.

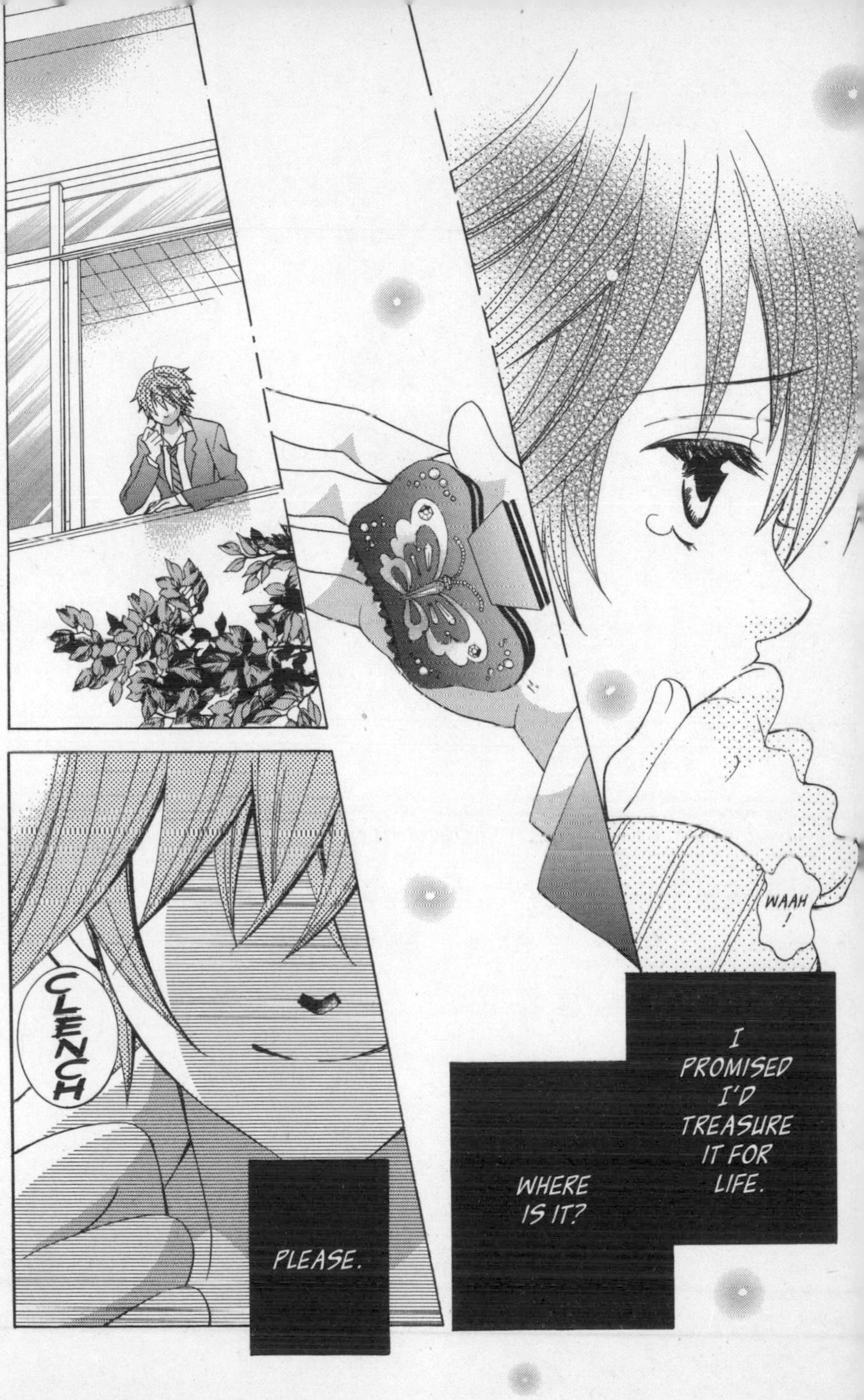
WAAH!
I PROMISED I'D TREASURE IT FOR LIFE.
WHERE IS IT?
CLENCH
PLEASE.

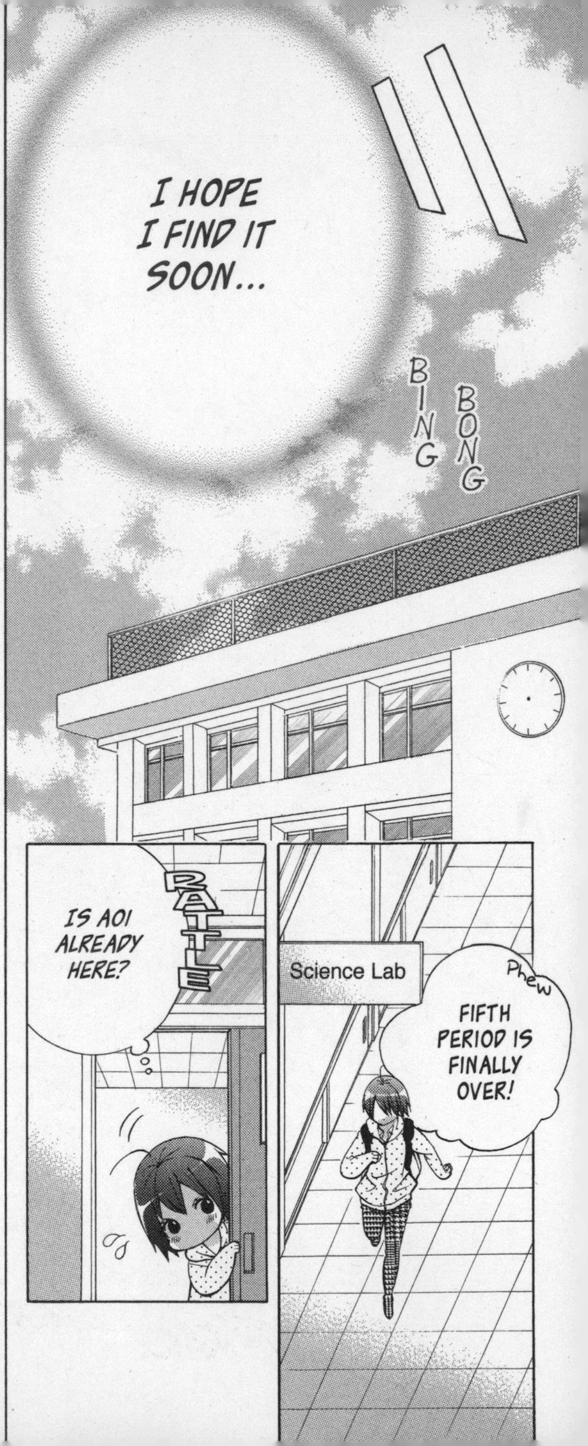
I HOPE I FIND IT SOON...
BING
BONG
Phew
FIFTH PERIOD IS FINALLY OVER!
Science Lab
RATTLE
IS AOI ALREADY HERE?

SPECIAL THANKS

Yuka Ito-sama,
Rieko Hirai-sama,
Kayoko Takahashi-sama,
Yukako Kawasaki-sama,
Nagisa Sato Sensei.

Rei Nanase Sensei,
Arisu Fujishiro Sensei,
Mumi Mimura Sensei,
Masayo Nagata-sama,
Naochan-sama,
Asuka Sakura Sensei and many others.

Bookstore Dan Kinshicho branch, Kinokuniya Shinjuku branch, LIBRO Ikebukuro branch, Kinokuniya Hankyu 32-bangai branch.

Sendai Hachimonjiya Bookstore, Books HOSHINO Kintetsu Pass'e branch, Asahiya Tennnoji MiO branch, Kurashiki Kikuya Bookstore.

Salesperson:
Hata-sama

Previous salesperson:
Honma-sama

Previous editor:
Nakata-sama

Current editor:
Shoji-sama

I also sincerely express my gratitude to everyone who picked up this volume.

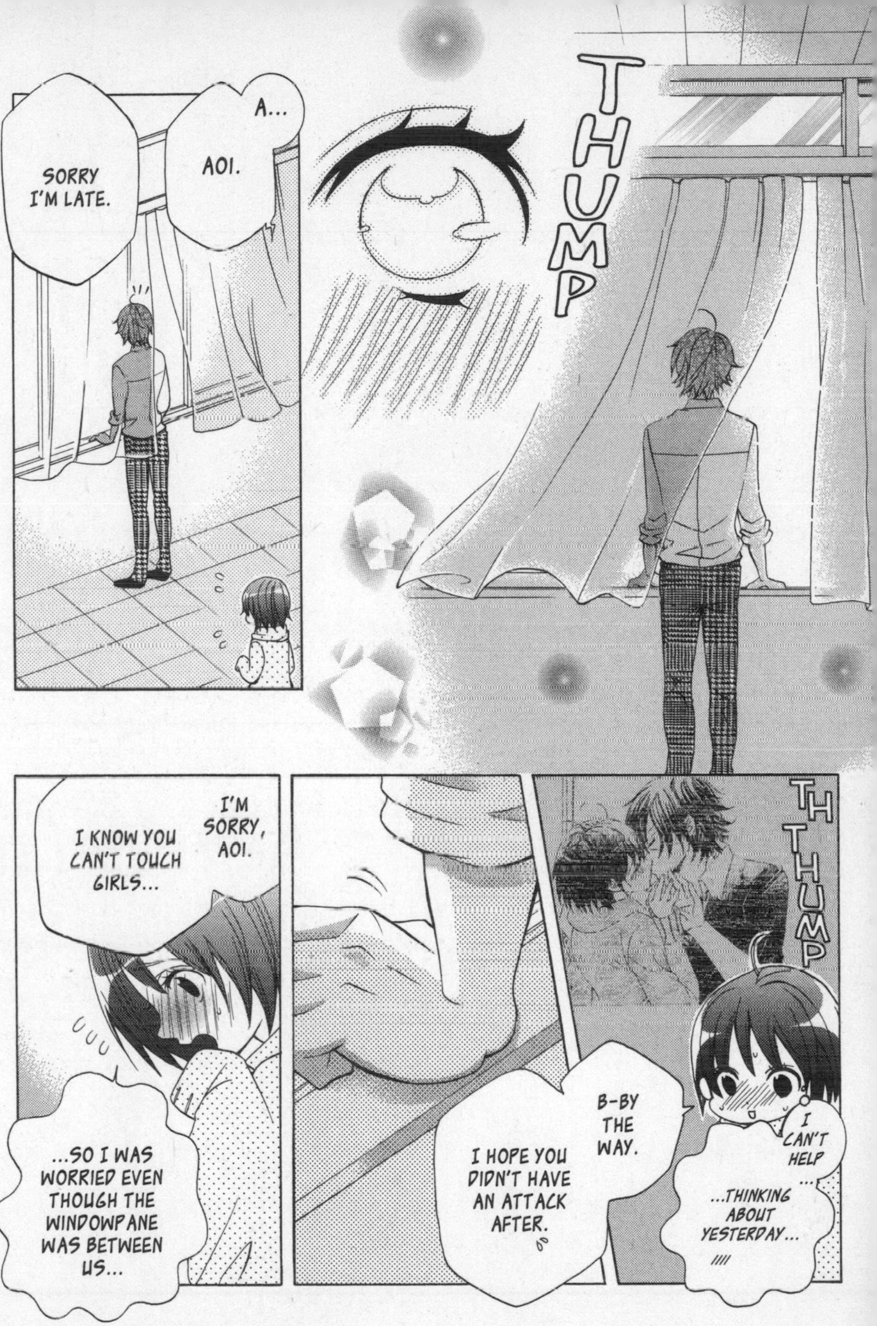
THUMP
A... AOI.
SORRY I'M LATE.
TH THUMP
I CAN'T HELP... ...THINKING ABOUT YESTERDAY...
B-BY THE WAY.
I HOPE YOU DIDN'T HAVE AN ATTACK AFTER.
I'M SORRY, AOI.
I KNOW YOU CAN'T TOUCH GIRLS...
...SO I WAS WORRIED EVEN THOUGH THE WINDOWPANE WAS BETWEEN US...

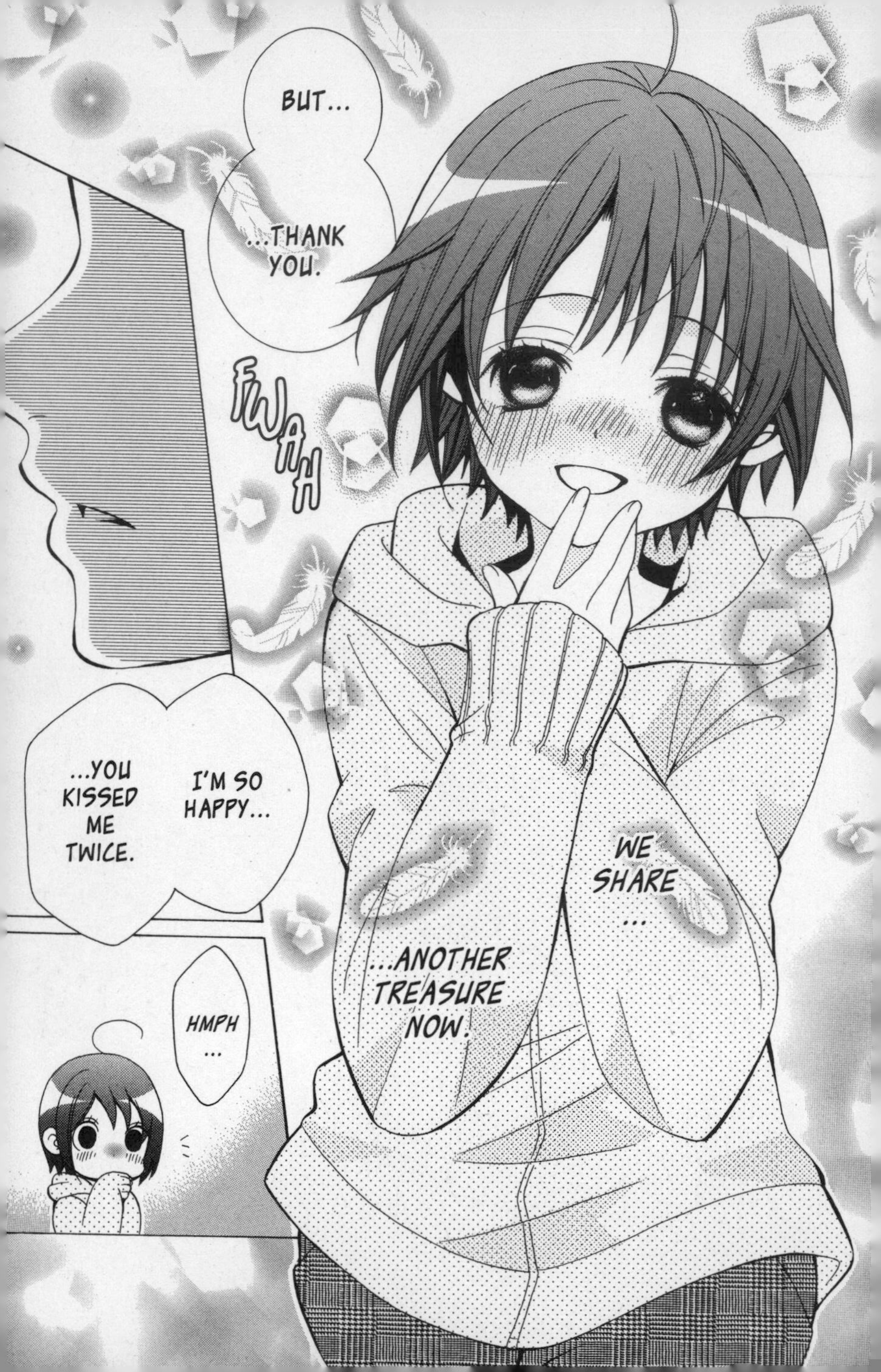
BUT...
...THANK YOU.
FWAH
I'M SO HAPPY...
...YOU KISSED ME TWICE.
WE SHARE...
...ANOTHER TREASURE NOW.
HMPH...

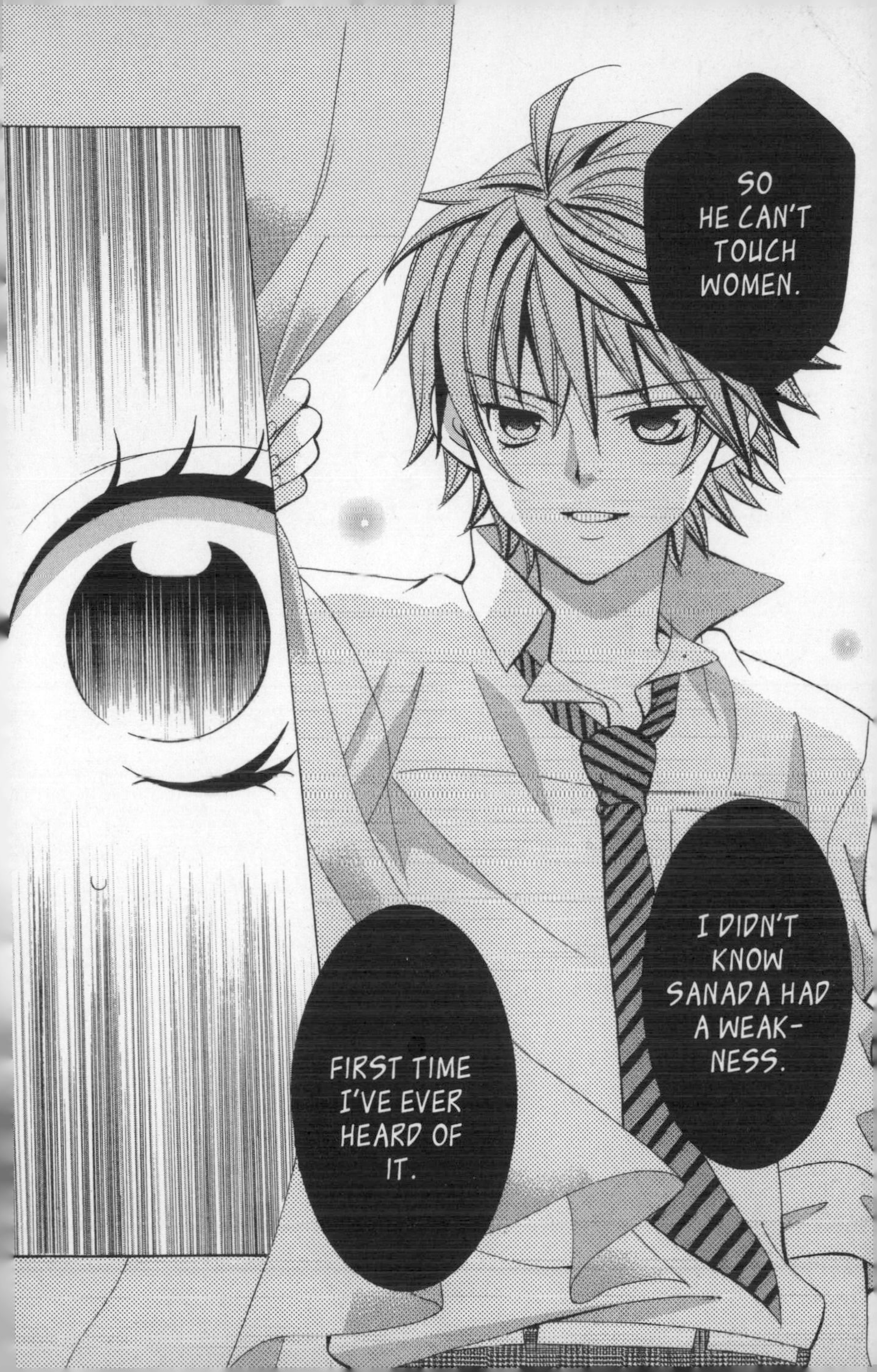
SO HE CAN'T TOUCH WOMEN.
I DIDN'T KNOW SANADA HAD A WEAK-NESS.
FIRST TIME I'VE EVER HEARD OF IT.

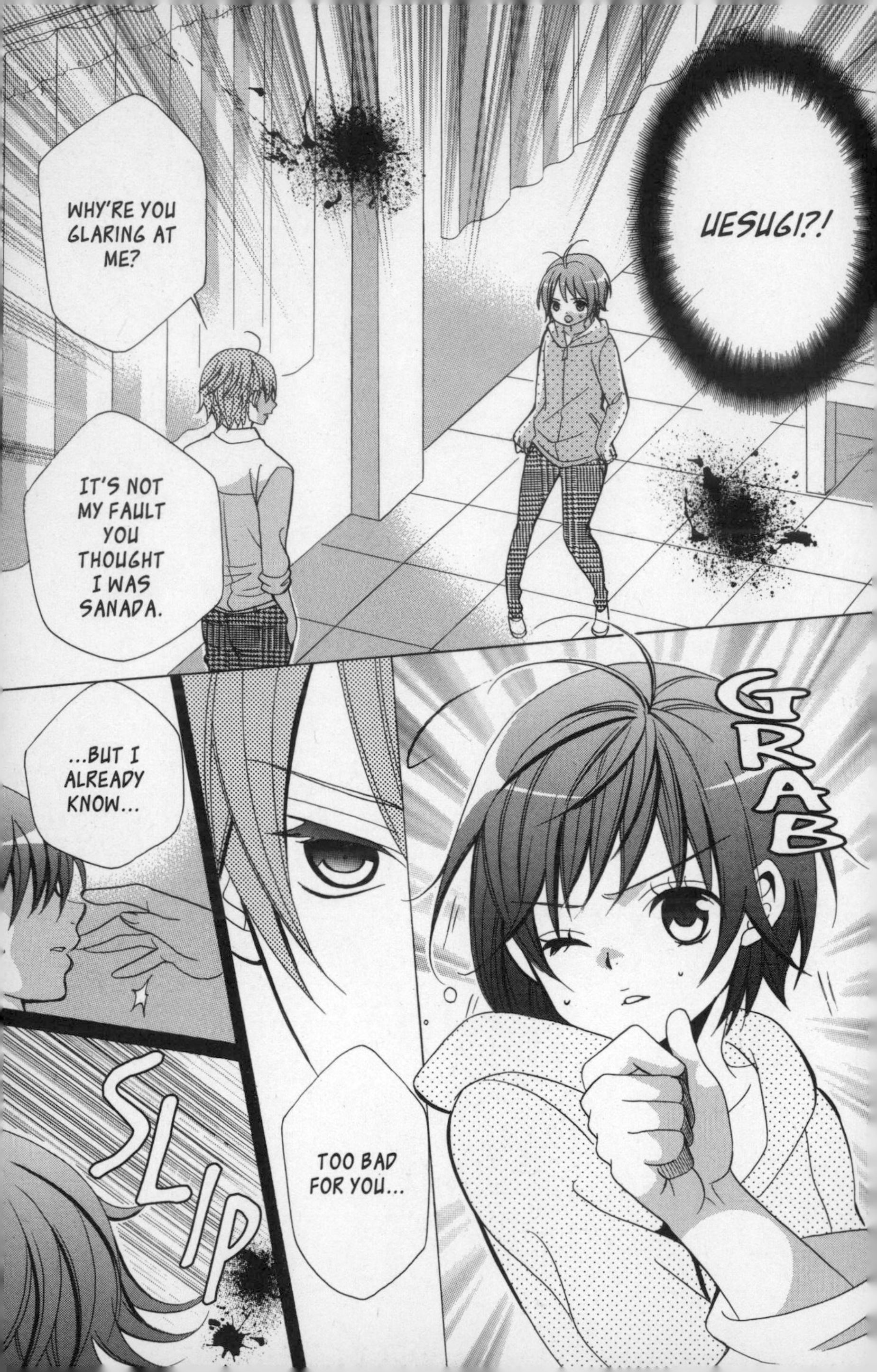
UESUGI?!
WHY'RE YOU GLARING AT ME?
IT'S NOT MY FAULT YOU THOUGHT I WAS SANADA.
GRAB
TOO BAD FOR YOU...
...BUT I ALREADY KNOW...
SLIP

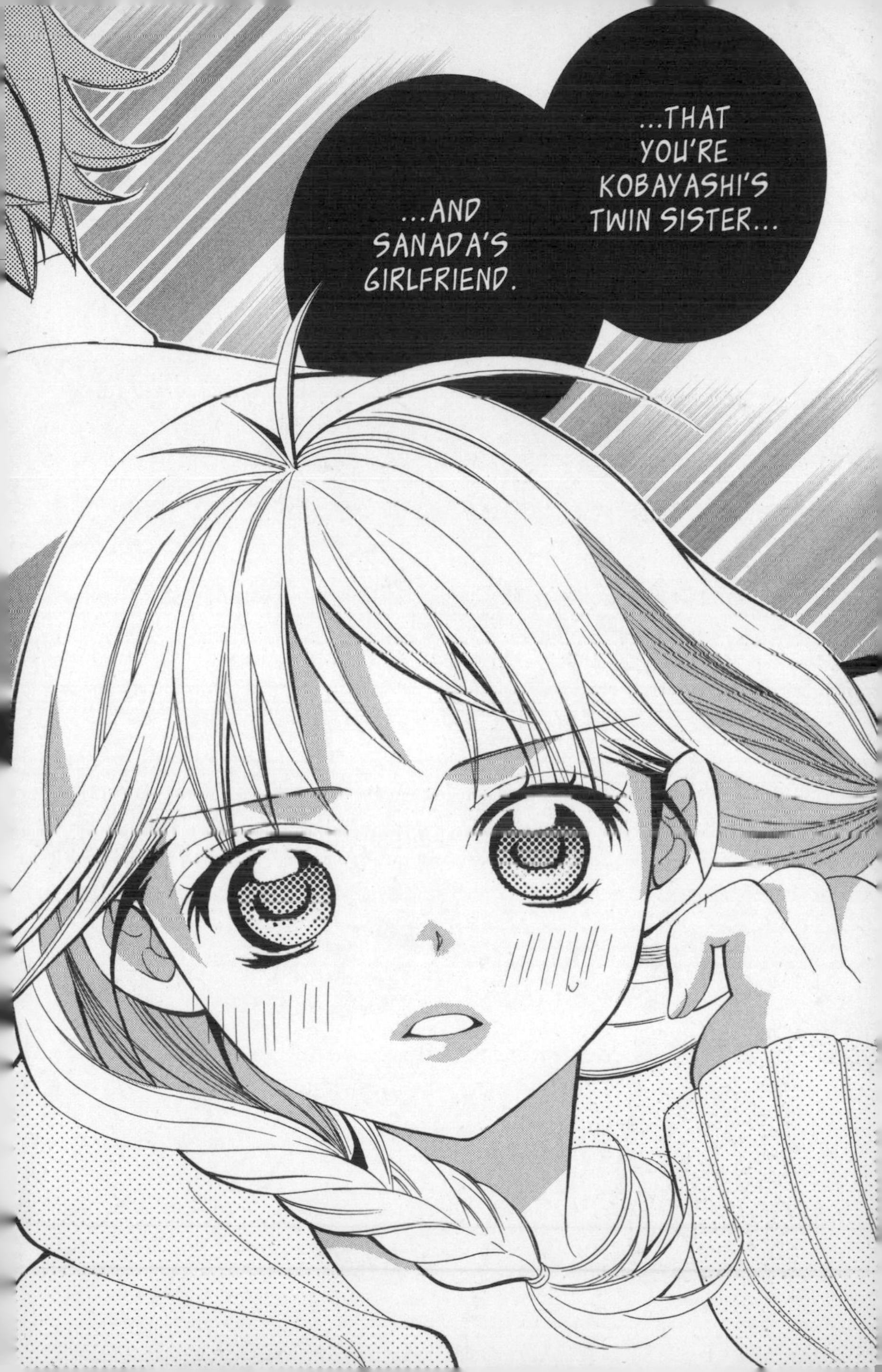
...THAT YOU'RE KOBAYASHI'S TWIN SISTER...
...AND SANADA'S GIRLFRIEND.

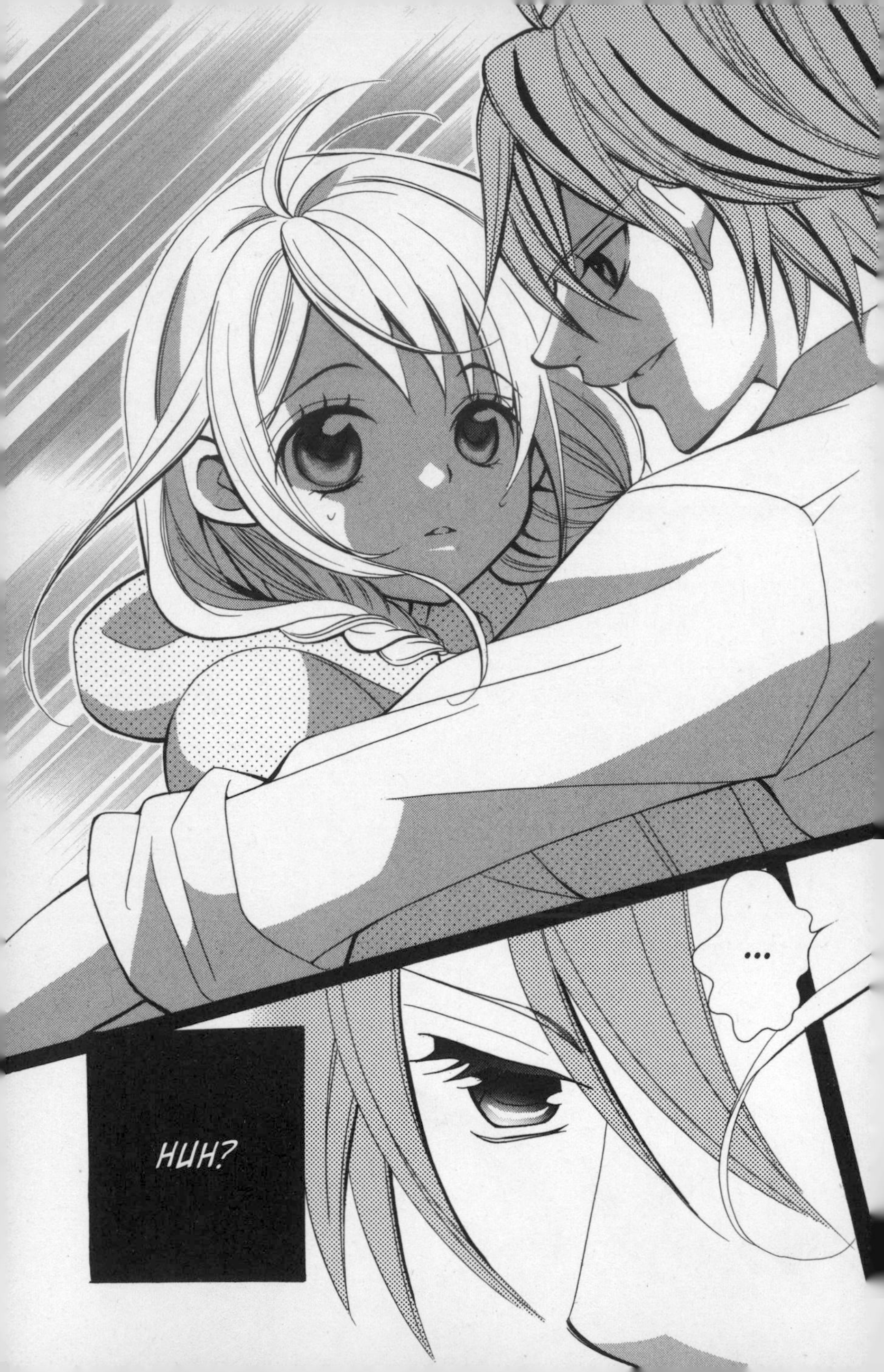
...
HUH?

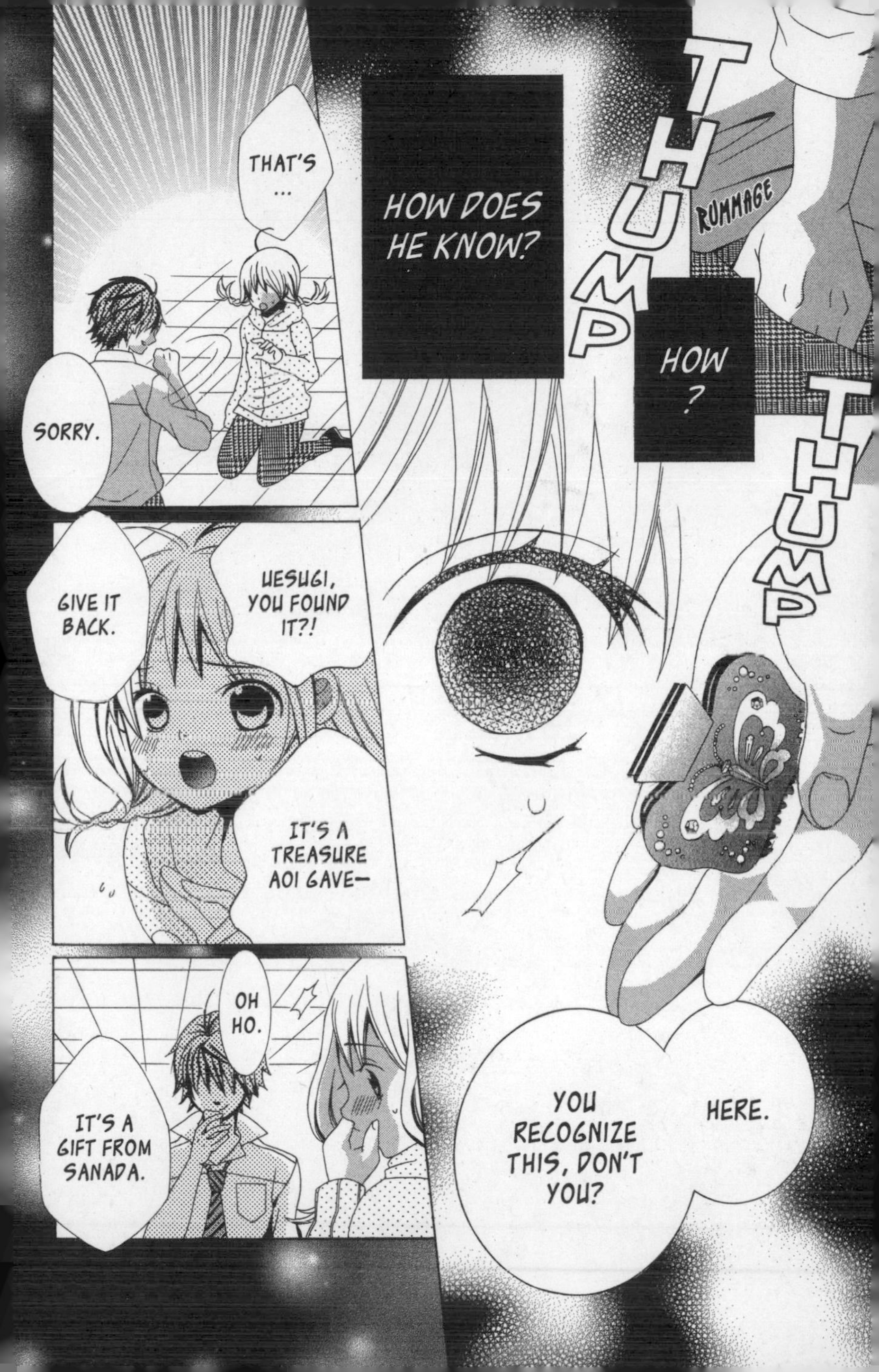
THUMP
RUMMAGE
HOW DOES HE KNOW?
HOW ?
THUMP
HERE.
YOU RECOGNIZE THIS, DON'T YOU?
THAT'S ...
SORRY.
UESUGI, YOU FOUND IT?!
GIVE IT BACK.
IT'S A TREASURE AOI GAVE—
OH HO.
IT'S A GIFT FROM SANADA.

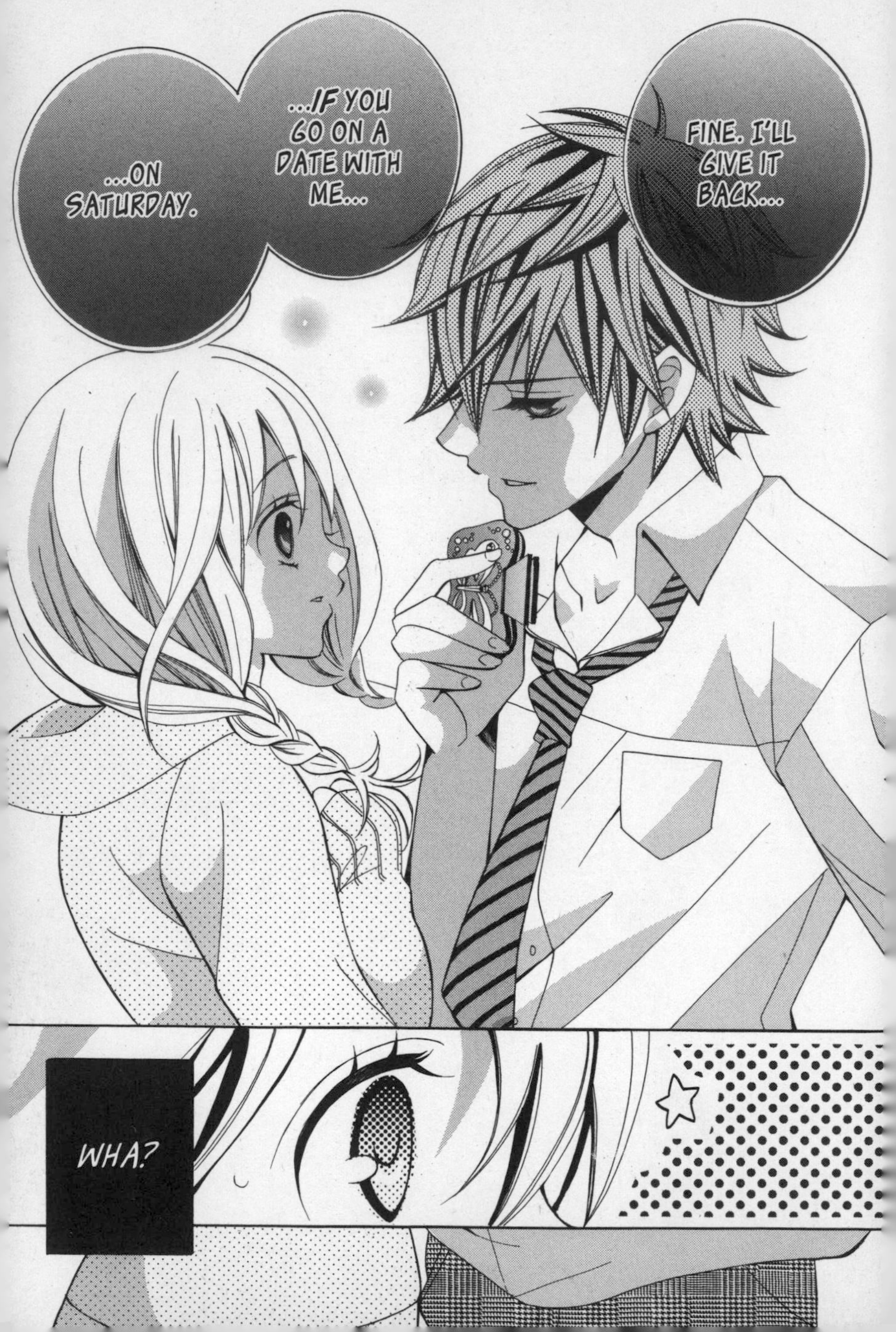
FINE. I'LL GIVE IT BACK...
...IF YOU GO ON A DATE WITH ME...
...ON SATURDAY.
WHA?

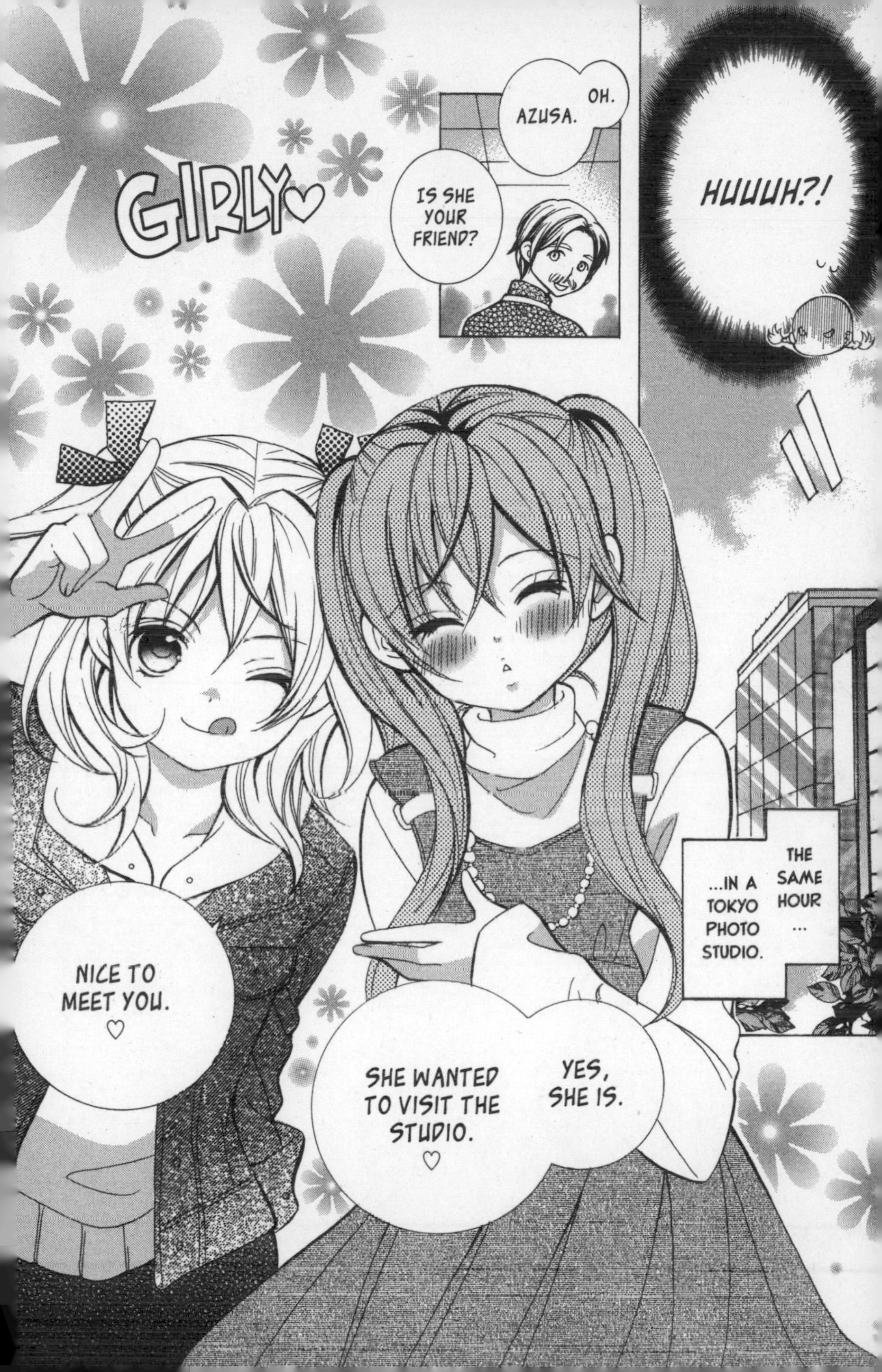
HUUUH?!
THE SAME HOUR ...
...IN A TOKYO PHOTO STUDIO.
OH. AZUSA.
IS SHE YOUR FRIEND?
YES, SHE IS.
SHE WANTED TO VISIT THE STUDIO. ♡
NICE TO MEET YOU. ♡
GIRLY♡

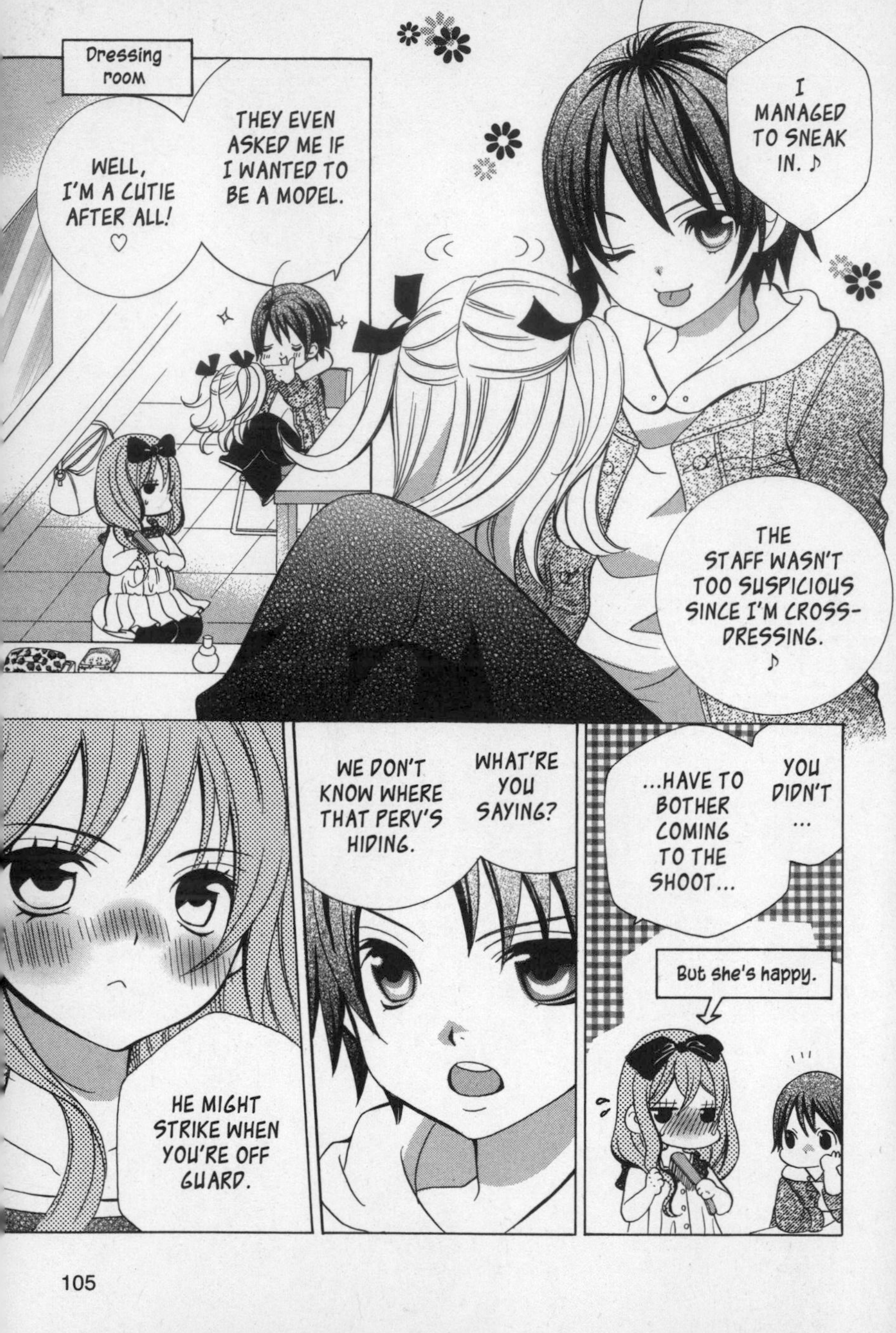
Dressing room
I MANAGED TO SNEAK IN. ♪
THE STAFF WASN'T TOO SUSPICIOUS SINCE I'M CROSS-DRESSING. ♪
THEY EVEN ASKED ME IF I WANTED TO BE A MODEL.
WELL, I'M A CUTIE AFTER ALL! ♡
YOU DIDN'T ...
...HAVE TO BOTHER COMING TO THE SHOOT...
But she's happy.
WHAT'RE YOU SAYING?
WE DON'T KNOW WHERE THAT PERV'S HIDING.
HE MIGHT STRIKE WHEN YOU'RE OFF GUARD.

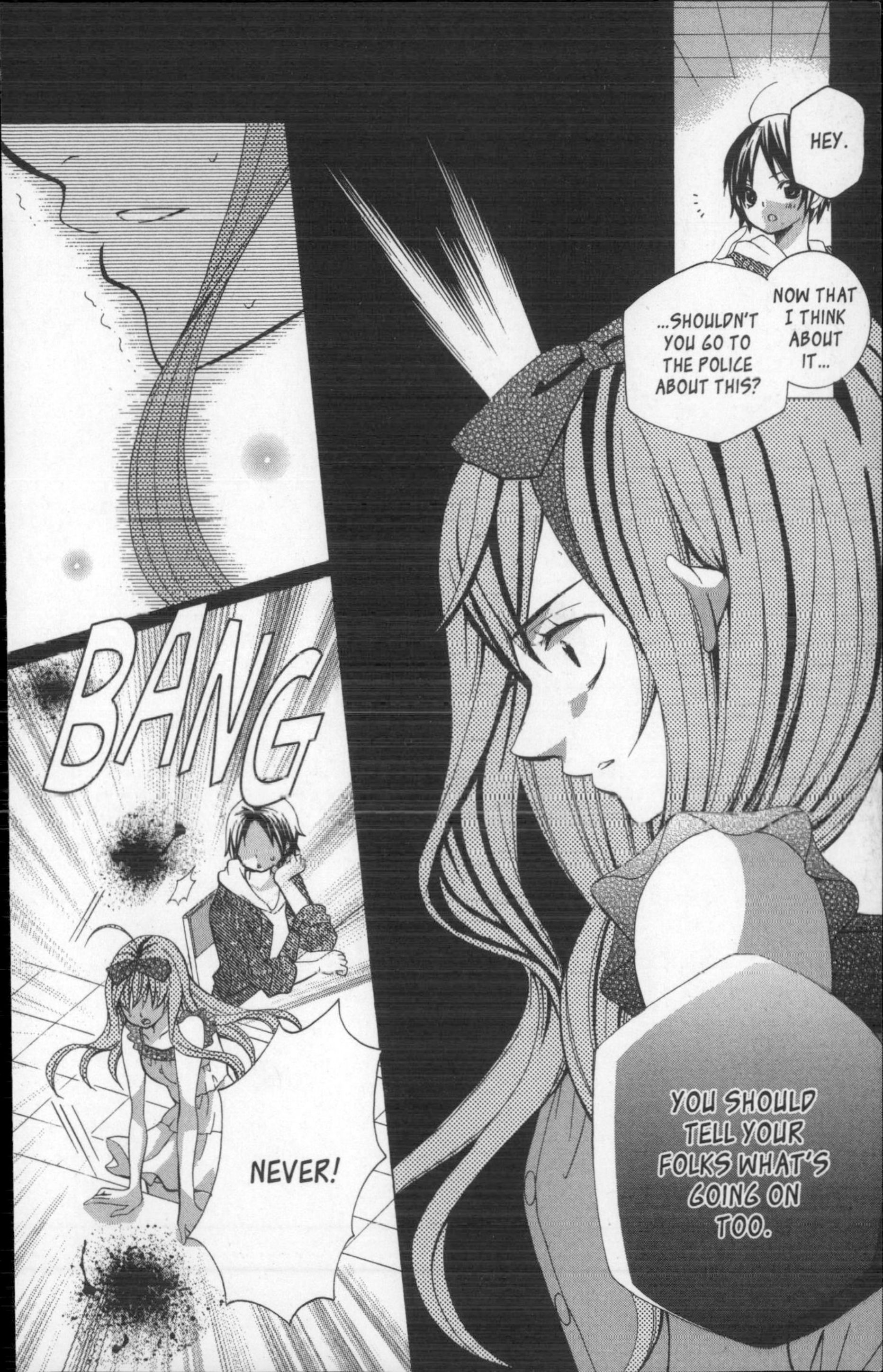
HEY.
NOW THAT I THINK ABOUT IT...
...SHOULDN'T YOU GO TO THE POLICE ABOUT THIS?
YOU SHOULD TELL YOUR FOLKS WHAT'S GOING ON TOO.
BANG
NEVER!

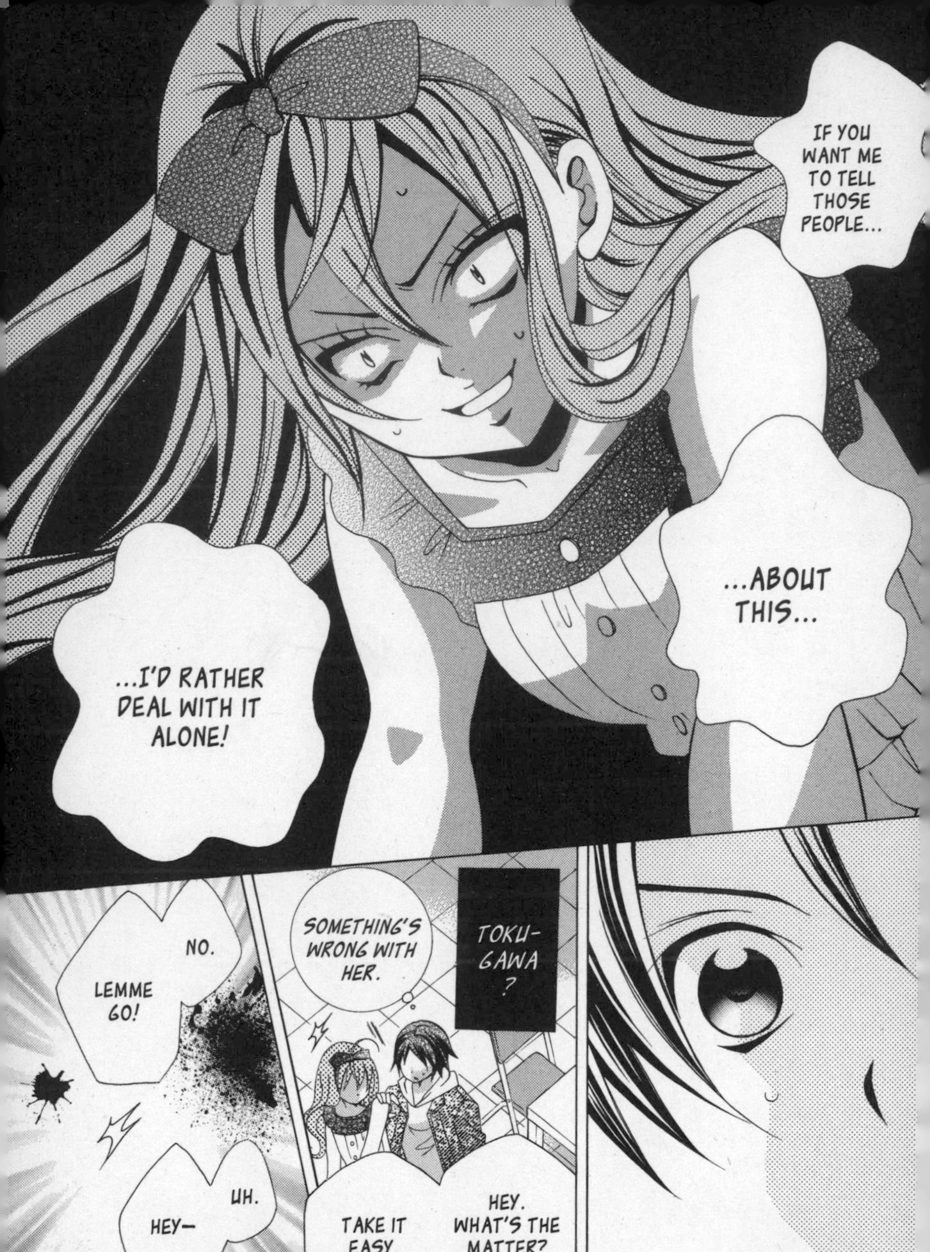
IF YOU WANT ME TO TELL THOSE PEOPLE...
...ABOUT THIS...
...I'D RATHER DEAL WITH IT ALONE!
TOKU-GAWA?
SOMETHING'S WRONG WITH HER.
HEY. WHAT'S THE MATTER?
TAKE IT EASY.
NO.
LEMME GO!
UH.
HEY—

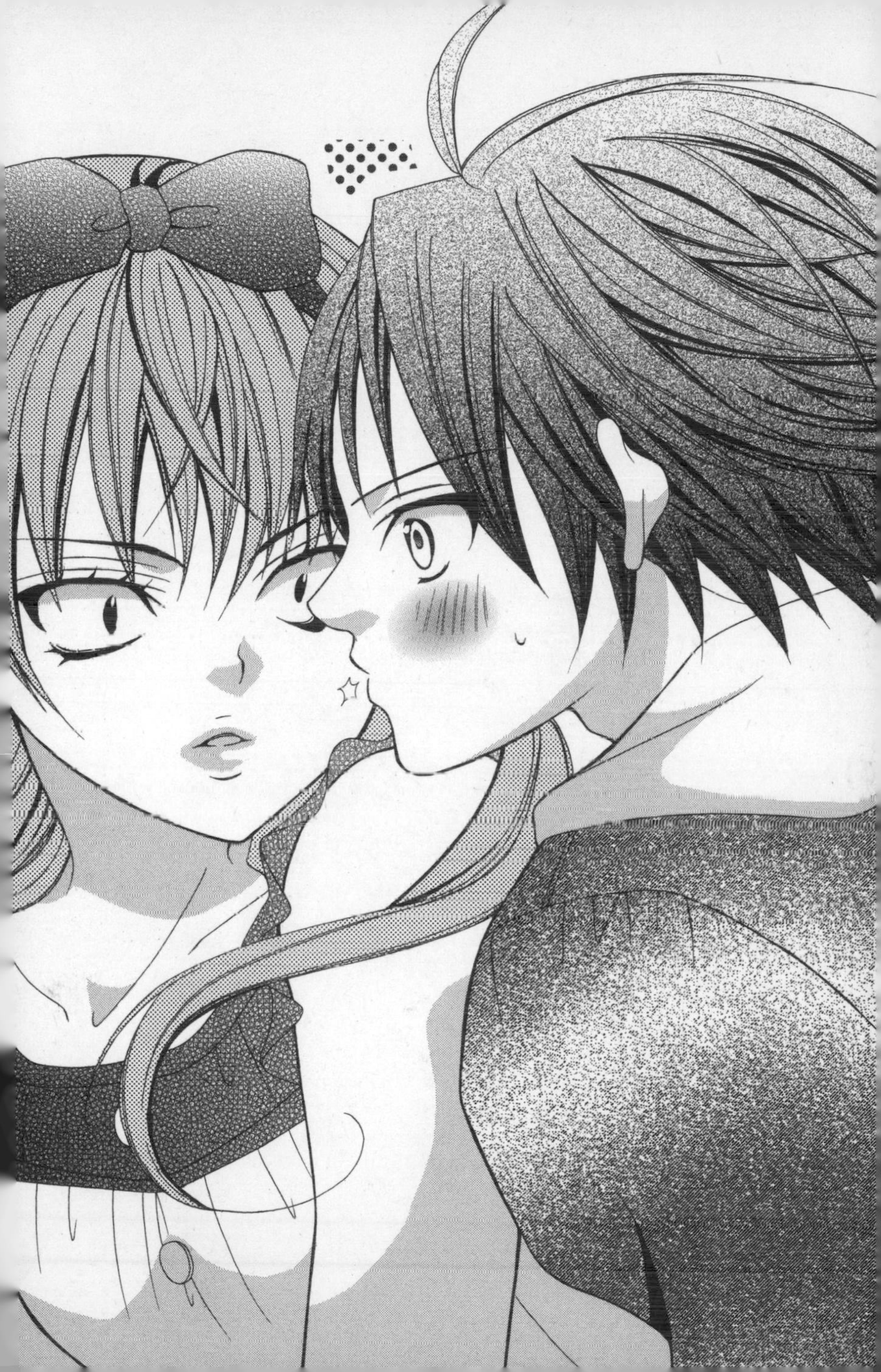

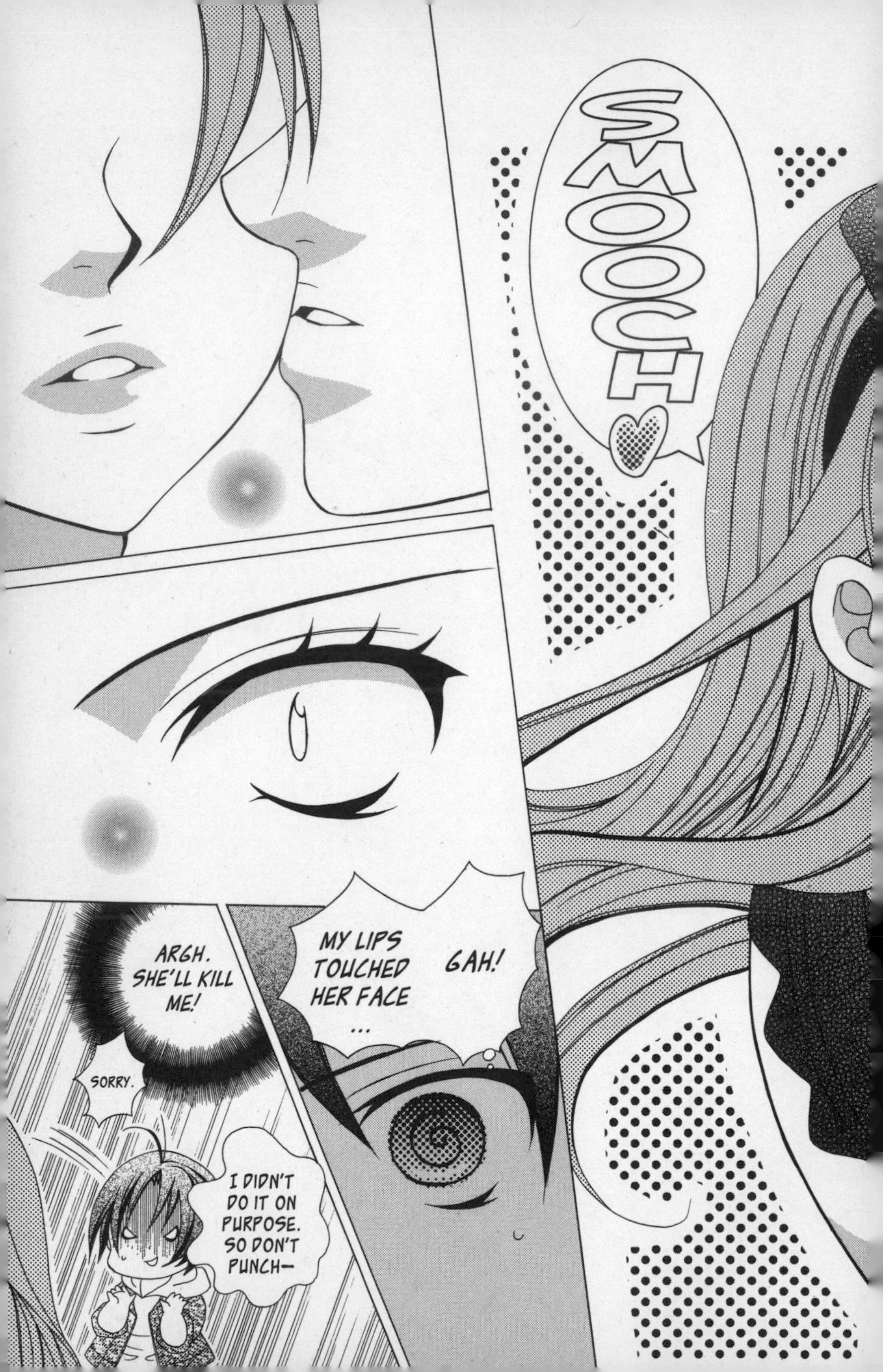
SMOOCH
GAH!
MY LIPS TOUCHED HER FACE ...
ARGH. SHE'LL KILL ME!
SORRY.
I DIDN'T DO IT ON PURPOSE. SO DON'T PUNCH—

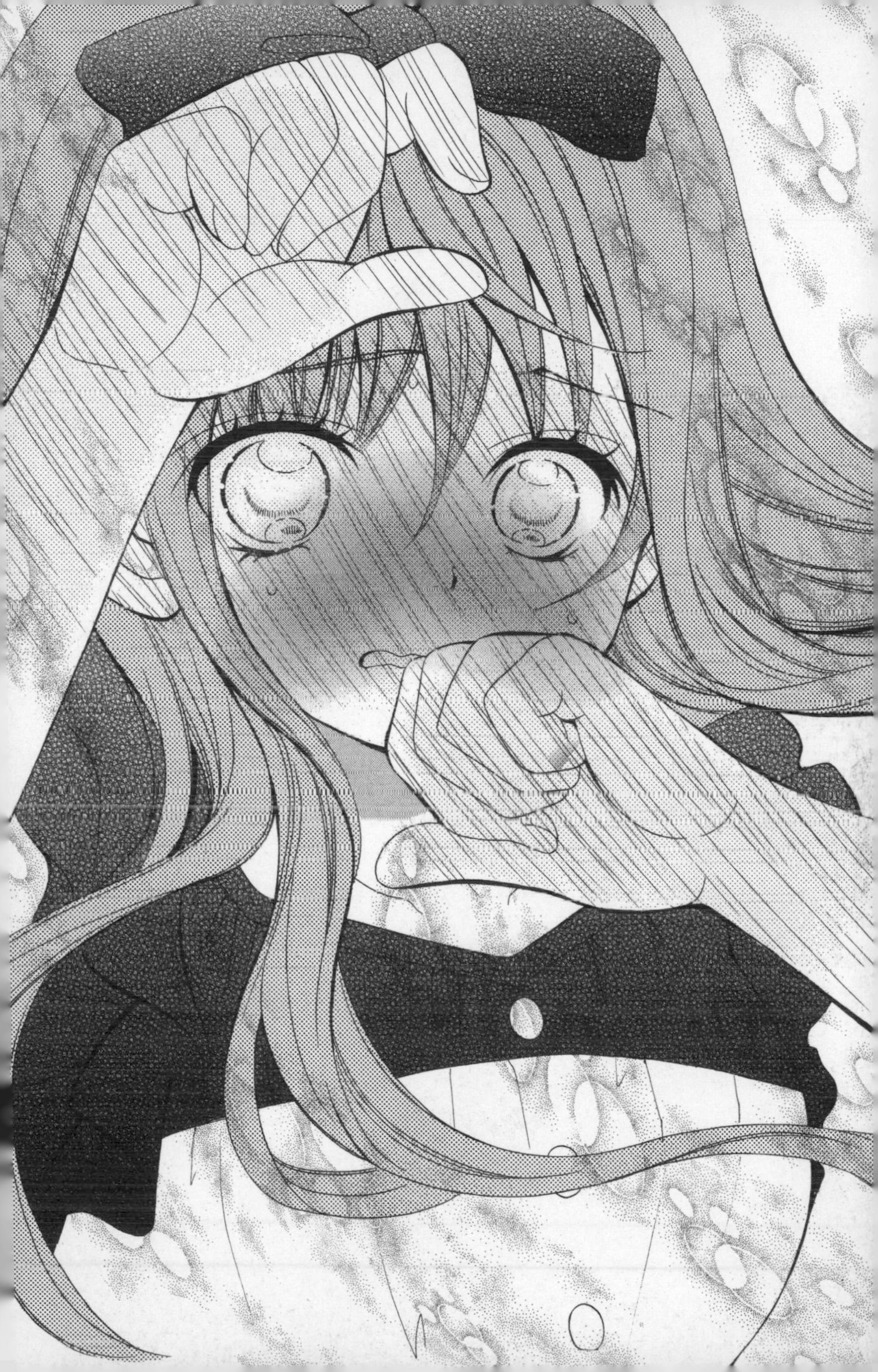

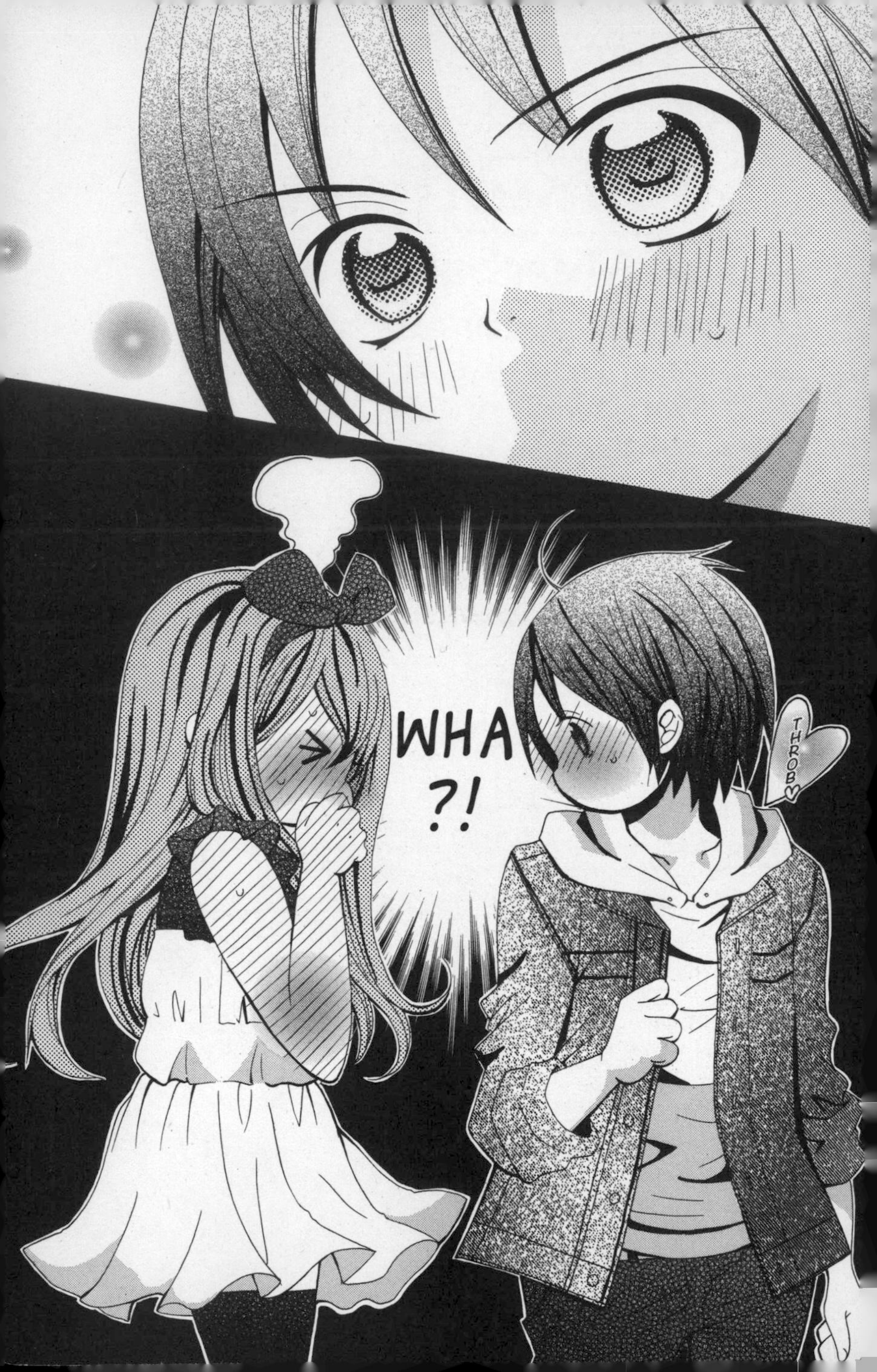
THROB♥
WHA ?!

The number one summer event!

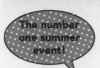

Summer Festival 2014

Summer Festival Merchandise!

This *So Cute!* merchandise was made for the Summer Festival, a big annual event! Every item is so cute it hurts!! ♪

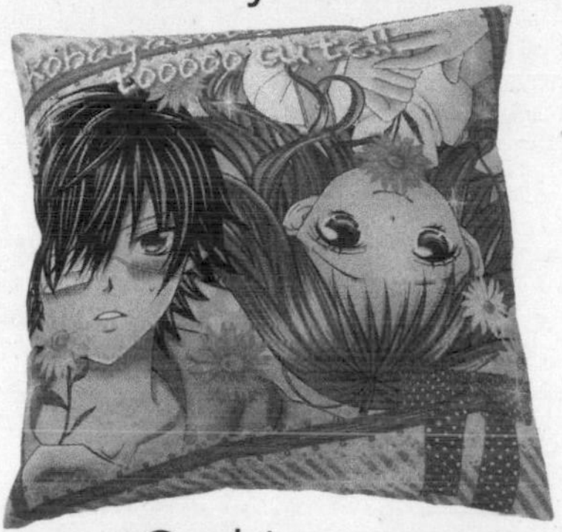

Cushion

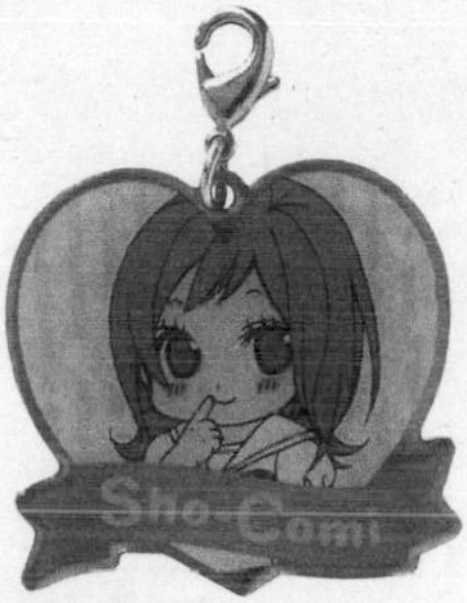
Sho-Comi

Love charm

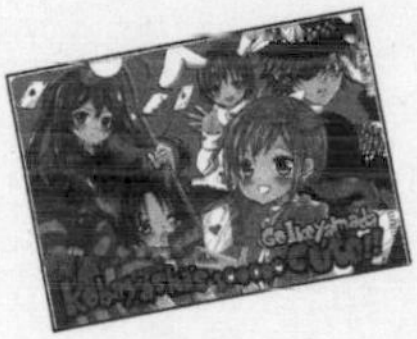

Folder

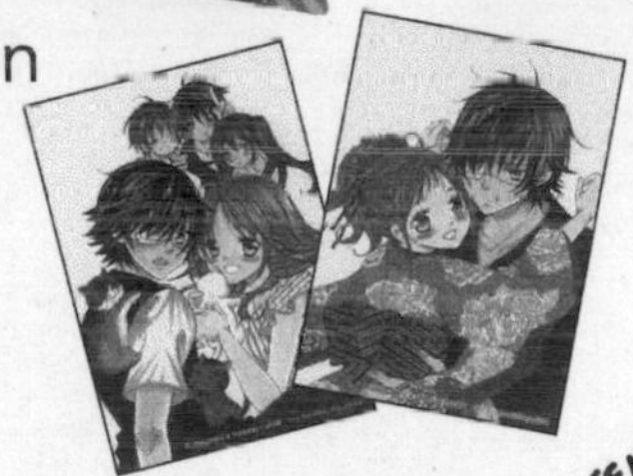

Photo cards

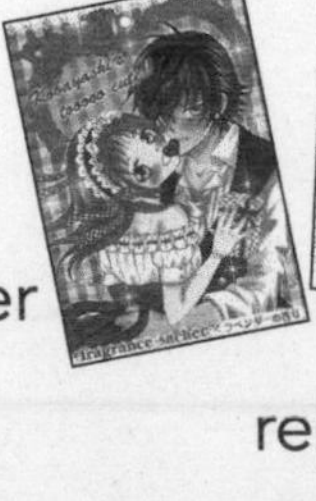

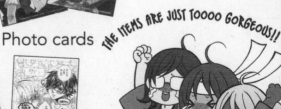

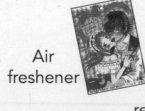

Air freshener

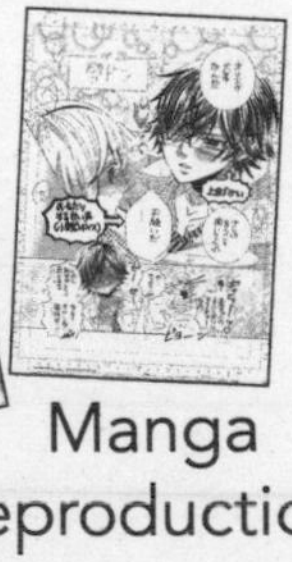

Manga reproduction

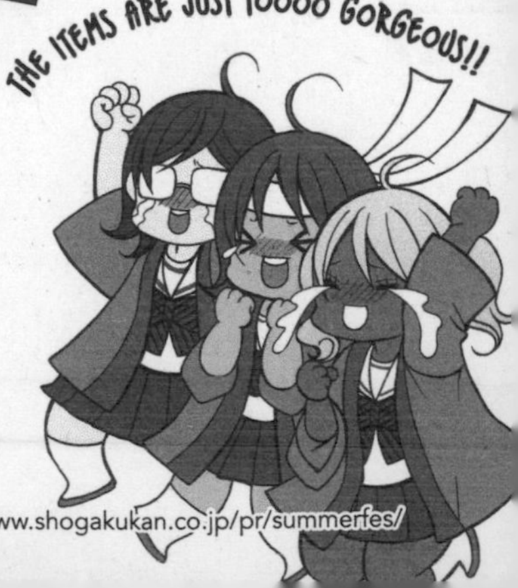
THE ITEMS ARE JUST TOOOO GORGEOUS!!

Details about the Summer Festival→ http://www.shogakukan.co.jp/pr/summerfes/

Chapter 34

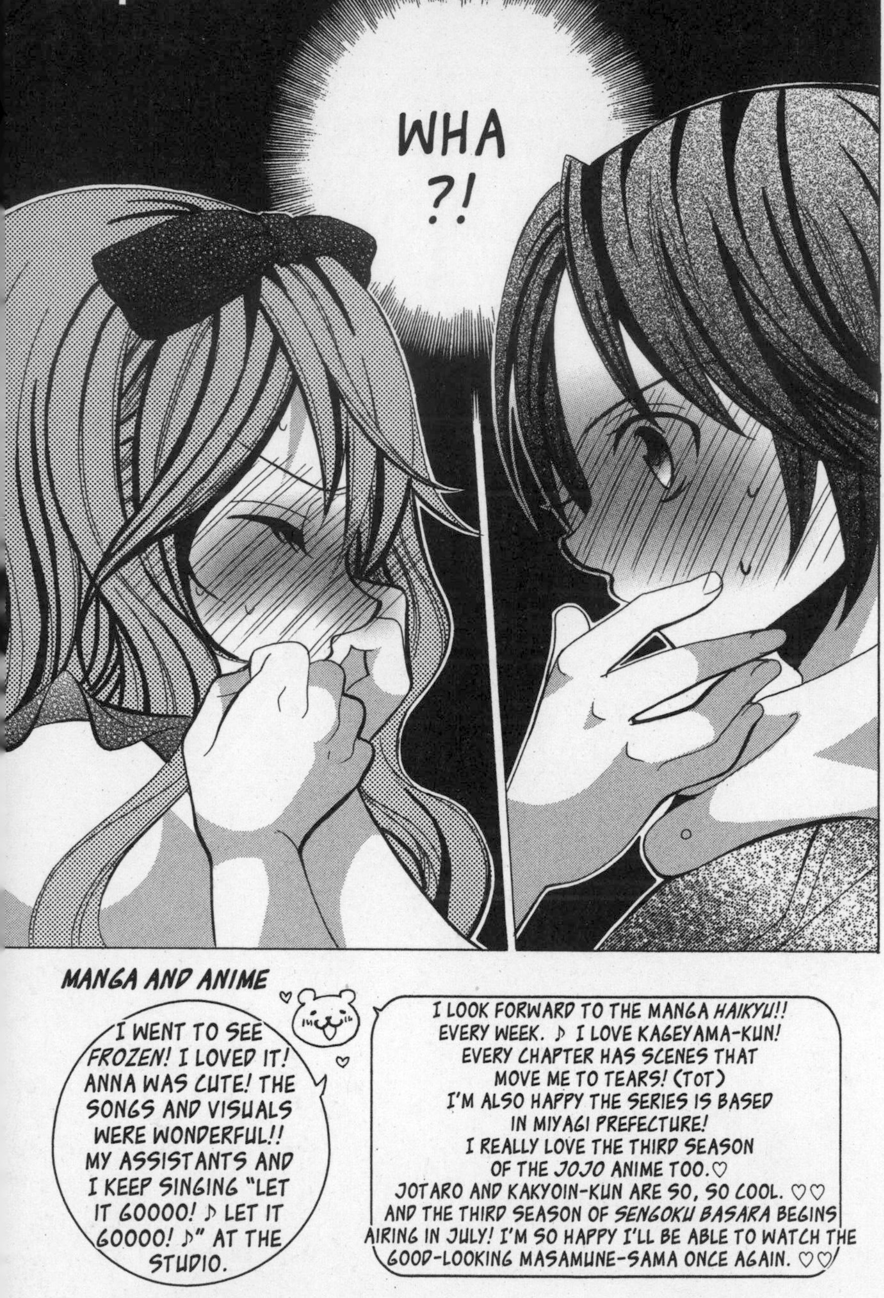
WHA ?!

MANGA AND ANIME

I WENT TO SEE *FROZEN*! I LOVED IT! ANNA WAS CUTE! THE SONGS AND VISUALS WERE WONDERFUL!! MY ASSISTANTS AND I KEEP SINGING "LET IT GOOOO! ♪ LET IT GOOOO! ♪" AT THE STUDIO.

I LOOK FORWARD TO THE MANGA *HAIKYU!!* EVERY WEEK. ♪ I LOVE KAGEYAMA-KUN! EVERY CHAPTER HAS SCENES THAT MOVE ME TO TEARS! (TOT) I'M ALSO HAPPY THE SERIES IS BASED IN MIYAGI PREFECTURE! I REALLY LOVE THE THIRD SEASON OF THE *JOJO* ANIME TOO.♡ JOTARO AND KAKYOIN-KUN ARE SO, SO COOL. ♡♡ AND THE THIRD SEASON OF *SENGOKU BASARA* BEGINS AIRING IN JULY! I'M SO HAPPY I'LL BE ABLE TO WATCH THE GOOD-LOOKING MASAMUNE-SAMA ONCE AGAIN. ♡♡

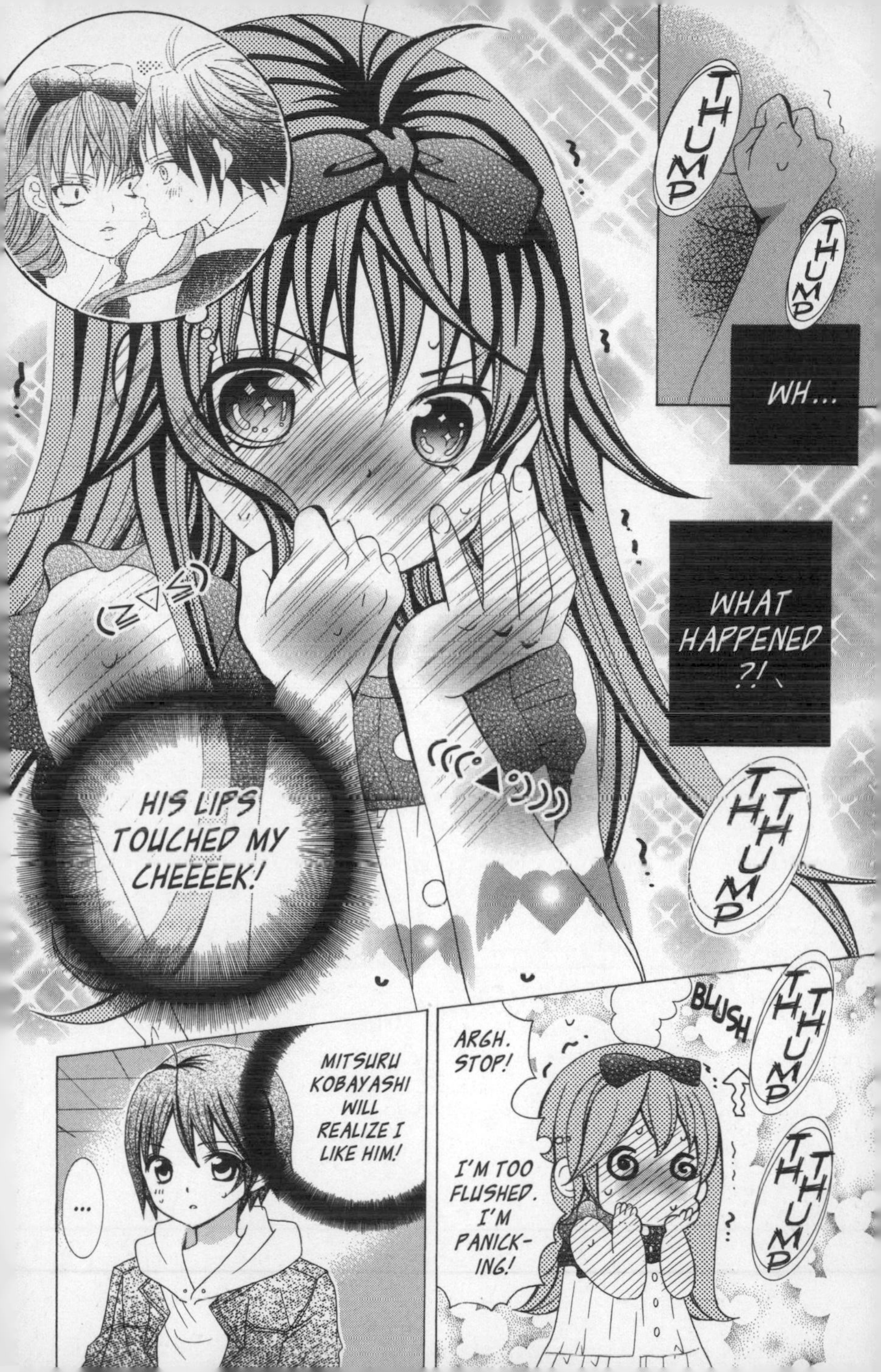
THUMP
THUMP
WH...
WHAT HAPPENED?!
THUMP THUMP
HIS LIPS TOUCHED MY CHEEEEK!
BLUSH
THUMP THUMP
ARGH. STOP!
I'M TOO FLUSHED. I'M PANICK-ING!
THUMP THUMP
MITSURU KOBAYASHI WILL REALIZE I LIKE HIM!
...

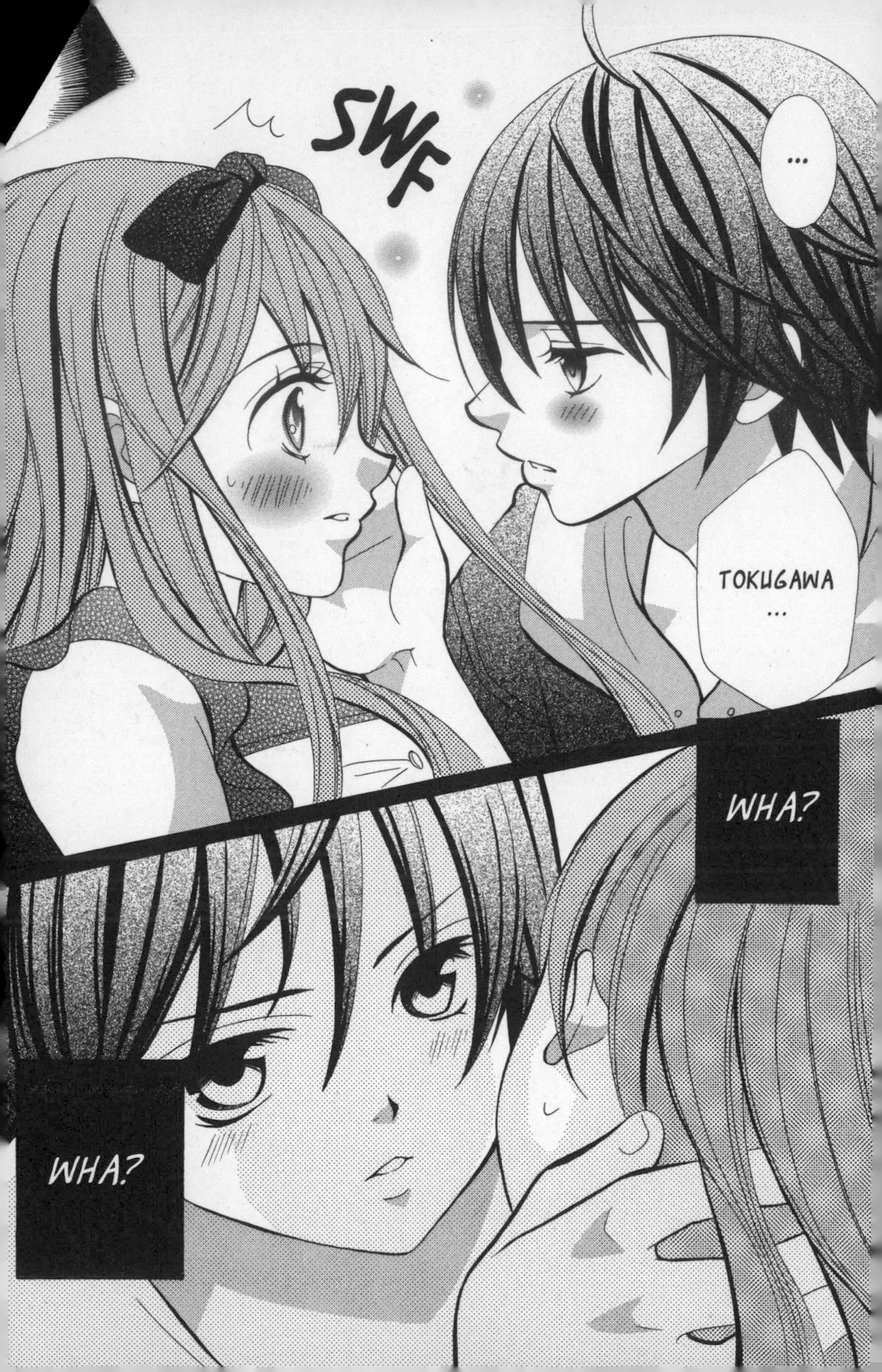
...
SWF
TOKUGAWA ...
WHA?
WHA?

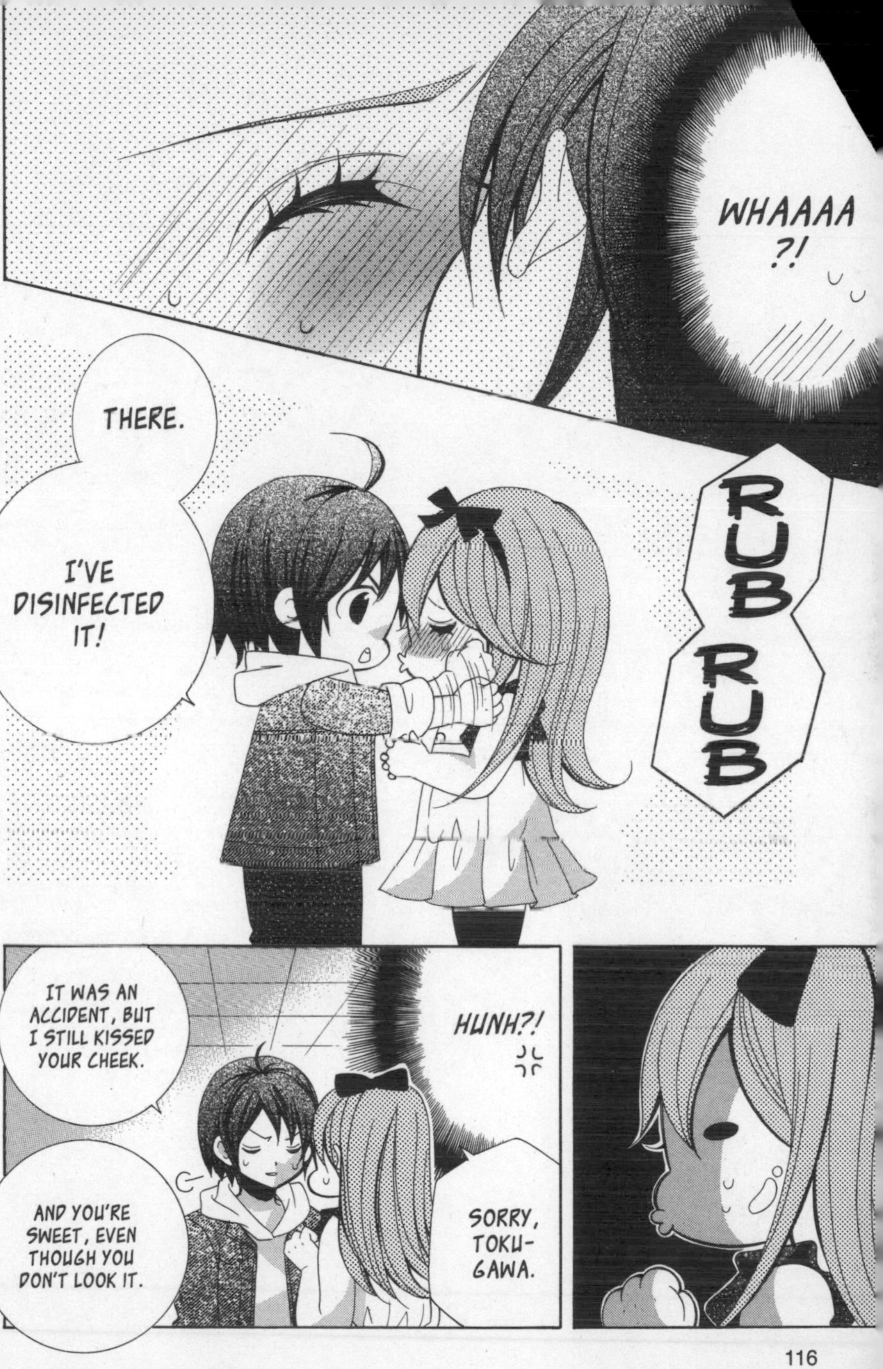
WHAAAA ?!
RUB RUB
THERE.
I'VE DISINFECTED IT!
HUNH?!
IT WAS AN ACCIDENT, BUT I STILL KISSED YOUR CHEEK.
SORRY, TOKU-GAWA.
AND YOU'RE SWEET, EVEN THOUGH YOU DON'T LOOK IT.

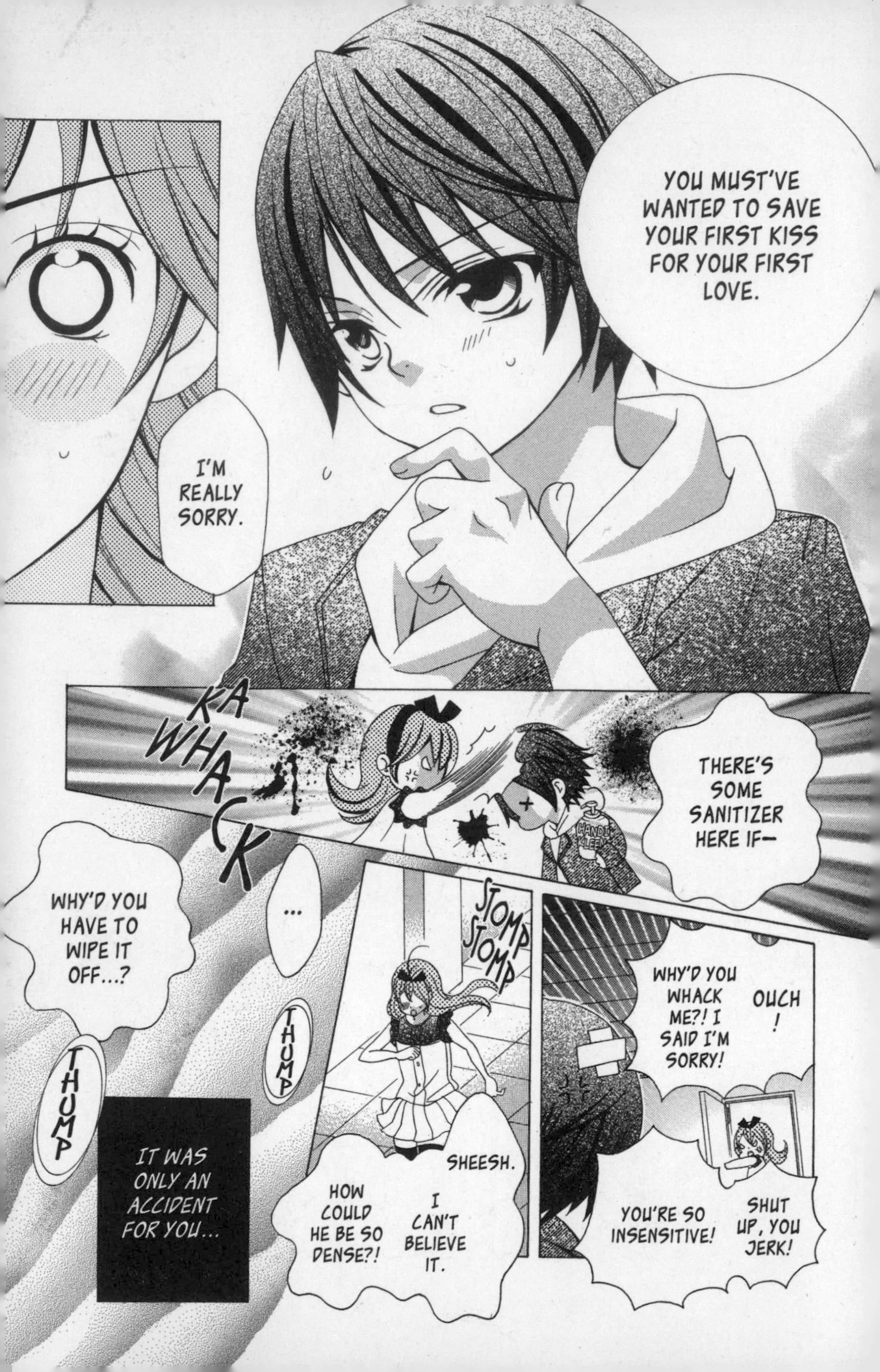
YOU MUST'VE WANTED TO SAVE YOUR FIRST KISS FOR YOUR FIRST LOVE.
I'M REALLY SORRY.
THERE'S SOME SANITIZER HERE IF—
HANDI KLEEN
KA WHACK
OUCH!
WHY'D YOU WHACK ME?! I SAID I'M SORRY!
SHUT UP, YOU JERK!
YOU'RE SO INSENSITIVE!
STOMP STOMP
SHEESH.
I CAN'T BELIEVE IT.
HOW COULD HE BE SO DENSE?!
...
WHY'D YOU HAVE TO WIPE IT OFF...?
THUMP
THUMP
IT WAS ONLY AN ACCIDENT FOR YOU...

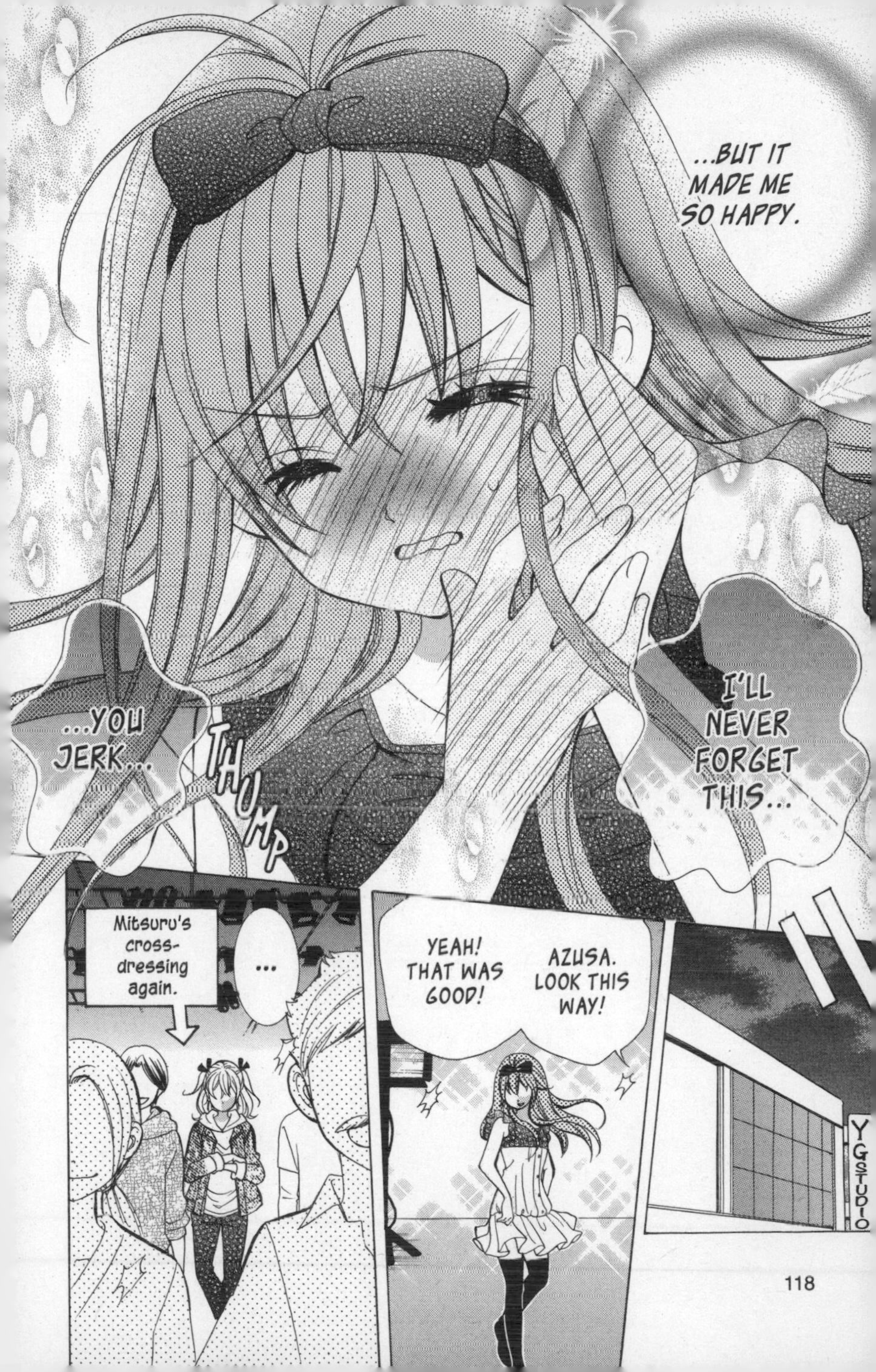
...BUT IT MADE ME SO HAPPY.
I'LL NEVER FORGET THIS...
...YOU JERK...
THUMP
YG STUDIO
AZUSA. LOOK THIS WAY!
YEAH! THAT WAS GOOD!
...
Mitsuru's cross-dressing again.

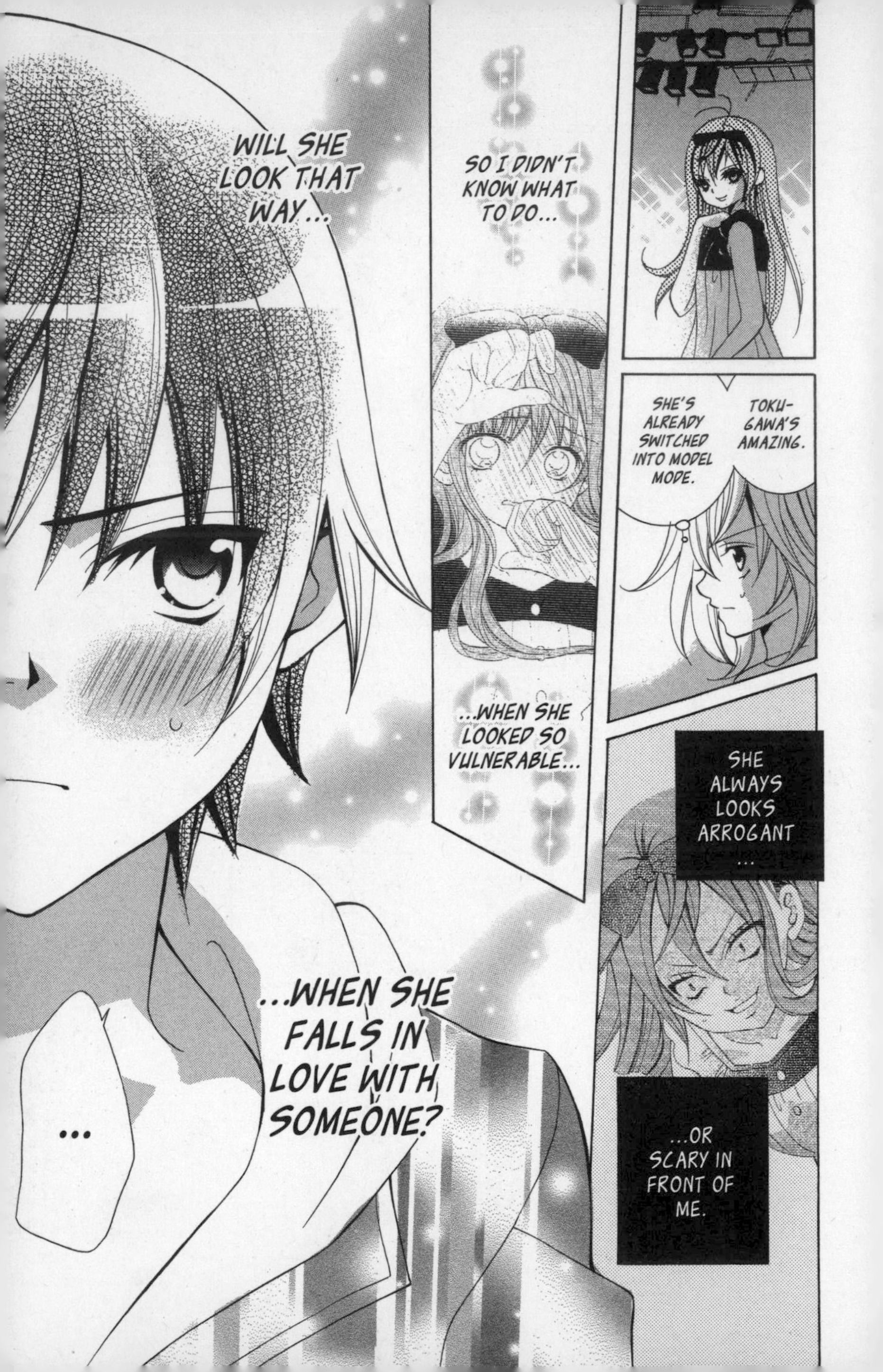
TOKU-GAWA'S AMAZING.
SHE'S ALREADY SWITCHED INTO MODEL MODE.
SHE ALWAYS LOOKS ARROGANT ...
...OR SCARY IN FRONT OF ME.
SO I DIDN'T KNOW WHAT TO DO...
...WHEN SHE LOOKED SO VULNERABLE...
WILL SHE LOOK THAT WAY...
...WHEN SHE FALLS IN LOVE WITH SOMEONE?
...

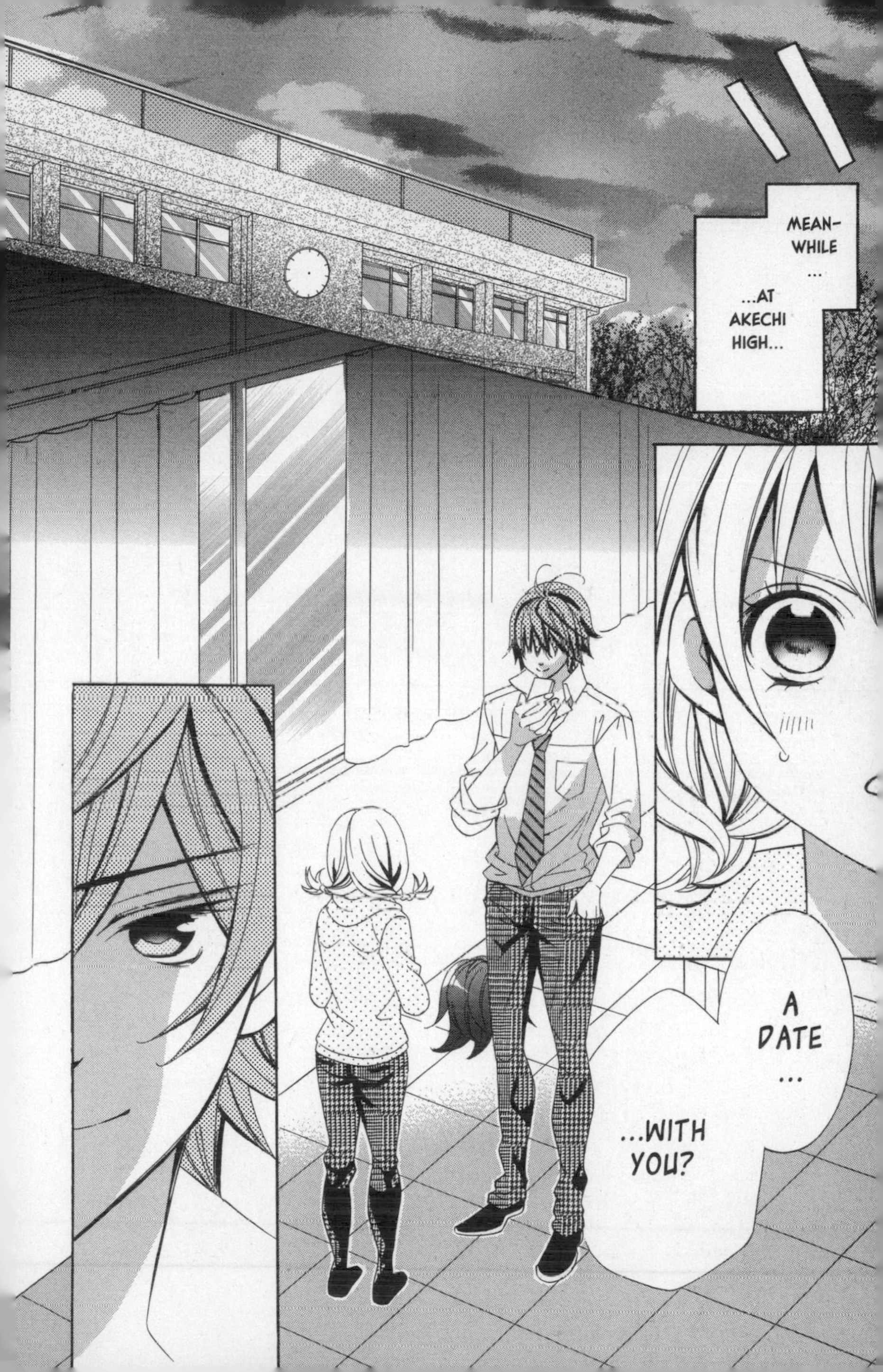
MEAN-WHILE ...
...AT AKECHI HIGH...
A DATE ...
...WITH YOU?

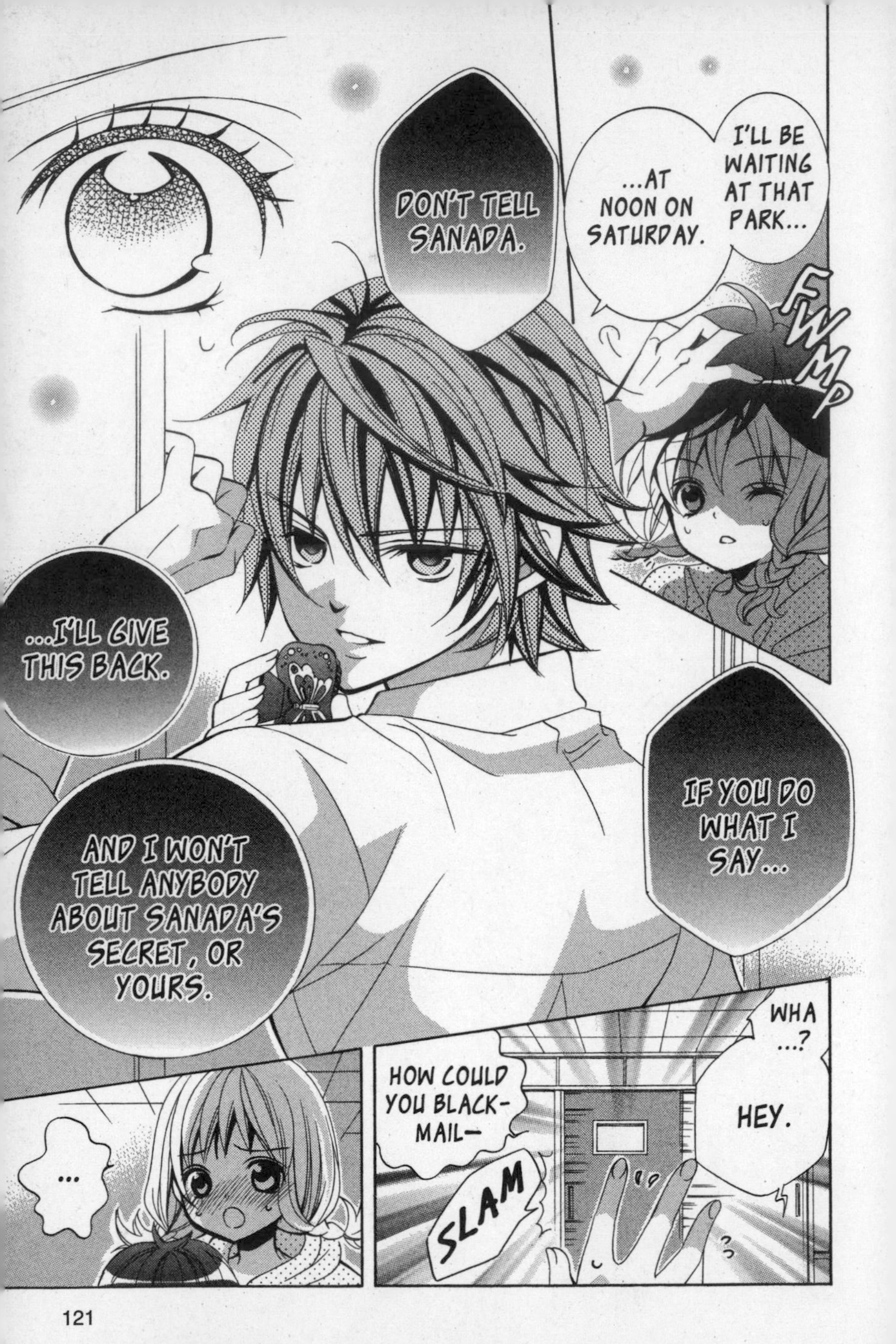
I'LL BE WAITING AT THAT PARK...
...AT NOON ON SATURDAY.
FWMP
DON'T TELL SANADA.
IF YOU DO WHAT I SAY...
...I'LL GIVE THIS BACK.
AND I WON'T TELL ANYBODY ABOUT SANADA'S SECRET, OR YOURS.
WHA ...?
HEY.
HOW COULD YOU BLACK-MAIL—
SLAM
...

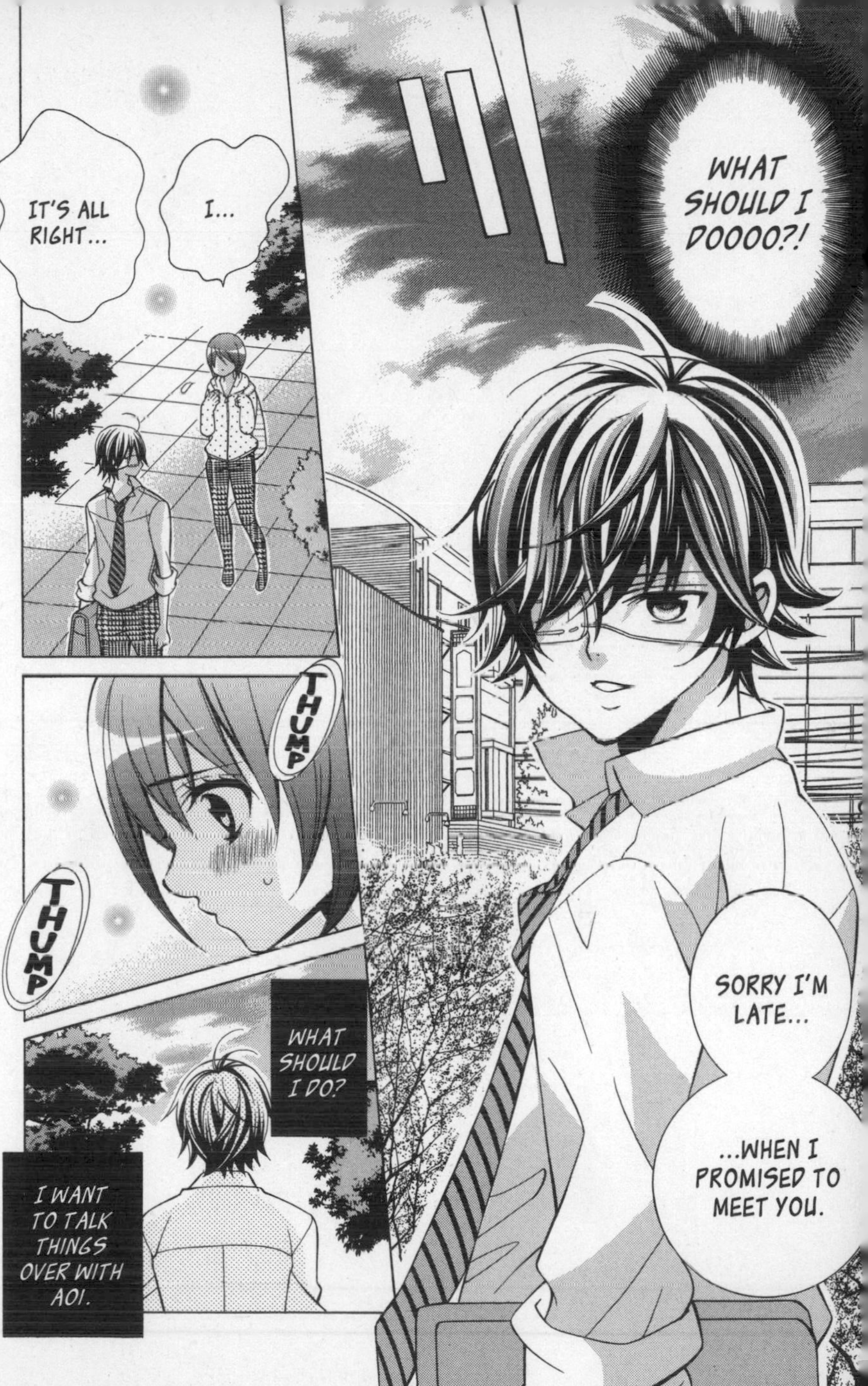
WHAT SHOULD I DOOOO?!
SORRY I'M LATE...
...WHEN I PROMISED TO MEET YOU.
I...
IT'S ALL RIGHT...
THUMP
THUMP
WHAT SHOULD I DO?
I WANT TO TALK THINGS OVER WITH AOI.

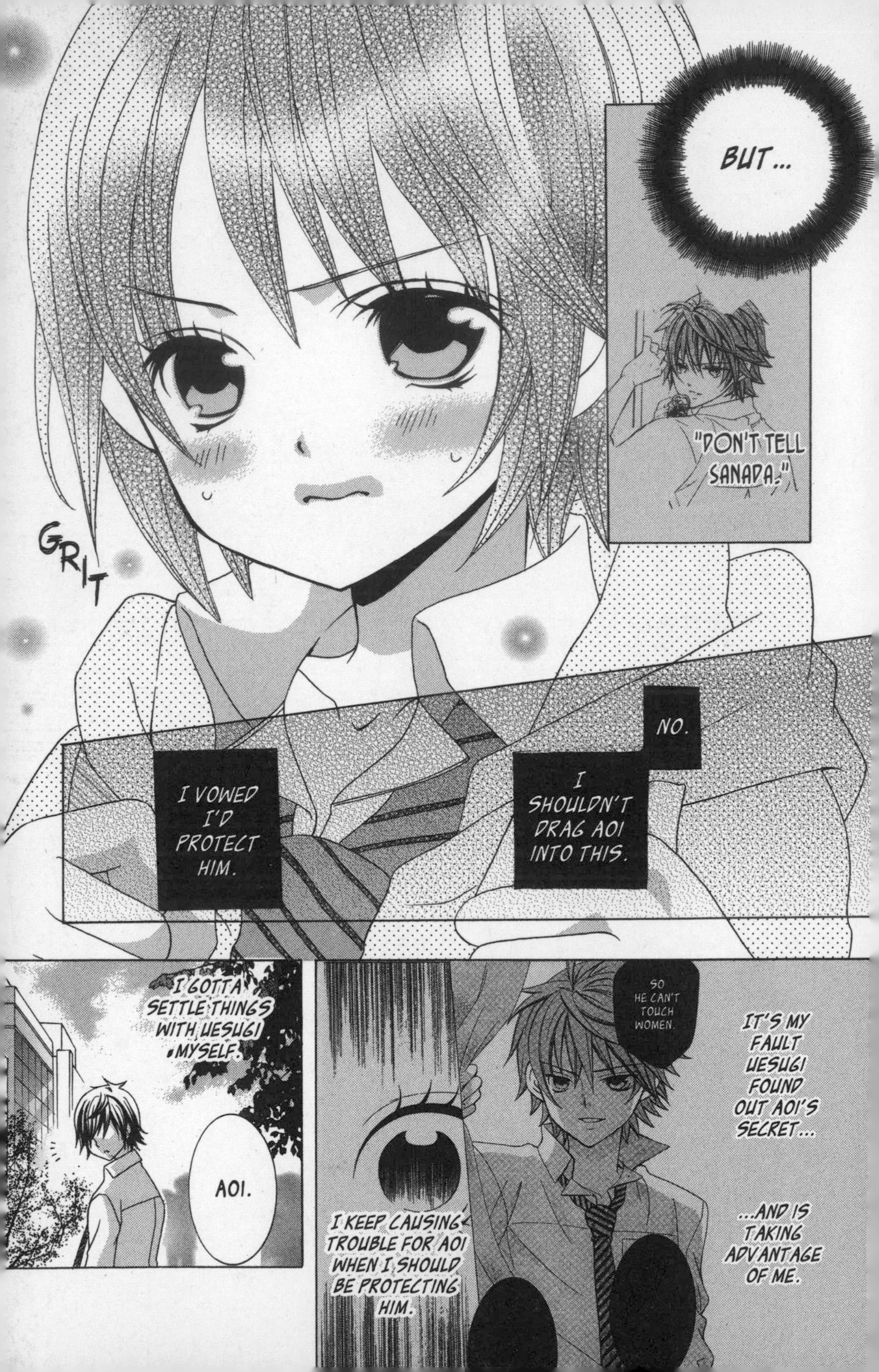
BUT...
"DON'T TELL SANADA."
GRIT
NO.
I SHOULDN'T DRAG AOI INTO THIS.
I VOWED I'D PROTECT HIM.
IT'S MY FAULT UESUGI FOUND OUT AOI'S SECRET...
SO HE CAN'T TOUCH WOMEN.
...AND IS TAKING ADVANTAGE OF ME.
I KEEP CAUSING TROUBLE FOR AOI WHEN I SHOULD BE PROTECTING HIM.
I GOTTA SETTLE THINGS WITH UESUGI MYSELF.
AOI.

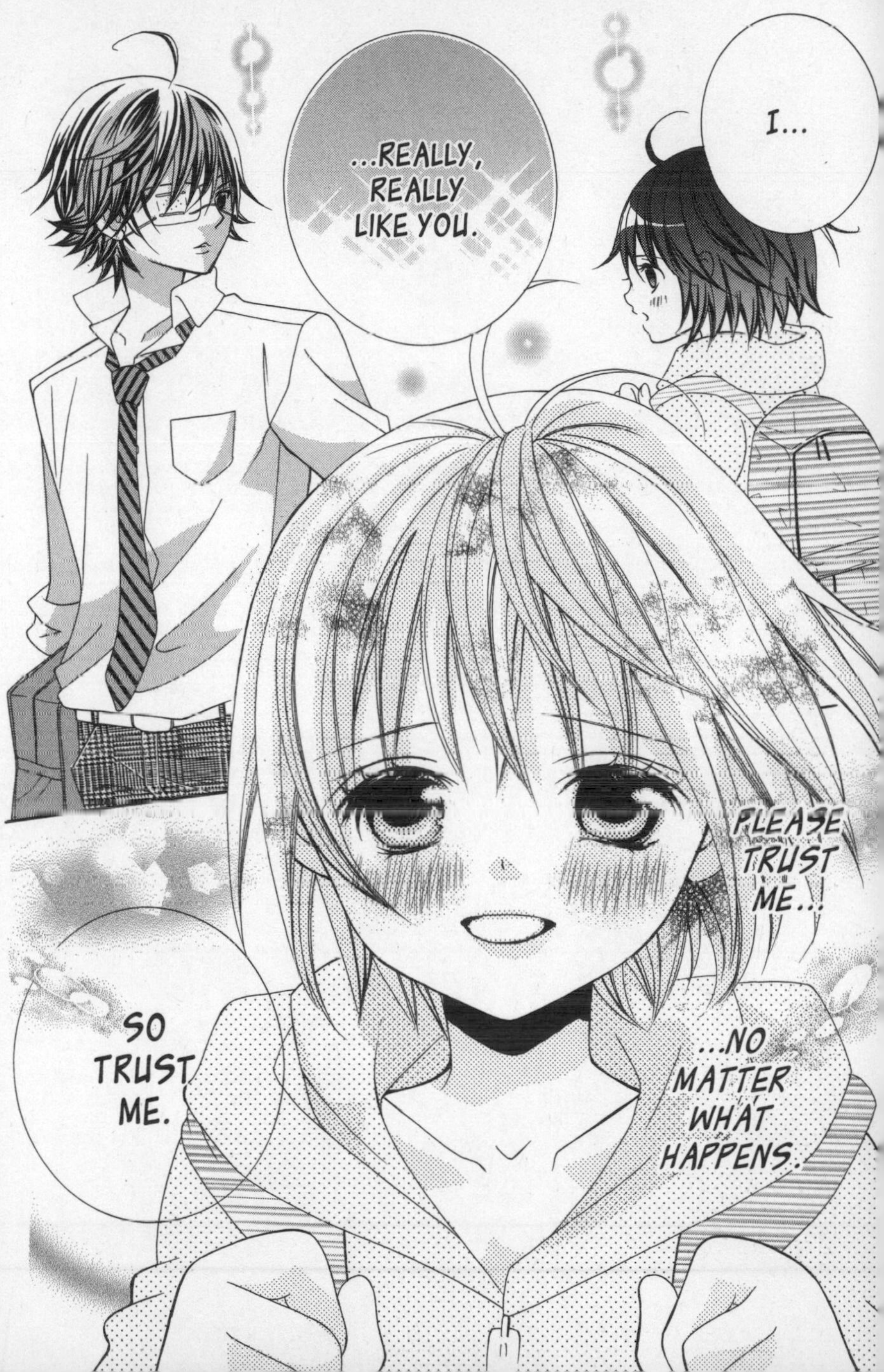
I...
...REALLY, REALLY LIKE YOU.
PLEASE TRUST ME...
...NO MATTER WHAT HAPPENS..
SO TRUST ME.

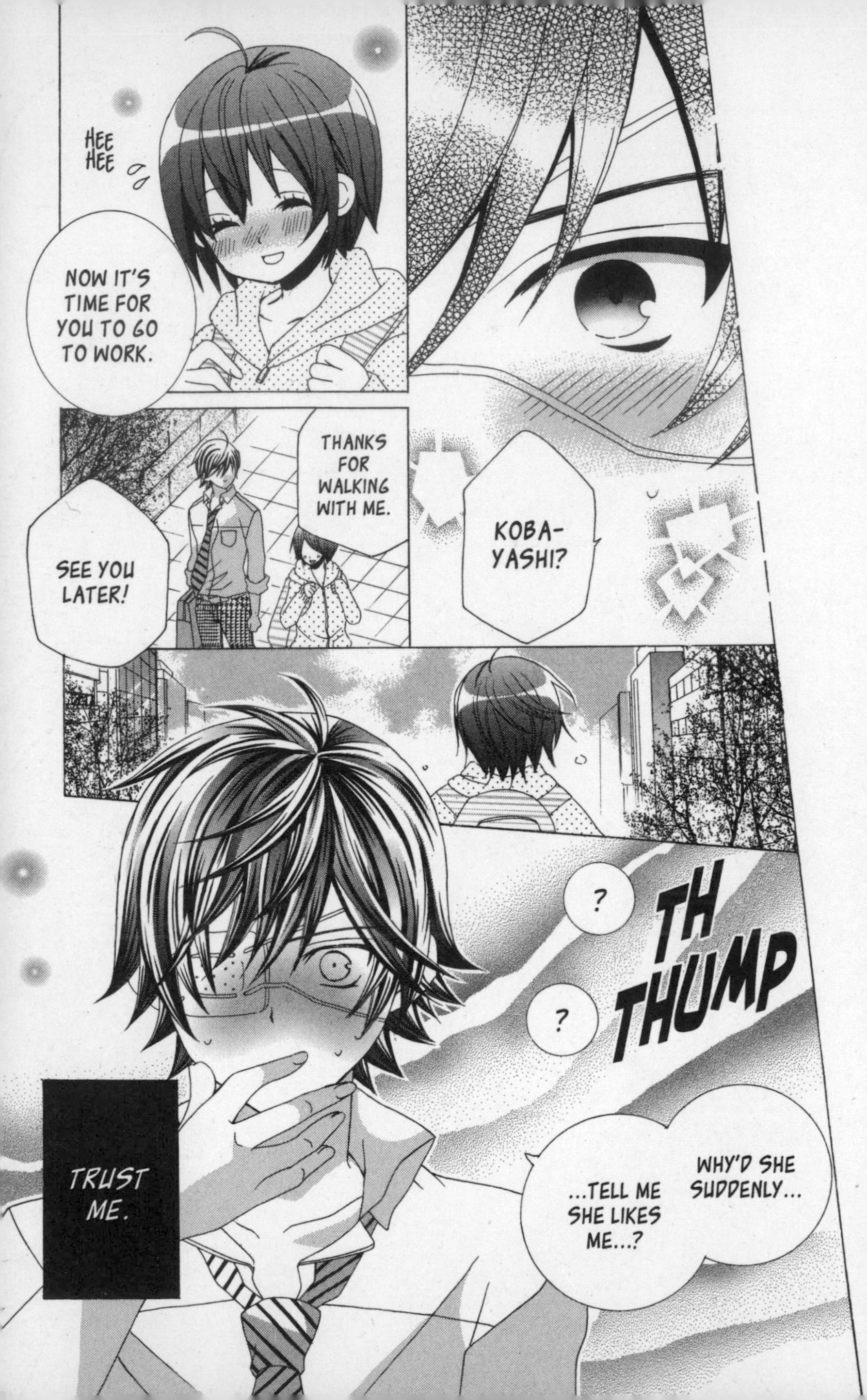
KOBA-YASHI?
HEE HEE
NOW IT'S TIME FOR YOU TO GO TO WORK.
THANKS FOR WALKING WITH ME.
SEE YOU LATER!
?
?
TH THUMP
WHY'D SHE SUDDENLY...
...TELL ME SHE LIKES ME...?
TRUST ME.

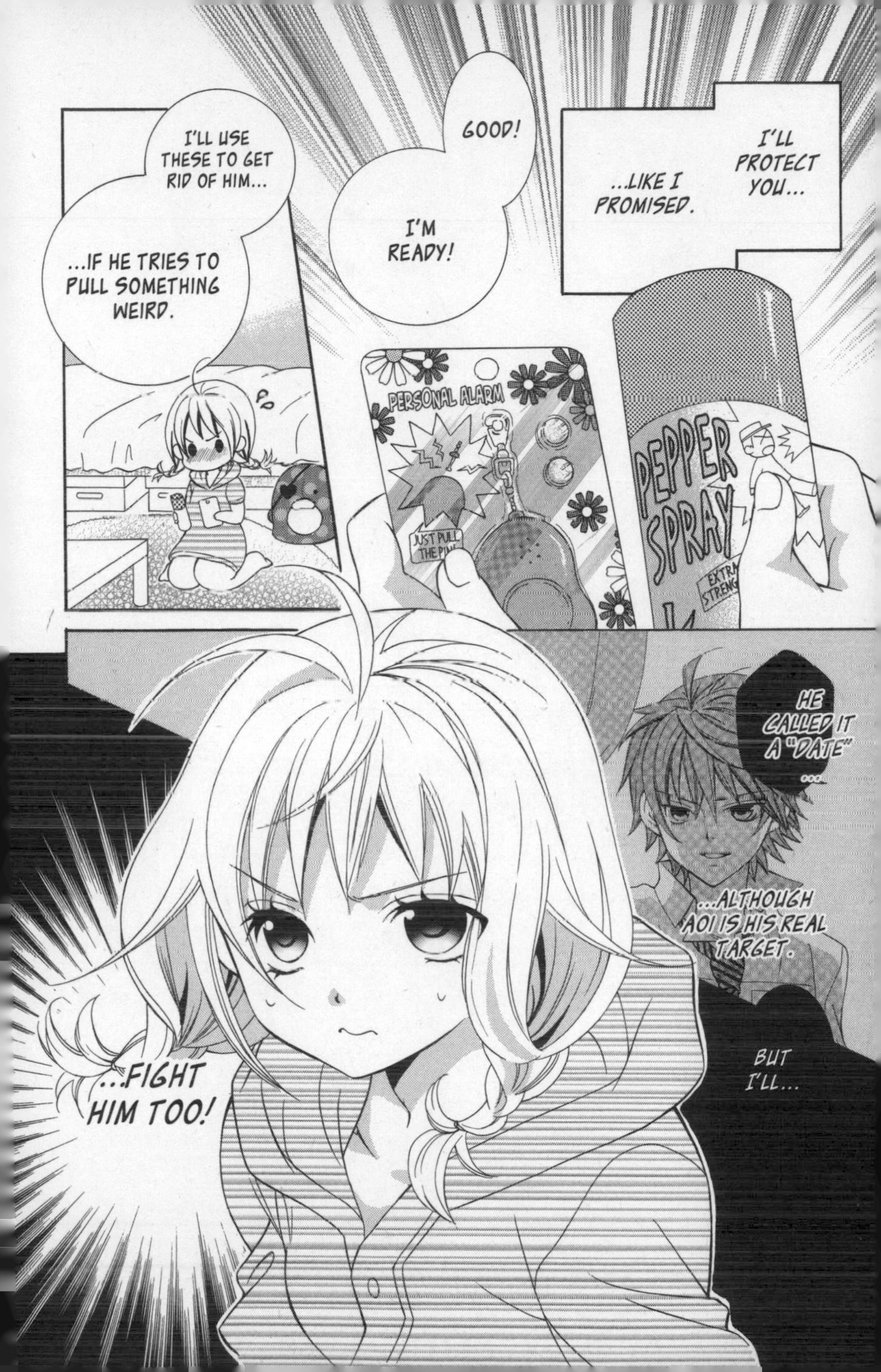
I'LL PROTECT YOU...
...LIKE I PROMISED.
PEPPER SPRAY
GOOD!
I'M READY!
PERSONAL ALARM
JUST PULL THE PIN
I'LL USE THESE TO GET RID OF HIM...
...IF HE TRIES TO PULL SOMETHING WEIRD.
HE CALLED IT A "DATE"...
...ALTHOUGH AOI IS HIS REAL TARGET.
BUT I'LL...
...FIGHT HIM TOO!

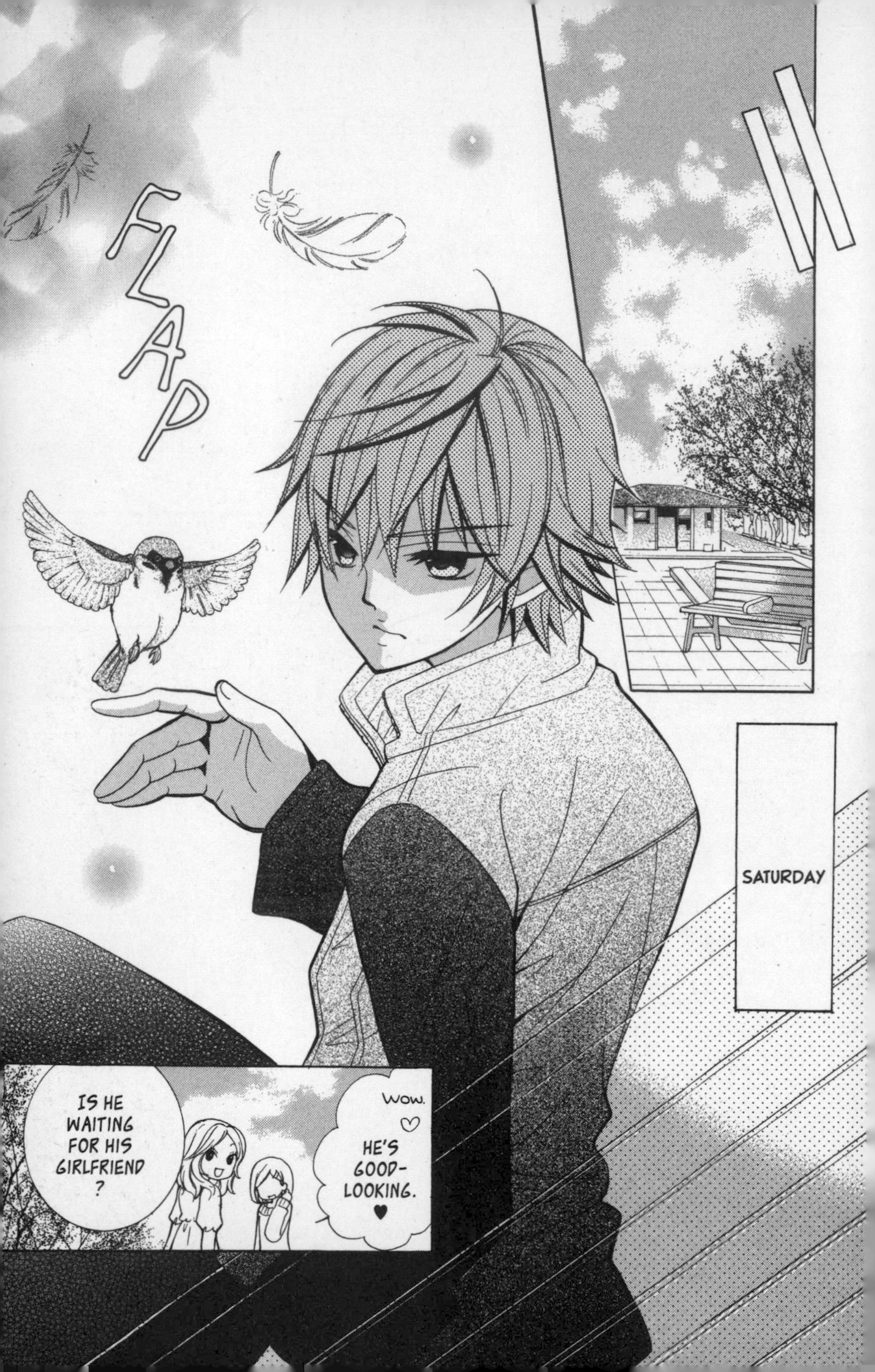
SATURDAY
FLAP
WOW. ♡ HE'S GOOD-LOOKING. ♥
IS HE WAITING FOR HIS GIRLFRIEND?

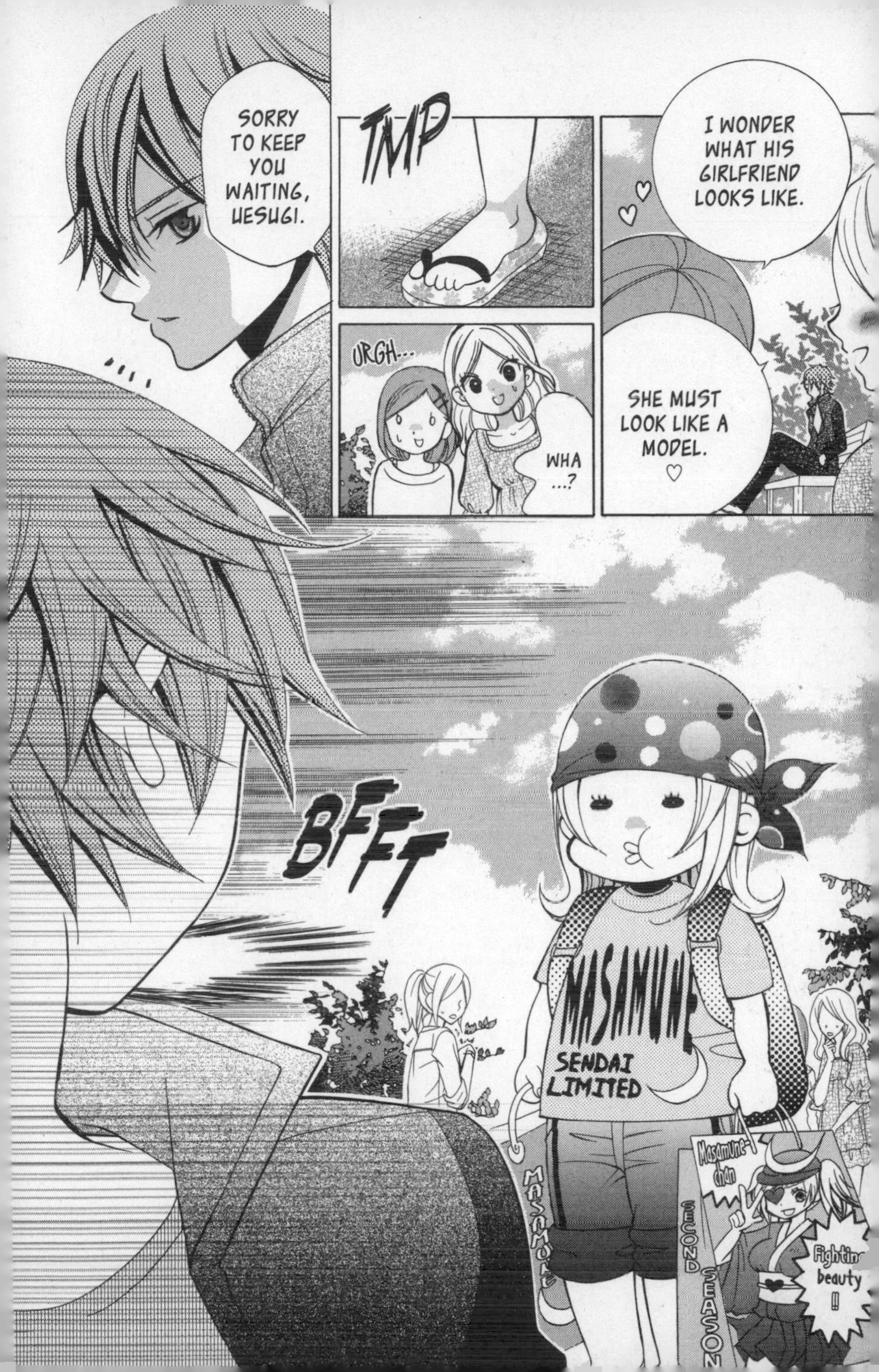

I WONDER WHAT HIS GIRLFRIEND LOOKS LIKE.
SHE MUST LOOK LIKE A MODEL.
TMP
URGH...
WHA ...?
SORRY TO KEEP YOU WAITING, UESUGI.
BFFT
MASAMUNE
SENDAI LIMITED
MASAMUNE
SECOND SEASON
Masamune-chan
Fightin beauty !!

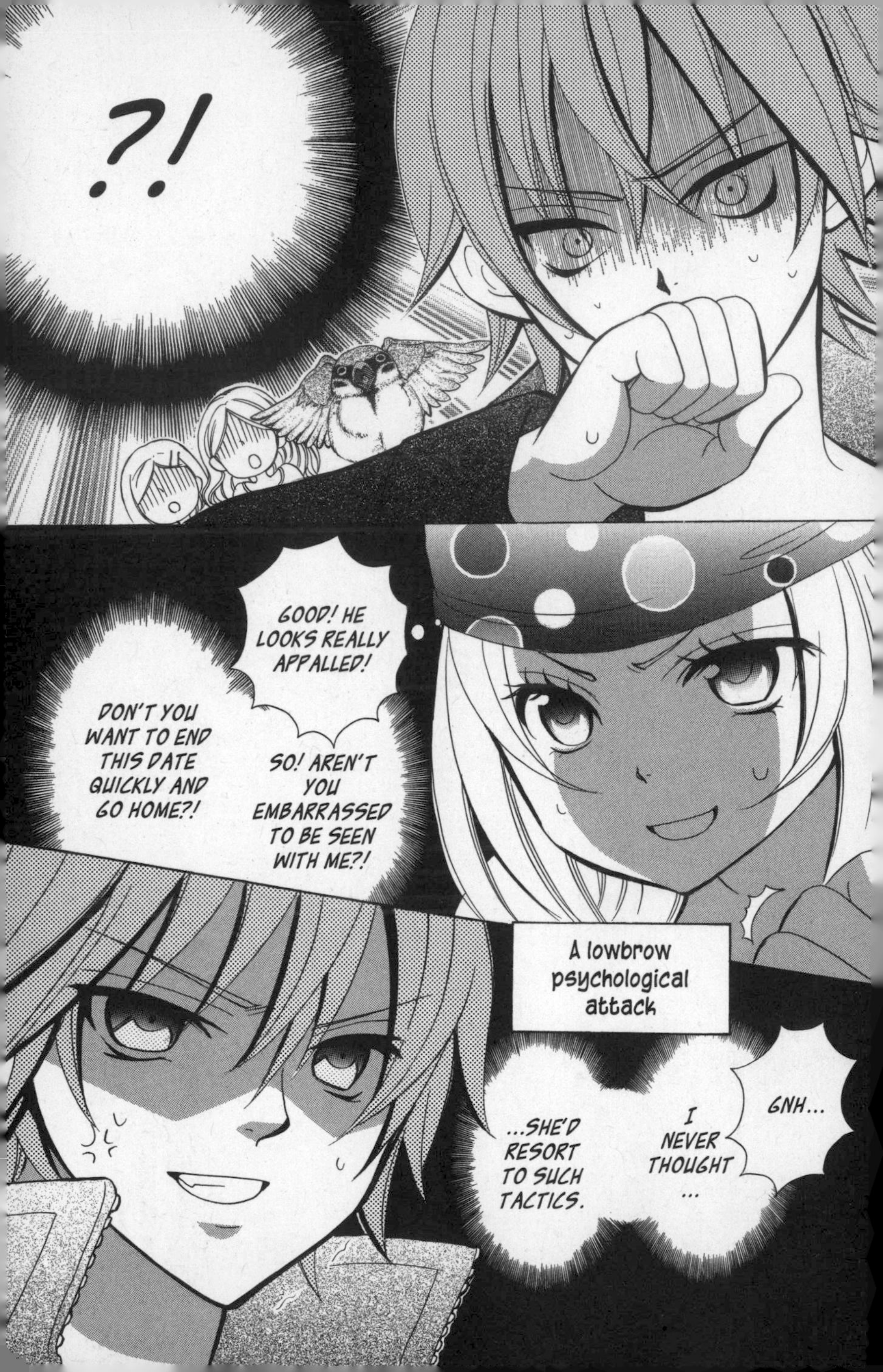
?!
GOOD! HE LOOKS REALLY APPALLED!
SO! AREN'T YOU EMBARRASSED TO BE SEEN WITH ME?!
DON'T YOU WANT TO END THIS DATE QUICKLY AND GO HOME?!
A lowbrow psychological attack
GNH...
I NEVER THOUGHT ...
...SHE'D RESORT TO SUCH TACTICS.

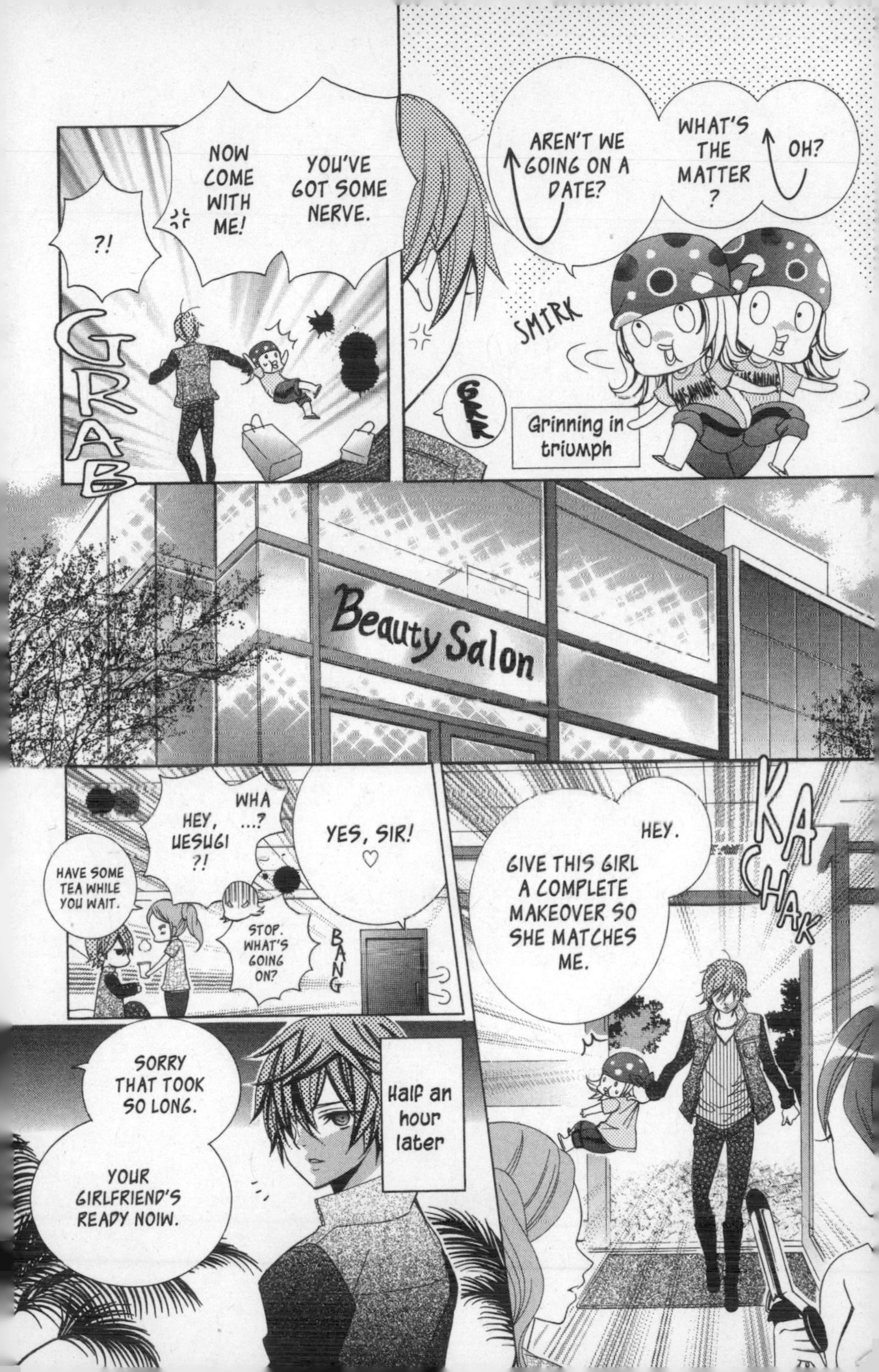
OH?
WHAT'S THE MATTER ?
AREN'T WE GOING ON A DATE?
SMIRK
GRRR
Grinning in triumph
YOU'VE GOT SOME NERVE.
NOW COME WITH ME!
?!
GRAB
Beauty Salon
KA CHAK
HEY.
GIVE THIS GIRL A COMPLETE MAKEOVER SO SHE MATCHES ME.
YES, SIR! ♡
WHA ...?
HEY, UESUGI ?!
STOP. WHAT'S GOING ON?
BANG
HAVE SOME TEA WHILE YOU WAIT.
Half an hour later
SORRY THAT TOOK SO LONG.
YOUR GIRLFRIEND'S READY NOIW.

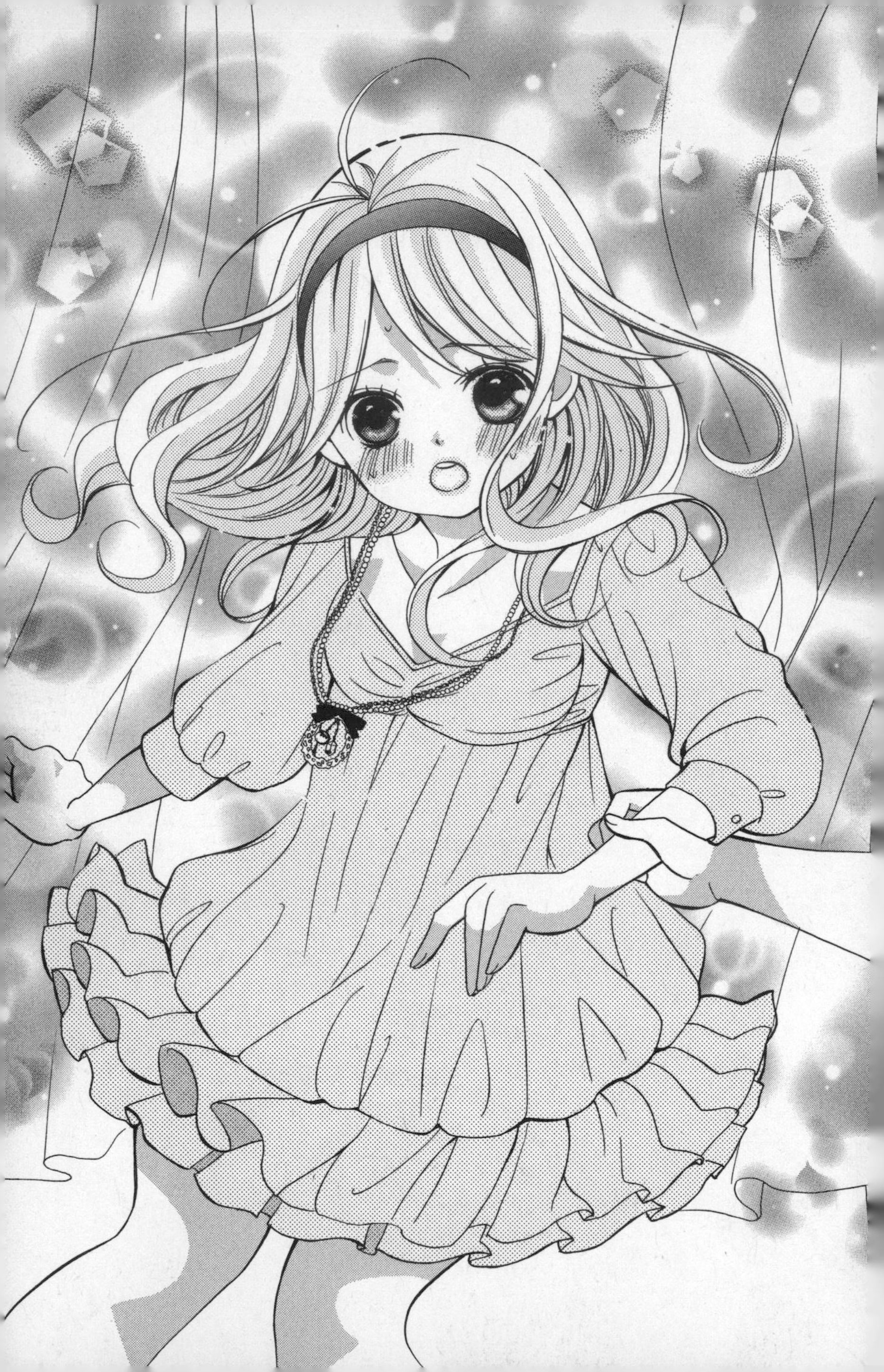

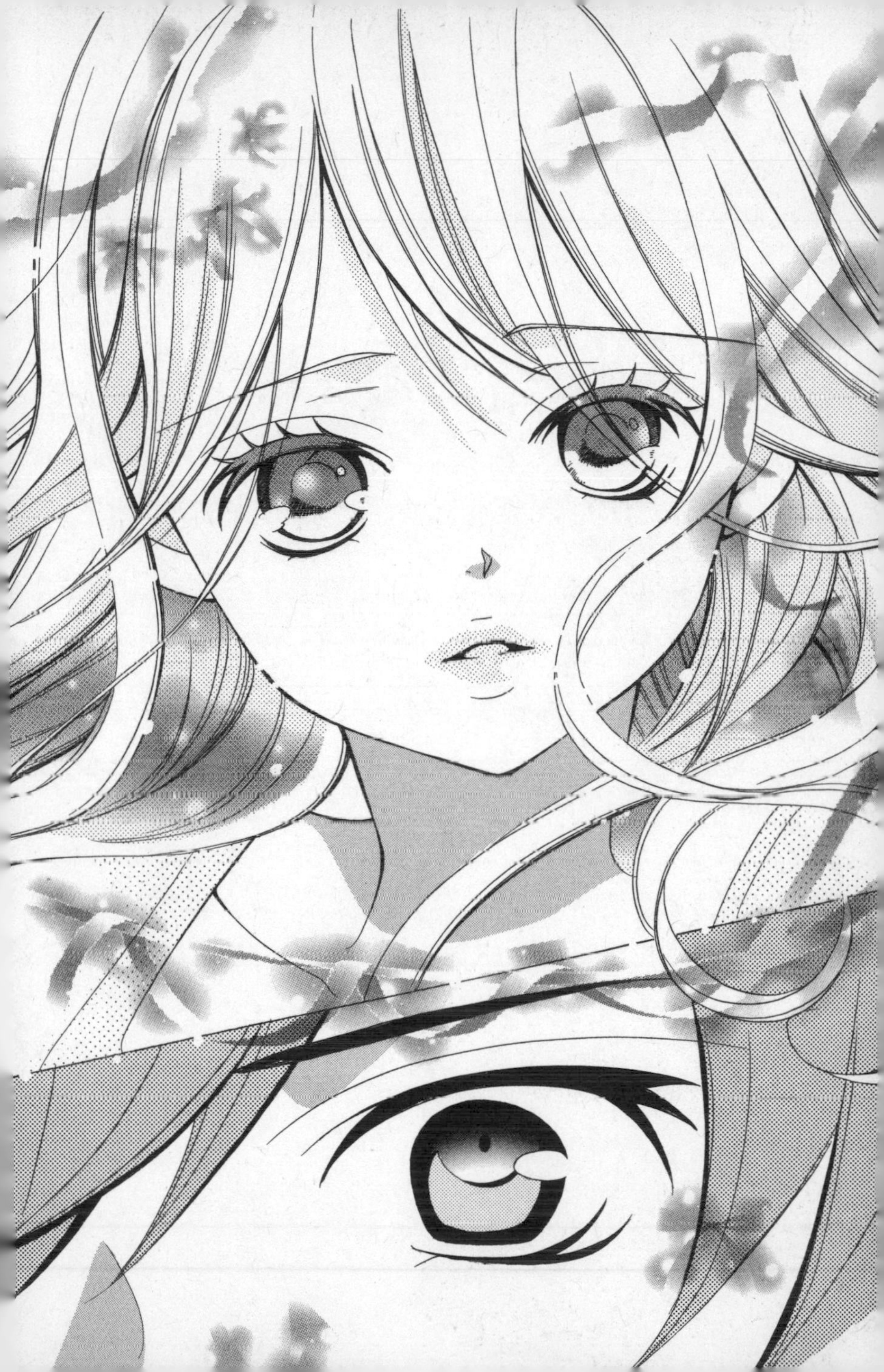

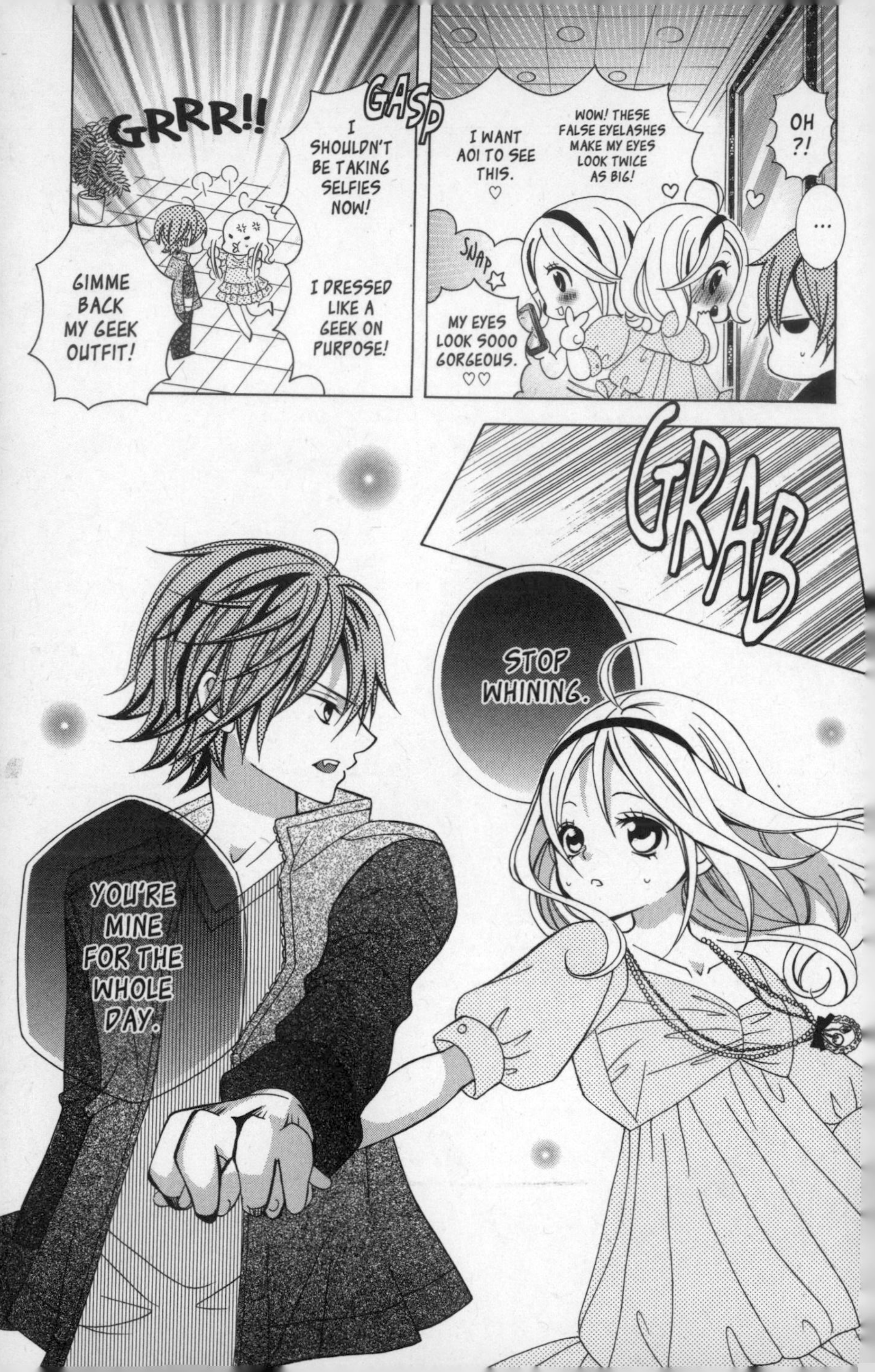
OH ?!
...
WOW! THESE FALSE EYELASHES MAKE MY EYES LOOK TWICE AS BIG! ♡
I WANT AOI TO SEE THIS. ♡
SNAP
MY EYES LOOK SOOO GORGEOUS. ♡♡
GASP
I SHOULDN'T BE TAKING SELFIES NOW!
I DRESSED LIKE A GEEK ON PURPOSE!
GRRR!!
GIMME BACK MY GEEK OUTFIT!
GRAB
STOP WHINING.
YOU'RE MINE FOR THE WHOLE DAY.

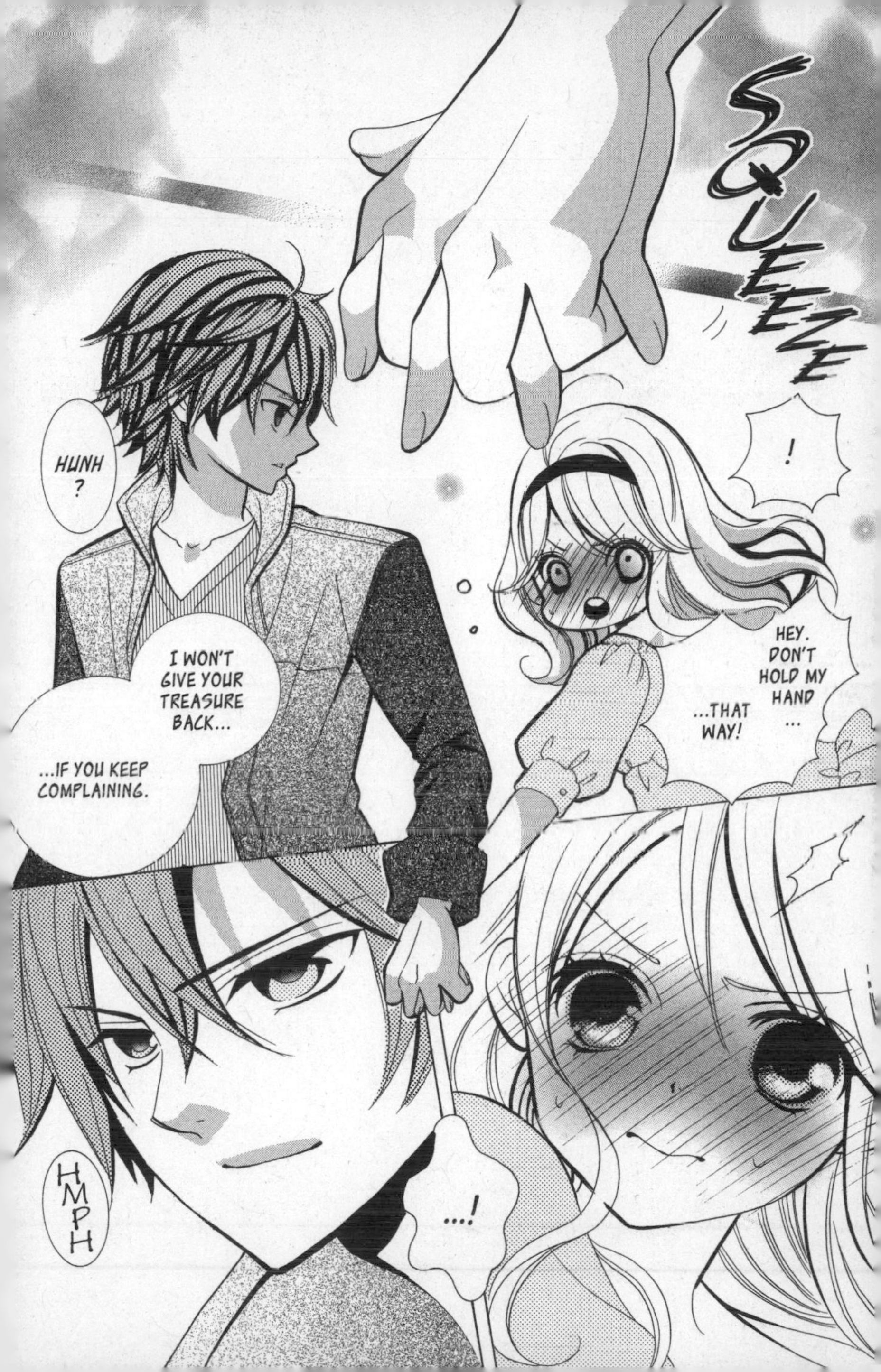
SQUEEZE
!
HEY. DON'T HOLD MY HAND ...
...THAT WAY!
HUNH ?
I WON'T GIVE YOUR TREASURE BACK...
...IF YOU KEEP COMPLAINING.
...!
HMPH

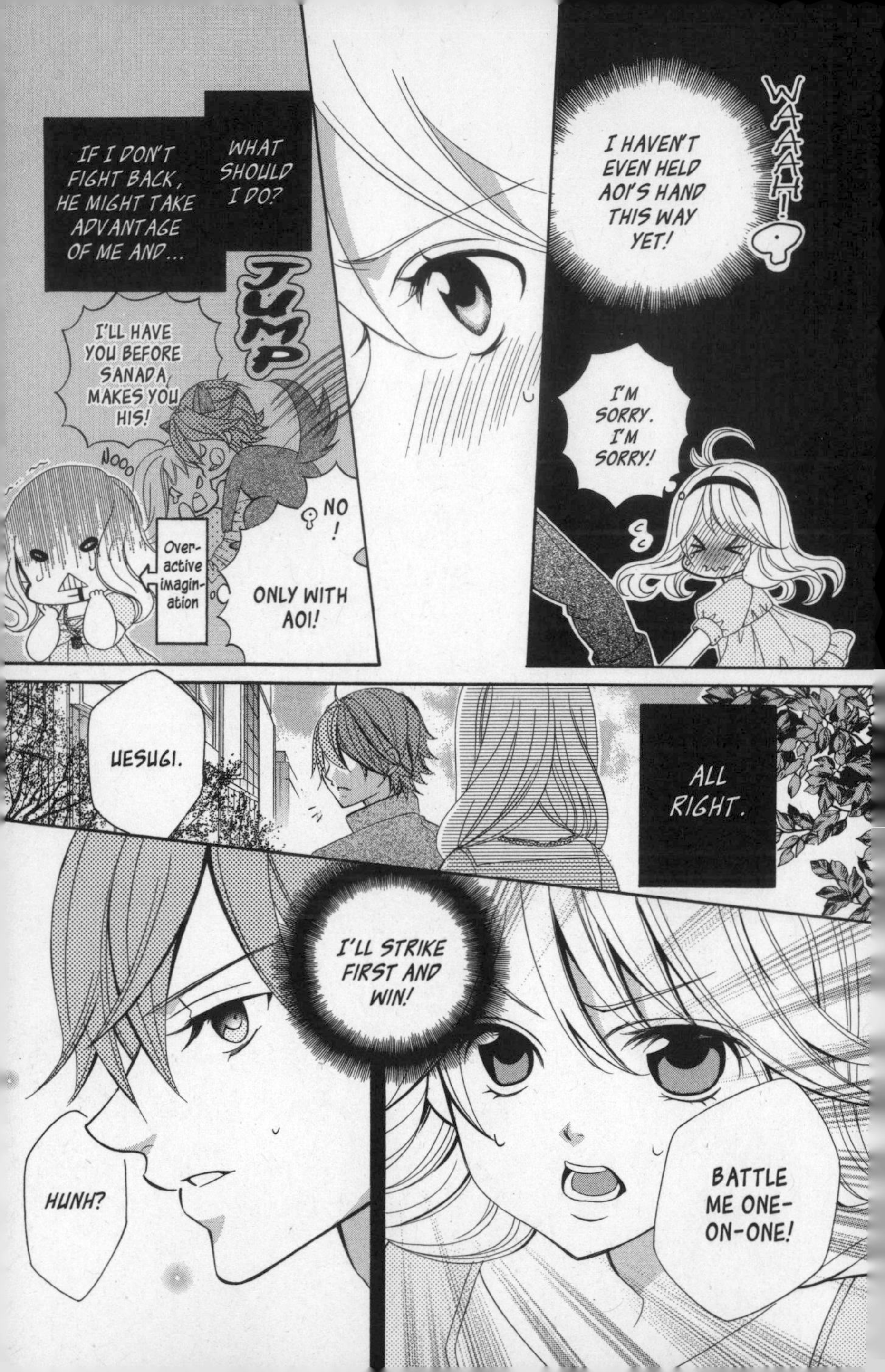
WAAAH!
I HAVEN'T EVEN HELD AOI'S HAND THIS WAY YET!
I'M SORRY. I'M SORRY!
WHAT SHOULD I DO?
IF I DON'T FIGHT BACK, HE MIGHT TAKE ADVANTAGE OF ME AND...
JUMP
I'LL HAVE YOU BEFORE SANADA MAKES YOU HIS!
NOOO
NO!
ONLY WITH AOI!
Over-active imagination
ALL RIGHT.
UESUGI.
BATTLE ME ONE-ON-ONE!
I'LL STRIKE FIRST AND WIN!
HUNH?

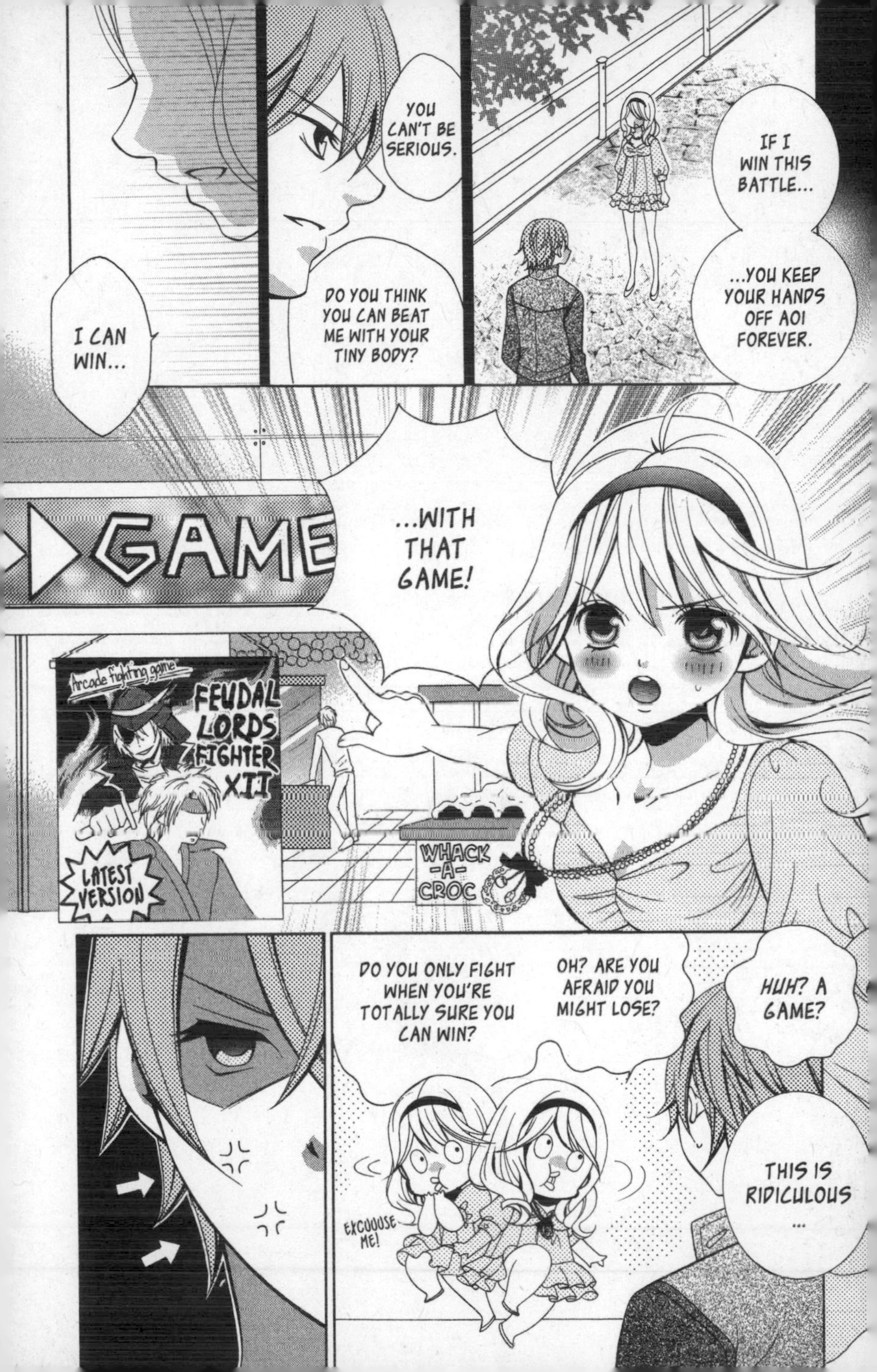
IF I WIN THIS BATTLE...
...YOU KEEP YOUR HANDS OFF AOI FOREVER.
YOU CAN'T BE SERIOUS.
DO YOU THINK YOU CAN BEAT ME WITH YOUR TINY BODY?
I CAN WIN...
...WITH THAT GAME!
GAME
Arcade fighting game
FEUDAL LORDS FIGHTER XII
LATEST VERSION
WHACK-A-CROC
HUH? A GAME?
THIS IS RIDICULOUS...
OH? ARE YOU AFRAID YOU MIGHT LOSE?
DO YOU ONLY FIGHT WHEN YOU'RE TOTALLY SURE YOU CAN WIN?
EXCUUUSE ME!

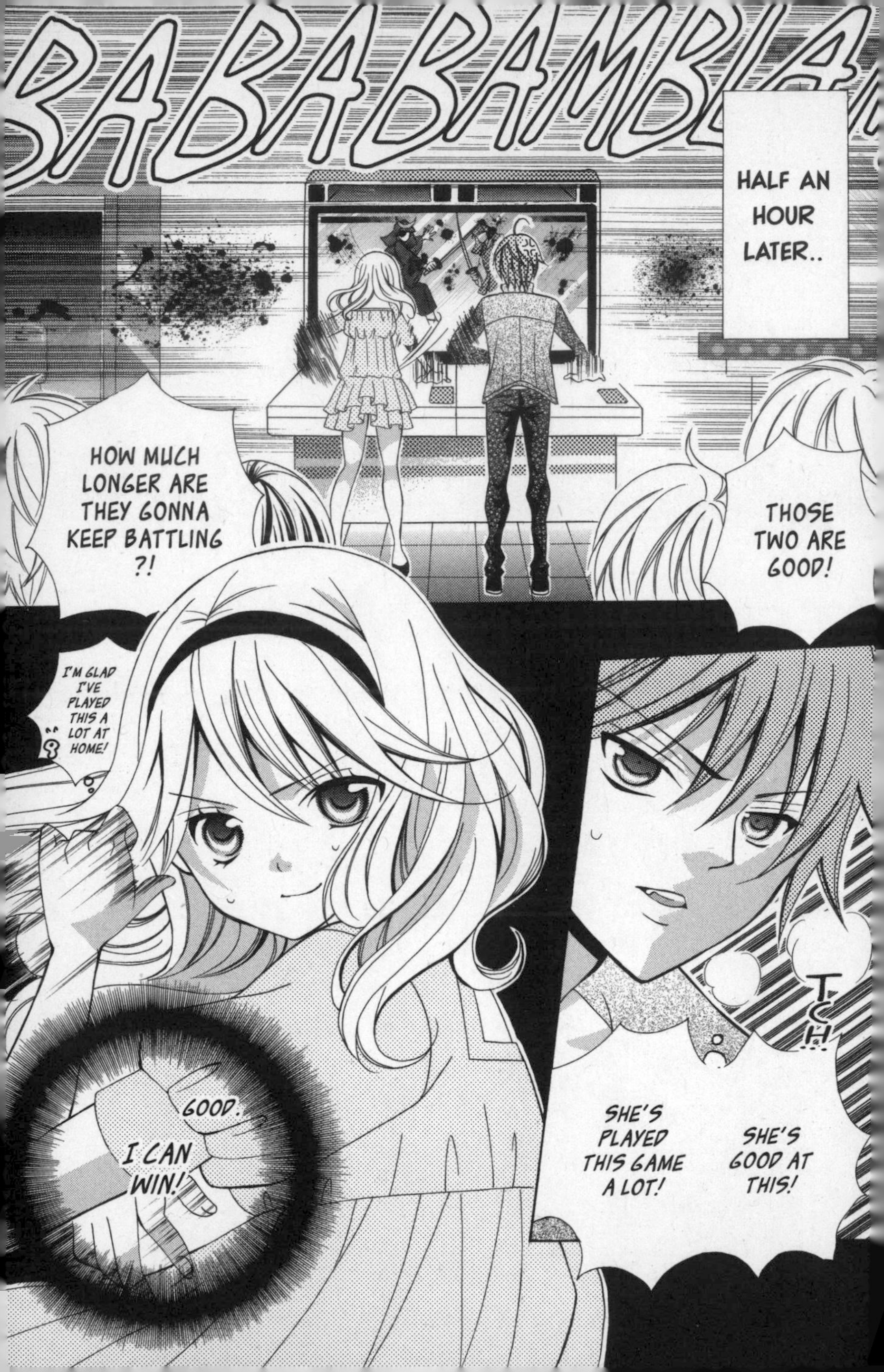
BABABAMBL
HALF AN HOUR LATER..
THOSE TWO ARE GOOD!
HOW MUCH LONGER ARE THEY GONNA KEEP BATTLING?!
TCH...
SHE'S GOOD AT THIS!
SHE'S PLAYED THIS GAME A LOT!
I'M GLAD I'VE PLAYED THIS A LOT AT HOME!
GOOD.
I CAN WIN!

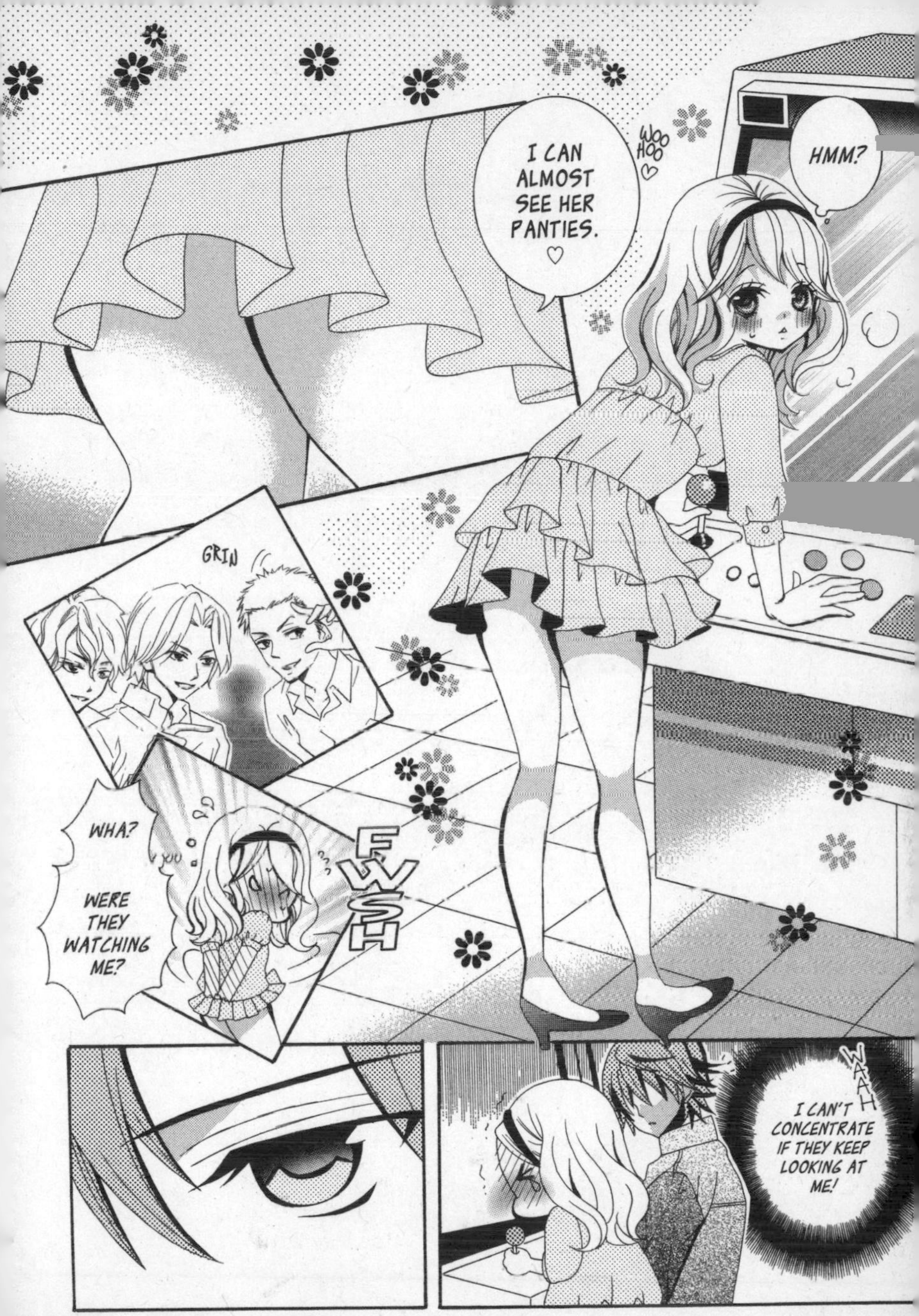
HMM?
WOO HOO ♡
I CAN ALMOST SEE HER PANTIES. ♡
GRIN
FWSH
WHA?
WERE THEY WATCHING ME?
WAAH
I CAN'T CONCENTRATE IF THEY KEEP LOOKING AT ME!

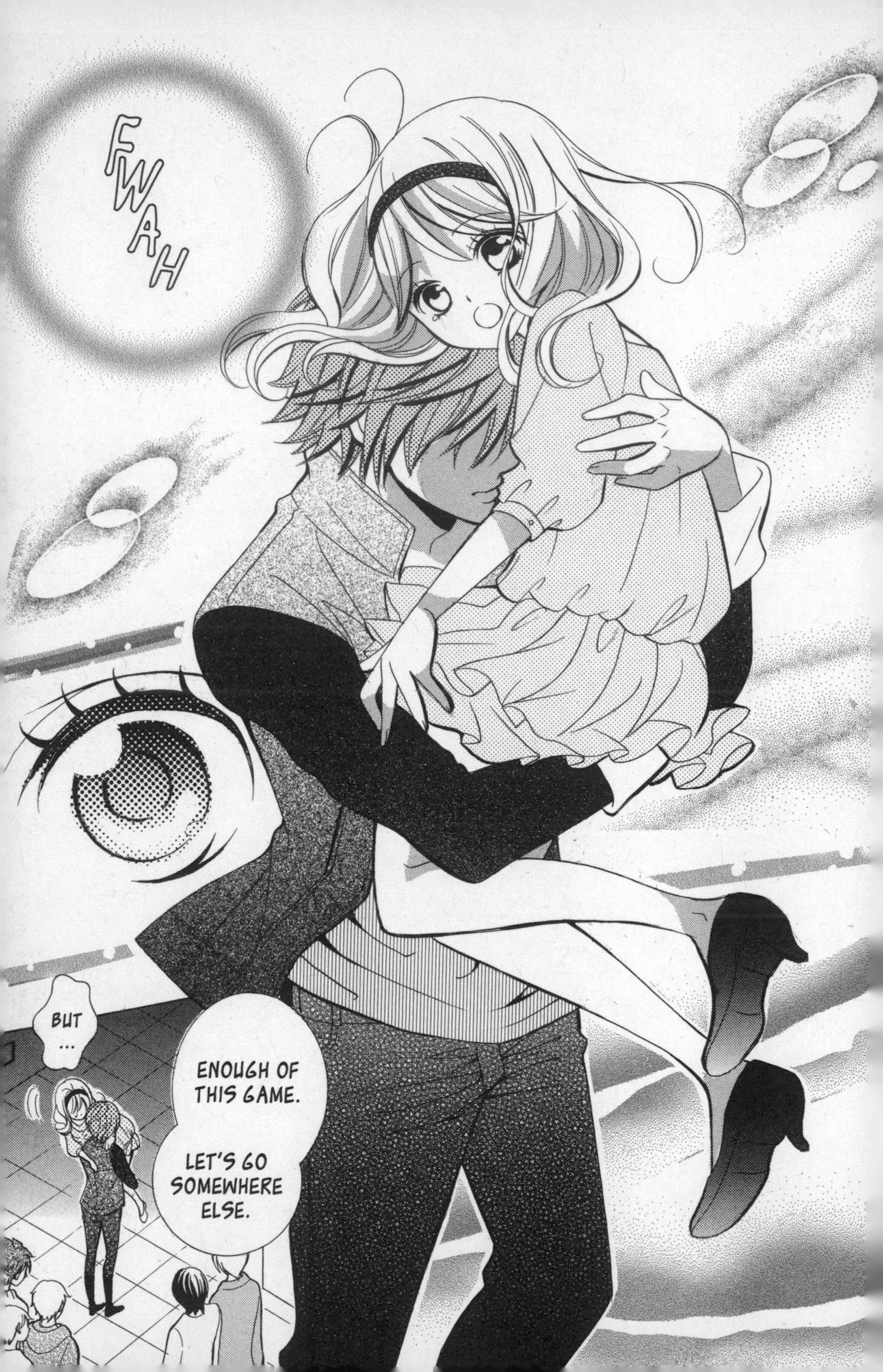
FWAH
ENOUGH OF THIS GAME.
LET'S GO SOMEWHERE ELSE.
BUT ...

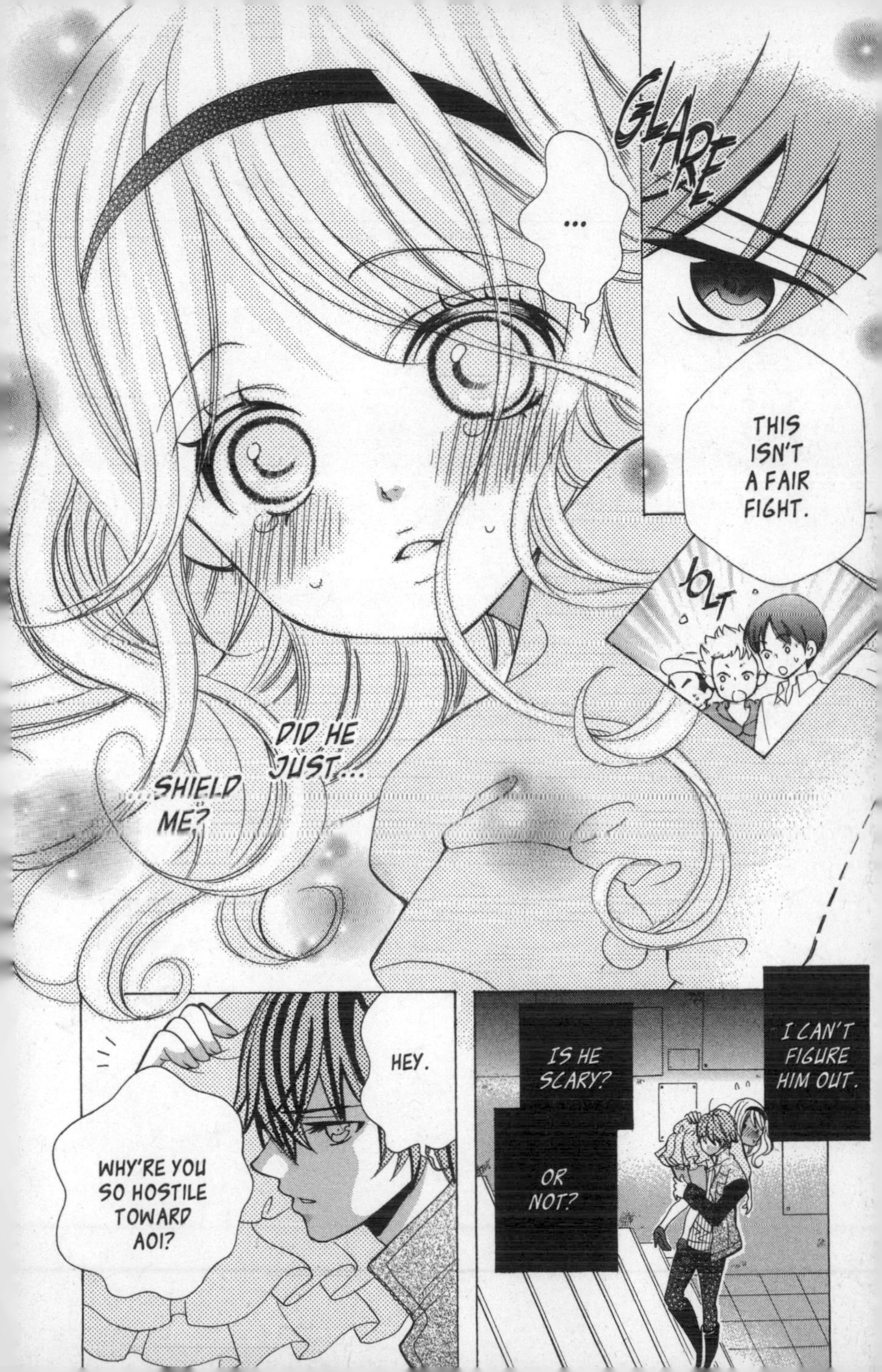
GLARE
THIS ISN'T A FAIR FIGHT.
JOLT
...
DID HE JUST...
...SHIELD ME?
I CAN'T FIGURE HIM OUT.
IS HE SCARY?
OR NOT?
HEY.
WHY'RE YOU SO HOSTILE TOWARD AOI?

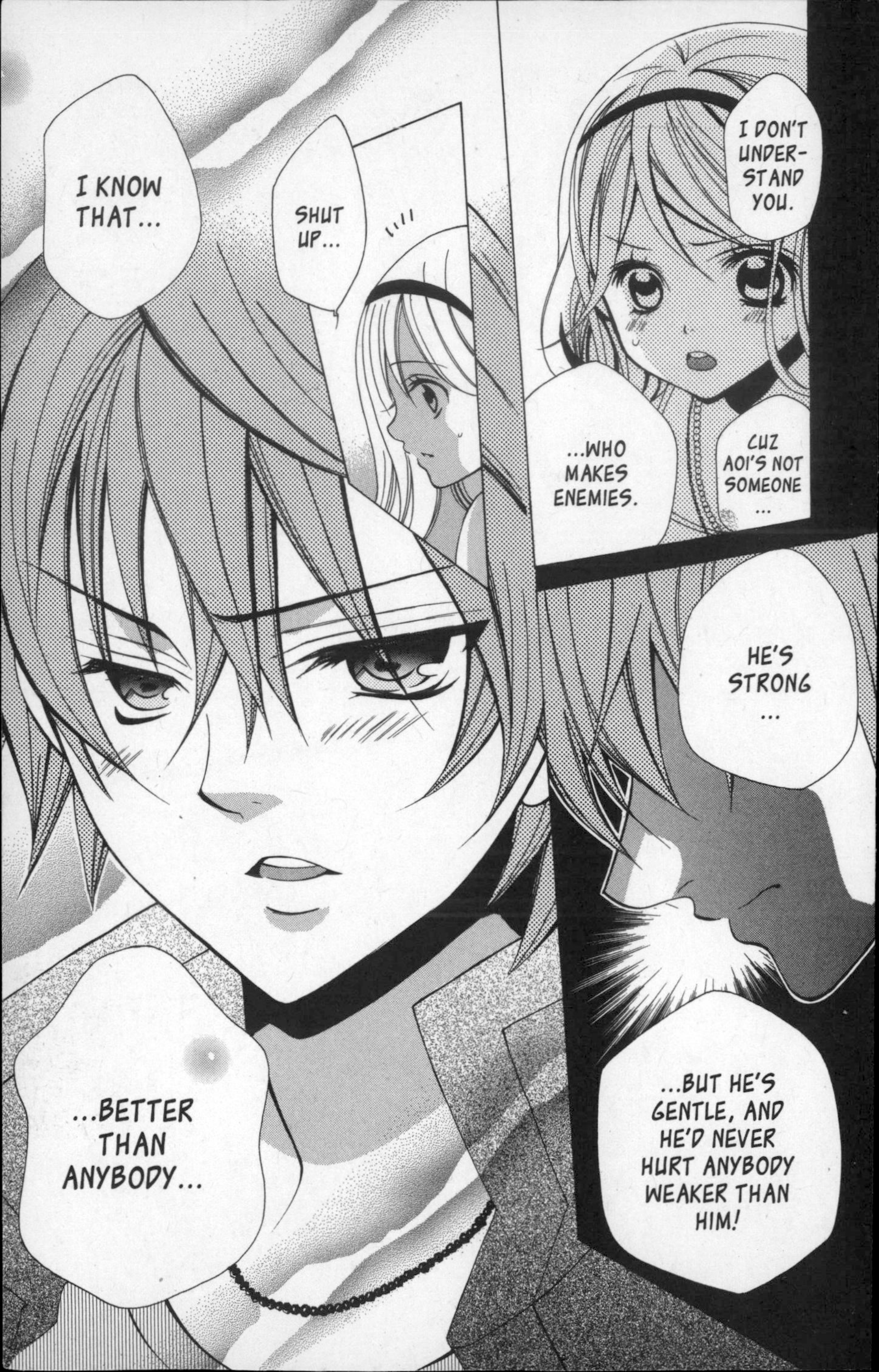
I DON'T UNDER-STAND YOU.
CUZ AOI'S NOT SOMEONE ...
...WHO MAKES ENEMIES.
HE'S STRONG ...
...BUT HE'S GENTLE, AND HE'D NEVER HURT ANYBODY WEAKER THAN HIM!
SHUT UP...
I KNOW THAT...
...BETTER THAN ANYBODY...

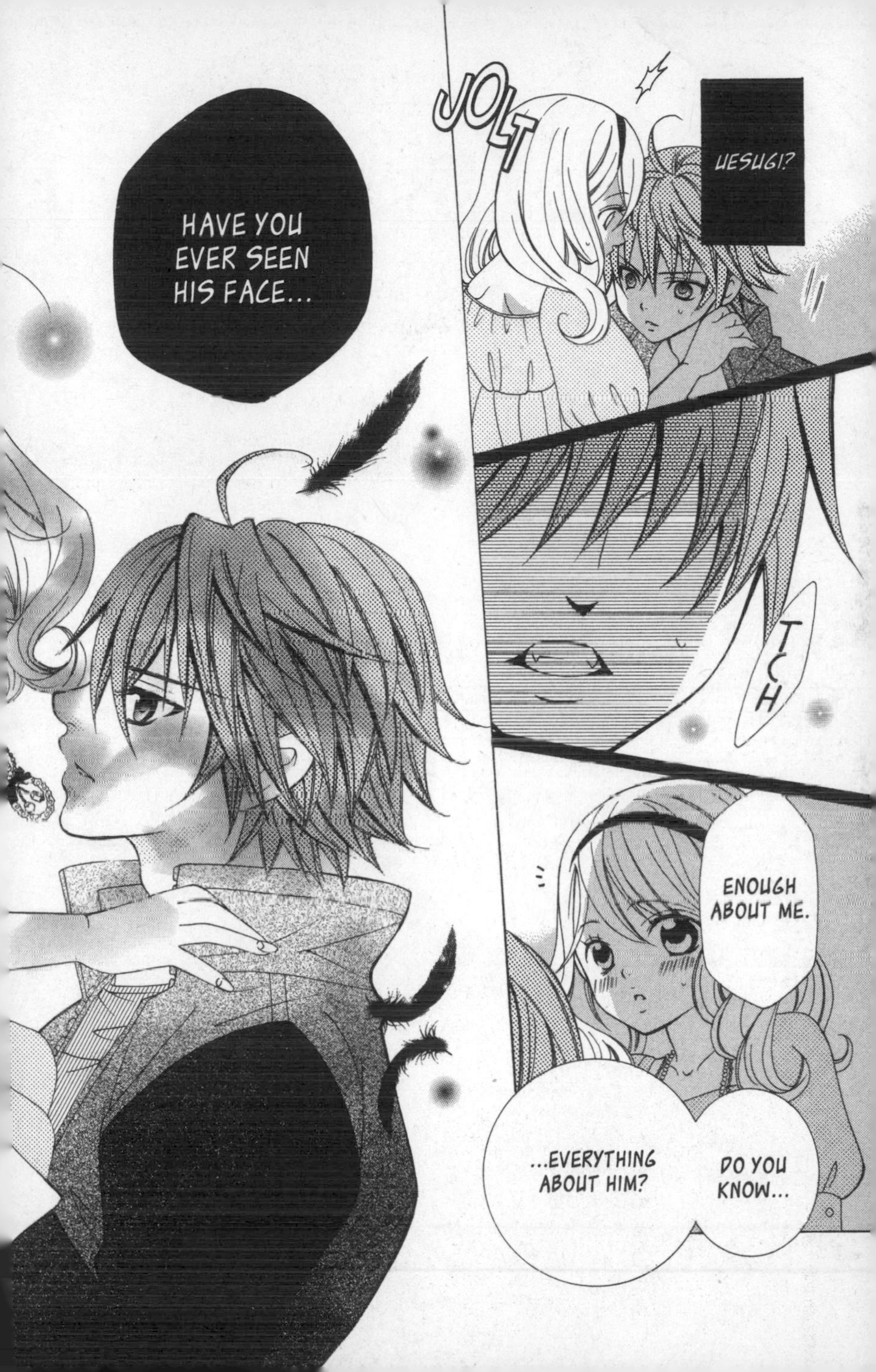
JOLT
UESUGI!?
TCH
ENOUGH ABOUT ME.
DO YOU KNOW...
...EVERYTHING ABOUT HIM?
HAVE YOU EVER SEEN HIS FACE...

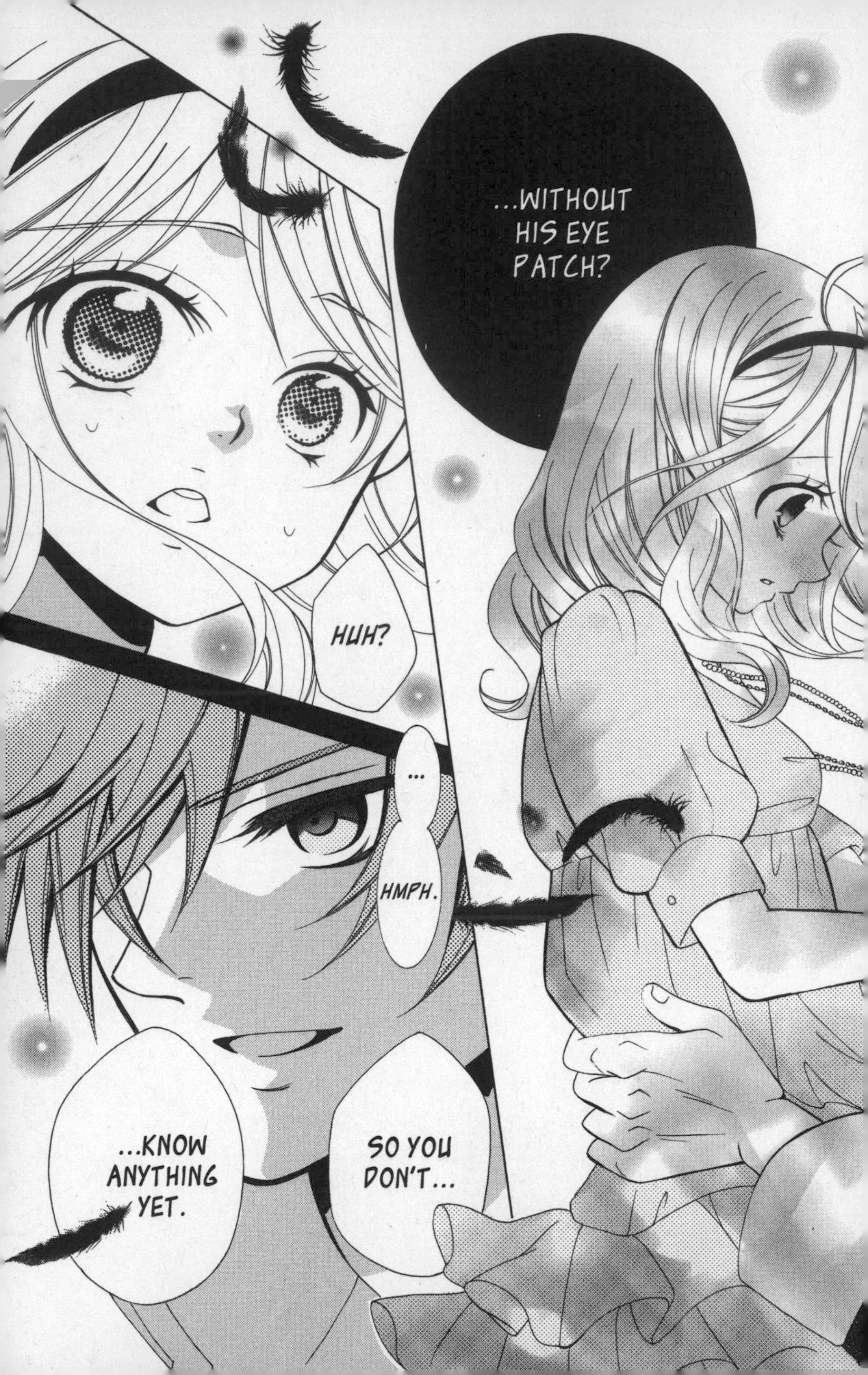
...WITHOUT HIS EYE PATCH?
HUH?
...
HMPH.
SO YOU DON'T...
...KNOW ANYTHING YET.

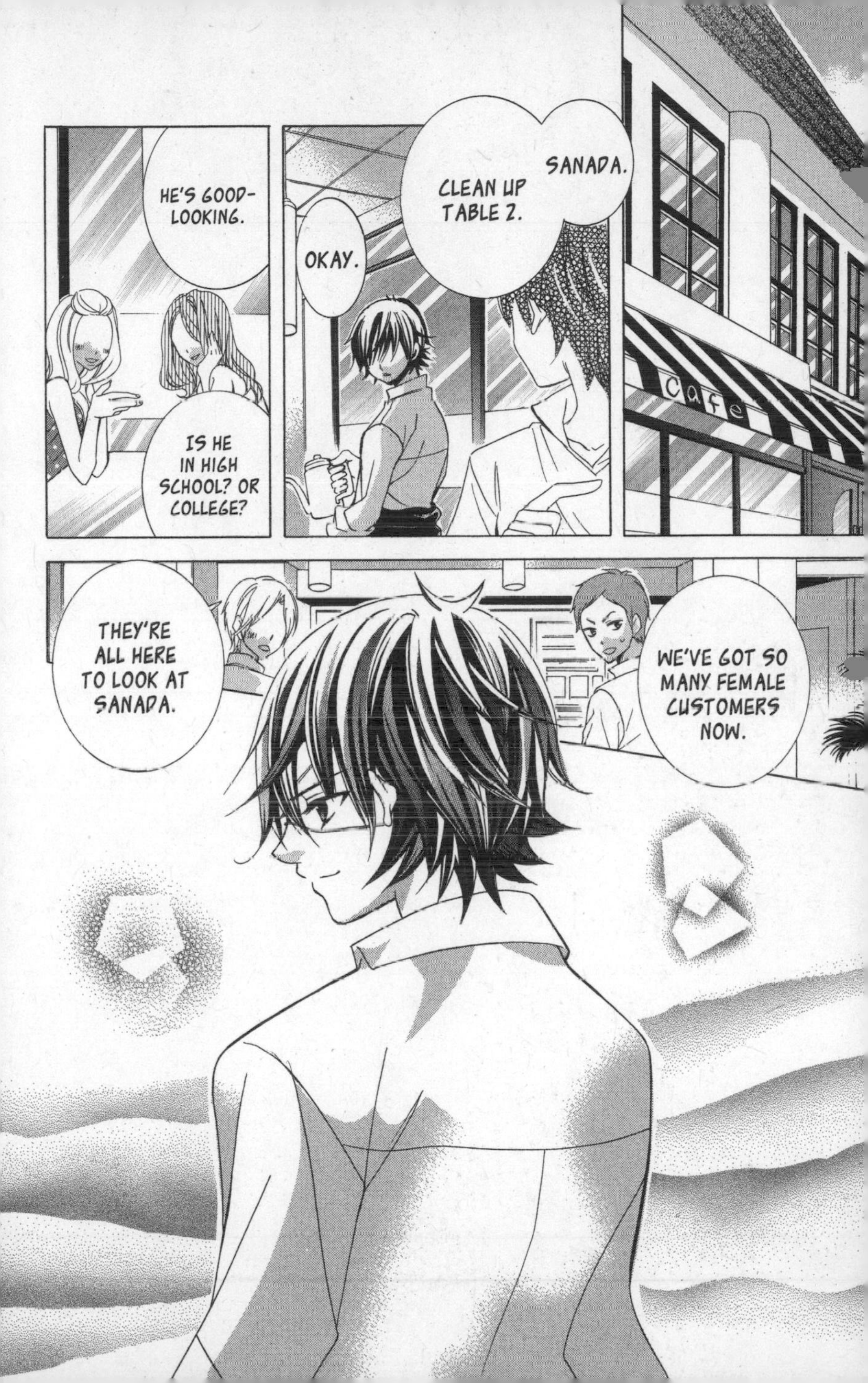
cafe
SANADA.
CLEAN UP TABLE 2.
OKAY.
HE'S GOOD-LOOKING.
IS HE IN HIGH SCHOOL? OR COLLEGE?
WE'VE GOT SO MANY FEMALE CUSTOMERS NOW.
THEY'RE ALL HERE TO LOOK AT SANADA.

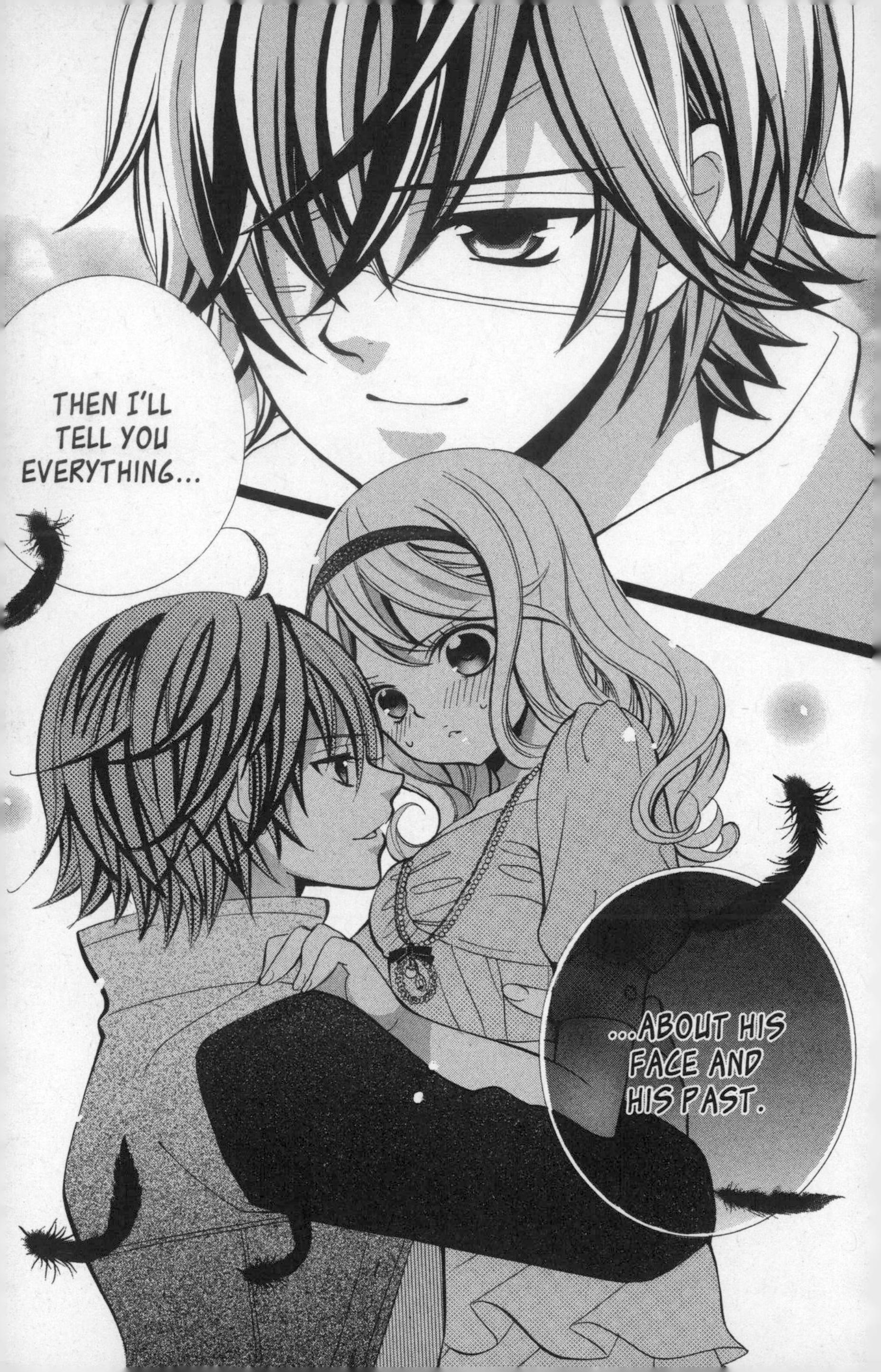
THEN I'LL TELL YOU EVERYTHING...
...ABOUT HIS FACE AND HIS PAST.

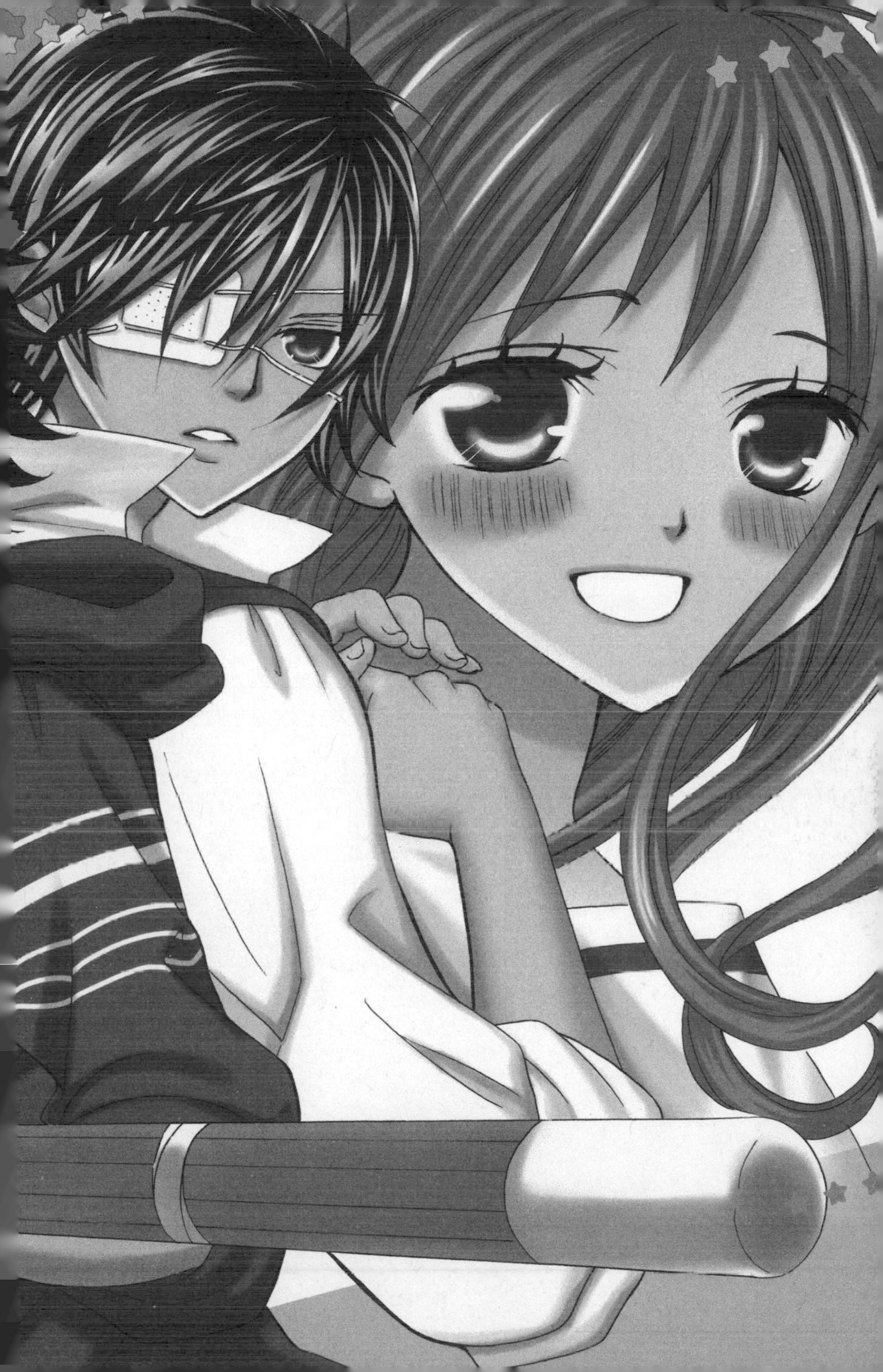

Chapter 35

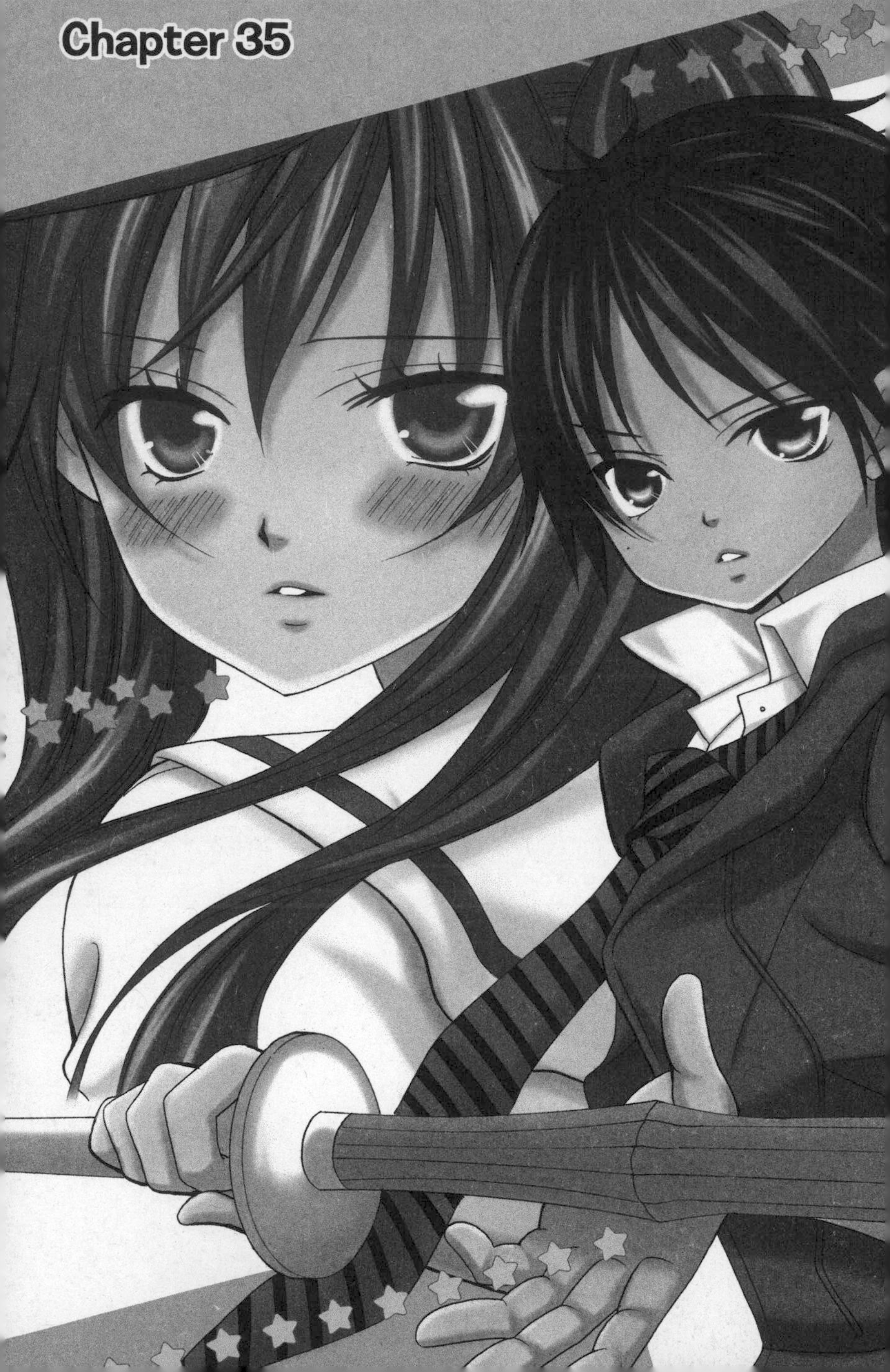

Idol group

pålet

Their second single is the *So Cute!* theme song

"Keep on Lovin' You"

Congrats! #6 on the ORICON singles chart!!!!

Idol group **pålet**'s single hit #6 on the ORICON weekly singles chart!! They sang the *So Cute!* anime DVD theme song that was included in the limited edition of the Japanese release of volume 6.

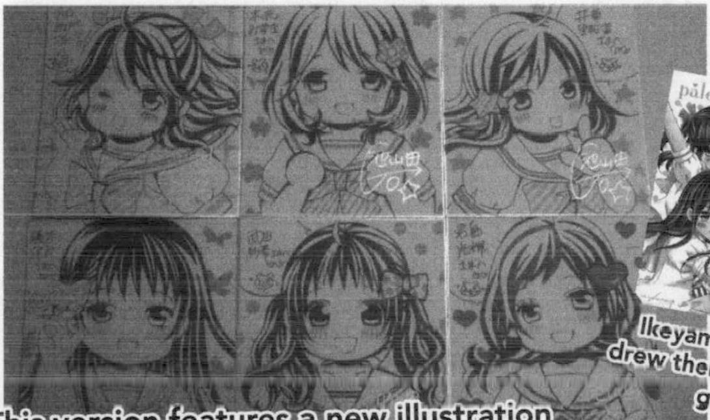

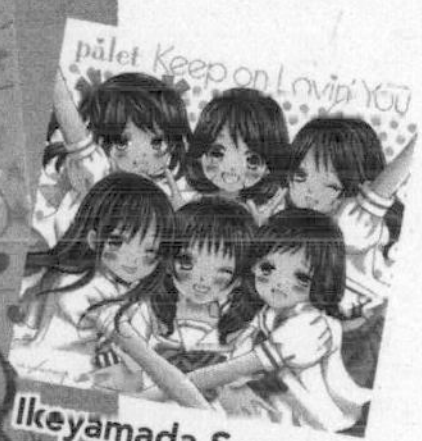
pålet Keep on Lovin' You

Ikeyamada Sensei drew their portraits as gifts!!

This version features a new illustration drawn by Ikeyamada Sensei. ♪

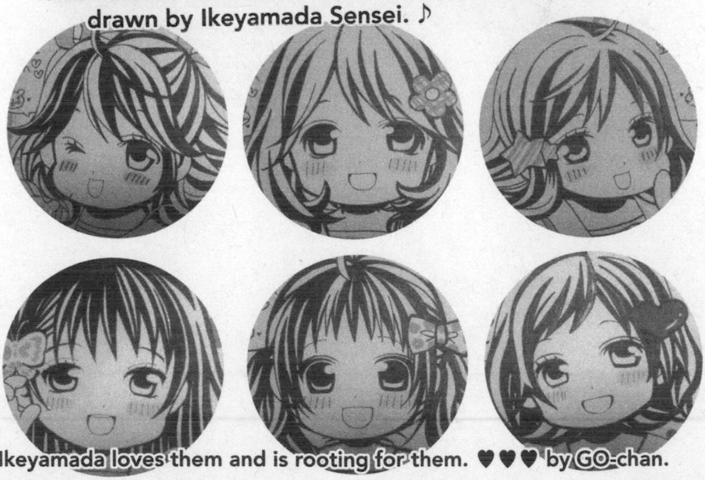

Ikeyamada loves them and is rooting for them. ♥♥♥ by GO-chan.

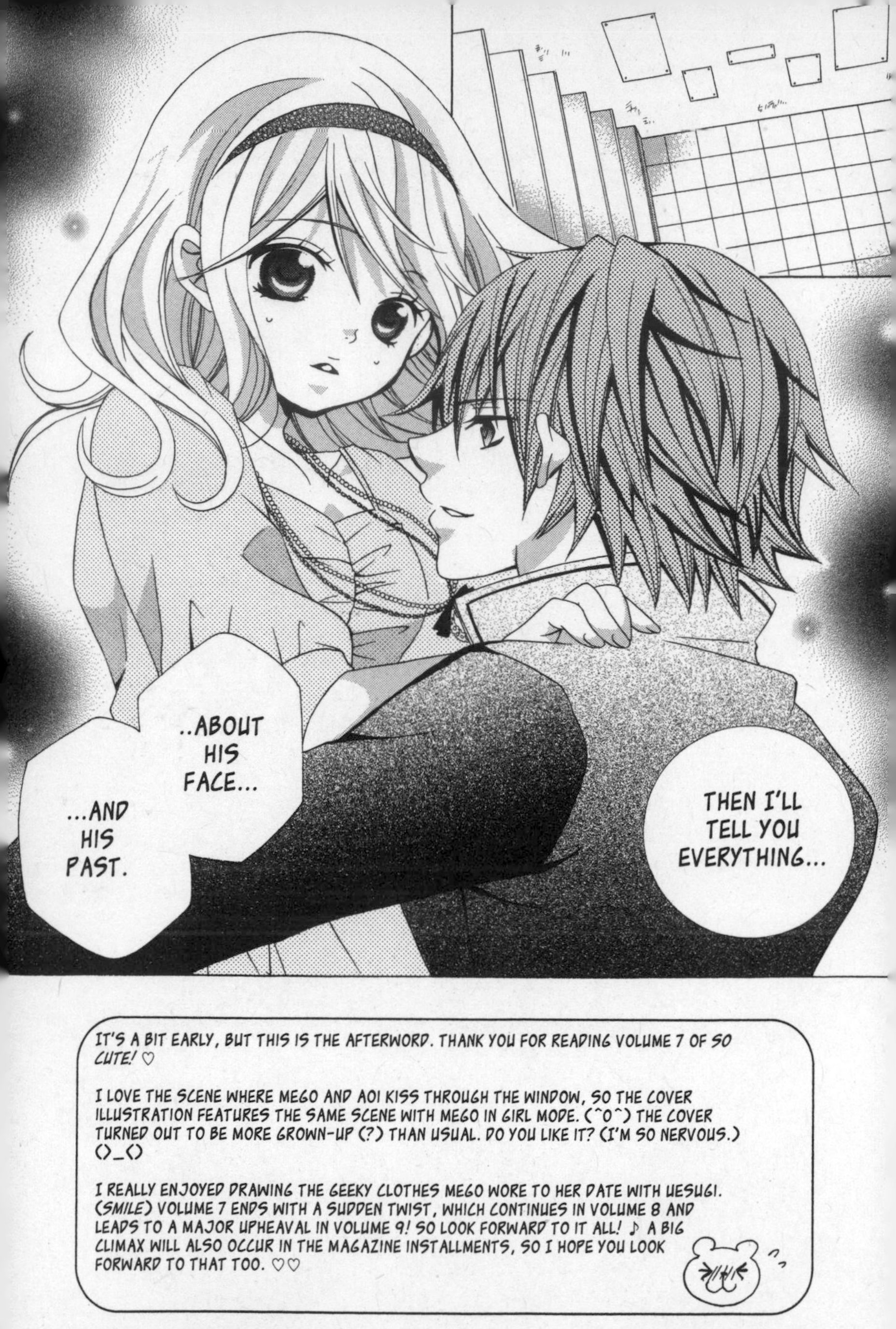
THEN I'LL TELL YOU EVERYTHING...
..ABOUT HIS FACE...
...AND HIS PAST.

IT'S A BIT EARLY, BUT THIS IS THE AFTERWORD. THANK YOU FOR READING VOLUME 7 OF *SO CUTE!* ♡

I LOVE THE SCENE WHERE MEGO AND AOI KISS THROUGH THE WINDOW, SO THE COVER ILLUSTRATION FEATURES THE SAME SCENE WITH MEGO IN GIRL MODE. (^O^) THE COVER TURNED OUT TO BE MORE GROWN-UP (?) THAN USUAL. DO YOU LIKE IT? (I'M SO NERVOUS.) ()_()

I REALLY ENJOYED DRAWING THE GEEKY CLOTHES MEGO WORE TO HER DATE WITH UESUGI. (*SMILE*) VOLUME 7 ENDS WITH A SUDDEN TWIST, WHICH CONTINUES IN VOLUME 8 AND LEADS TO A MAJOR UPHEAVAL IN VOLUME 9! SO LOOK FORWARD TO IT ALL! ♪ A BIG CLIMAX WILL ALSO OCCUR IN THE MAGAZINE INSTALLMENTS, SO I HOPE YOU LOOK FORWARD TO THAT TOO. ♡♡

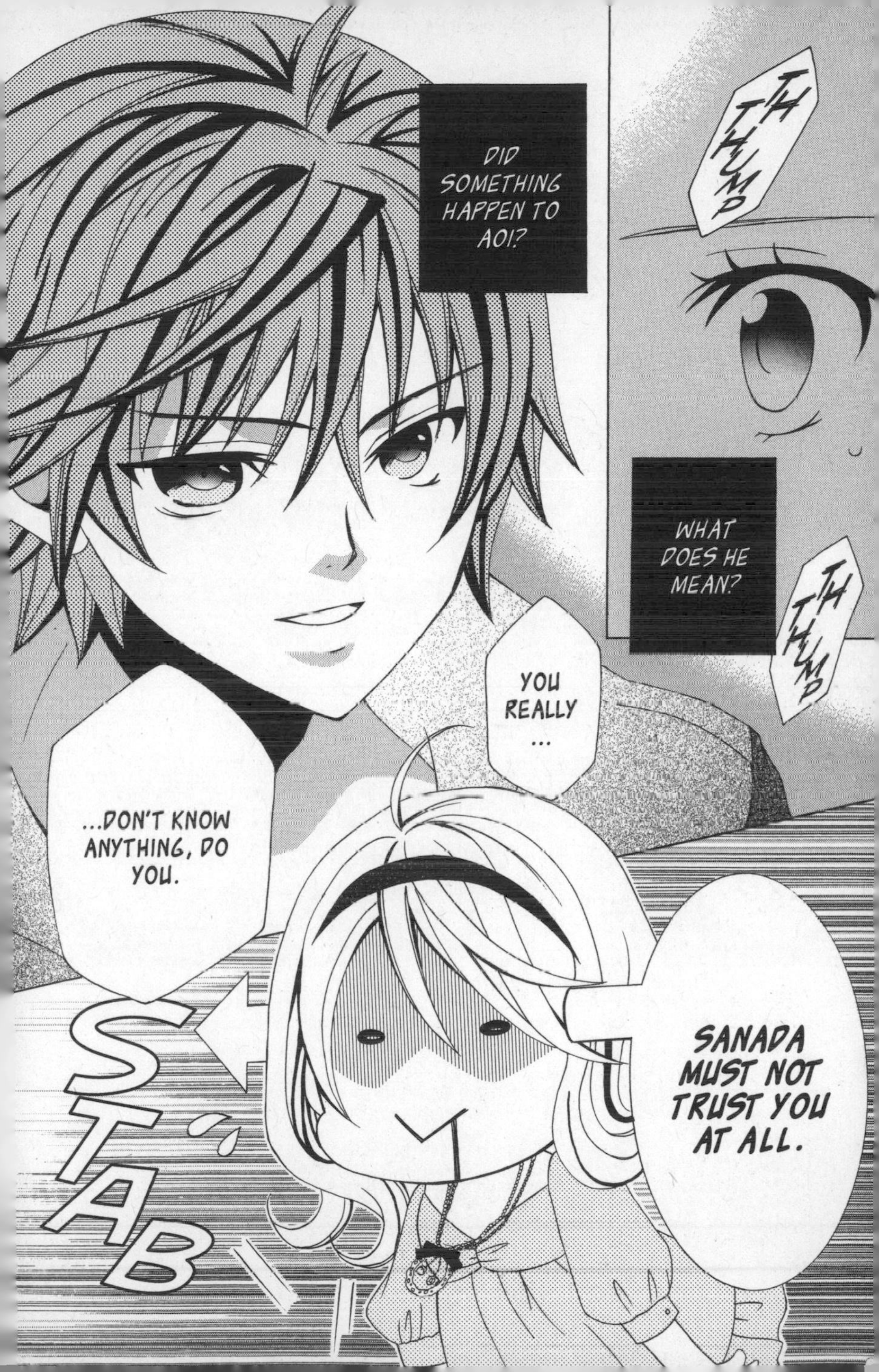
THTHUMP
WHAT DOES HE MEAN?
THTHUMP
DID SOMETHING HAPPEN TO AOI?
YOU REALLY ...
...DON'T KNOW ANYTHING, DO YOU.
SANADA MUST NOT TRUST YOU AT ALL.
STAB

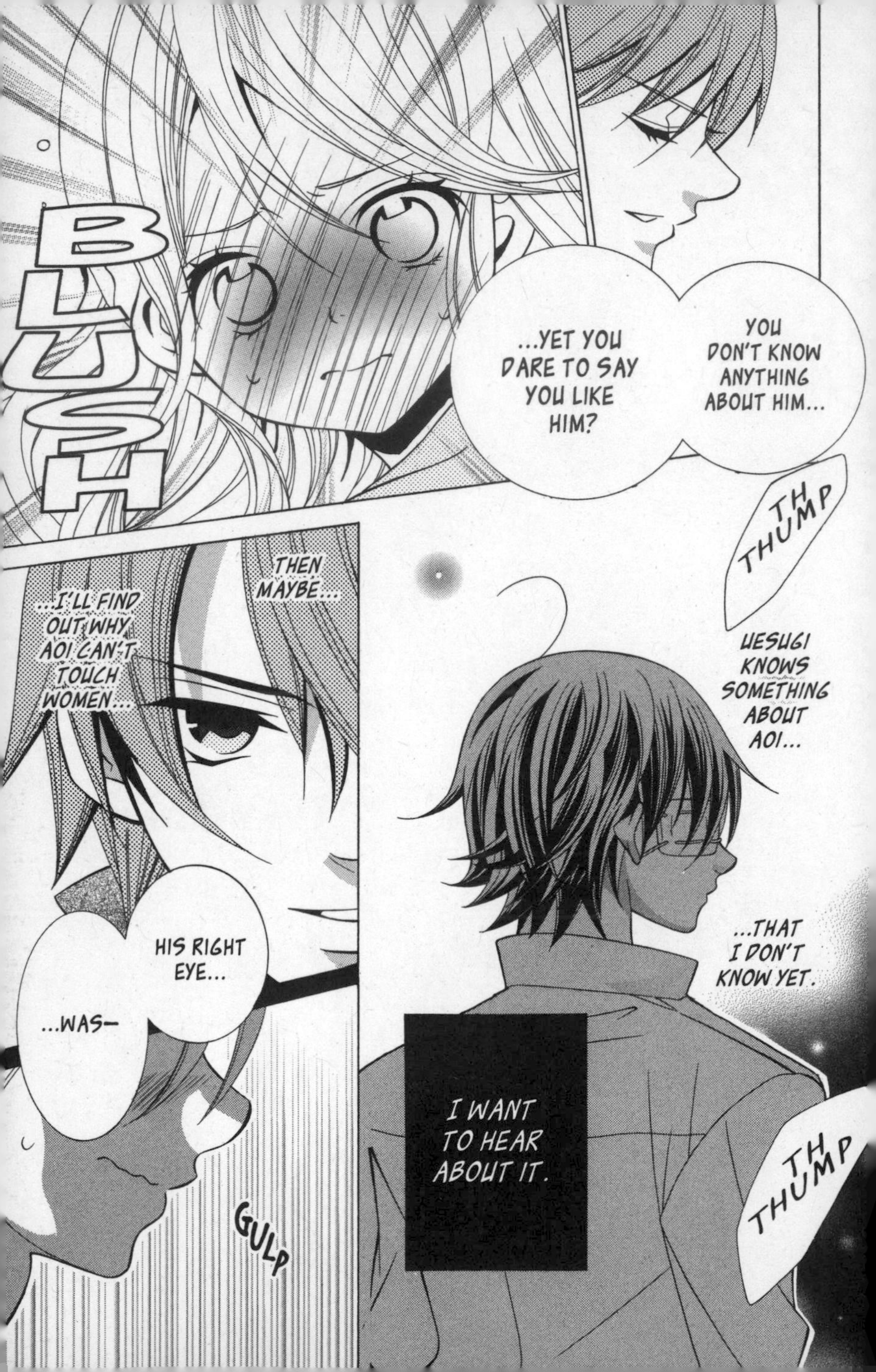
YOU DON'T KNOW ANYTHING ABOUT HIM...
...YET YOU DARE TO SAY YOU LIKE HIM?
BLUSH
TH THUMP
UESUGI KNOWS SOMETHING ABOUT AOI...
...THAT I DON'T KNOW YET.
I WANT TO HEAR ABOUT IT.
TH THUMP
THEN MAYBE...
...I'LL FIND OUT WHY AOI CAN'T TOUCH WOMEN...
HIS RIGHT EYE...
...WAS—
GULP

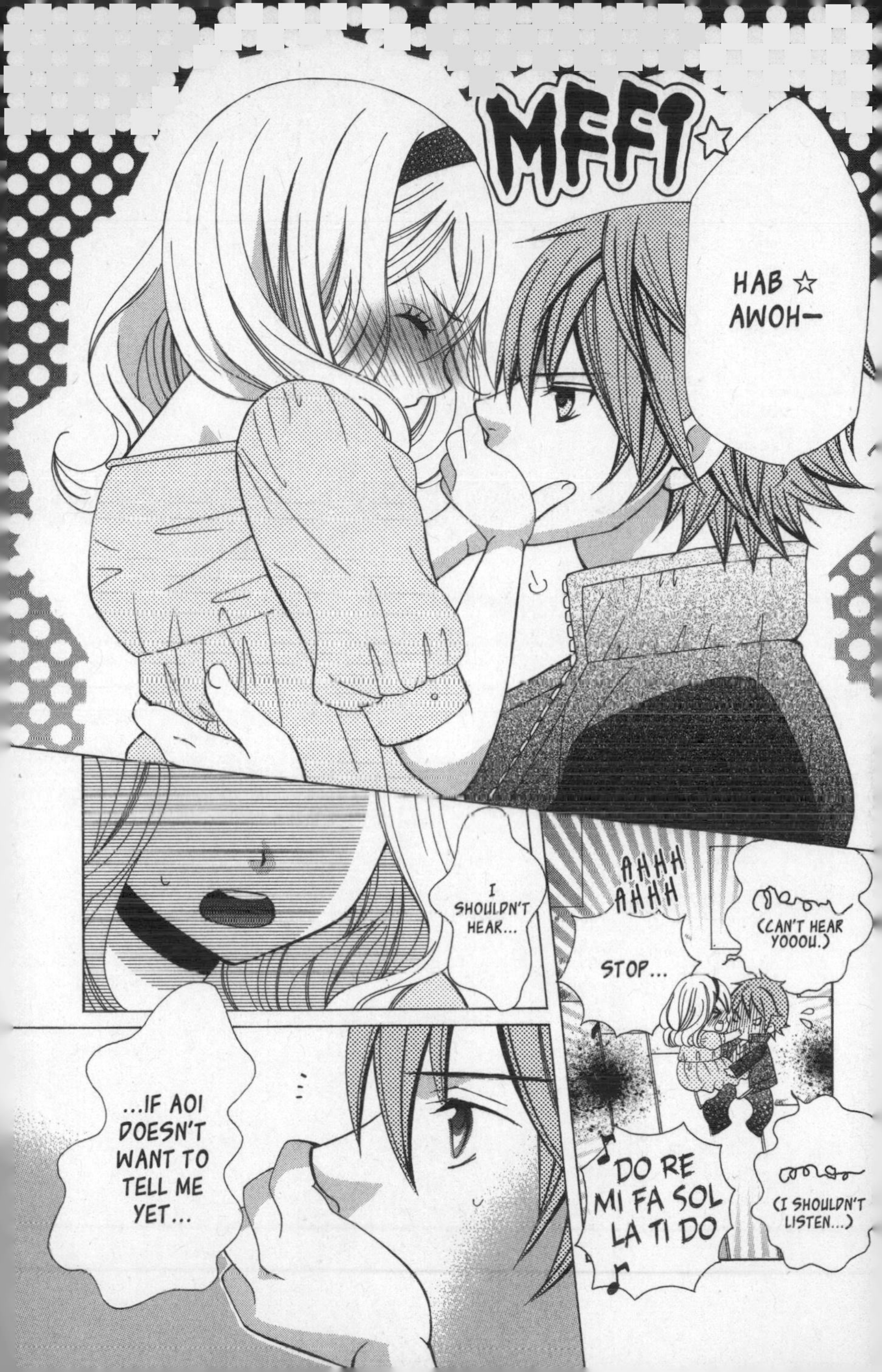
MFF!☆
HAB ☆ AWOH—
AHHH AHHH
(CAN'T HEAR YOOOU.)
STOP...
(I SHOULDN'T LISTEN...)
DO RE MI FA SOL LA TI DO
I SHOULDN'T HEAR...
...IF AOI DOESN'T WANT TO TELL ME YET...

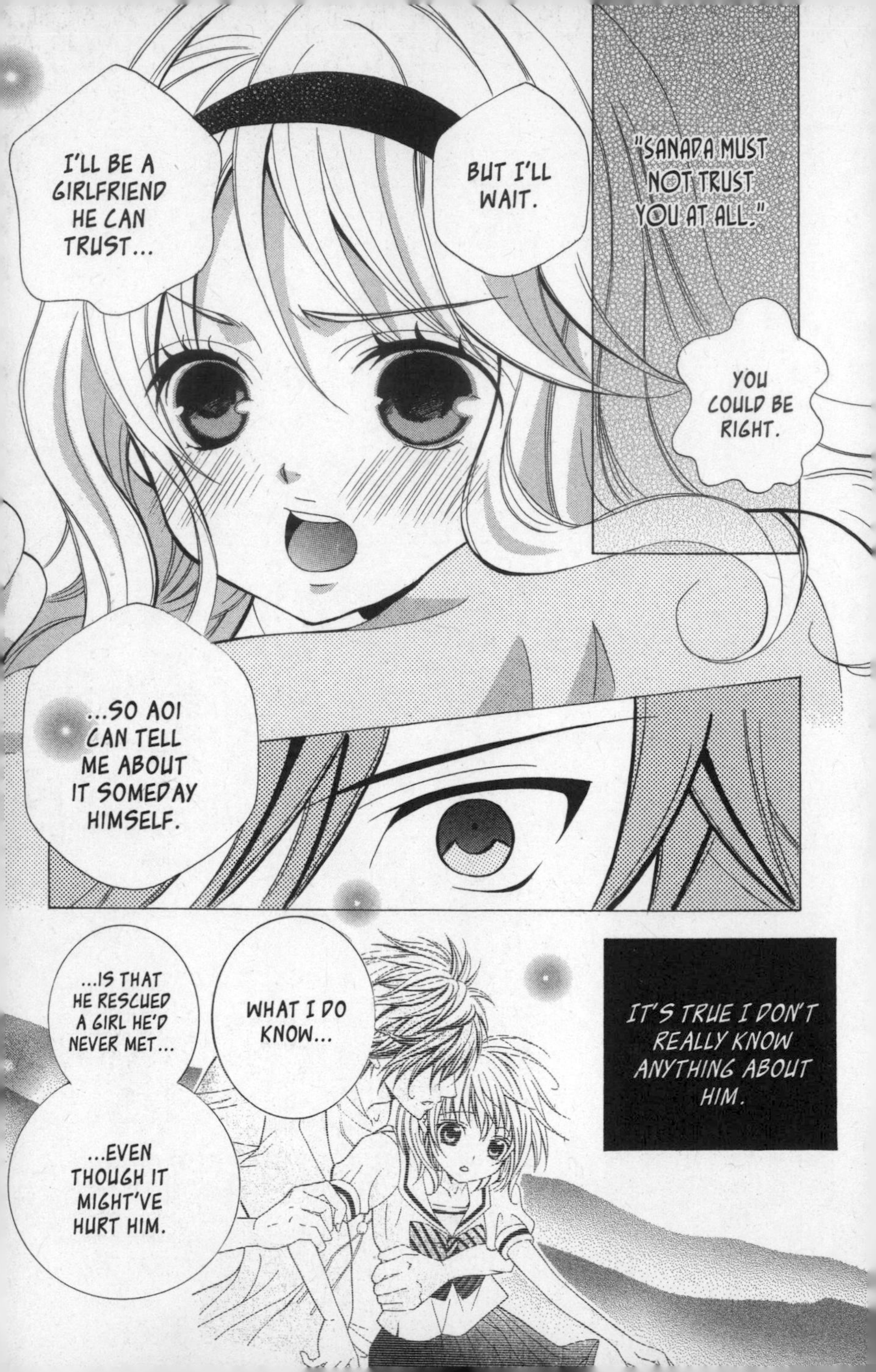
"SANADA MUST NOT TRUST YOU AT ALL."
YOU COULD BE RIGHT.
BUT I'LL WAIT.
I'LL BE A GIRLFRIEND HE CAN TRUST...
...SO AOI CAN TELL ME ABOUT IT SOMEDAY HIMSELF.
IT'S TRUE I DON'T REALLY KNOW ANYTHING ABOUT HIM.
WHAT I DO KNOW...
...IS THAT HE RESCUED A GIRL HE'D NEVER MET...
...EVEN THOUGH IT MIGHT'VE HURT HIM.

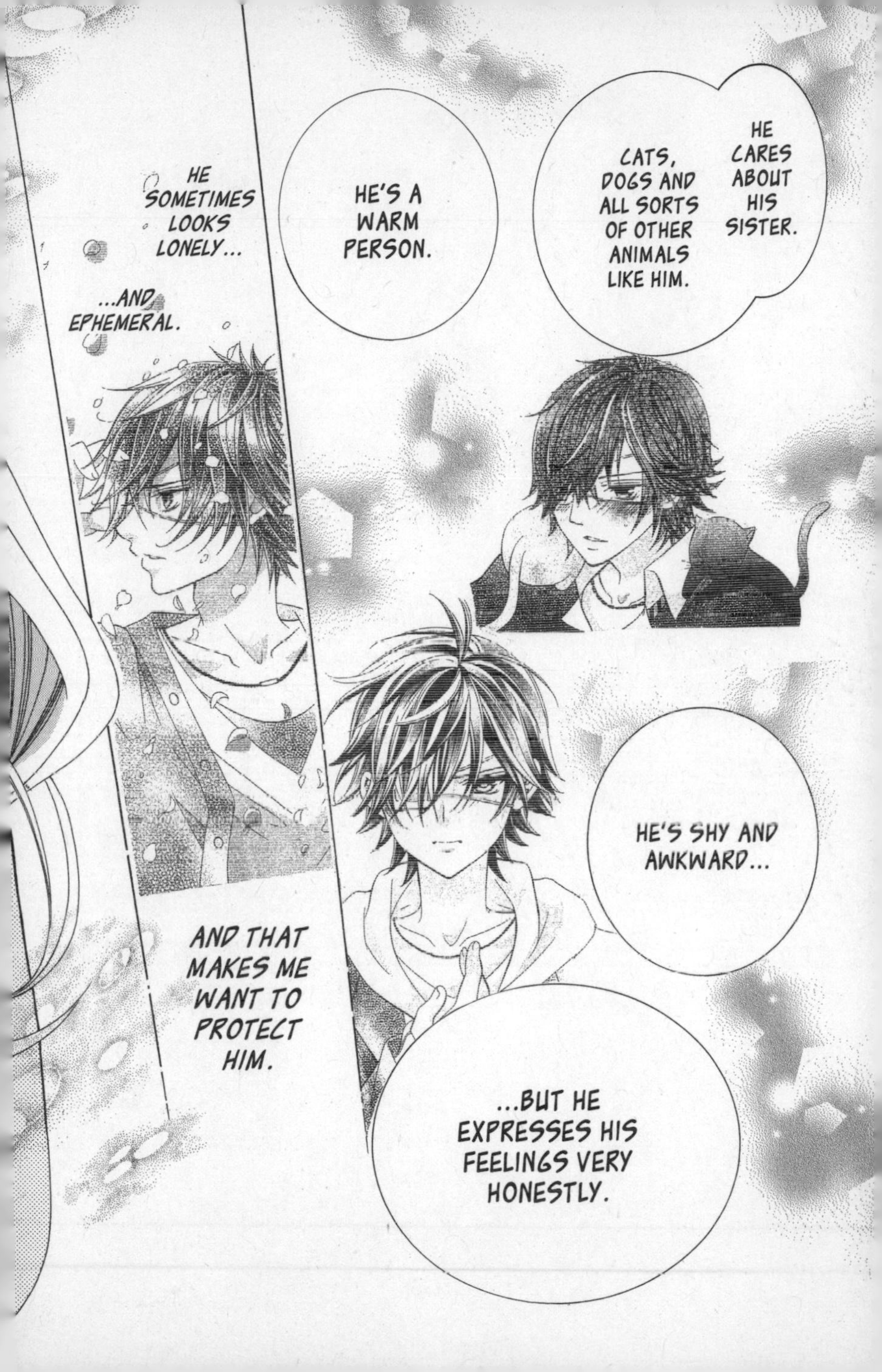
HE CARES ABOUT HIS SISTER.
CATS, DOGS AND ALL SORTS OF OTHER ANIMALS LIKE HIM.
HE'S A WARM PERSON.
HE'S SHY AND AWKWARD...
...BUT HE EXPRESSES HIS FEELINGS VERY HONESTLY.
HE SOMETIMES LOOKS LONELY...
...AND EPHEMERAL.
AND THAT MAKES ME WANT TO PROTECT HIM.

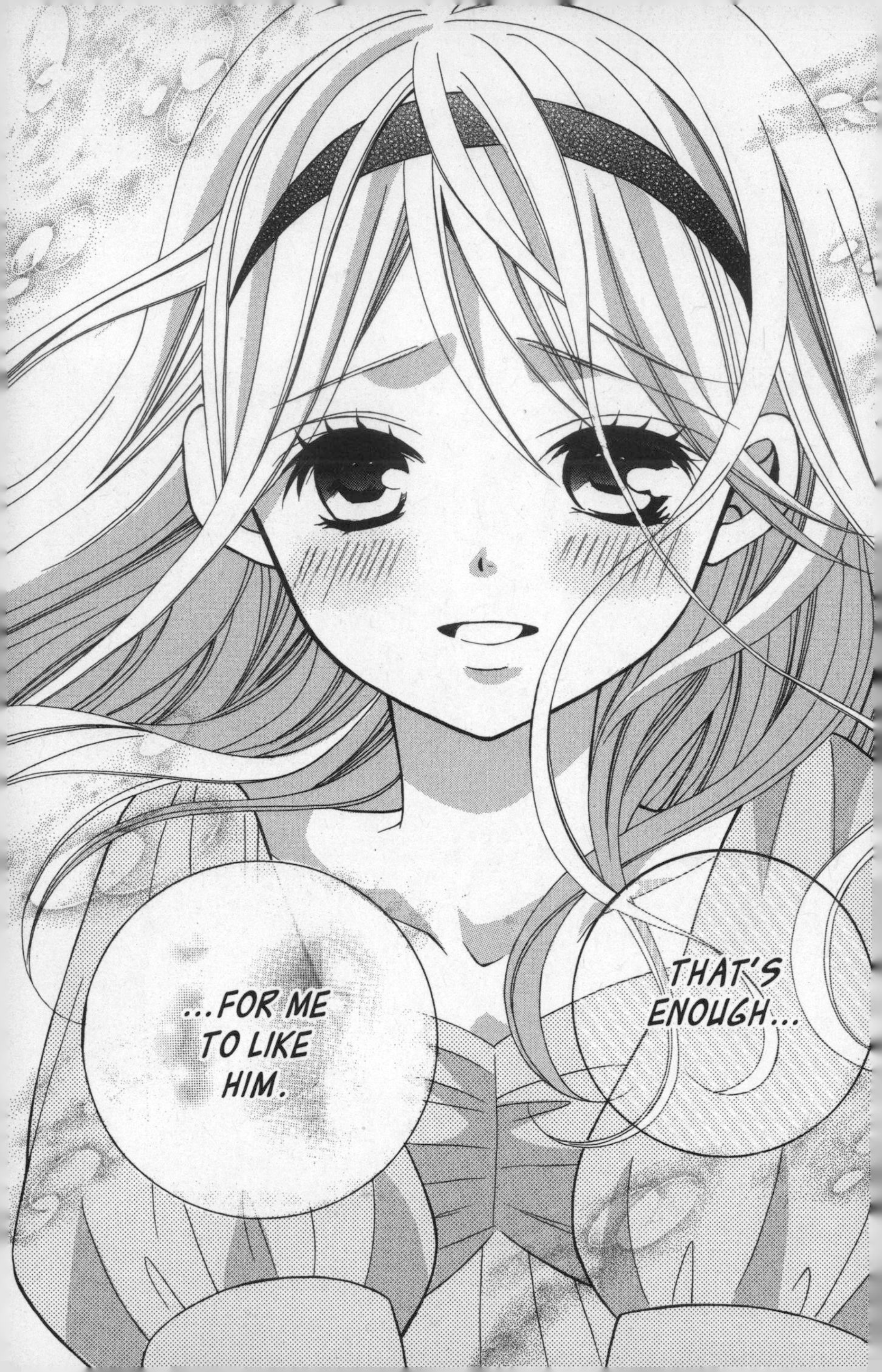
THAT'S ENOUGH...
...FOR ME TO LIKE HIM.

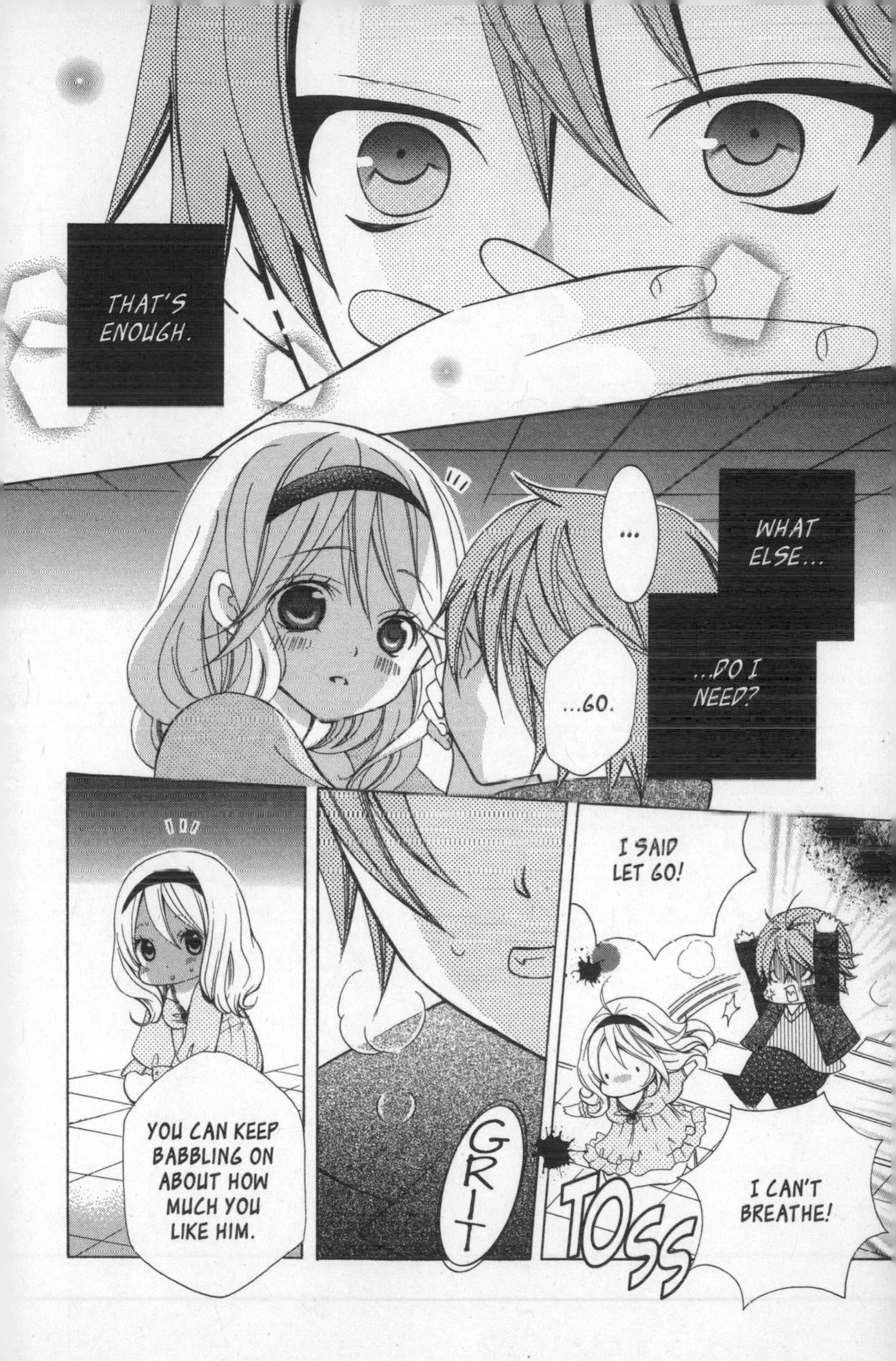
THAT'S ENOUGH.
WHAT ELSE...
...
...DO I NEED?
...GO.
I SAID LET GO!
I CAN'T BREATHE!
TOSS
GRIT
YOU CAN KEEP BABBLING ON ABOUT HOW MUCH YOU LIKE HIM.

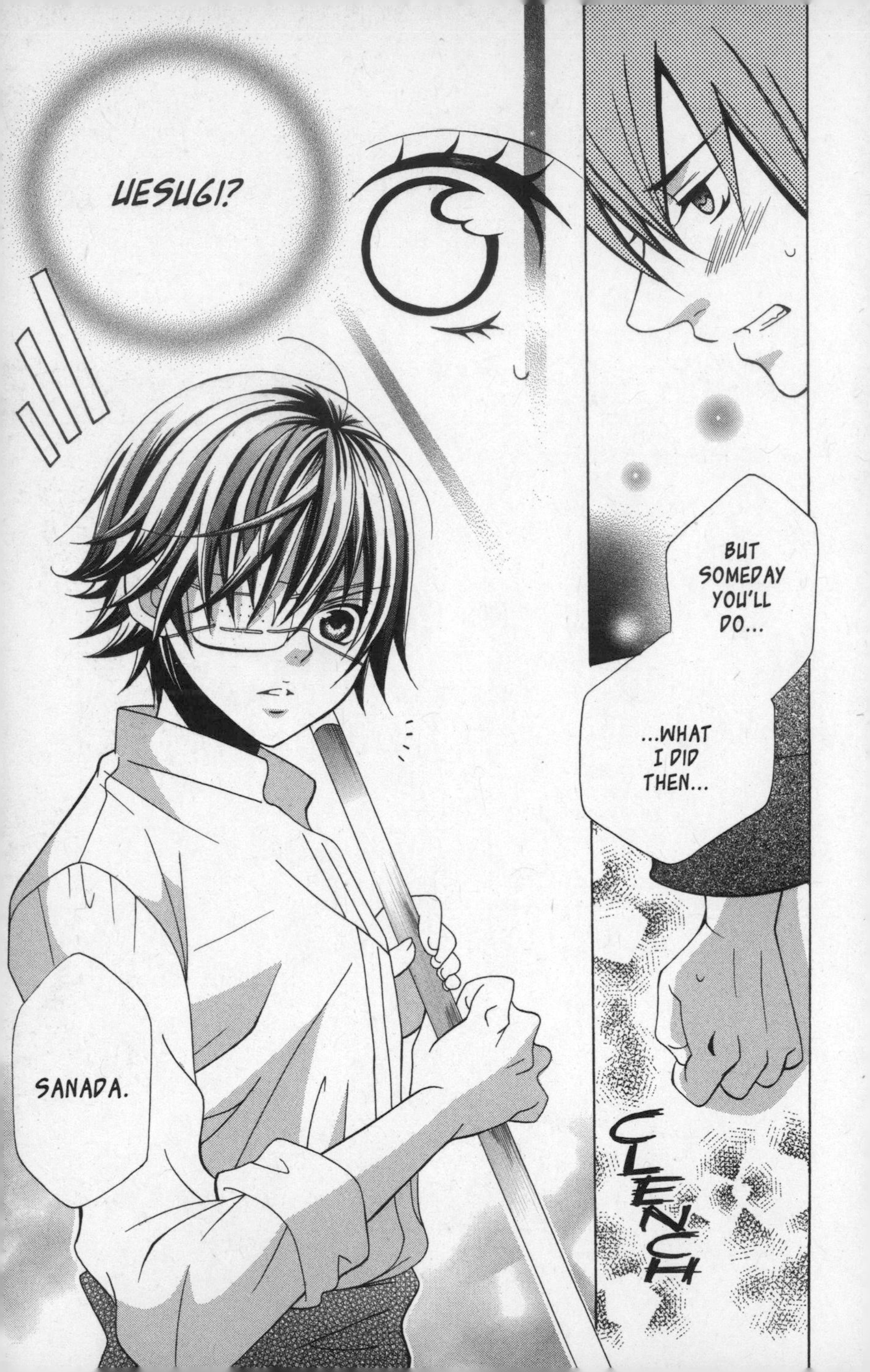
BUT SOMEDAY YOU'LL DO...
...WHAT I DID THEN...
CLENCH
UESUGI!?
SANADA.

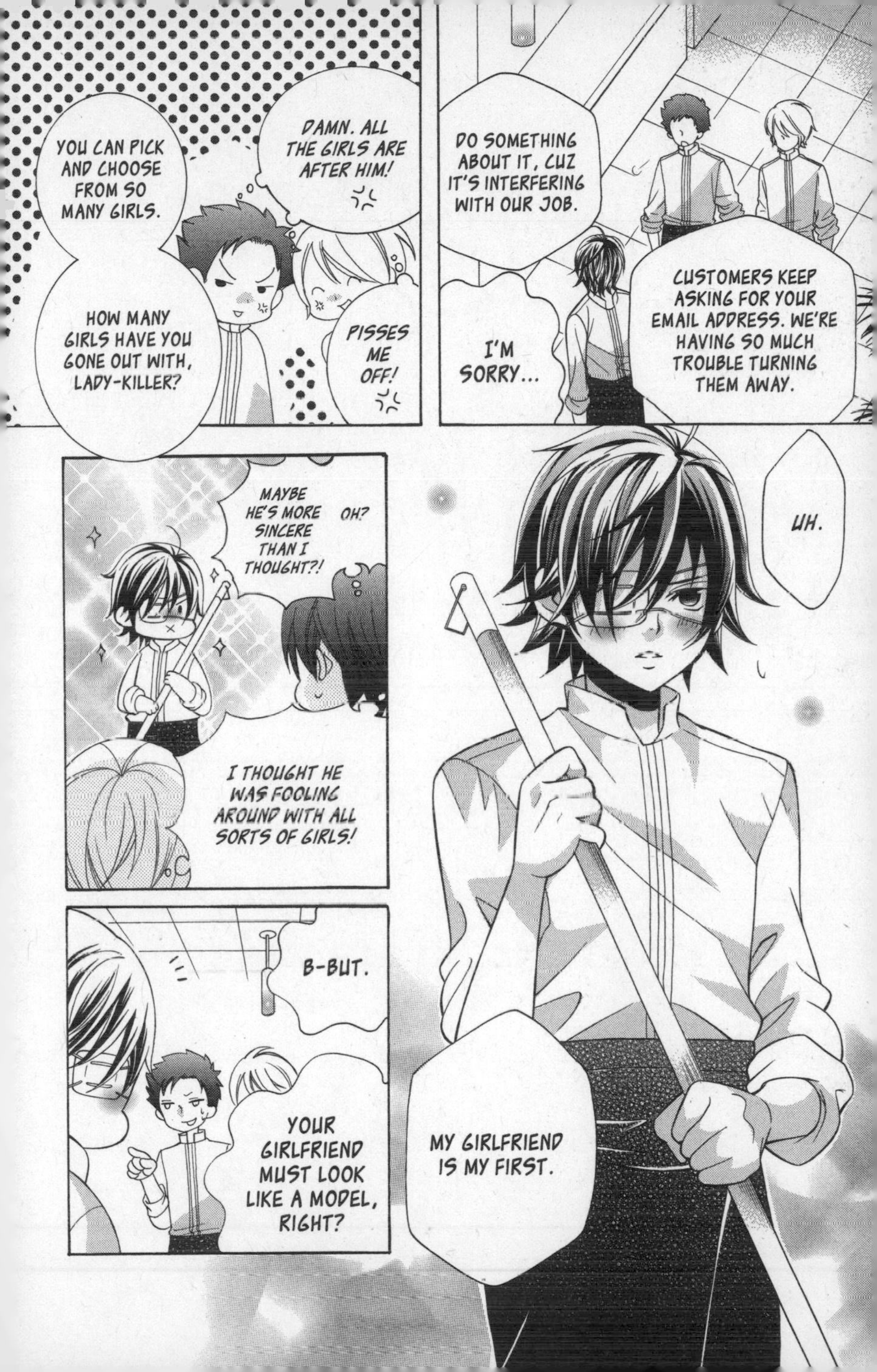
DO SOMETHING ABOUT IT, CUZ IT'S INTERFERING WITH OUR JOB.
CUSTOMERS KEEP ASKING FOR YOUR EMAIL ADDRESS. WE'RE HAVING SO MUCH TROUBLE TURNING THEM AWAY.
I'M SORRY...
DAMN. ALL THE GIRLS ARE AFTER HIM!
YOU CAN PICK AND CHOOSE FROM SO MANY GIRLS.
PISSES ME OFF!
HOW MANY GIRLS HAVE YOU GONE OUT WITH, LADY-KILLER?
UH.
MY GIRLFRIEND IS MY FIRST.
OH?
MAYBE HE'S MORE SINCERE THAN I THOUGHT?!
I THOUGHT HE WAS FOOLING AROUND WITH ALL SORTS OF GIRLS!
B-BUT.
YOUR GIRLFRIEND MUST LOOK LIKE A MODEL, RIGHT?

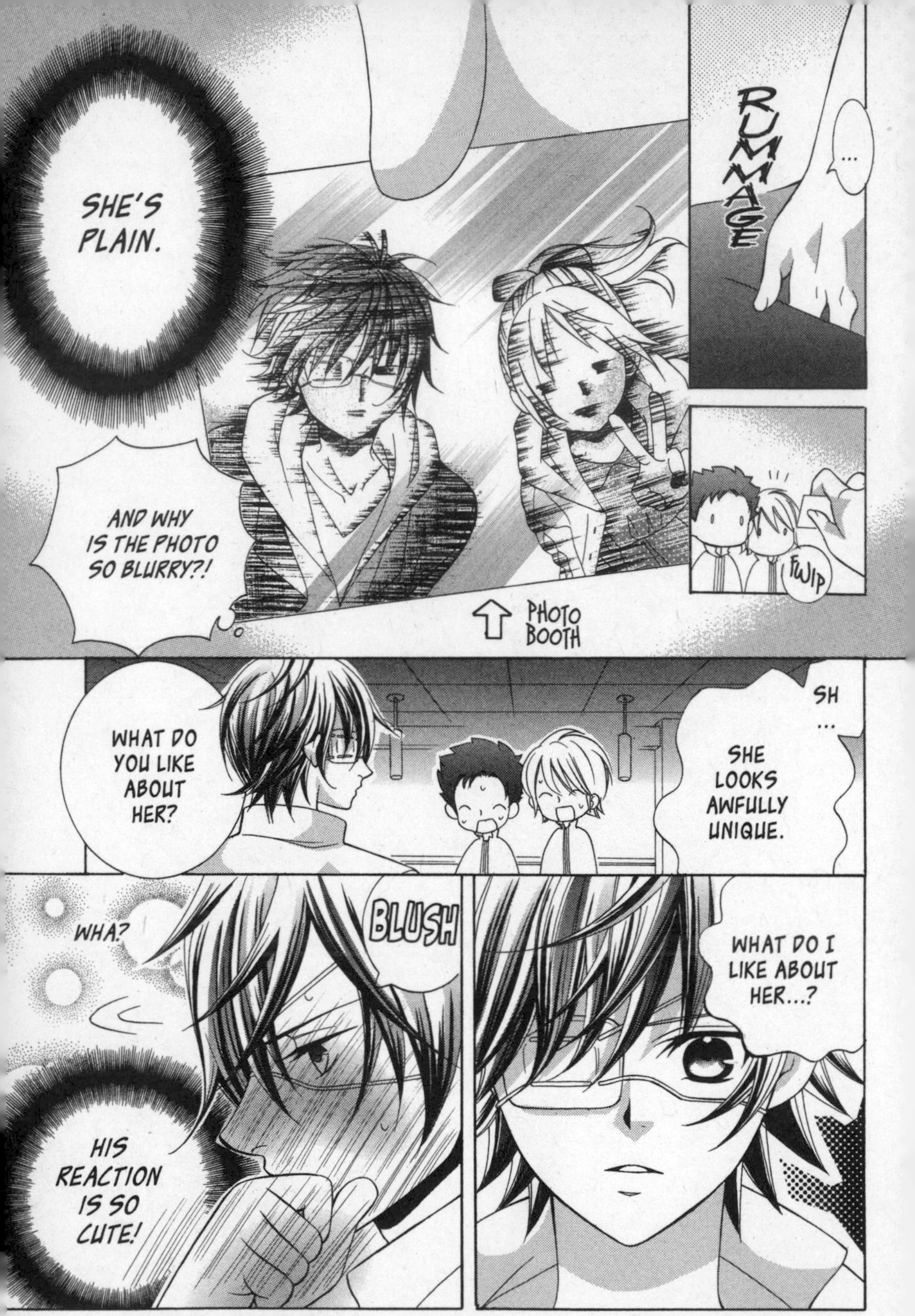
RUMMAGE
...
FWIP
SHE'S PLAIN.
AND WHY IS THE PHOTO SO BLURRY?!
PHOTO BOOTH
SH ...
SHE LOOKS AWFULLY UNIQUE.
WHAT DO YOU LIKE ABOUT HER?
WHAT DO I LIKE ABOUT HER...?
BLUSH
WHA?
HIS REACTION IS SO CUTE!

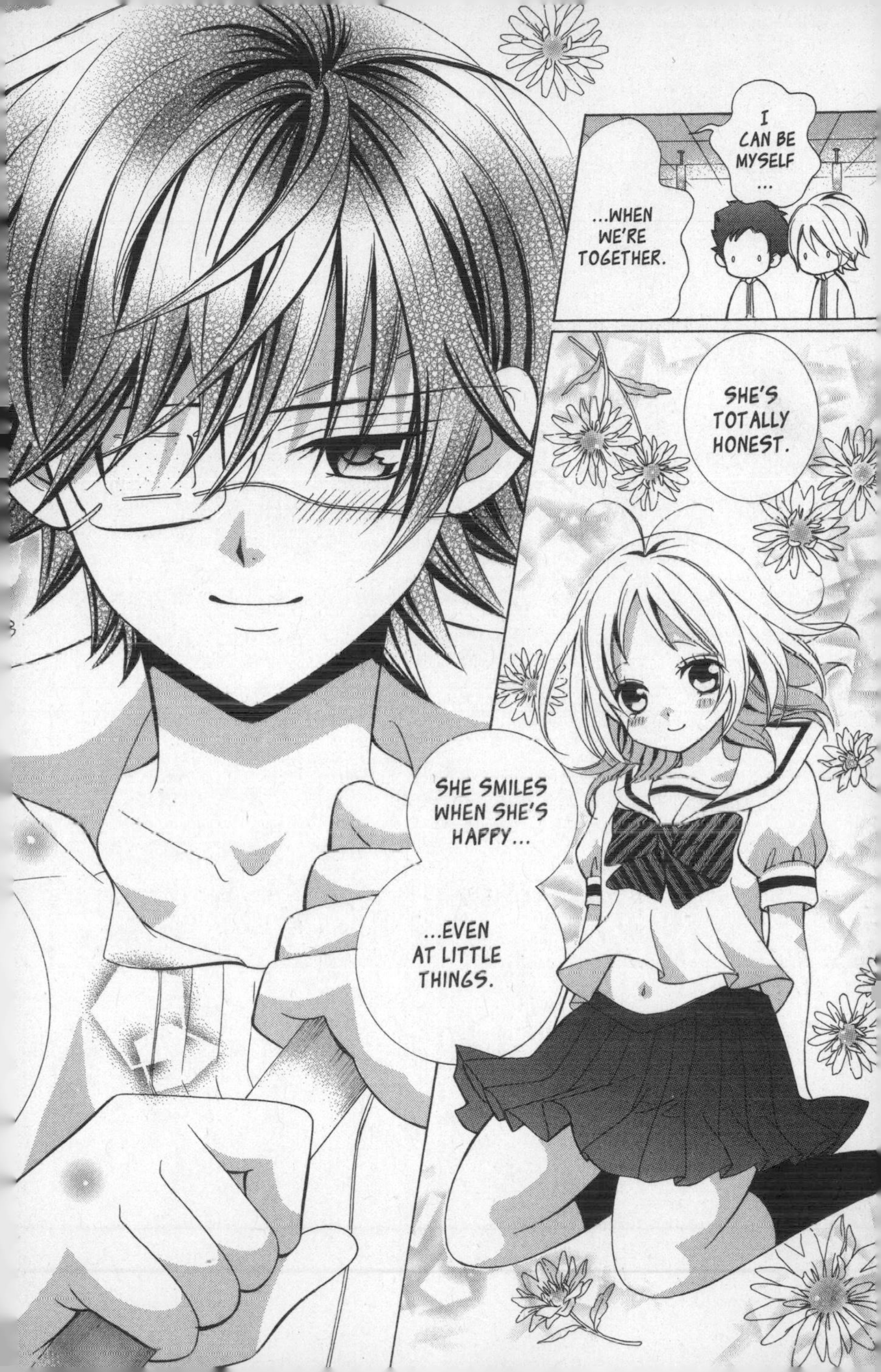
I CAN BE MYSELF ...
...WHEN WE'RE TOGETHER.
SHE'S TOTALLY HONEST.
SHE SMILES WHEN SHE'S HAPPY...
...EVEN AT LITTLE THINGS.

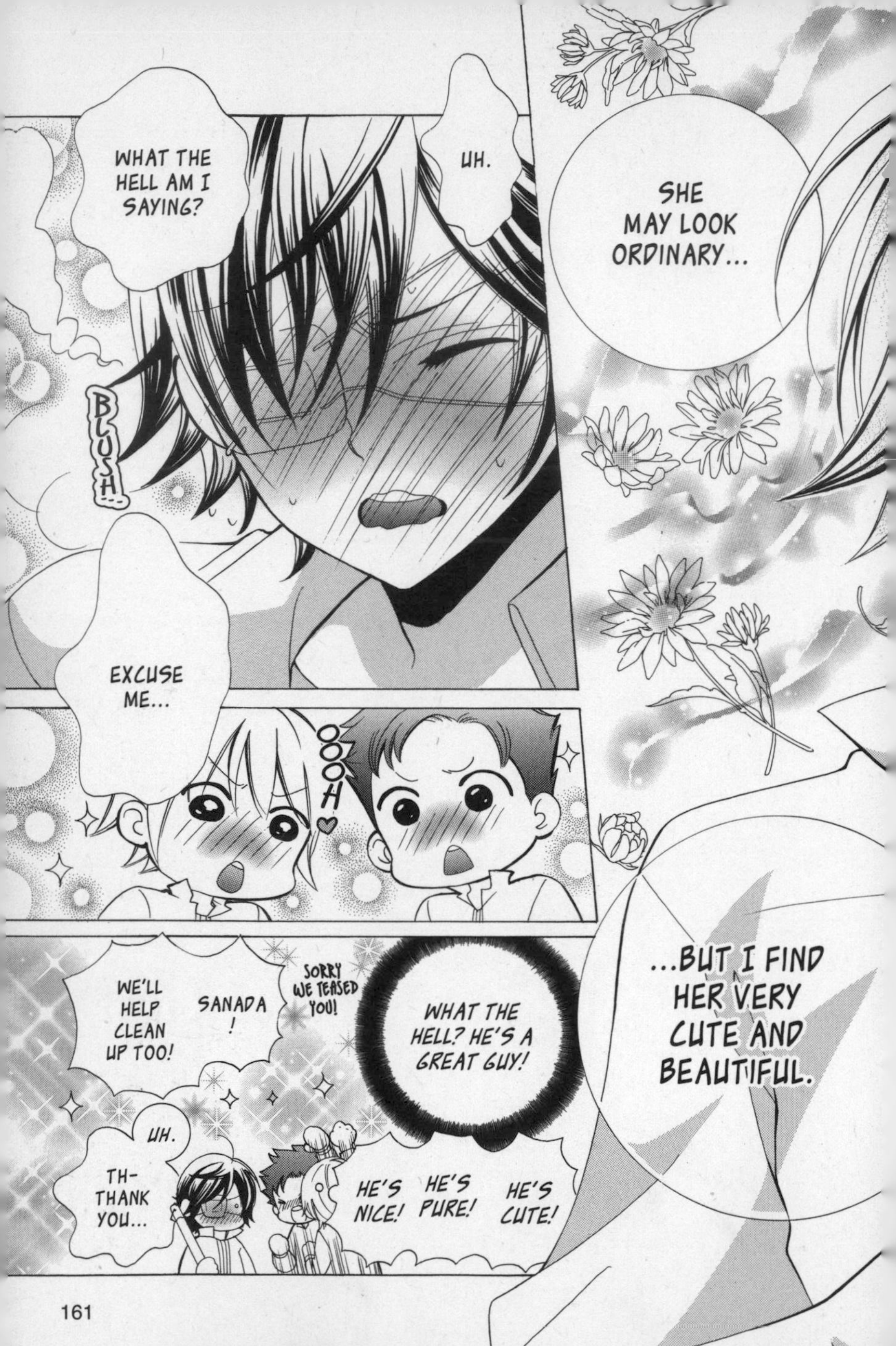

SHE MAY LOOK ORDINARY...
...BUT I FIND HER VERY CUTE AND BEAUTIFUL.
UH.
WHAT THE HELL AM I SAYING?
BLUSH
EXCUSE ME...
OOOH
SORRY WE TEASED YOU!
SANADA!
WE'LL HELP CLEAN UP TOO!
WHAT THE HELL? HE'S A GREAT GUY!
HE'S CUTE!
HE'S PURE!
HE'S NICE!
UH.
TH-THANK YOU...

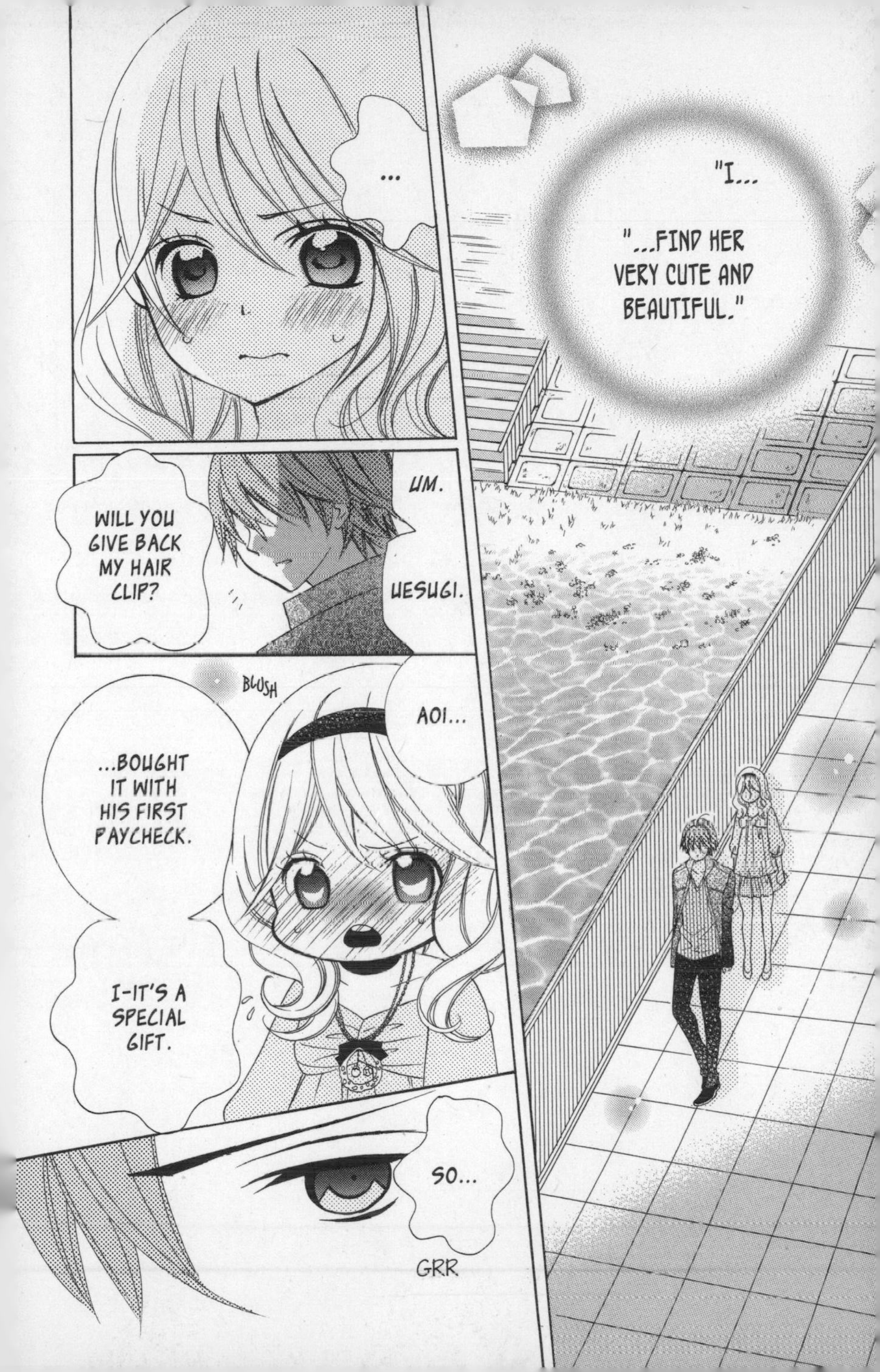
"I...
"...FIND HER VERY CUTE AND BEAUTIFUL."
...
UM.
UESUGI.
WILL YOU GIVE BACK MY HAIR CLIP?
BLUSH
AOI...
...BOUGHT IT WITH HIS FIRST PAYCHECK.
I-IT'S A SPECIAL GIFT.
SO...
GRR

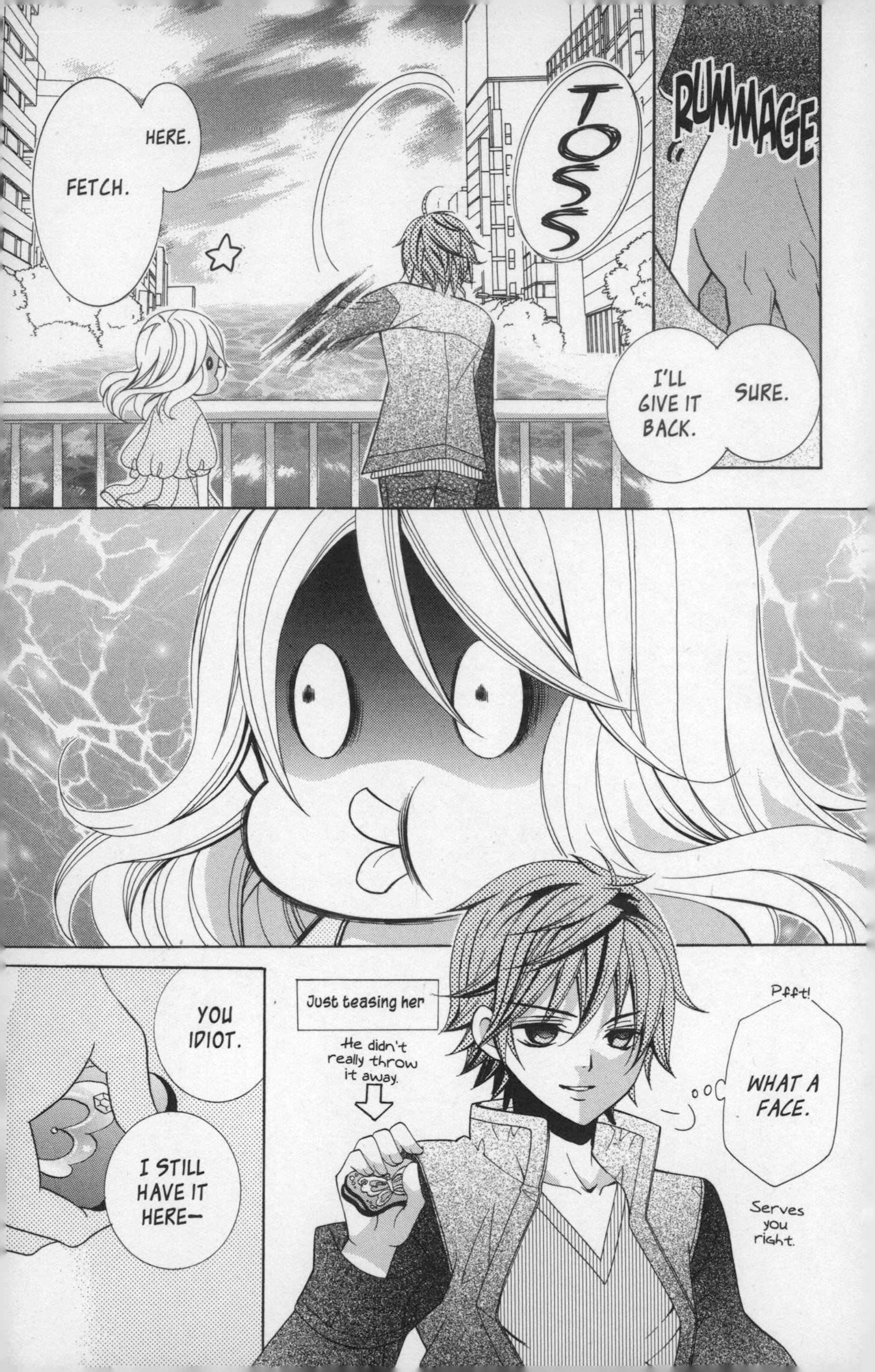
RUMMAGE
SURE.
I'LL GIVE IT BACK.
TOSS
HERE.
FETCH.
Pfft!
WHAT A FACE.
Serves you right.
Just teasing her
He didn't really throw it away.
YOU IDIOT.
I STILL HAVE IT HERE—

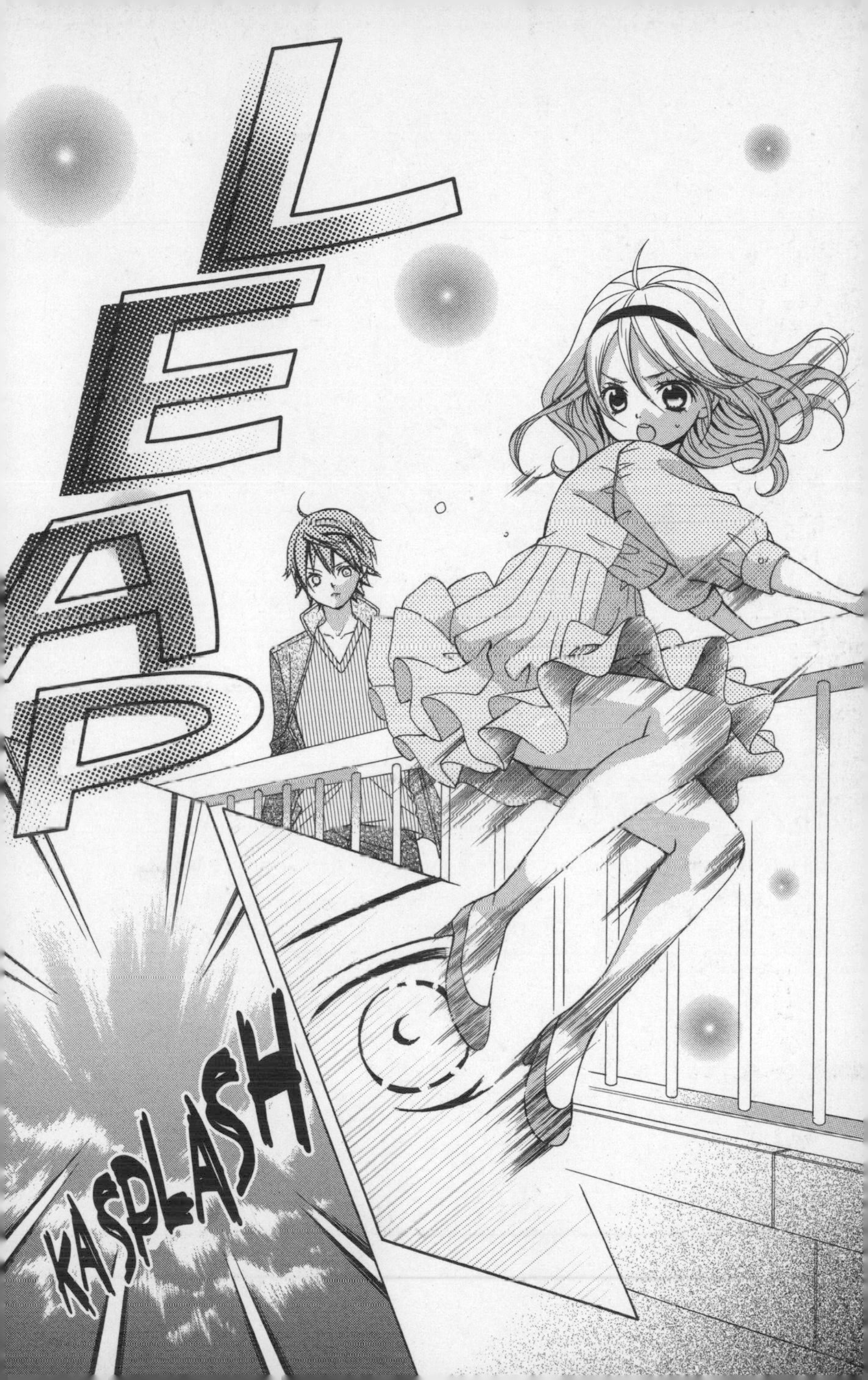
LEAP
KASPLASH

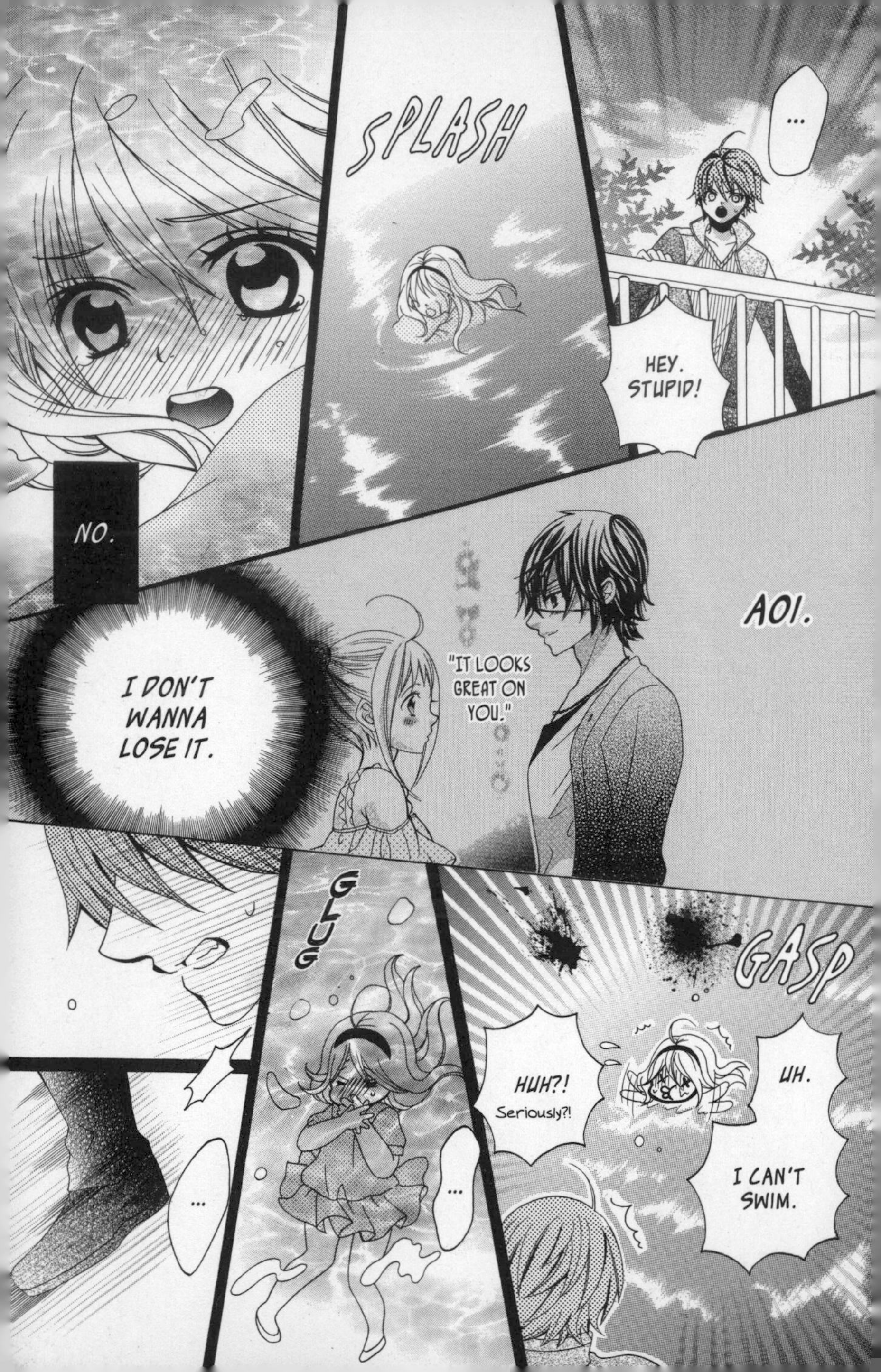
...
HEY. STUPID!
SPLASH
NO.
AOI.
"IT LOOKS GREAT ON YOU."
I DON'T WANNA LOSE IT.
GASP
UH.
I CAN'T SWIM.
HUH?!
Seriously?!
GLUG
...
...

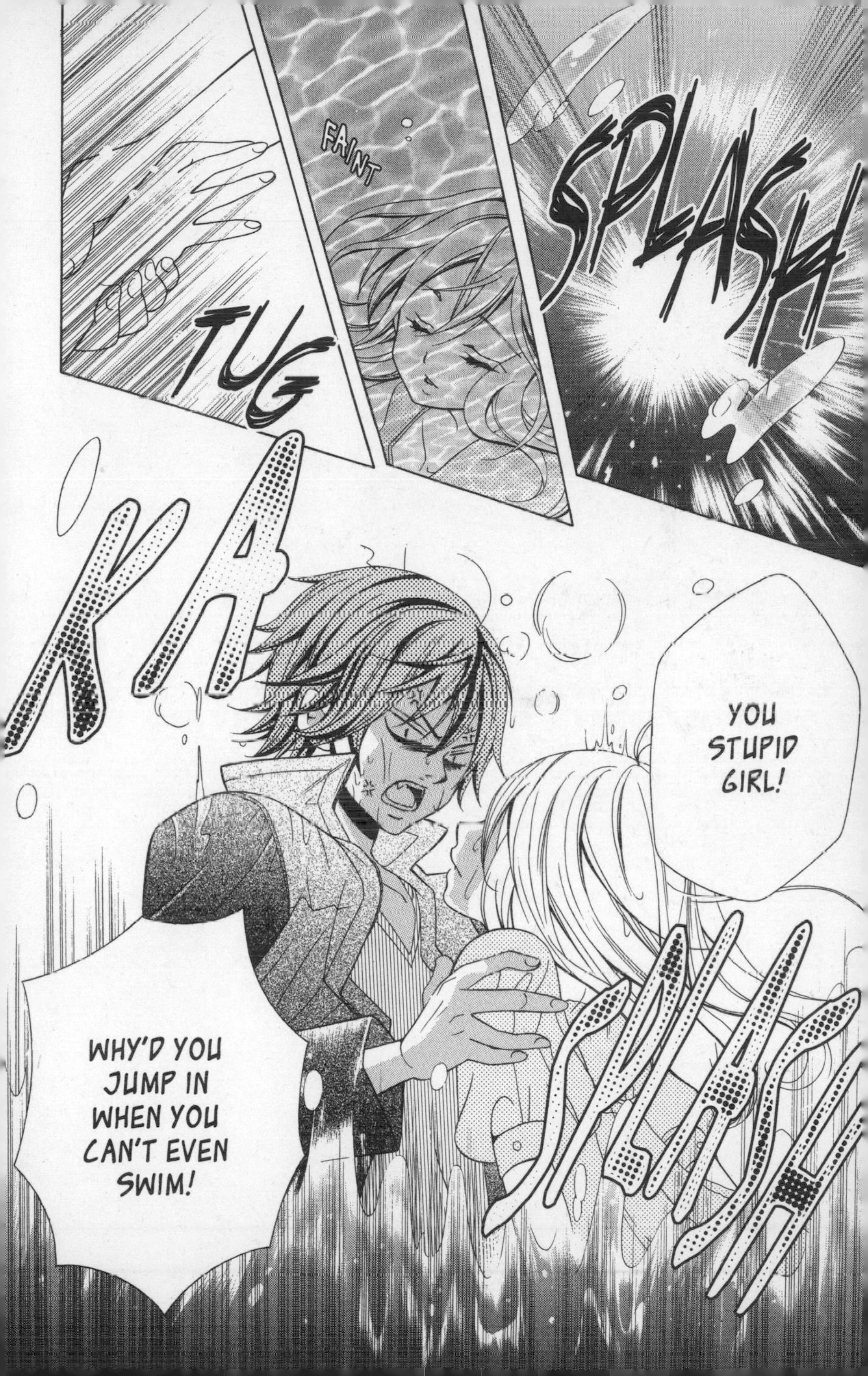
SPLASH
FAINT
TUG
YOU STUPID GIRL!
KA
SPLASH
WHY'D YOU JUMP IN WHEN YOU CAN'T EVEN SWIM!

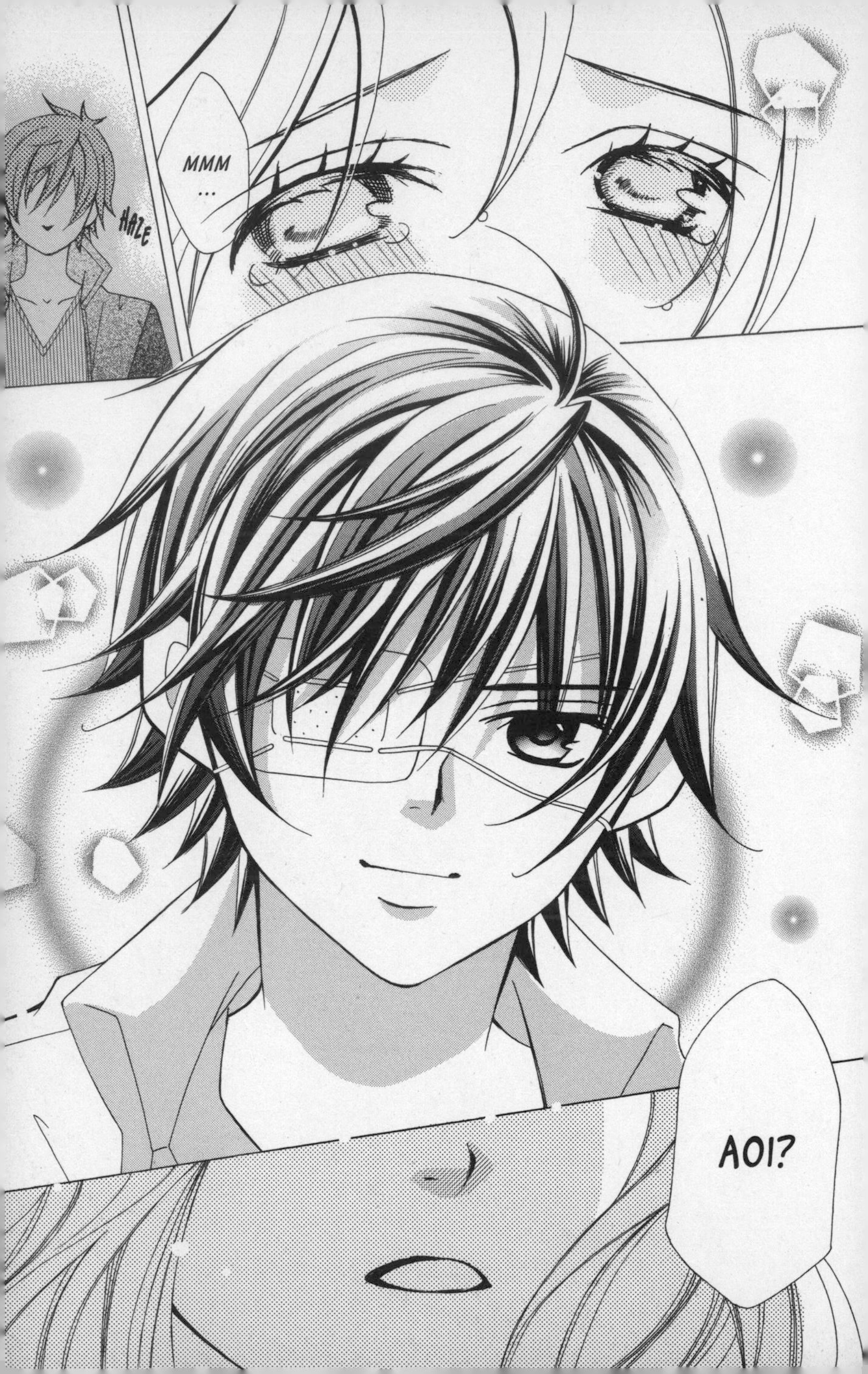
MMM
...
HAZE
AOI?

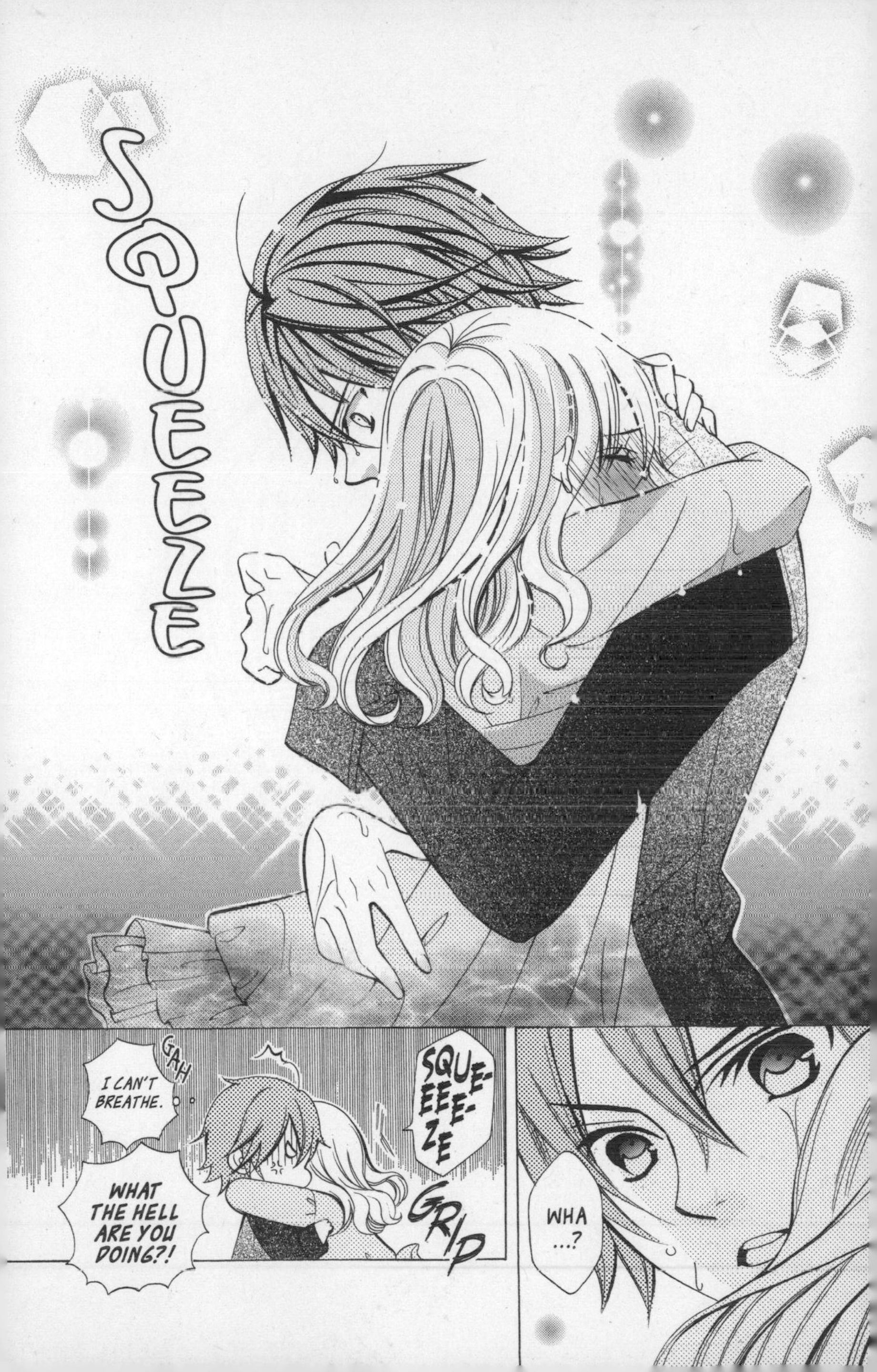
SQUEEZE
WHA ...?
SQUE-EEEE-ZE
GRIP
GAH
I CAN'T BREATHE.
WHAT THE HELL ARE YOU DOING?!

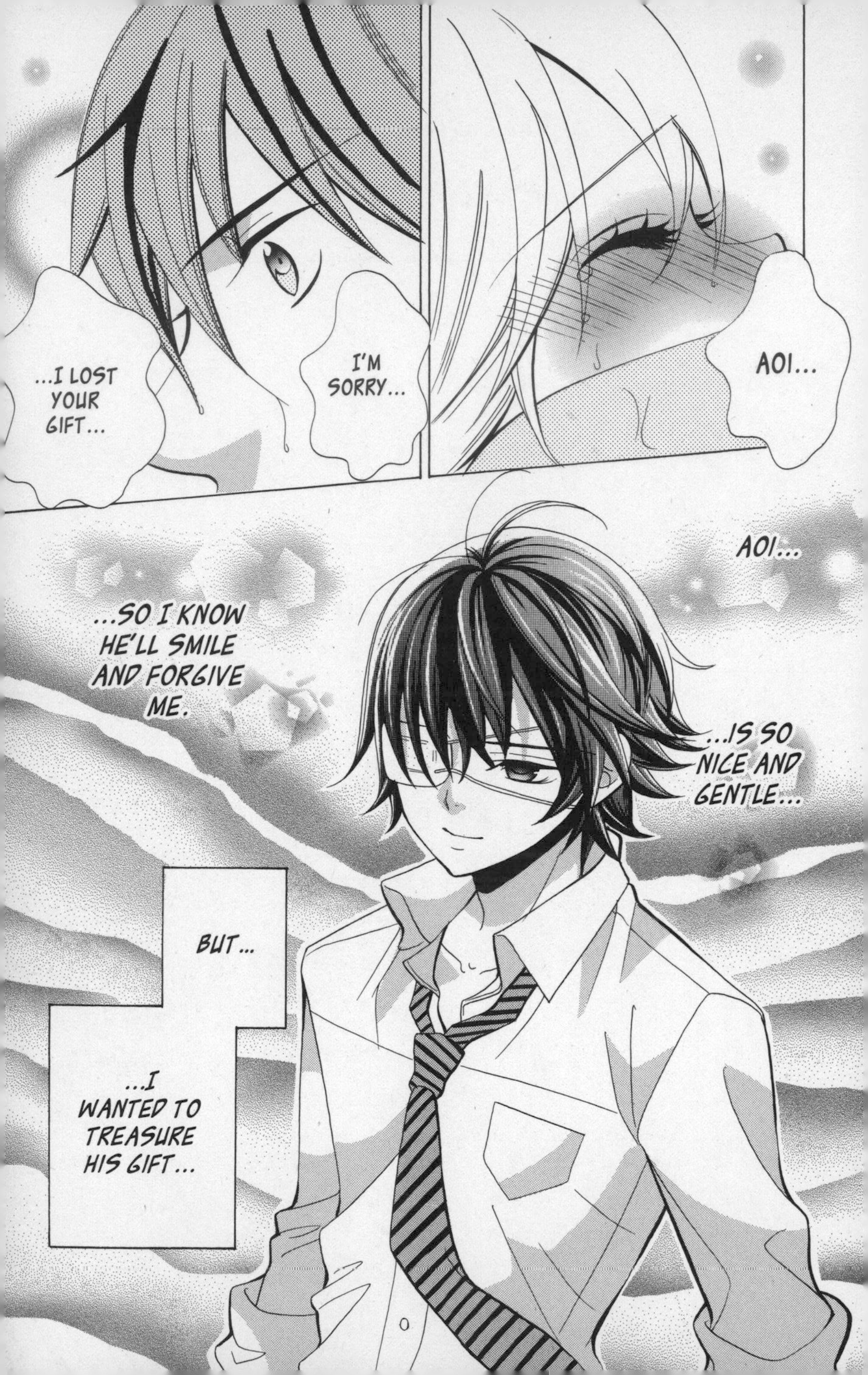
AOI...
I'M SORRY...
...I LOST YOUR GIFT...
AOI...
...IS SO NICE AND GENTLE...
...SO I KNOW HE'LL SMILE AND FORGIVE ME.
BUT...
...I WANTED TO TREASURE HIS GIFT...

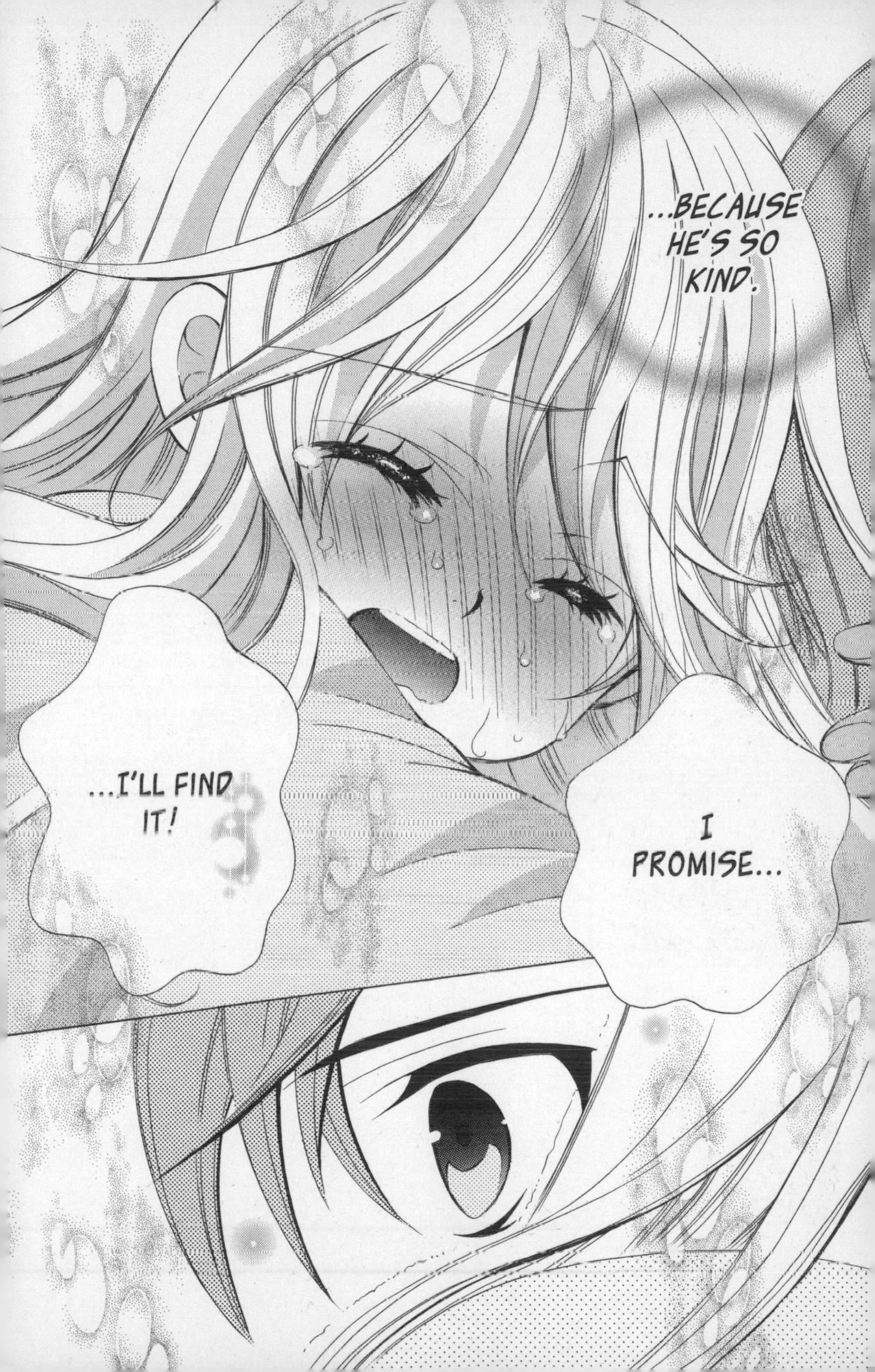
...BECAUSE HE'S SO KIND.
I PROMISE...
...I'LL FIND IT!

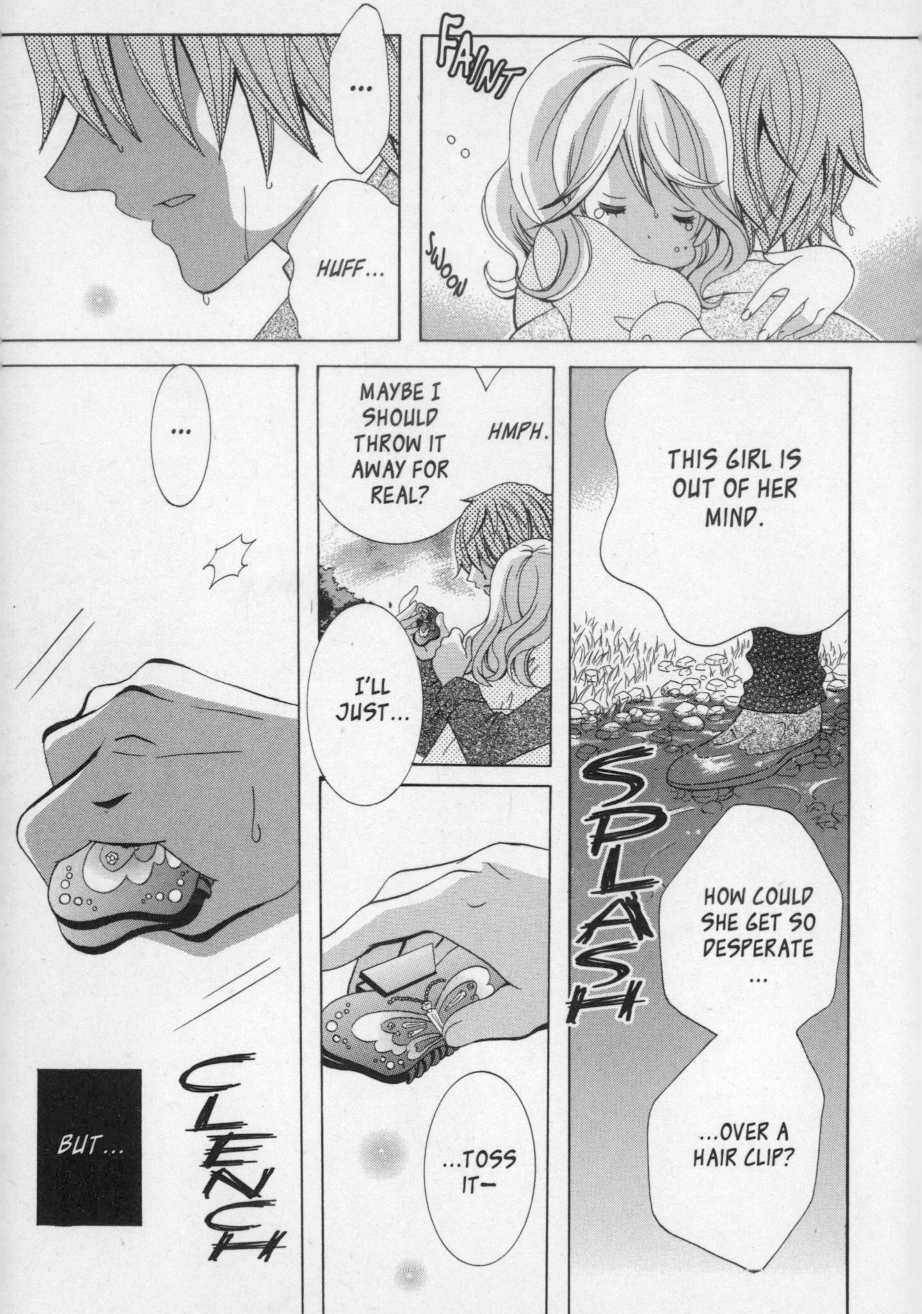
FAINT
SWOON
...
HUFF...
THIS GIRL IS OUT OF HER MIND.
SPLASH
HOW COULD SHE GET SO DESPERATE...
...OVER A HAIR CLIP?
MAYBE I SHOULD THROW IT AWAY FOR REAL?
HMPH.
I'LL JUST...
...TOSS IT—
...
CLENCH
BUT...

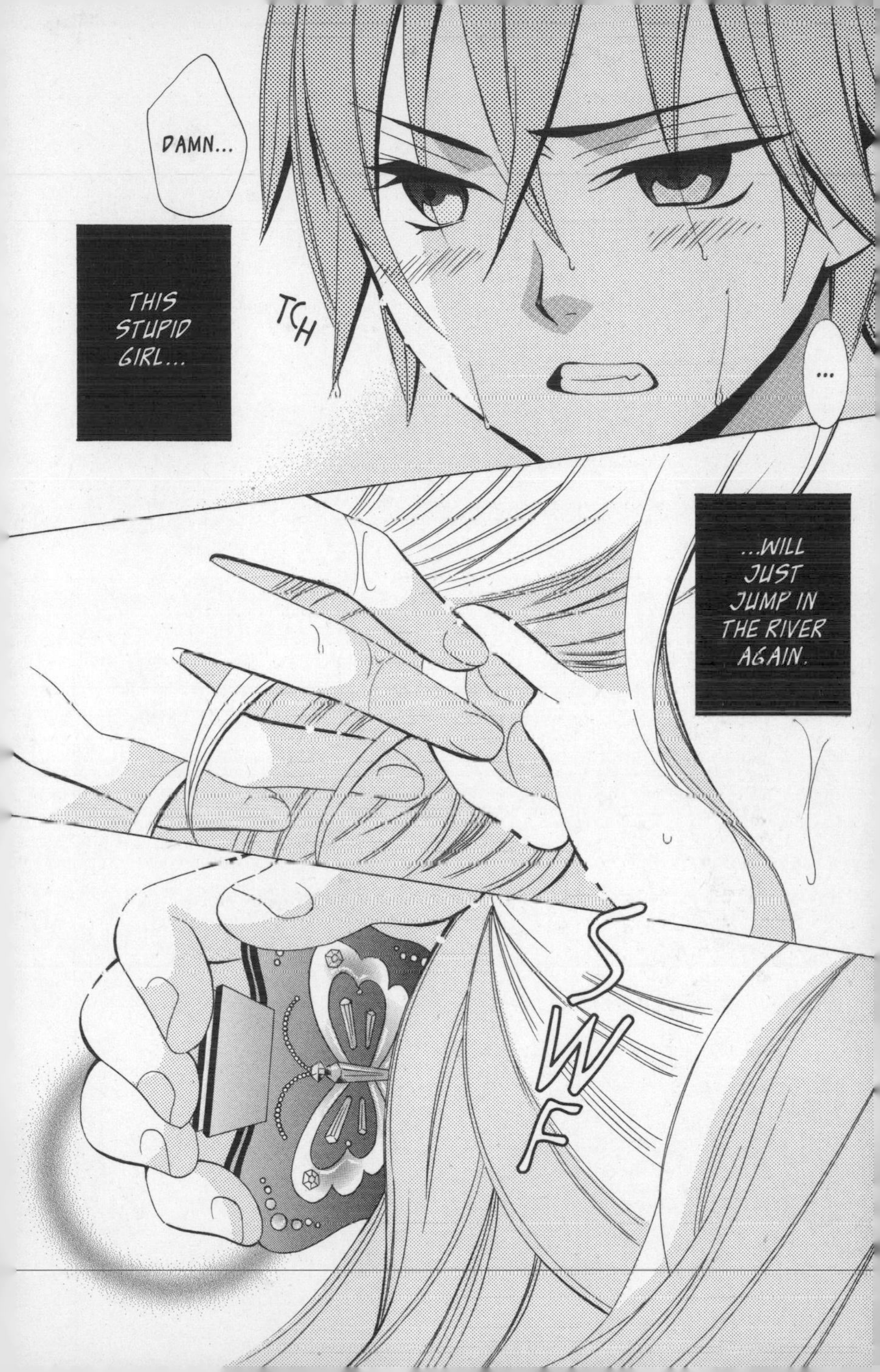
DAMN...
...
TCH
THIS STUPID GIRL...
...WILL JUST JUMP IN THE RIVER AGAIN.
SWF

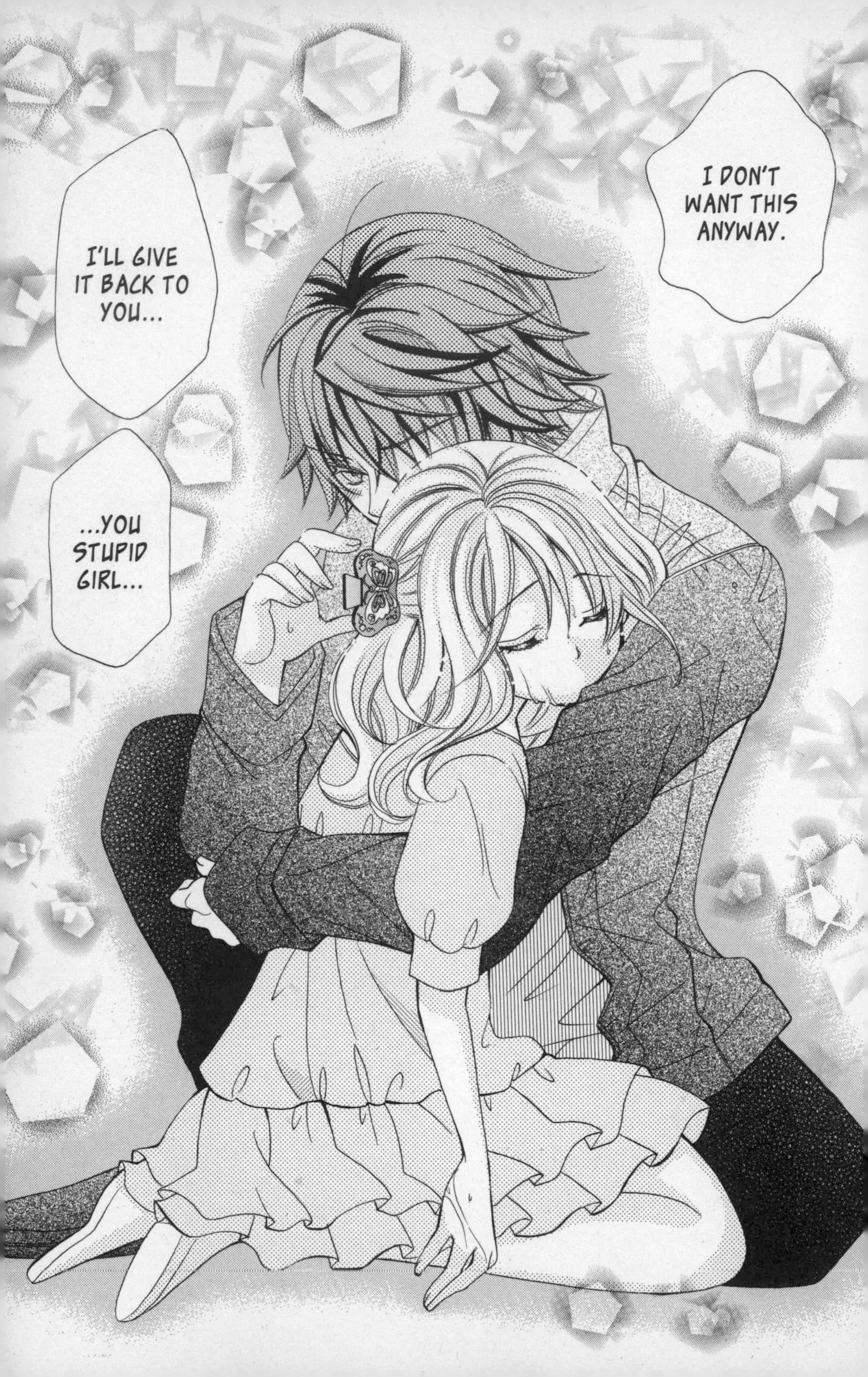
I DON'T WANT THIS ANYWAY.
I'LL GIVE IT BACK TO YOU...
...YOU STUPID GIRL...

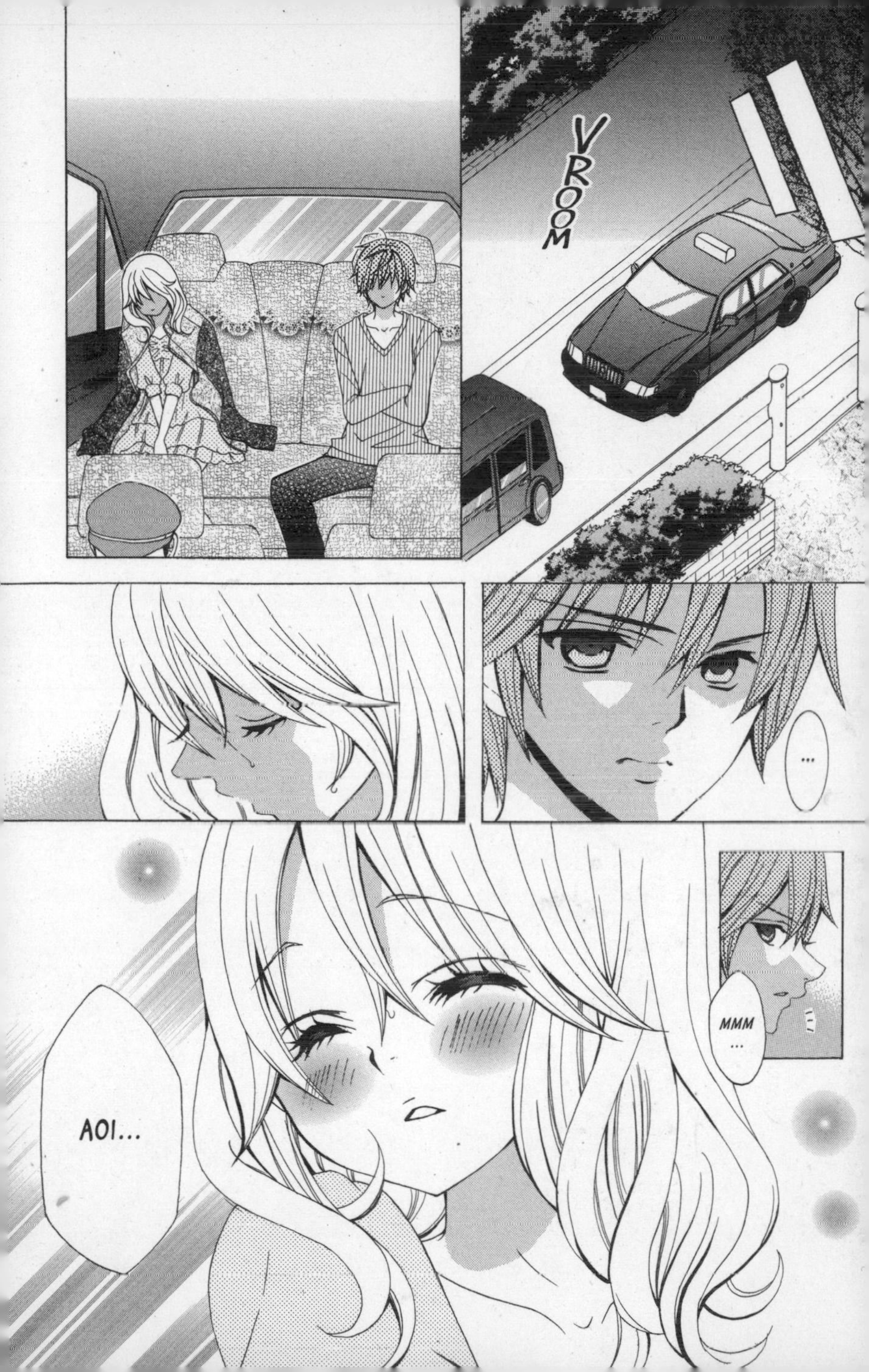
VROOM
...
MMM...
AOI...

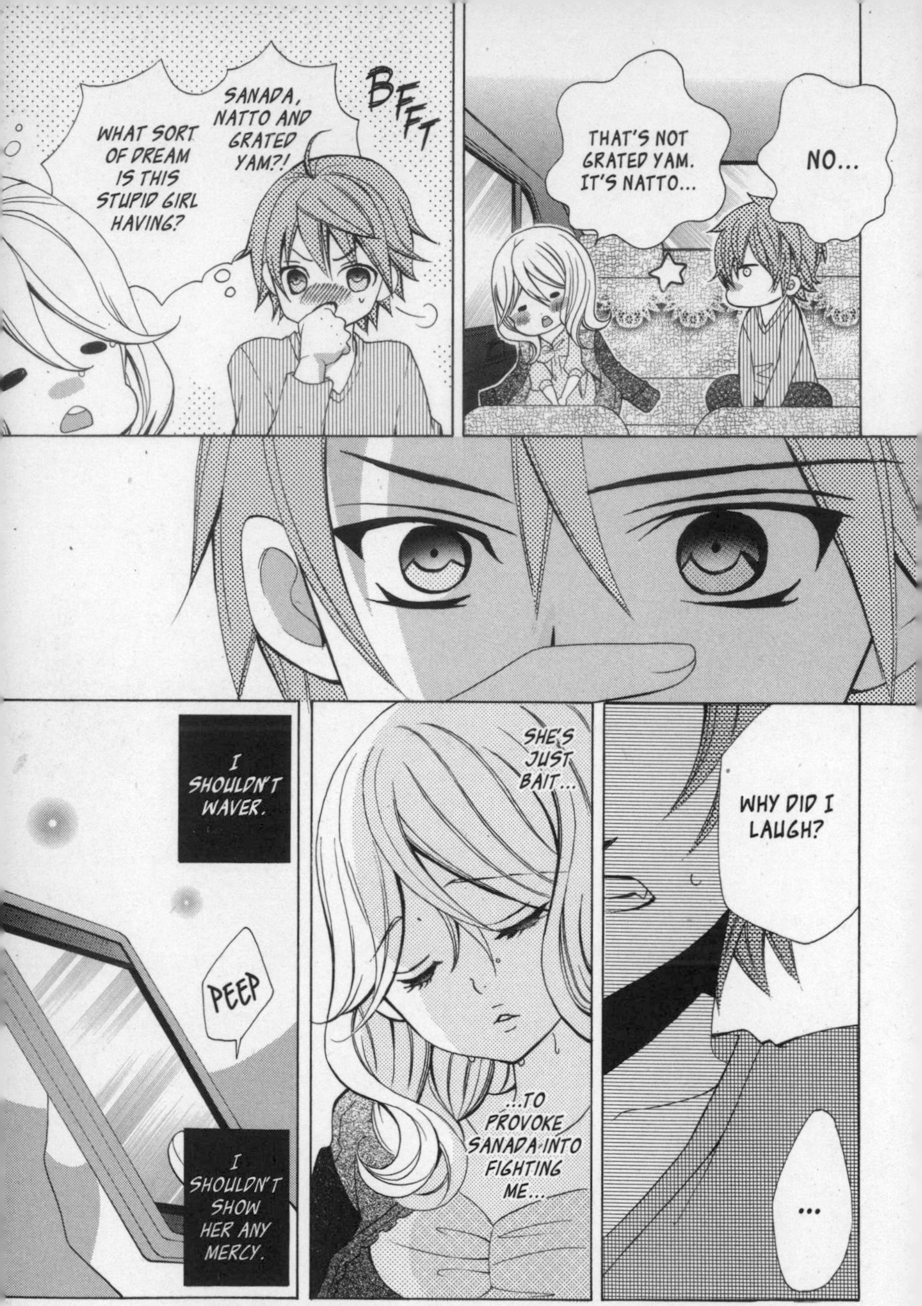

NO...
THAT'S NOT GRATED YAM. IT'S NATTO...
BFFT
SANADA, NATTO AND GRATED YAM?!
WHAT SORT OF DREAM IS THIS STUPID GIRL HAVING?
WHY DID I LAUGH?
...
SHE'S JUST BAIT...
...TO PROVOKE SANADA INTO FIGHTING ME...
I SHOULDN'T WAVER.
PEEP
I SHOULDN'T SHOW HER ANY MERCY.

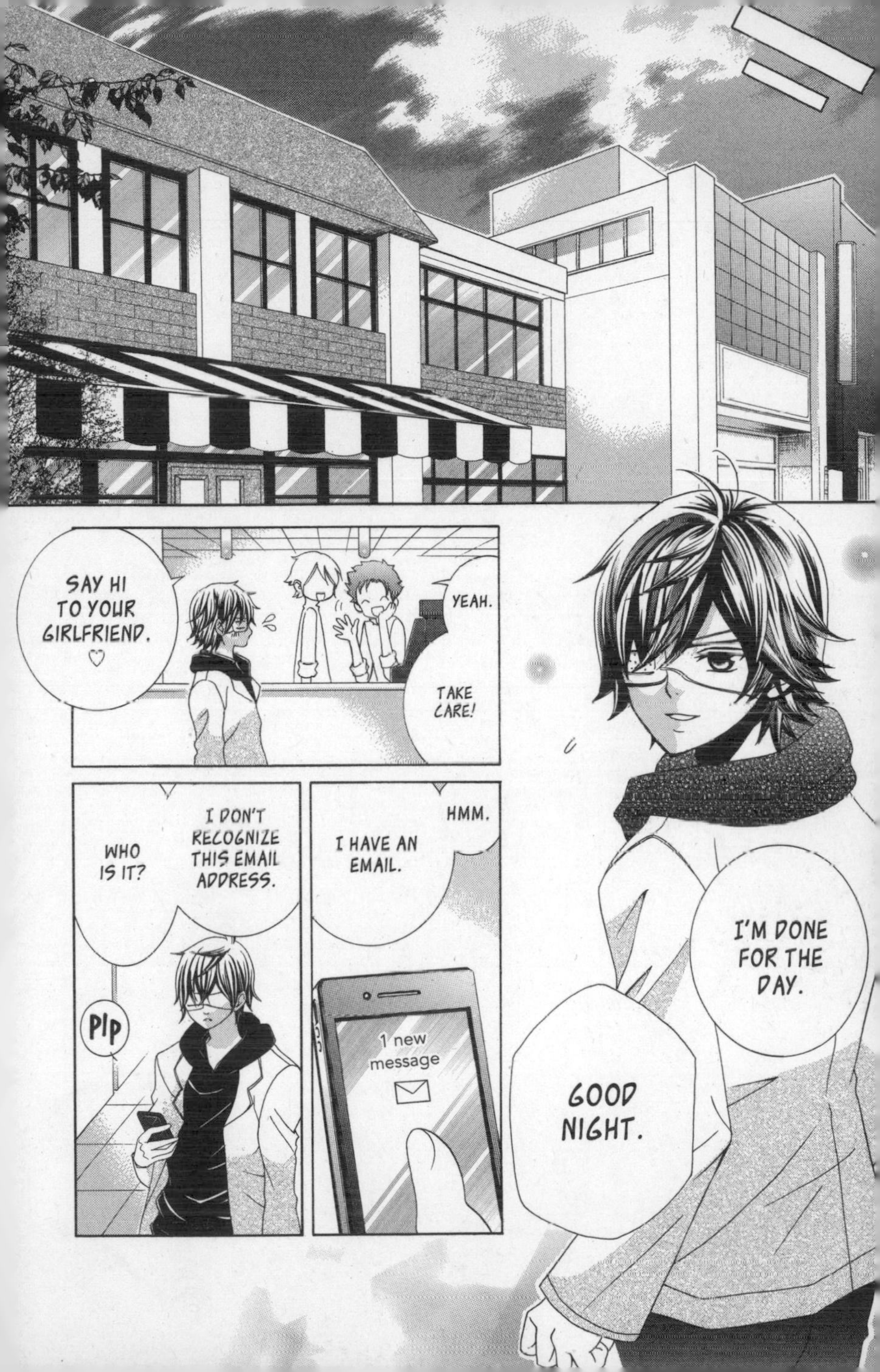
I'M DONE FOR THE DAY.
GOOD NIGHT.
YEAH.
TAKE CARE!
SAY HI TO YOUR GIRLFRIEND. ♡
HMM.
I HAVE AN EMAIL.
1 new message
I DON'T RECOGNIZE THIS EMAIL ADDRESS.
WHO IS IT?
PIP

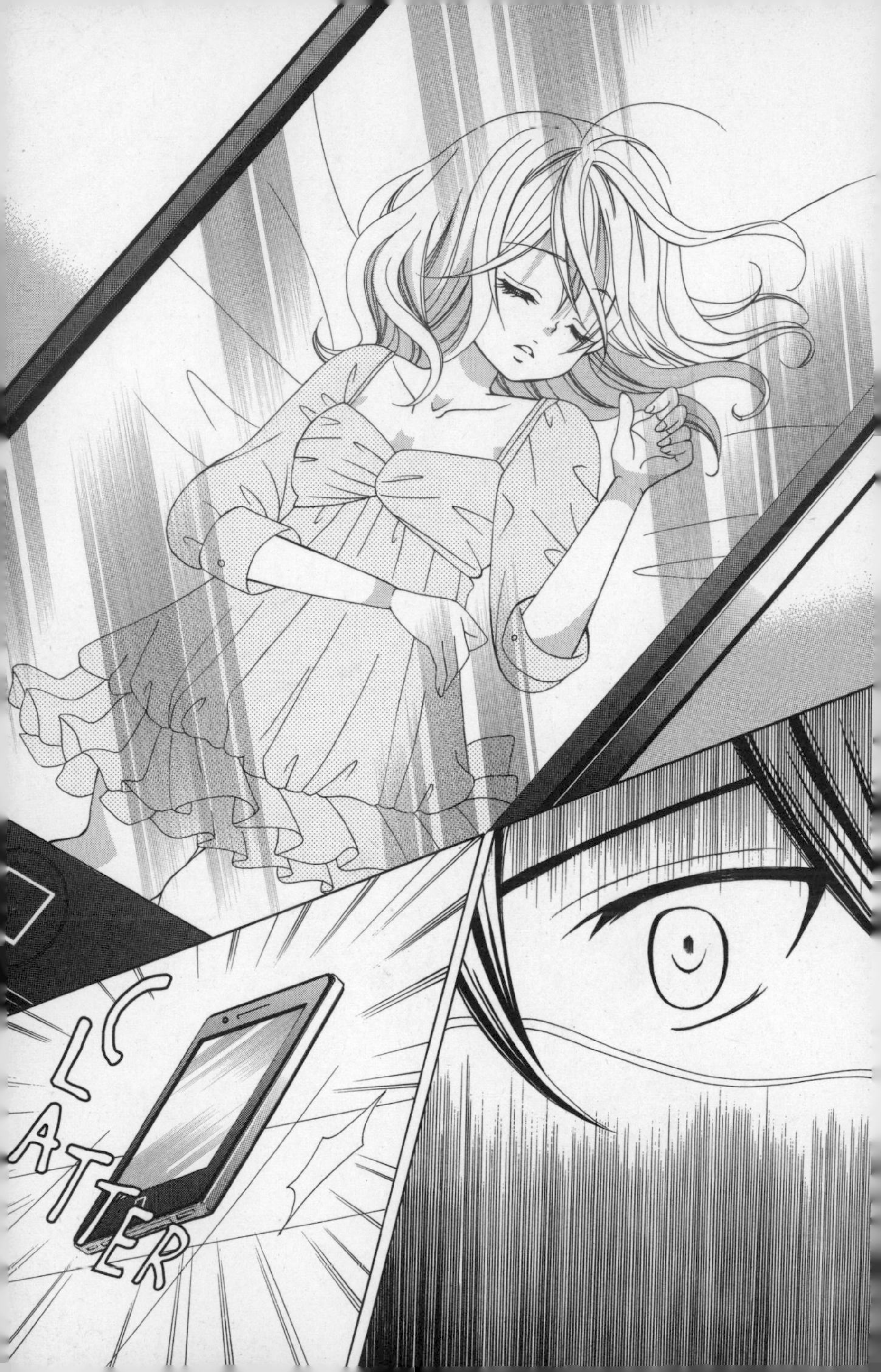
CLATTER

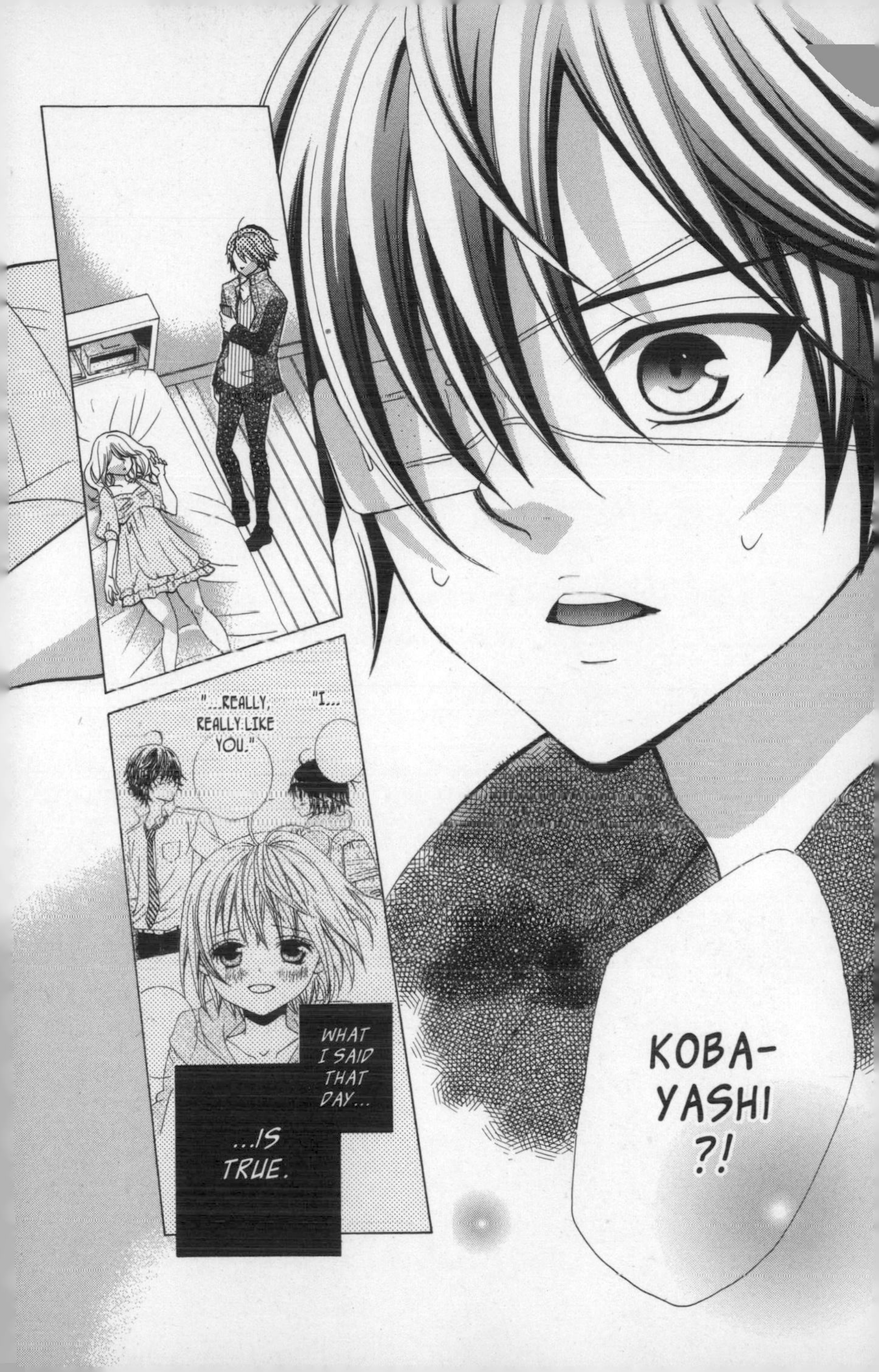
KOBA-YASHI ?!
"I...
"...REALLY, REALLY LIKE YOU."
WHAT I SAID THAT DAY...
...IS TRUE.

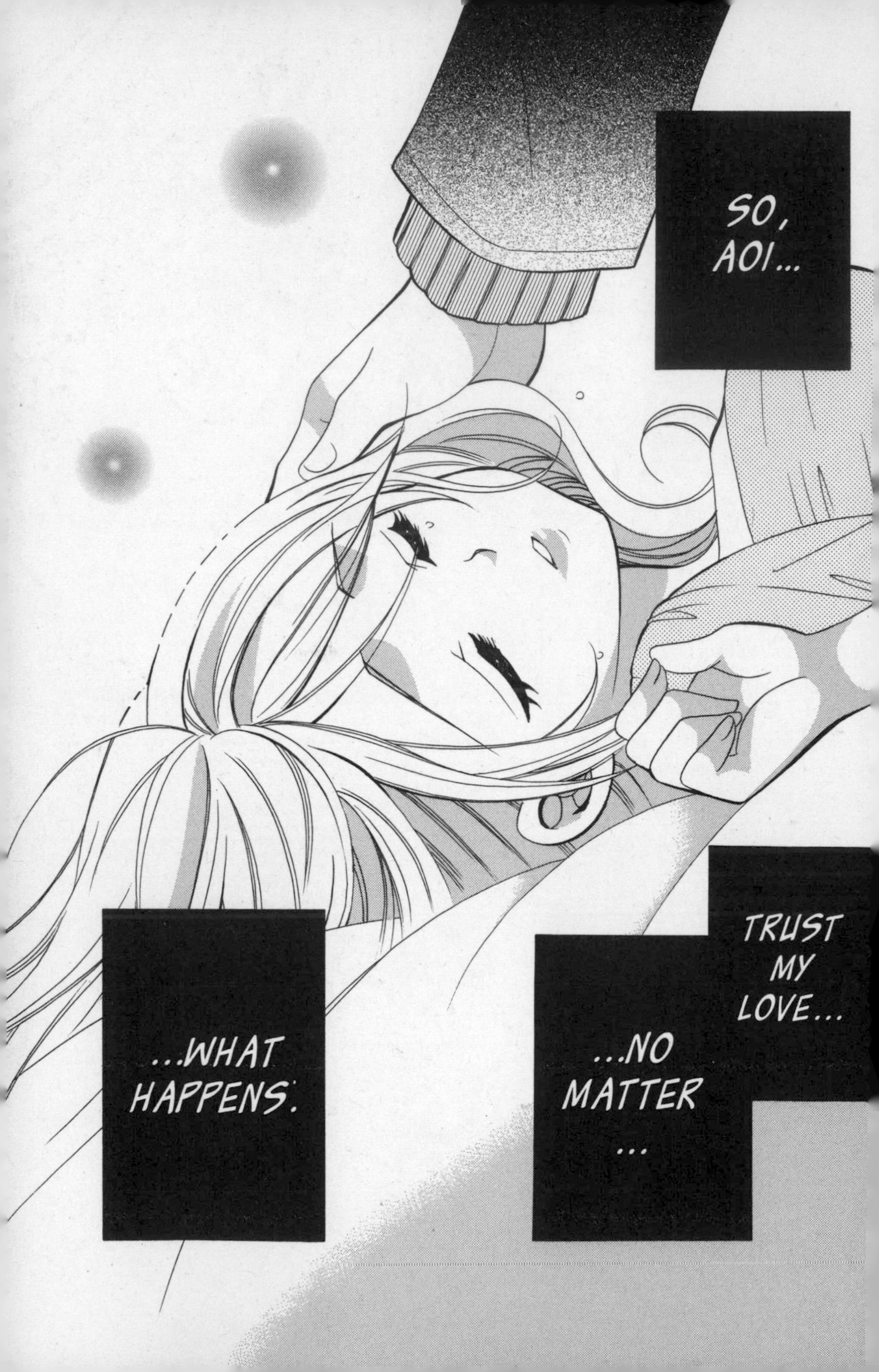
SO, AOI...
TRUST MY LOVE...
...NO MATTER ...
...WHAT HAPPENS.

EVERYONE'S DRAWINGS ARE SO CUTE, THEY HURT!!

SO CUTE! FAN ART FEATURE ♥

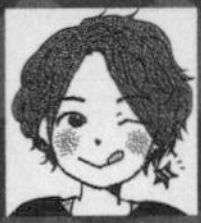

Editor: Shoji

Here we show you everyone's fan art. ♪
Editor Shoji has commented on each one this time too!!

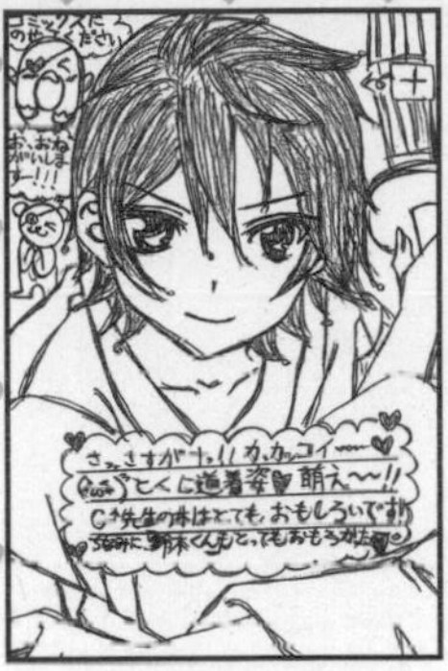

Ed.: Mitsuru is cool and cute here!!

Maaya (Aomori) ←

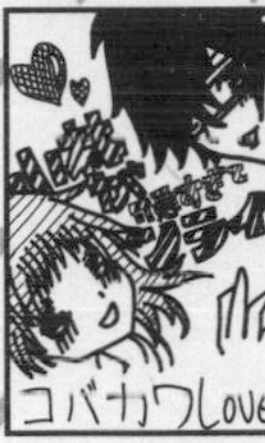

コバカワLove♡

Ed.: They're looking at each other... love-love. ♥

Harurun (Mie) ←

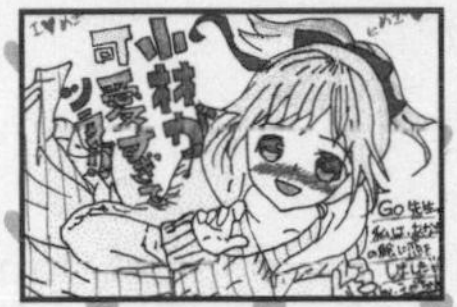

Ega-chan (Aomori) ↑

Ed.: Mego's just too cute!!

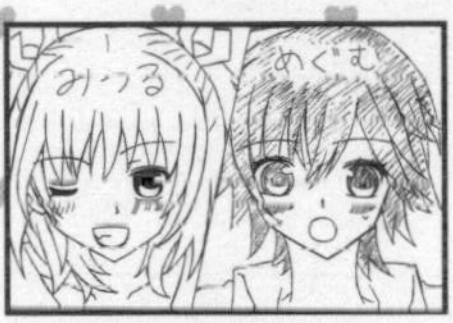

みつる
めぐむ

Madoka Inoue ↑
(Kagoshima)

Ed.: People love drawing the twins!!

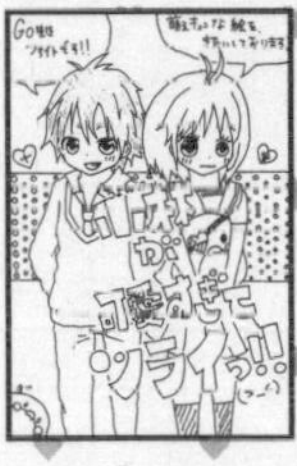

Ed.: W... we'll do our best. (><)

Kabocha (Gifu) ←

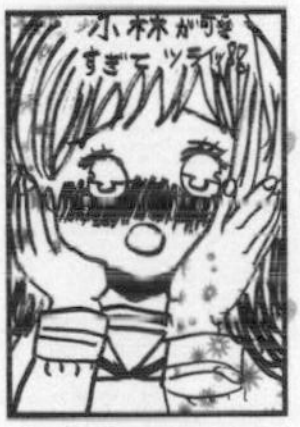

Ed.: The blushing Mego is cute!!

Arisa Tokura (Tokyo) ←

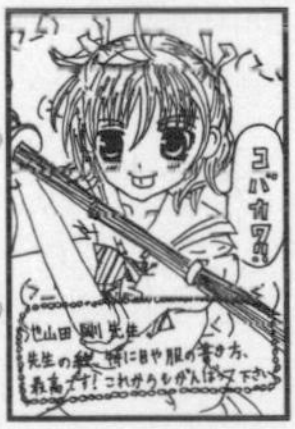

Ed.: The cross-dressed Mitsuru is super cute!!

Hina (Hyogo) ←

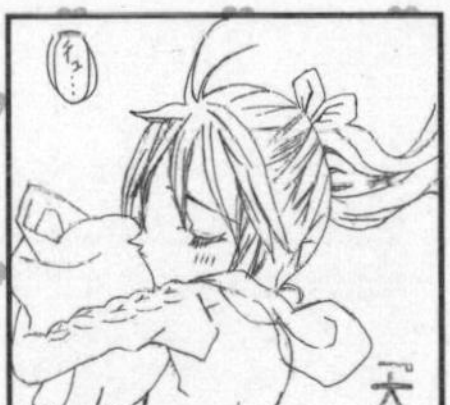

大好き

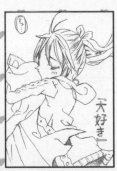

Ed.: This scene...makes my heart flutter. ♥

Kouko Nakata (Tottori) ↑

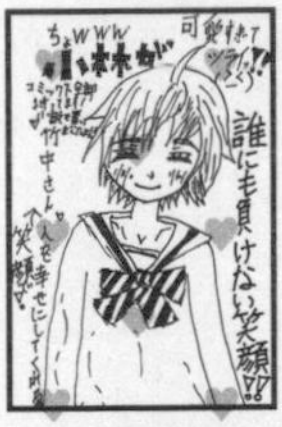

誰にも負けない笑顔!!

Ed.: Shino's smile makes me smile too!!

Sakura Neko ★
(Tokyo) ↑

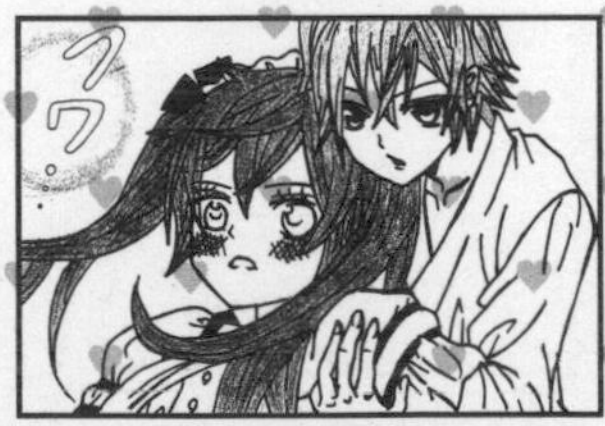

Ed.: Look forward to their relationship too!!

Junna
(Saitama) ↑

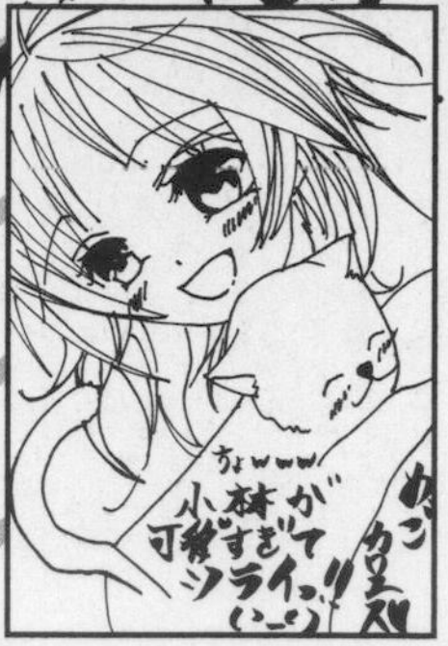
小林が可愛すぎてツライっ!!

Ed.: Mego and Mego Two are both so cute. (>_<)

Maya Takizawa (Gunma) ←

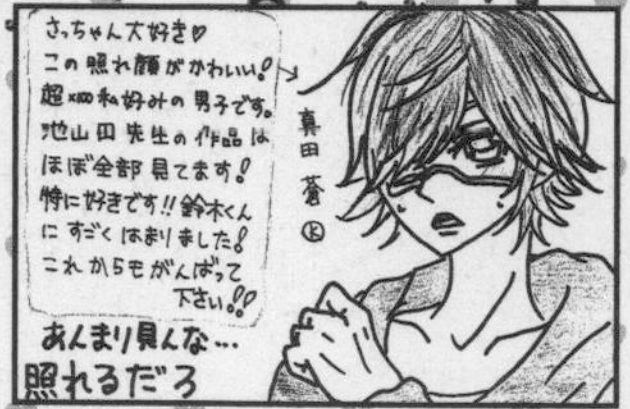
さっちゃん大好き♡
この照れ顔がかわいい!
真田蒼
これからもがんばって下さい!!
あんまり見んな…
照れるだろ

Ed.: The ★ shy-looking Aoi makes my heart throb!

Shiho Saito (Aomori) ←

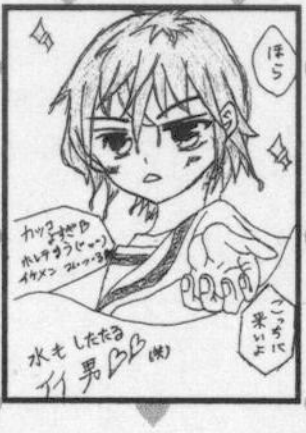
ほら
水もしたたるイイ男♡

Ed.: He looks handsome even when he's cross-dressed!!

← Love Yu Kitagaya (Chiba)

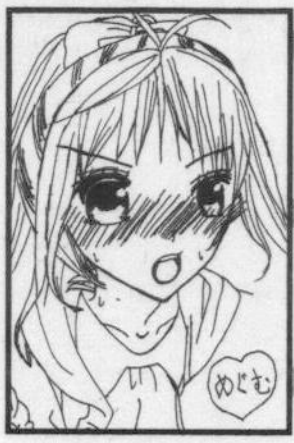
めぐむ

Ed.: Mego looks cool when she looks gallant!! (>_<)

↑ Momoka Mizoguchi (Osaka-fu)

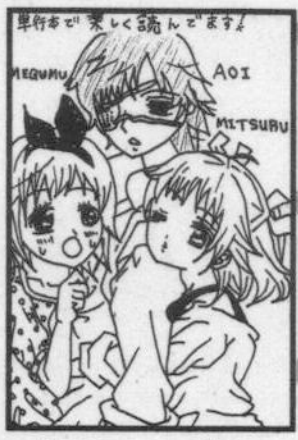
MEGUMU
AOI
MITSURU

Ed.: Aoi has a beauty on each side!

Rizu (Nagasaki) ←

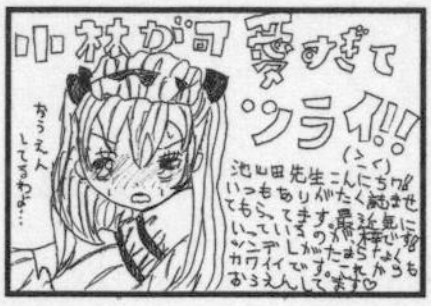
小林が可愛すぎてツライ!!

Ed.: I love Azusa when she looks sweet...

← Ichigo-chan (Aichi)

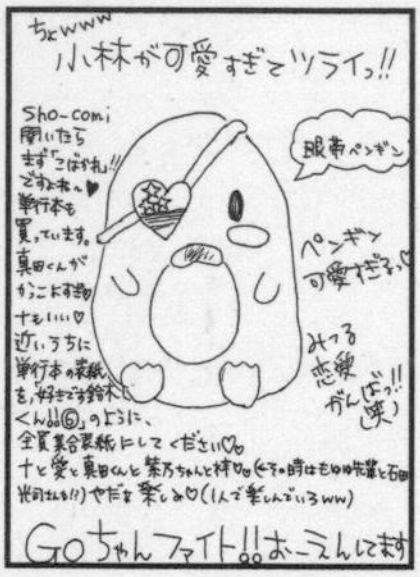
小林が可愛すぎてツライっ!!
眼帯ペンギン
Goちゃんファイト!!おーえんしてます

Ed.: The eye-patch penguin is so popular I'm jealous!!

Sana Oota (Aichi) ←

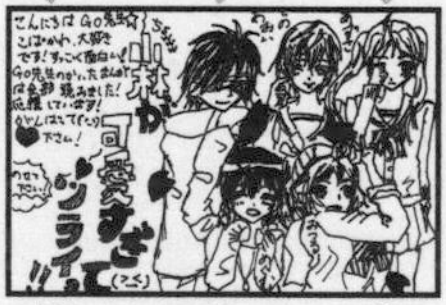

Ed.: Everyone's here!!

Airinko (Aichi) ↑

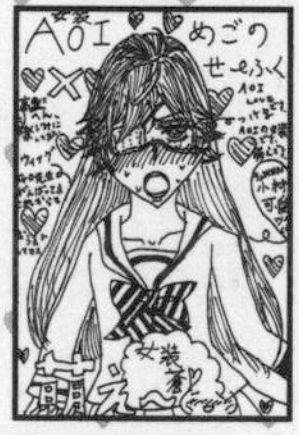
AOI

Ed.: Aoi is cross-dressing?!

I LOVE Aoi ♡ (Tokyo) ↑

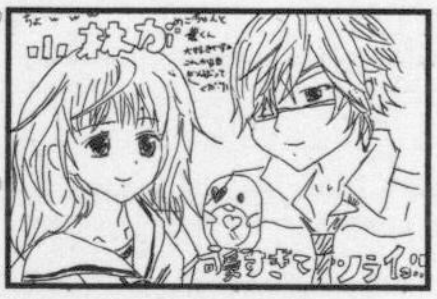

Ed.: They're looking at each other warmly ♥ and that makes me wanna smile!

Asami Kato (Aichi) ↑

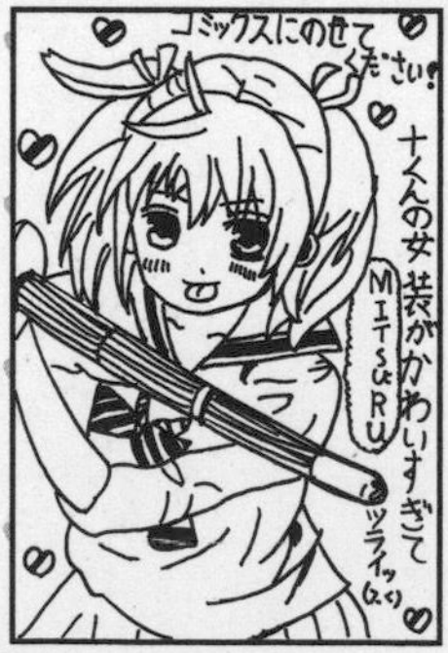
コミックスにのせてください!
MITSURU

Ed.: This pose is so like Mitsuru!!

Yuu (Osaka) ←

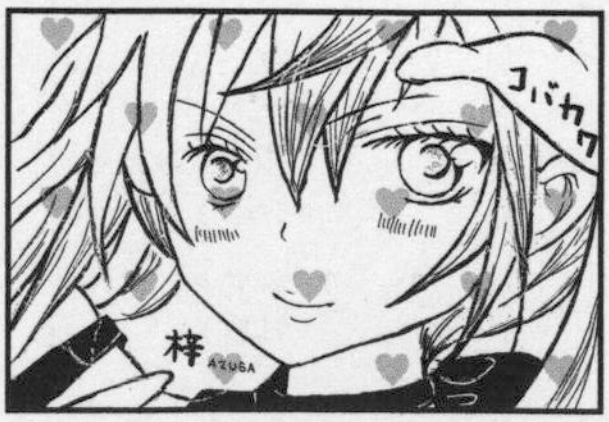
梓
AZUSA

Ed.: Azusa's popularity is suddenly soaring!

Aina Uki (Hyogo) ←

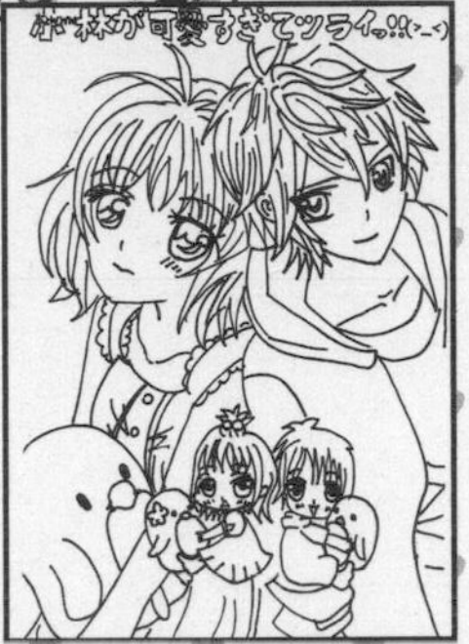

Ed.: The tiny Mego and Mitsuru are so cute!!

Airi Nemoto (Hyogo) ←

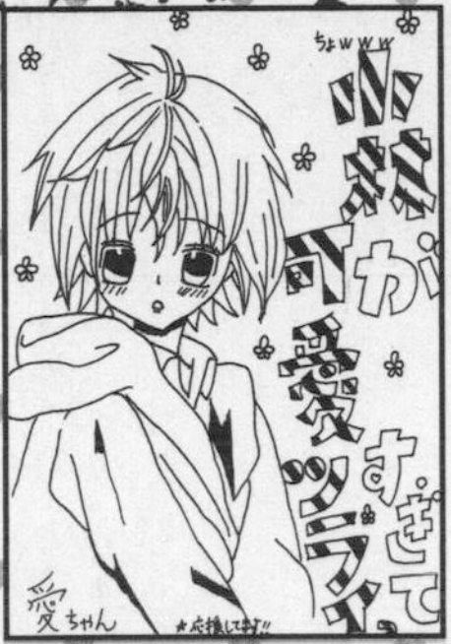

Ed.: The pure Mego's really like an angel!!

Yuria Okada (Ehime) ←

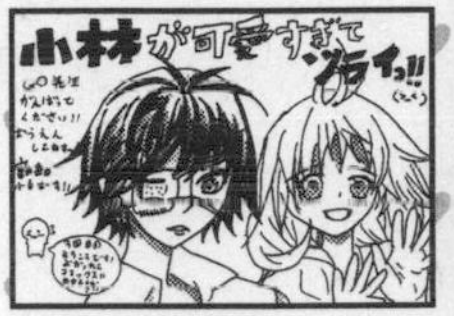
小林が可愛すぎてツライっ!!

Ed.: The two are lovey-dovey. ♥

Narumi (Miyazaki) ↑

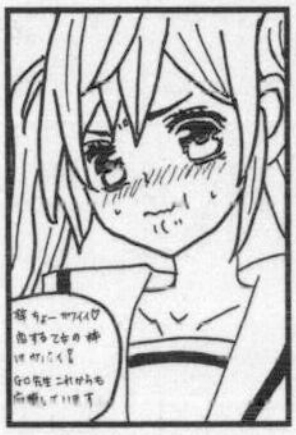

Ed.: The way her lips are quivering... ooh!!

Rika Maeda (Oita) ←

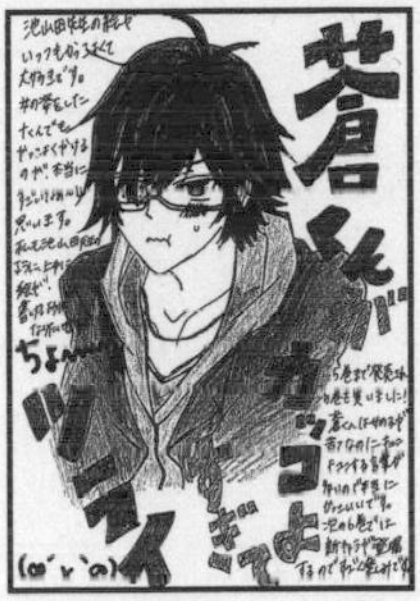

Ed.: My lips are quivering too. Twinge. ♡

UVERworld (Chiba) ←

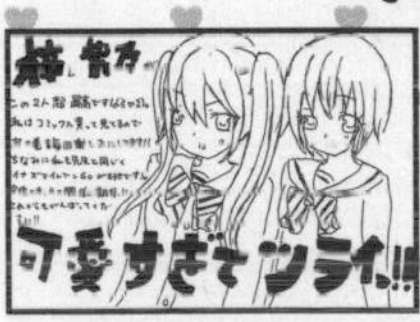
可愛すぎてツライっ!!

Ed.: What is the true relationship between these two?!

Ono-chan (Ehime) ↑

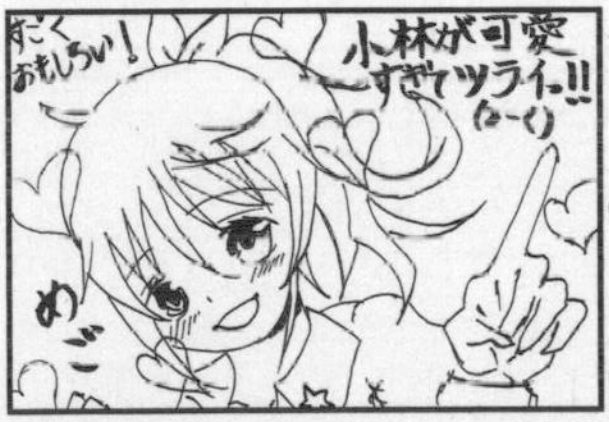
すごくおもしろい!
小林が可愛すぎてツライ!!

Ed.: The lovely ♪ Mego makes me smile.

Nanami Ueki (Tochigi) ←

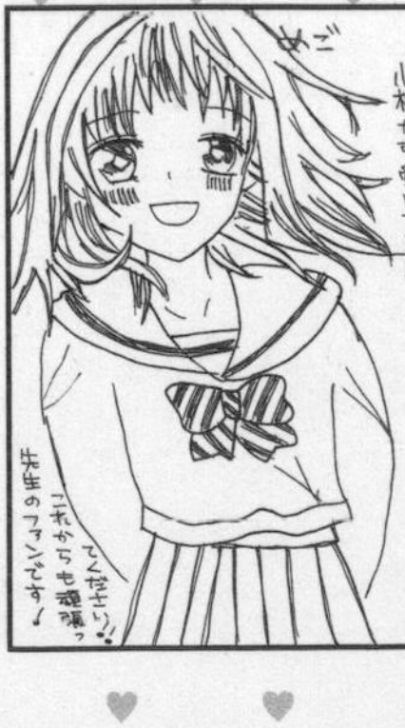

Ed.: I love the way Mego's so honest!

Non (Gifu) ←

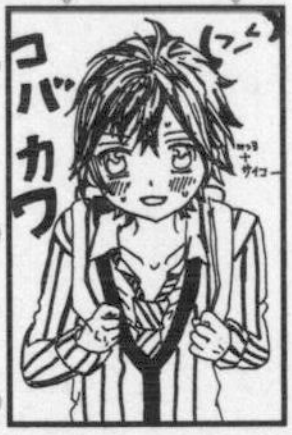

Ed.: Mitsuru. You're sweating too much!

Yuna Takahashi (Miyazaki) ←

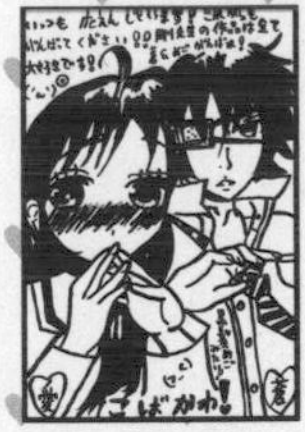

Ed.: Mego looks cute in black hair too!!

Pocky (Tokyo) ←

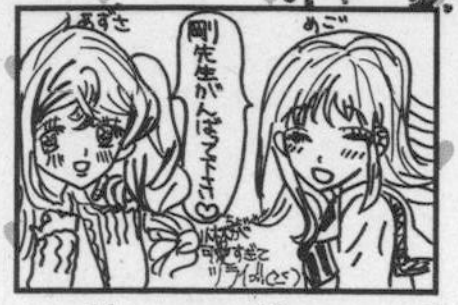

Ed.: These two look lovely!!
I love Azusa ☆
(Saitama) ↑

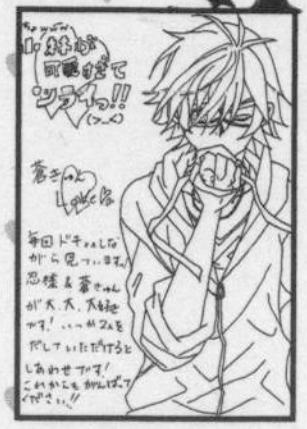

Ed.: A kiss on the ribbon... makes my heart flutter. ♥

Fruit punch
(Higashi Osaka) ↑

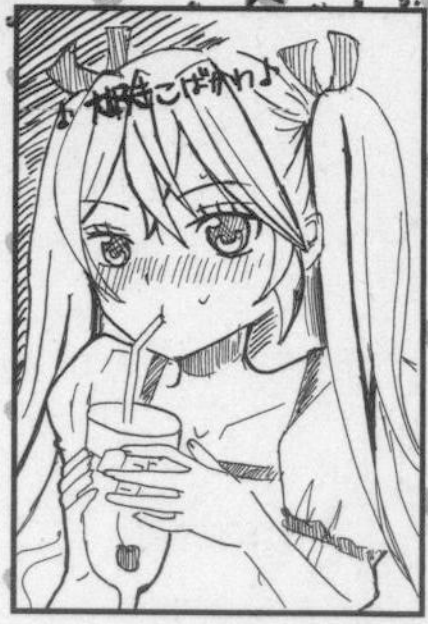

Ed.: Azusa's popularity is suddenly soaring!

Rio Yoneyama
(Kanagawa)
←

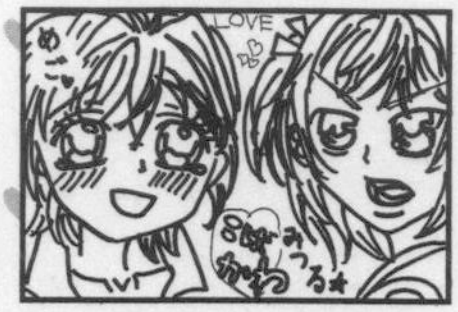

Ed.: The twins' smiles are magnum-force!!
Harurun♥ (Gunma) ↑

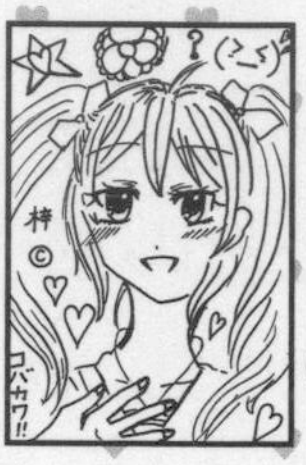

Ed.: I fell for Azusa's smile!!

Chisato Okada
(Ishikawa)
←

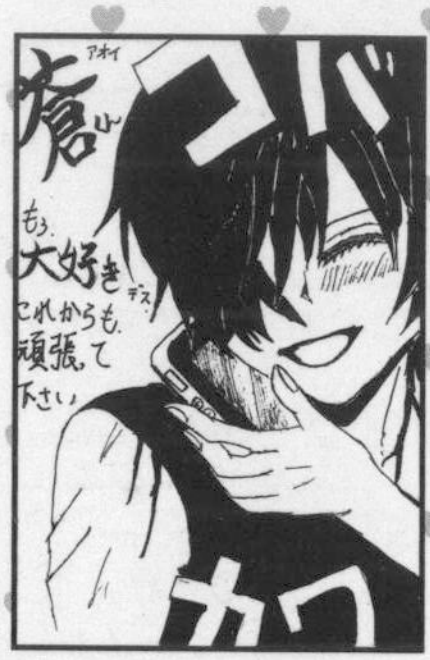

Ed.: This smile wil knock Mego out for sure. ♥

You Miyashiro
(Okinawa)
←

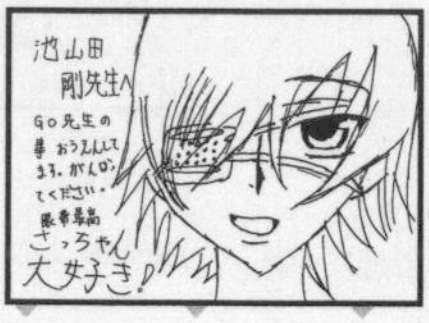

Ed.: Yeah, yeah. Eye patches are the best!!
← Kiririn ☆
(Gunma)

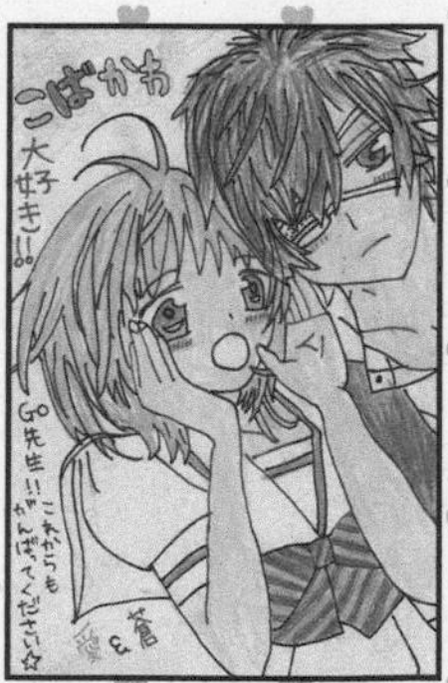

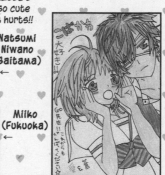

Ed.: The way they're in love gives me heartburn (says the mean side of me).

Mayu Yoshida
(Shiga)
←

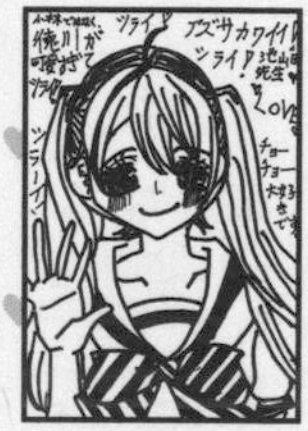

Ed.: Azusa's so cute it hurts!!

Natsumi Niwano
(Saitama)
←

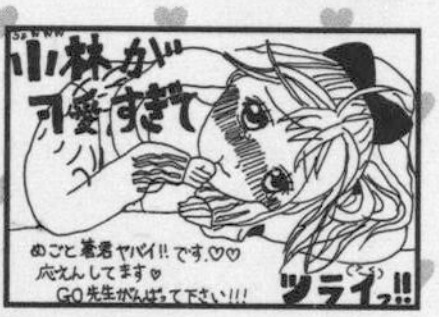

Ed.: Mego, don't cry! Don't cry!! You look just too cute!!
Terurin (Tochigi) ↑

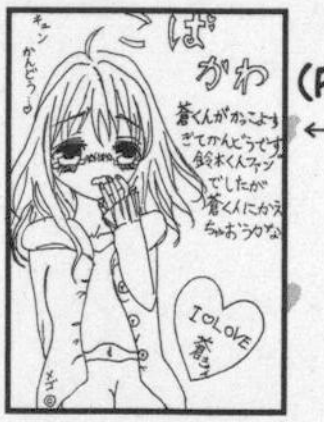

Miiko
(Fukuoka)
←

Ed.: My heart flutters cuz Mego's so cute. ♥

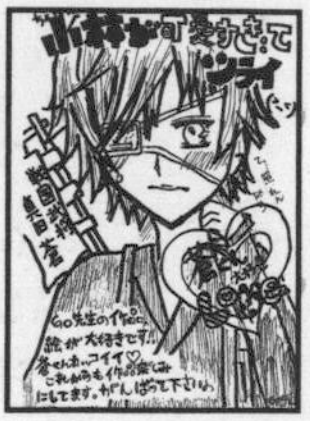

Ed.: Aoi's cosplay looks real cool!!

Sayaka Suzuki
(Hyogo)
←

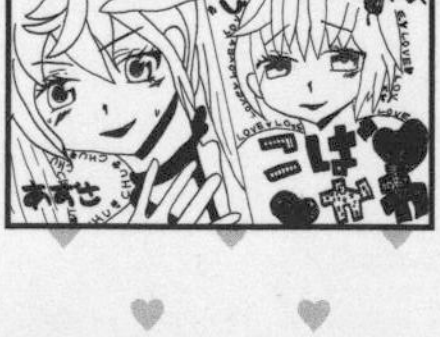

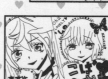

Ed.: Azusa and Shino just look too beautiful!! (>_<)

Mucchan
(Iwate)
←

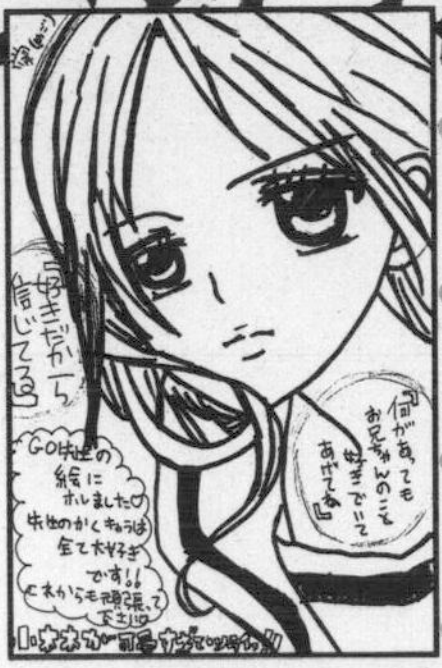

Ed.: My heart thumps at the mature-looking Mego. ♥

Tsubasa (Miyazaki)

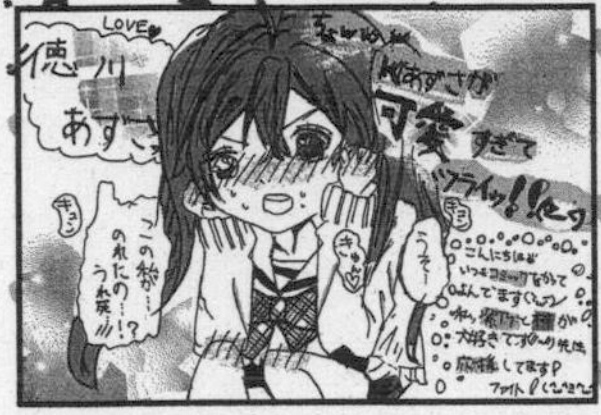

Ed.: Thank you for Azusa's sweet look!

Akari Tsuzaki (Wakayama)

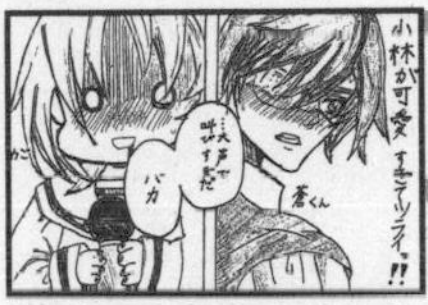

Ed.: The heroines won't switch places...

Kanako (Gifu)

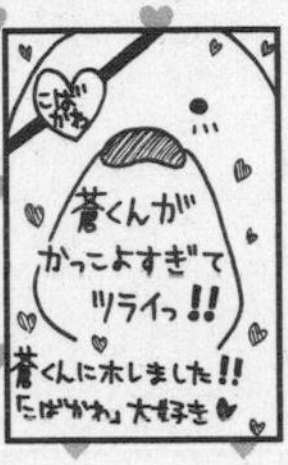
蒼くんがかっこよすぎてツライっ!!

Ed.: Readers love the eye-patch penguin too!!

Ayukuma (Tochigi)

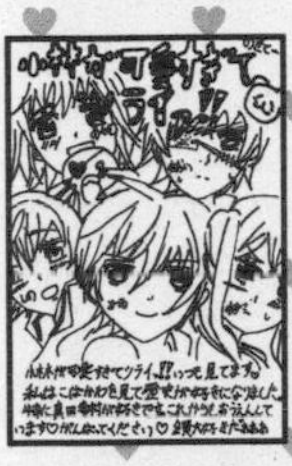

Ed.: A gorgeous shot! Of the five characters!!

Sumiren Yamamoto (Hyogo)

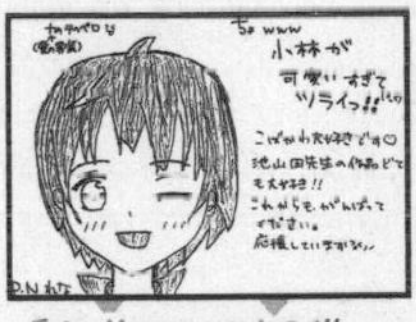

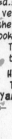

Ed.: Mego my bad!!

Rena (Kumamoto)

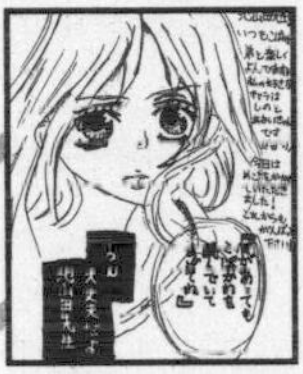

Ed.: A memorable scene!! ♥

Karin Nakase (Hyogo)

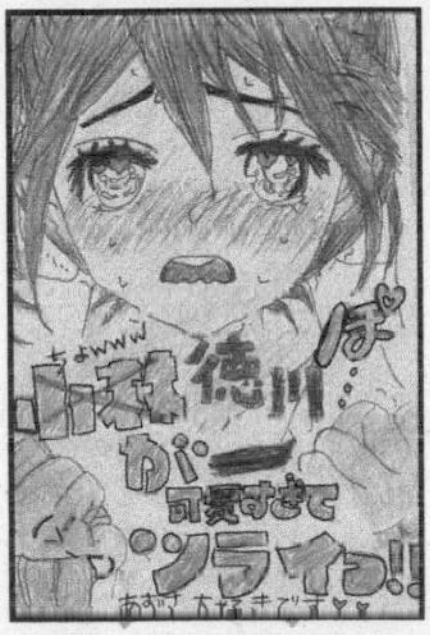

Ed.: Another version of the mature-looking Mego! Thump-thump.

Haruka Tanno (Yamagata)

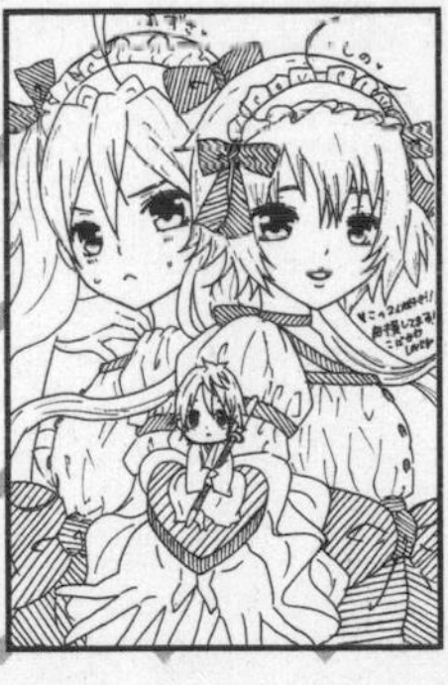

Ed.: Mitsuru's on Azusa's and Shino's palms?! Switch places with me!!

Kin no Hiyoko (Chiba)

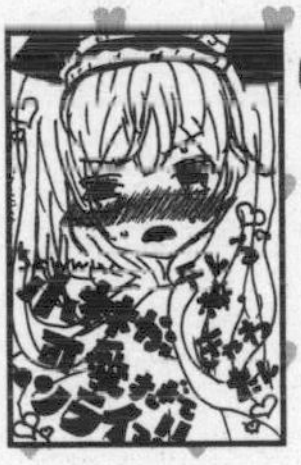

Ed.: Azusa's sweet face is so powerful...

Anju (Tokyo)

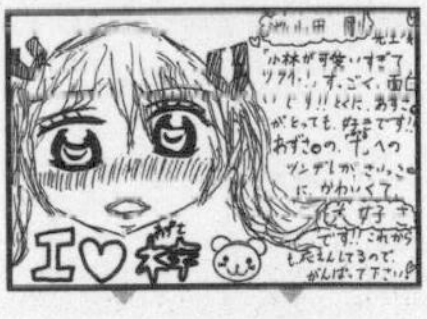

Ed.: Mego's cute, but Azusa's cute too! I love both of them. ♥

Retsu Nabeshima (Kochi)

Send your fan mail to:

Go Ikeyamada
c/o Shojo Beat
VIZ Media, LLC
P.O. Box 77010
San Francisco, CA
94107

AUTHOR BIO

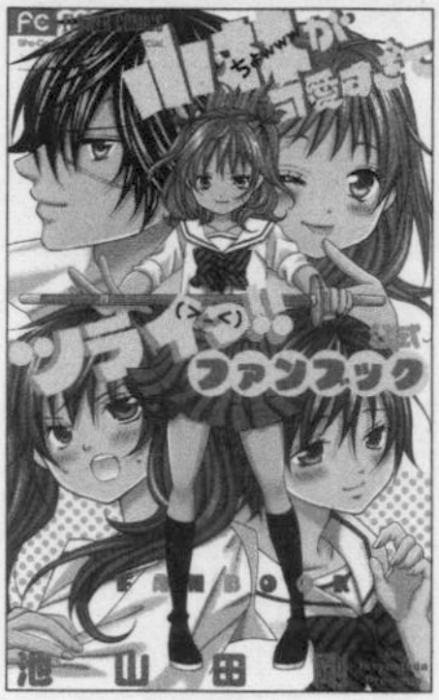
ファンブック

So Cute! volume 7 was released in Japan with a fan book! ♪ I love the cover illustration where all five main characters (Mego, Mitsuru, Aoi, Shino and Azusa) are together. ♥

The manga will soon be celebrating its second anniversary. The story is going to rapidly develop and get even more exciting, so I do hope you enjoy reading it. ♥

Go Ikeyamada is a Gemini from Miyagi Prefecture whose hobbies include taking naps and watching movies. Her debut manga *Get Love!!* appeared in *Shojo Comic* in 2002, and her current work *So Cute It Hurts!!* (*Kobayashi ga Kawai Suguite Tsurai!!*) is being published by VIZ Media.

SO CUTE IT HURTS!!

Volume 7

Shojo Beat Edition

STORY AND ART BY
GO IKEYAMADA

English Translation & Adaptation/Tomo Kimura
Touch-Up Art & Lettering/Evan Waldinger
Design/Izumi Evers
Editor/Pancha Diaz

KOBAYASHI GA KAWAISUGITE TSURAI!! Vol.7
by Go IKEYAMADA
© 2012 Go IKEYAMADA
All rights reserved.
Original Japanese edition published by SHOGAKUKAN.
English translation rights in the United States of America, Canada,
United Kingdom and Ireland arranged with SHOGAKUKAN.

Printed in the U.S.A.

Published by VIZ Media, LLC
P.O. Box 77010
San Francisco, CA 94107

10 9 8 7 6 5 4 3 2 1
First printing, June 2016

www.viz.com   www.shojobeat.com

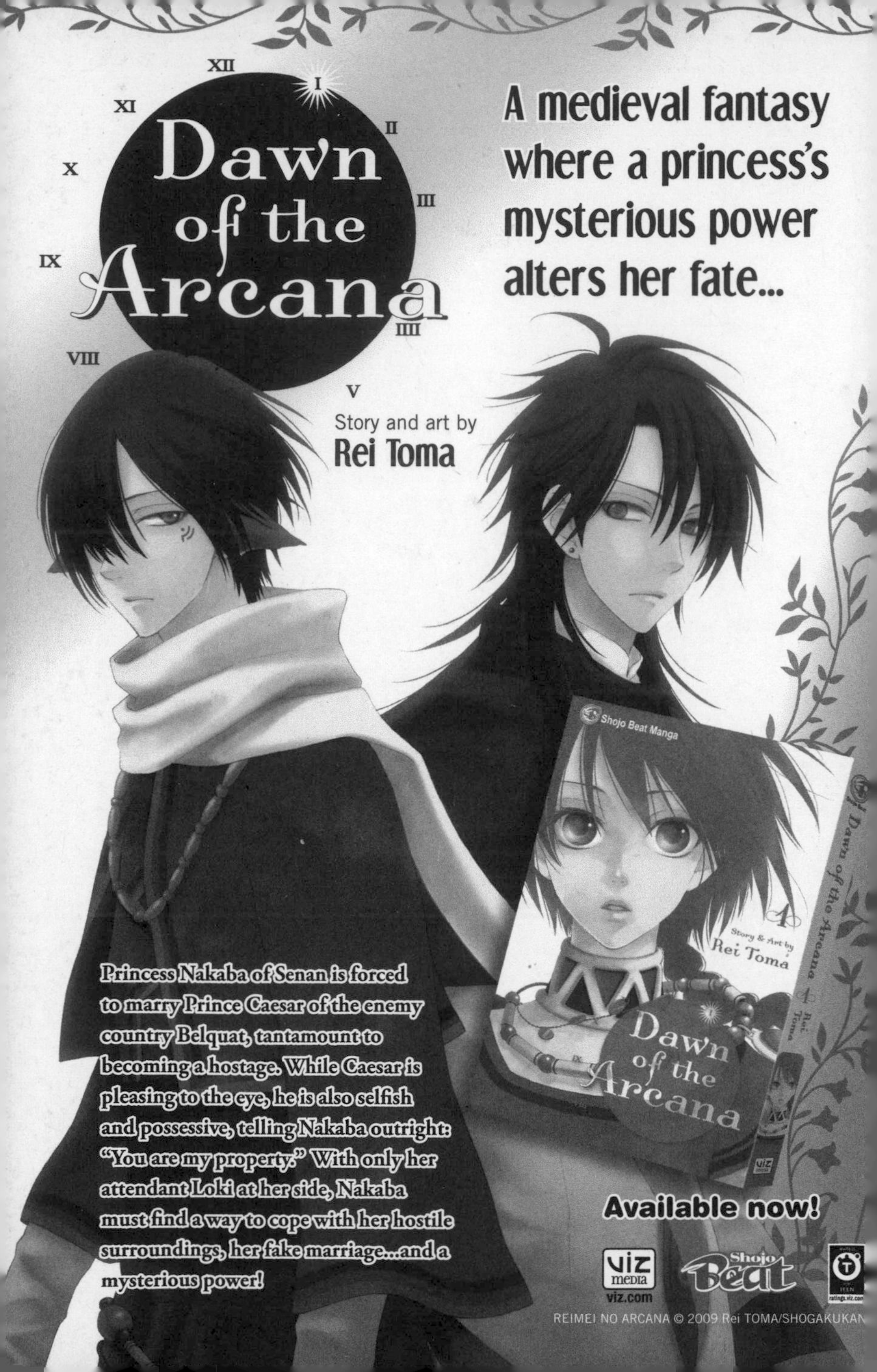
Dawn of the Arcana
A medieval fantasy where a princess's mysterious power alters her fate...
Story and art by
Rei Toma
Shojo Beat Manga
Dawn of the Arcana 1
Story & Art by Rei Toma
Princess Nakaba of Senan is forced to marry Prince Caesar of the enemy country Belquat, tantamount to becoming a hostage. While Caesar is pleasing to the eye, he is also selfish and possessive, telling Nakaba outright: "You are my property." With only her attendant Loki at her side, Nakaba must find a way to cope with her hostile surroundings, her fake marriage...and a mysterious power!
Available now!
viz media
viz.com
Shojo Beat
REIMEI NO ARCANA © 2009 Rei TOMA/SHOGAKUKAN

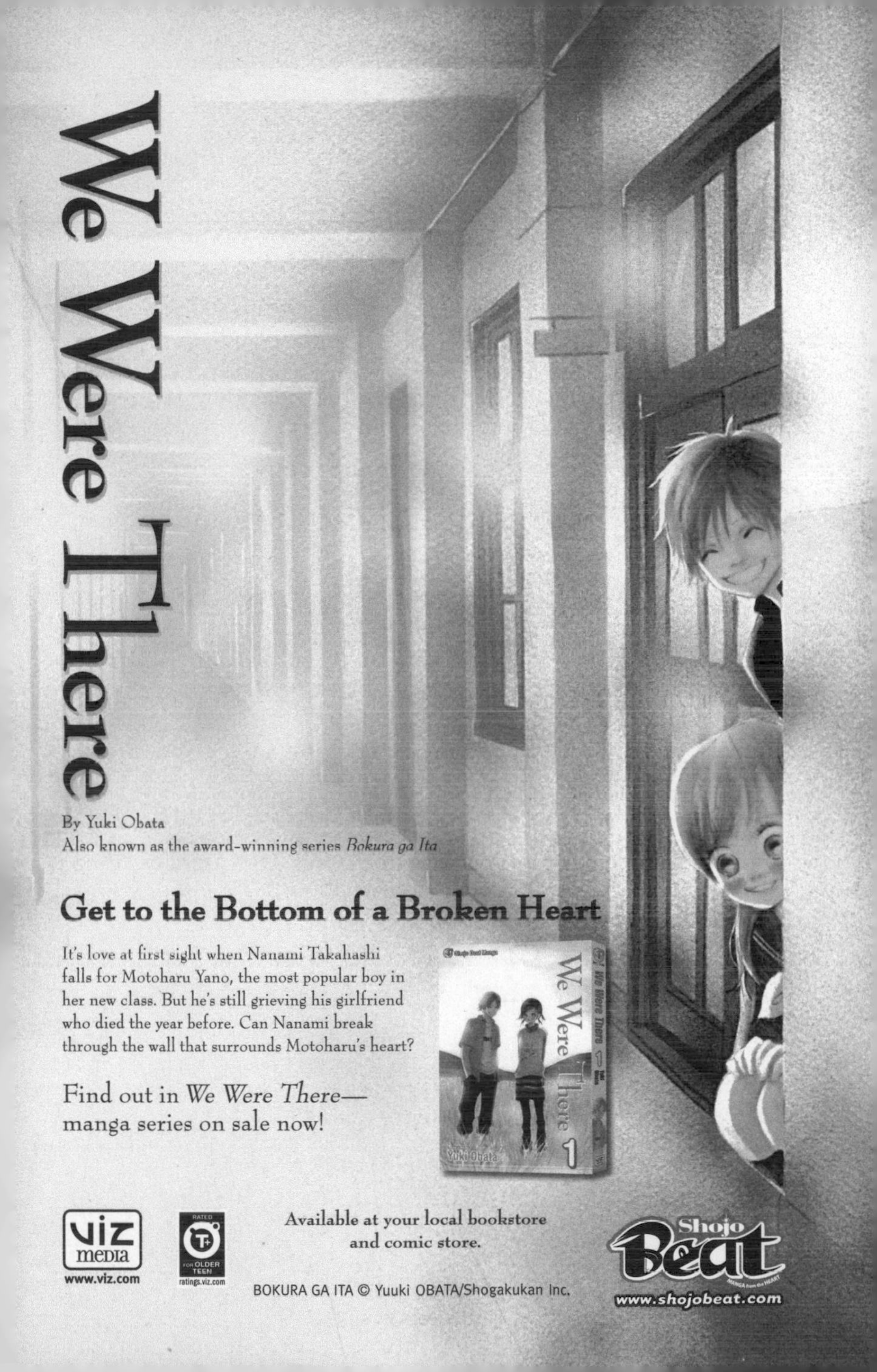
We Were There
By Yuki Obata
Also known as the award-winning series *Bokura ga Ita*
Get to the Bottom of a Broken Heart
It's love at first sight when Nanami Takahashi falls for Motoharu Yano, the most popular boy in her new class. But he's still grieving his girlfriend who died the year before. Can Nanami break through the wall that surrounds Motoharu's heart?
Find out in *We Were There*— manga series on sale now!
Shojo Beat Manga
We Were There
Yuki Obata
1
VIZ media
www.viz.com
RATED T+ FOR OLDER TEEN
ratings.viz.com
Available at your local bookstore and comic store.
BOKURA GA ITA © Yuuki OBATA/Shogakukan Inc.
Shojo Beat
MANGA from the HEART
www.shojobeat.com

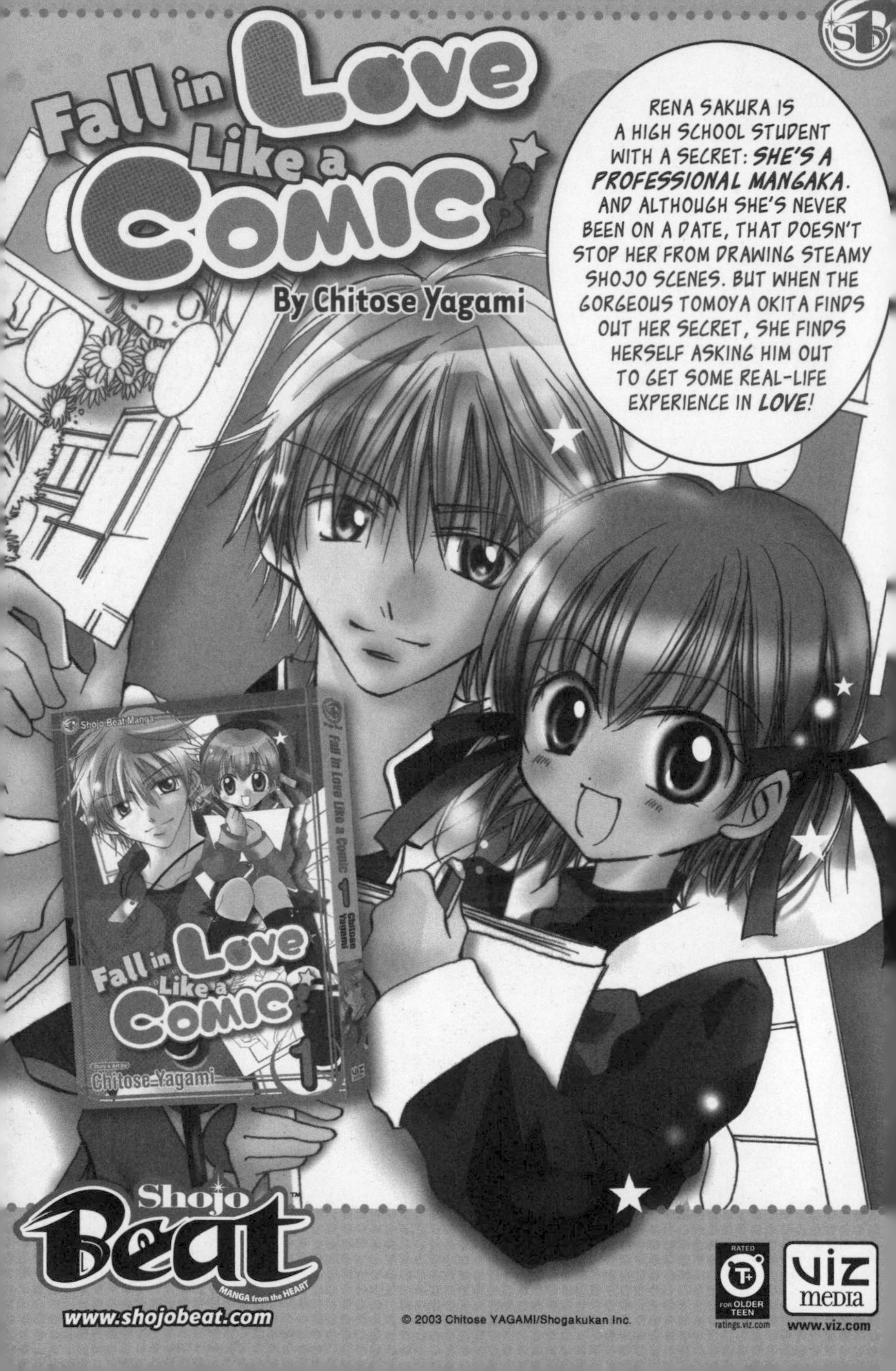

Fall in Love Like a Comic
By Chitose Yagami
RENA SAKURA IS A HIGH SCHOOL STUDENT WITH A SECRET: ***SHE'S A PROFESSIONAL MANGAKA***. AND ALTHOUGH SHE'S NEVER BEEN ON A DATE, THAT DOESN'T STOP HER FROM DRAWING STEAMY SHOJO SCENES. BUT WHEN THE GORGEOUS TOMOYA OKITA FINDS OUT HER SECRET, SHE FINDS HERSELF ASKING HIM OUT TO GET SOME REAL-LIFE EXPERIENCE IN ***LOVE***!
Shojo Beat Manga
Fall in Love Like a Comic 1 Chitose Yagami
Fall in Love Like a Comic
1
Chitose Yagami
Shojo Beat™
MANGA from the HEART
www.shojobeat.com
© 2003 Chitose YAGAMI/Shogakukan Inc.
RATED T+ FOR OLDER TEEN
ratings.viz.com
VIZ media
www.viz.com

Honey Blood

Story & Art by Miko Mitsuki

Hinata can't help but be drawn to Junya, but could it be that he's actually a vampire?

When a girl at her school is attacked by what seems to be a vampire, high school student Hinata Sorazono refuses to believe that vampires even exist. But then she meets her new neighbor, Junya Tokinaga, the author of an incredibly popular vampire romance novel... Could it be that Junya's actually a vampire—and worse yet, the culprit?!

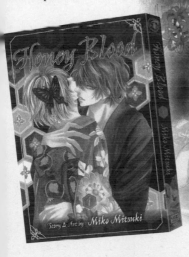

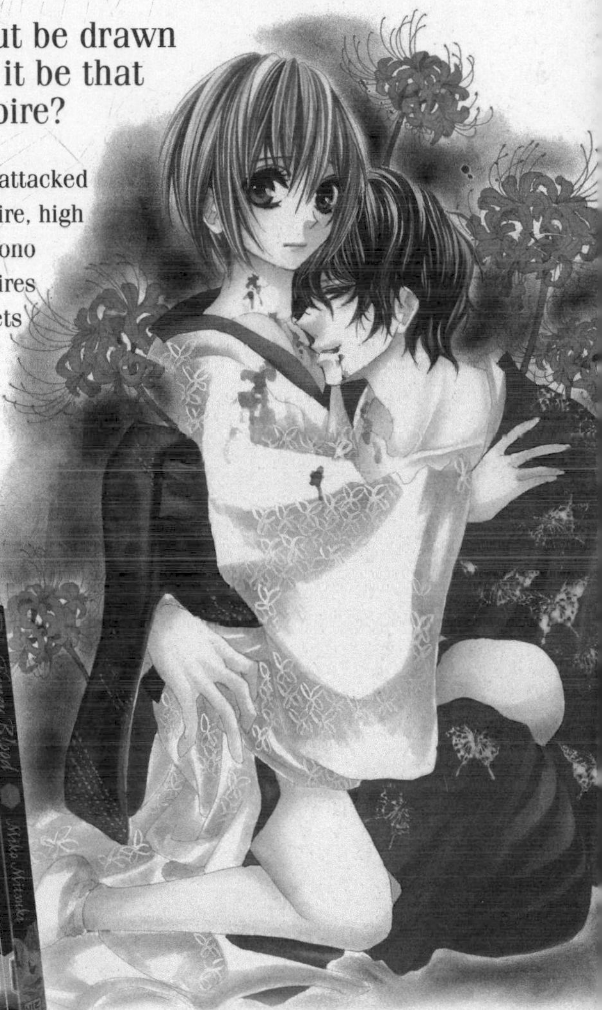

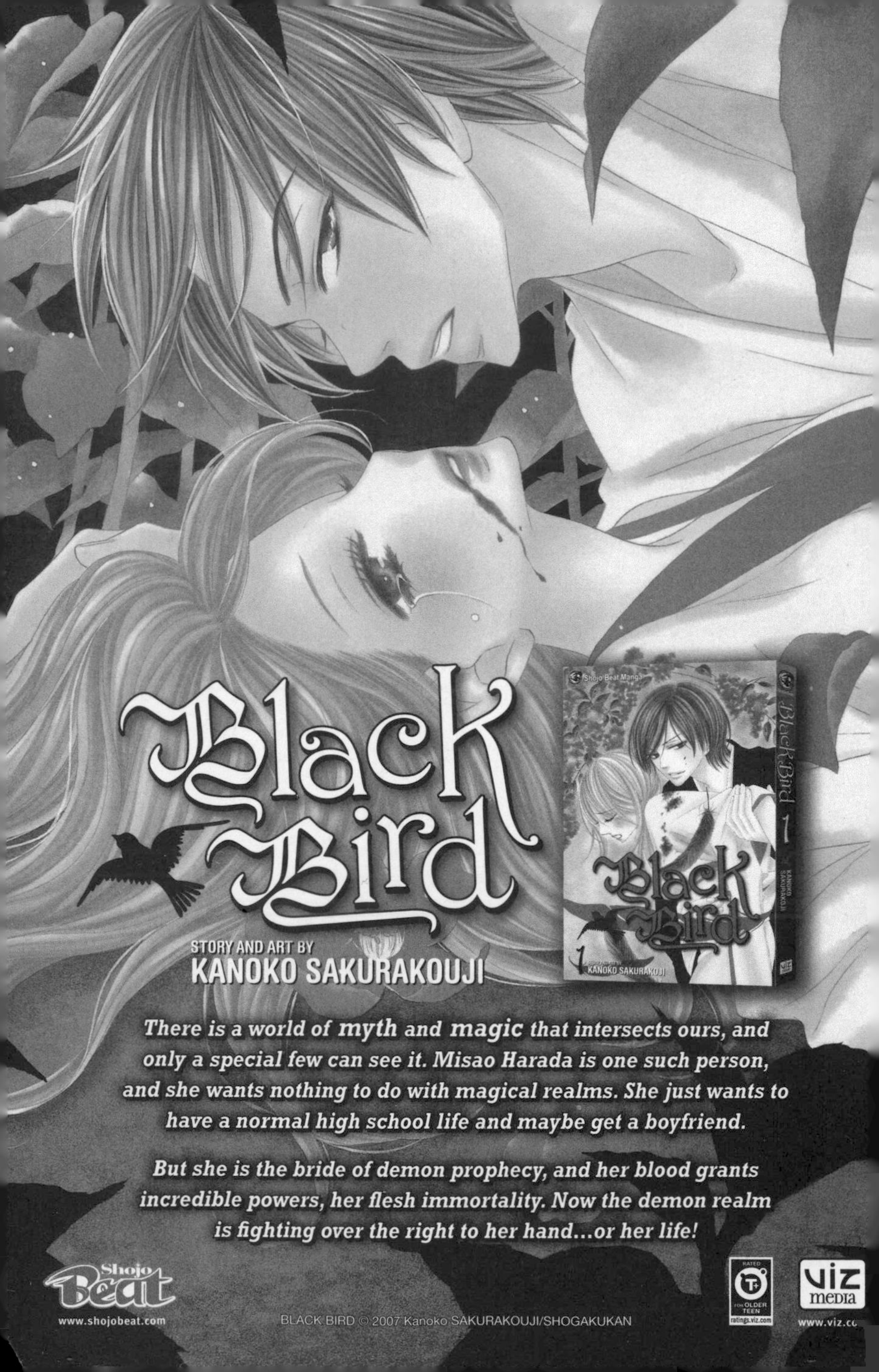
Black Bird
STORY AND ART BY
KANOKO SAKURAKOUJI
There is a world of myth and magic that intersects ours, and only a special few can see it. Misao Harada is one such person, and she wants nothing to do with magical realms. She just wants to have a normal high school life and maybe get a boyfriend.
But she is the bride of demon prophecy, and her blood grants incredible powers, her flesh immortality. Now the demon realm is fighting over the right to her hand...or her life!
Shojo Beat
www.shojobeat.com
BLACK BIRD © 2007 Kanoko SAKURAKOUJI/SHOGAKUKAN
RATED T+ FOR OLDER TEEN
ratings.viz.com
VIZ MEDIA
www.viz.co

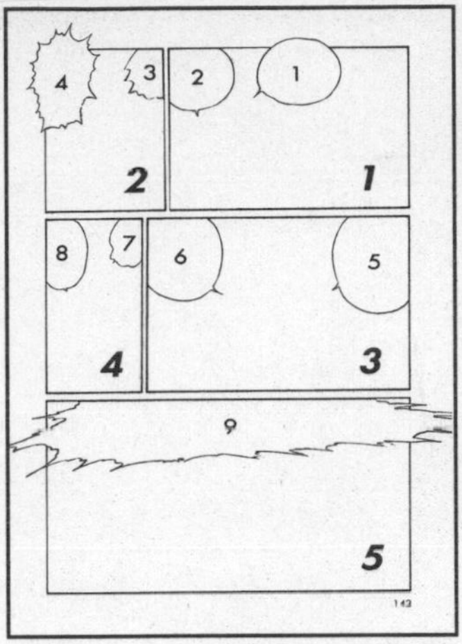
1
1
2
2
3
4
3
5
6
4
7
8
5
9

This is the last page.

In keeping with the original Japanese comic format, this book reads from right to left—so action, sound effects and word balloons are completely reversed. This preserves the orientation of the original artwork—plus, it's fun! Check out the diagram shown here to get the hang of things, and then turn to the other side of the book to get started!

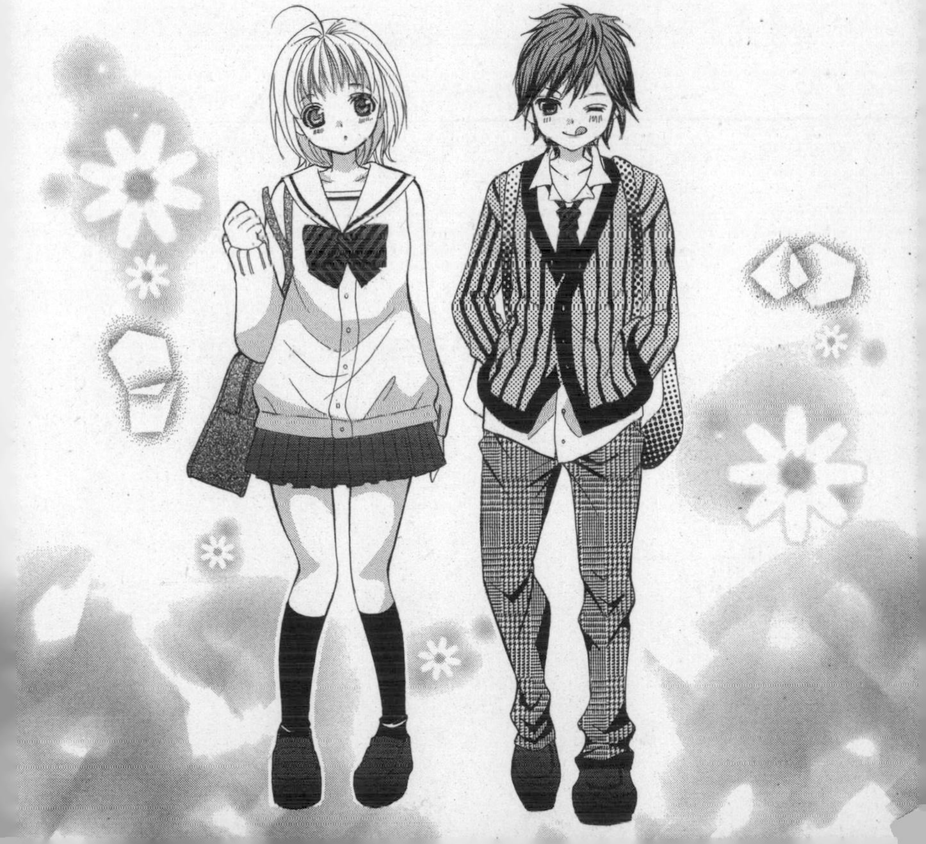